Beyond the Handshake

# Beyond the Handshake

*Multilateral Cooperation
in the Arab-Israeli Peace Process, 1991–1996*

Dalia Dassa Kaye

COLUMBIA UNIVERSITY PRESS   NEW YORK

COLUMBIA UNIVERSITY PRESS
*Publishers Since 1893*
New York Chichester, West Sussex

Copyright © 2001 Columbia University Press
All rights reserved

Library of Congress Cataloging-in-Publication Data

Kaye, Dalia Dassa.
   Beyond the handshake : multilateral cooperation in the Arab-Israeli peace process 1991-1996 / Dalia Dassa Kaye.
      p. cm.
   Includes bibliographical references and index.
   ISBN 978-0-231-12002-9 (cloth:alk. paper)
   ISBN 978-0-231-12003-6 (pbk.: alk. paper)
   ISBN 978-0-231-50532 (ebook)
   1. Arab-Israeli conflict—1993—Peace.  2. Arab countries—Foreign economic relations—Israel.  3. Israel–Foreign economic relations—Arab countries.  I. Title.

DS119.76.K354 2000
   956.05'3—dc21
                                                                    00–059031

Casebound editions of Columbia University Press books are printed on permanent and durable acid-free paper.
Printed in the United States of America

# Contents

*Preface* vii

*Introduction* xi

1. Explaining Regional Multilateral Cooperation   1

2. The Historical Record: Pre-Madrid Regional Cooperation   30

3. The Origins of the Arab-Israeli Multilateral Talks   44

4. Regional Security Cooperation   76

5. Regional Economic Cooperation   110

6. Water and Environmental Cooperation   158

7. Conclusion   184

*Appendix A: Concluding Remarks by Secretary of State James A. Baker III Before the Organizational Meeting for Multilateral Negotiations on the Middle East*   199

*Appendix B: Article 4: Security. Treaty of Peace Between the State of Israel and the Hashemite Kingdom of Jordan*   203

*Appendix C: Declaration of Principles and Statements of Intent on Arms Control and Regional Security* 206

*Appendix D: Statement by the Cooperation Council of the Arab States of the Gulf on the Cancellation by the GCC of the Secondary/Tertiary Arab Boycott of Israel* 210

*Appendix E: Casablanca Declaration* 211

*Appendix F: Amman Declaration* 216

*Appendix G: Cairo Declaration* 220

*Appendix H: Declaration on Principles for Cooperation Among the Core Parties on Water-Related Matters and New and Additional Water Resources* 223

*Appendix I: The Bahrain Environmental Code of Conduct for the Middle East* 230

Notes  235

Selected Bibliography  294

Index  311

# Preface

By the summer of 1994, nearly a year had passed since The Handshake on the White House Lawn, that is to say, the September 1993 Israeli-PLO breakthrough known to history as the Oslo Accord. The Handshake itself—an eager Yasir Arafat pumping the hand of a somewhat sheepish Yitzhak Rabin—seemed to mark the endgame for a Palestinian-Israeli settlement. History—or better, regional politics—proved the optimism premature in many respects. But the Handshake did initiate a period of intense bilateral peacemaking that dominated the news from the region and led to a comprehensive framework for Palestinian-Israeli peace as well as the Israel-Jordan peace treaty. The powerful image of the Handshake dominated the perception of change in Middle East politics so thoroughly that other profound shifts in regional thinking and dialogue went nearly unnoticed by the mainstream media in the United States, Europe, and even the region. It was thus with very good fortune that in the summer of 1994, as a summer staffer in the U.S. Department of State's Office of Policy Planning, I stumbled upon the graduate student's holy grail—a dissertation topic. That topic, the subject of this book, was the Arab-Israeli multilateral peace process, which, by mid-1994, had a momentum and vitality not matched by its press coverage. The multilaterals, I recognized early on, provided just the right framework for understanding Arab-Israeli regional politics in the 1990s, as well as a number of theoretically important developments emerging in the wake of the Cold War.

Focusing on this relatively unknown and mysterious aspect of the peace process offered an opportunity to move beyond the daily headlines and speculations so pervasive in the bilateral arena and offer an assessment of regional relations that would contribute to both the Middle East and International Relations (IR) communities. Because the multilaterals address issues of long-term concern to regional players (arms control, economics, water, the environment, and refugees) rather than the immediate bilateral conflicts between Israel and its neighbors, the process offered an interesting prism for examining the changing nature of regional relations and a concrete set of cases to assess the strengths and weaknesses of various theories explaining regional cooperation more generally.

As with most novel empirical developments, the emergence of multilateral cooperation among Arabs and Israelis raised a number of important questions. Why, after decades of armed conflict and rivalry, did Arabs and Israelis agree to sit down together to discuss regional problems in a multilateral setting? And once this process originated, what drove the regional parties to continue such cooperation or, in some cases, what prompted them to halt their cooperative efforts? Why would many international relations scholars dismiss this type of cooperation despite its significance in the Arab-Israeli arena? It is my hope that the answers to these questions, the central ones addressed in this book, contribute both empirical knowledge about a relatively unknown Arab-Israeli process and a reconceptualization of how international relations scholars can view cooperative processes in regions like the Middle East.

I argue that traditional understandings of cooperation based on outcomes, while important, neglect the equally significant view of cooperation as a process. Cooperation is not just about producing policy adjustment among actors with a given set of interests; it is also about creating a process in which new interests and understandings can coalesce. Cooperation, as viewed in this book, is about a process in which international actors work together to achieve common understandings. Of course, cooperation defined as process can still fail. In the cases of the Arab-Israeli multilaterals, for example, some groups have been more successful than others in reaching common understandings about the nature of their issue area and the value of regional cooperation itself. The varied success of the working groups was related in part to their ability to transform highly politically charged issues into "technical" problems. By viewing cooperation as a process rather than solely an outcome, we can better explain international developments in regions like the Middle East and appreciate their significance. While, as this study shows, a great power like the United States may be needed to initiate such processes, the formation of new interactive settings may influence how regional actors conceptualize regional challenges and inspire regional activism in shaping the nature of relations in ways not originally intended.

This book was written partly in the interest of narrowing the ever-present divide between regional specialists and IR theorists, and in the hope that scholars and students in both communities will take an interest in all aspects of the book. Still, students of Middle East politics and IR theory may find different parts of this book interesting or relevant to their work. Middle East scholars may take a particular interest in chapter 2 (the historical overview of regional cooperation) and the initial sections of the succeeding chapters, which provide the empirical narrative of the developments in the multilateral working groups covered in the book. IR scholars will likely find chapter 1 (the theoretical framework) of greater interest, as well as the latter sections of chapters 3 through 6, which consider the theoretical explanation for the empirical narrative.

A number of individuals have taken an active interest in this study over a number of years and I am very grateful to them. Beginning with my support network at Berkeley, I cannot thank enough Steve Weber, Ernie Haas, and Elizabeth Kier for their wise counsel and for reading numerous versions of the text. Nelson Polsby and David Caron also provided advice and critical readings of early versions of the manuscript. For introducing me to the multilaterals and becoming another helpful reader of this work and collaborator in the arms control area, I owe a great debt to Bruce Jentleson.

I would also like to thank a number of individuals who read various parts and versions of the manuscript and provided helpful comments in the revision process: Tamar Gutner, Jeff Sosland, Marty Finnemore, Deborah Avant, Susan Sell, Jim Lebovic, Jim Goldgeier, Jay Smith, and Henry Nau. A special note of gratitude is due to Michael Barnett, who not only read the entire manuscript but also helped me to reconceptualize the project with invaluable advice and encouragement as it was transformed from a dissertation into a book. Kevin Wein and Kelci Gershon provided excellent research assistance. Many thanks also to Kate Wittenberg and Anne McCoy at Columbia University Press, and to Robert Hemenway for copyediting the manuscript. And I am particularly grateful to the over seventy policymakers and regional specialists in the United States and the Middle East who shared their insights with me, sometimes in multiple interviews.

It is thanks, above all, to their generosity that this book could take the form that it has.

I conducted much of the research for this book as a Foreign Policy Research Fellow at the Brookings Institution and as an Institute on Global Conflict and Cooperation/MacArthur Regional Relations Scholar. Many thanks to both of these institutions, particularly to the helpful library staff at Brookings. The Washington, D.C. center of the University of California at Davis provided me with office space as a graduate student and the University of California at Berkeley's Center for Middle Eastern Studies awarded a Mellon grant, which supported one of my research trips to the Middle East.

It is most difficult to thank the person who deserves it most, David Kaye. Without his scrutiny of every word of this manuscript (or so I'm told), and most importantly his steady encouragement and support and his caring for our daughter Danielle while I worked on the manuscript, this book would hardly have been possible. I am forever grateful to him. Of course, all errors are ultimately mine. Finally, I dedicate this book to my parents, Judy and Dani Dassa.

# Introduction

> There is an enormous gap, in my view, between what I would call the hypnosis of the present, or hypnosis towards the past, and a real understanding of the fundamental changes occurring today, in our lifetimes, which ultimately will find expression in the books written in academia or in history books, much more than in the day to day press. I think we all suffer from political or psychological jet-lag, where we don't harmonize what we see, the new images and pictures and rhetoric and actions over the last 40 years, with what exists and doesn't exist in the Middle East.
>
> —Uri Savir[1]

Arabs and Israelis have battled one another in political and military arenas, seemingly continuously, for some fifty years. Yet recently, and within the span of only a few years, a broad group of Arab states sat down with Israel and began to cooperate on a wide range of regional issues in a multilateral setting. Why? How did enemies reluctant even to recognize one another choose to cooperate on substantive problems? What changed to enable such cooperation? How do such cooperative processes operate? And what forces stood, or stand, in the way of continuing cooperation? This book systematically addresses these fundamental questions, which cut to the heart of the evolving politics of the Middle East, the emergence and development of cooperative processes in regions of conflict, and the way international relations scholars examine the practice of regional cooperation at the turn of the century. I argue that multilateral cooperation in the Middle East must be understood as a process of interaction rather than solely a set of outcomes, and I demonstrate how interaction influences the way states view the region and the value of cooperation itself. The book's focus on multilateral cooperation in the Middle East thus contributes empirical knowledge about the development of Arab-Israeli relations after the Gulf War as well as theoretical comment on the prospects for regional multilateral cooperation among former adversaries; it provides a window into how Middle East politics are evolving and how IR theory can shed light on that evolution.

## What Are the Multilaterals?

The day-to-day pattern of Palestinian-Israeli relations—crisis, negotiation, resolution, crisis—often overshadows regional efforts to establish cooperative relations among Arabs and Israelis. Yet, in the aftermath of the 1990–91 Persian Gulf War new regional alignments and opportunities for changing regional relations emerged. The Gulf War itself generated a shared sense of common threats facing Arabs and Israelis alike as they found themselves on the same side of the conflict. And with the Cold War over, the United States and the Soviet Union sought to cooperate rather than compete in order to establish new opportunities for Arab-Israeli peacemaking. One result, and the focus of this study, was the Arab-Israeli multilateral peace process, among the most important efforts in the history of Arab-Israeli peacemaking to overcome the regional "hypnosis towards the past."

The multilaterals might be seen as the quieter, less prominent of two siblings. The other sibling is, of course, the bilateral Arab-Israeli peace process. Both were born at the Madrid Middle East Peace Conference in October 1991, cosponsored by the United States and the Soviet Union principally to launch direct, bilateral negotiations between Israel and its immediate neighbors in an attempt to bring the Arab-Israeli conflict to a conclusion. As Secretary of State James A. Baker III observed after months of shuttle diplomacy to bring Israel and the Arab parties to Madrid, "Even in a period of dramatic and far-reaching change around the world, this conference stands apart. . . . For decades, agreement on whether to negotiate eluded the parties. This weekend, direct, bilateral negotiations aimed at a comprehensive, genuine peace will start."[2] In the end, Israel, Jordan, the Palestinians, Syria, and Lebanon attended the Madrid conference and agreed to participate in direct negotiations in efforts to reach a comprehensive peace.

The U.S. vision, however, was clearly broader than a series of bilateral peace treaties. President George Bush specified that the American quest was for a comprehensive regional peace:

> We come to Madrid on a mission of hope—to begin work on a just, lasting, and comprehensive settlement to the conflict in the Middle

East. We come here to seek peace for a part of the world that in the long memory of man has known far too much hatred, anguish, and war.... Our objective must be clear.... It is not simply to end the state of war in the Middle East and replace it with a state of nonbelligerency. This is not enough; this would not last. Rather, we seek peace, real peace. And by real peace I mean treaties. Security. Diplomatic relations. Economic relations. Trade. Investment. Cultural exchange. Even tourism.... What we seek is a Middle East where vast resources are no longer devoted to armaments.... A Middle East where normal men and women lead normal lives.[3]

The American vision was, in some ways, broad and radical for the Middle East, but certainly not the stuff of daily news items. As expected, Madrid's bilateral tracks and the Israeli-Palestinian negotiations that followed the 1993 Oslo Accord captured the daily headlines.

Meanwhile, a less heralded and relatively unknown track of the Madrid process evolved simultaneously between Israel and a large segment of the Arab world.[4] The letter of invitation to the Madrid conference invited regional parties to join also a multilateral peacemaking track that would "focus on region-wide issues such as arms control and regional security, water, refugee issues, environment, economic development, and other subjects of mutual interest."[5] The Arab-Israeli multilateral peace talks (the "multilaterals") offered a novel and unprecedented approach to Middle East peacemaking.[6]

Unlike the bilateral tracks, the multilateral talks established a *regional* framework for Arab-Israeli peacemaking which included Arab states beyond Israel's borders. The United States and Russia sponsored a conference in Moscow in January 1992 to launch the multilateral track formally, a conference attended by thirty-six parties, including eleven Arab states and Israel.[7] After forty-four years of official nonrecognition by all Arab states except Egypt, Israel was joined not only by three of its immediate neighbors (Egypt, Jordan, and the Palestinians) but also by Arab states from the Gulf (including key states like Saudi Arabia) and North Africa to address a broad range of regional issues.[8] While the bilaterals were designed to "resolve the core bilateral issues at the heart of the Arab-Israeli dispute: namely, land, peace, and security," the multilaterals were intended to "address functional issues on a region-wide basis . . . to foster broader human contact between Israelis and Arabs."⁹ The bilaterals would resolve the conflicts of the past while the multilaterals would address the regional problems of the present and future.

As the first regional forum where such a wide array of Arab states sat with Israel to discuss common regional problems, the multilaterals marked a turning point in regional relations, the first tangible sign of a possible change in the way regional actors saw themselves and the region. Less than a year before, in the midst of the Gulf crisis, such a meeting would have been unthinkable. In his concluding remarks at the 1992 Moscow organizational meeting, Secretary Baker noted both the challenge and the promise of a new multilateral forum:

> No one should expect immediate breakthroughs toward multilateral cooperation in the Middle East, but neither should we neglect the possibilities for cooperation which exist at this unique moment in the history of the region. . . . Look around you. . . . Who would have imagined 50 years ago that the nations of Europe, many of whom were for centuries the fiercest of enemies, would find lasting common purpose in a vibrant European Community? And, who would have imagined even 5 years ago that the United States would launch a new partnership with a democratizing Russia? Who really knows what kinds of cooperation, however improbable it might seem today, might be possible in the Middle East.¹⁰

The Moscow meeting initiated five working groups focused on regional problems, each chaired by an extraregional party (a "gavelholder"): Arms Control and Regional Security (ACRS), chaired by the United States and Russia; Regional Economic Development (REDWG), chaired by the European Union; the Environment (EWG), chaired by Japan; Water Resources (WWG), chaired by the United States; and Refugees (RWG), chaired by Canada. A steering group co-chaired by the United States and Russia was also established to oversee the operations of the overall process and its respective working groups.

After Moscow, beginning in the spring of 1992, the multilateral working groups began to meet separately and developed distinct agendas and goals, with varying degrees of success. Israel and its Arab partners, with the encouragement and funding of their extraregional sponsors, developed regional projects, numerous confidence-building measures, and even new regional institutions [see figure 1]. The working groups began with occasional plenary

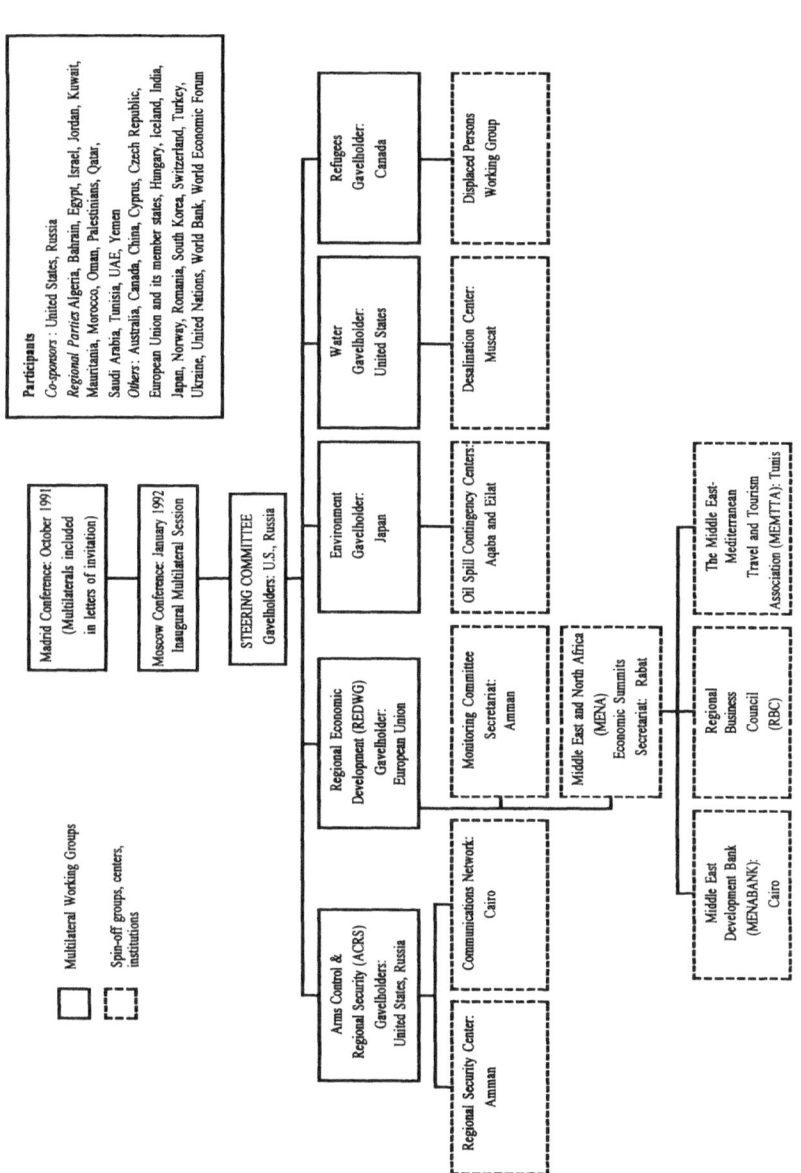

FIGURE 1 The Arab-Israeli Multilateral Peace Process

sessions where the entire range of issues within a particular group might be discussed at a fairly general level. Over time the working groups increased their interaction by meeting in smaller, more focused intersessionals between the larger plenaries, sometimes on a monthly basis. Many concepts discussed in the multilaterals found their way into Israel's bilateral peace agreements with Jordan and the Palestinian Authority (PA). A network of hundreds of regional and extraregional experts have participated in and organized the activities of the multilateral working groups, creating a nascent multilateral subculture. New working relations were formed among Israeli and Arab political elites and technical experts. Despite political limitations and numerous conflicts, the multilateral peace process has proven a unique and largely positive experiment in Arab-Israeli relations.

## Why the Multilaterals Matter

The multilaterals have significance for both theoretical and empirical reasons. First, the multilaterals demonstrate the need for IR scholars to reevaluate conventional understandings of cooperation and the functions that interactive forums and institutions serve. Specifically, the study suggests that the conventional understanding of cooperation as policy adjustment (focused on policy outcomes), while important, neglects the crucial *process* of cooperation. Reconceptualizing cooperation as a process of *working together in an effort to achieve common understandings* enhances our appreciation for new regional forums like the multilaterals. Such a reconceptualization of cooperation should also contribute to studies of other regions and institutions by highlighting dynamics overlooked by the traditional definition of cooperation. Most critically, viewing cooperation as a process allows us to determine how interaction within the process helps shape actor views and positions. It narrows the gap between what participants involved in international negotiations view as cooperation and how IR scholars study the phenomenon. Moreover, the criteria for success and failure change because cooperation is about working toward common understandings, not just producing specific policy outcomes. The multilaterals demonstrate that placing Arabs and Israelis in a novel multilateral process can change views and attitudes not only toward the specific issue areas but also toward regional relations more generally.

Second, the emergence and enlargement of regional forums and institutions since the late 1980s[11] argue for rich understandings and analyses of new forums for cooperation emerging in regions like the Middle East. As might be expected, the European dimension of this trend, certainly the most mature example of regional cooperation and integration, receives the most attention. Equally interesting are the new efforts at "regionalization" in other areas, such as Asia, Latin America and the Middle East, where former rivalries may be giving way to growing regional cooperation, or what some call "cooperative security."[12] While the durability of these new forums is uncertain, they hold the potential to create patterned expectations (or norms of acceptable behavior) among regional parties. These types of cooperative forums can never guarantee the absence of conflict, but they can contribute to limiting its prospects and controlling conflicts once they have begun.

Finally, multilateral interaction is essential for handling certain regional problems—such as arms proliferation, economic development, water scarcity, environmental degradation, and refugee crises—that have been largely neglected because of the politically divisive nature of the Arab-Israeli conflict and its tendency to dominate the regional agenda throughout the Cold War. However, these and similar types of problems must be addressed because bilateral Arab-Israeli peace treaties are not sufficient to bring about an enduring regional peace. Without multilateral forums, critical regional problems will continue to be neglected, leaving sources for regional conflict in place.

New multilateral interaction addressing common issue areas can also contribute to normalizing Arab-Israeli relations, moving from the unnatural state of nonrecognition and exclusion to regular dialogue, cooperation, and even disagreements that fall short of armed conflict. While many obstacles remain to the full normalization of the region and regular multilateral relationships that include Israel, the shift toward multilateral cooperation has been definite. Of course, the pace and substantive outcomes of Arab-Israeli multilateralization are not foregone conclusions, with a variety of factors pushing the process in different directions. In this study I will explore and explain the foundations of this process and the factors facilitating and impeding Arab-Israeli multilateral cooperation, with the intention of contributing to both our general understanding of how cooperation works and our awareness of the specific dynamics of Arab-Israeli peacemaking.

## The Relationship Between the Bilateral and Multilateral Tracks

Many observers may assume that the fate of the multilaterals and related regional cooperation efforts is contingent on progress in the bilaterals, especially the Palestinian track. According to this logic, the multilaterals were created solely to support the bilateral tracks, and their development hinges on bilateral progress. If the bilaterals falter, so do the multilaterals. To some extent, this assumption has held, as exemplified by the suspension of many regional activities following the freeze in Israeli-Palestinian relations during the administration of Israeli Prime Minister Benjamin Netanyahu beginning in mid-1996. However, gaps between bilateral and multilateral progress are also apparent, suggesting that the bilaterals—while certainly a critical force—leave much unexplained about the multilaterals and the requisites for further Arab-Israeli multilateral cooperation.

The major problem with such an assessment is empirical: the multilaterals have not, in fact, moved in tandem with the bilateral negotiating tracks at all times. To be sure, the 1993 Oslo breakthrough in the Israeli-Palestinian negotiations[13] significantly improved the regional environment and created new possibilities for Arab-Israeli multilateral cooperation, just as certain Israeli policies under Prime Minister Netanyahu contributed to a slowdown in these efforts. Yet even before Oslo the multilateral working groups were making steady progress, particularly in formulating consensus on working agendas. Given that the bilateral negotiations occurring in Washington during the two years between Madrid and Oslo were deadlocked, the multilateral track was a surprising success. In fact, the multilaterals played an important role in keeping the Madrid process afloat in this pre-Oslo period, emerging as a distinct force in the larger peace process. They did so in two central ways: 1) by providing a forum for continuous Arab-Israeli interaction when the bilateral tracks were stalled; and 2) by providing conceptual blueprints, and even language, for future bilateral accords between Israel, the Palestinians, and Jordan.

For example, while the Israeli-Palestinian track was stalled in the aftermath of the Israeli expulsion of several hundred Hamas activists from the West Bank and Gaza Strip in December 1992, the ACRS working group conducted a successful meeting the following May in Washington, where the group agreed to move to a more active work agenda, including the launching of focused intersessional activities (technical expert meetings).

Other working groups also expanded their work agendas and activities before Oslo, particularly the less contentious environment talks. The group's gavelholder, Japan, conducted a seminar on maritime disaster prevention, and the U.S. sponsored a workshop in the summer of 1993 on wastewater treatment facilities for small communities. Even after Oslo, the multilaterals continued to function during crisis periods in the bilateral tracks. For example, just two months after the massacre in Hebron of twenty-nine Arabs by an Israeli on February 25, 1994, which interrupted the bilateral negotiations, the water group held a "business as usual" plenary session in Oman, the first multilateral meeting to take place in the Gulf. The stability of the multilateral track throughout various crises gave the overall peace process continuity and momentum and demonstrated that the link between bilateral and multilateral progress was not always direct.

The bilateral negotiations did limit the scope of the multilateral talks (e.g., the multilaterals avoided issues concerning borders and sovereignty), but the multilaterals also influenced the bilateral peace agreements. For example, provisions relating to water and environment issues in the Oslo Accord, such as a Palestinian Water and Environmental Authority, were first discussed in the multilaterals. In the economic realm, the REDWG-commissioned World Bank study of the development needs of the West Bank and Gaza formed the basis for assistance to the Palestinians after Oslo. Similarly, the confidence-building measures (CBMs) included in ACRS's agenda contributed positively to the Israel-Jordan peace treaty, with the communication, notification, and maritime arrangements first studied in ACRS included in the final agreement. Indeed, the treaty refers to ACRS specifically, stressing the need for a multilateral dimension to regional security [see appendix B].

Thus, the causal arrow did not always flow from bilateral developments; at times, the reverse was true. That said, progress in the bilaterals, particularly the Oslo Accord, did favorably impact the multilateral working groups. Bilateral progress, then, may be a necessary condition for successful outcomes in multilateral cooperation, but it is not determinative. It alone cannot predict the pace of the multilaterals, particularly the variation across its working groups. For instance, why did different groups achieve varying degrees of success at the same juncture in the bilateral process? At the time of the Amman Economic Summit in October 1995, for example, the bilateral peace process had reached its peak, with the meeting convening on the heels of the signing of the second Oslo Accord (Oslo II) which began the process of Israeli troop redeployments in the West Bank. Yet while the economic working group and related activities were flourishing at that time, ACRS was beginning to face serious challenges, setting the stage for the Israeli-Egyptian rift over the Nuclear Nonproliferation Treaty (NPT) extension the following spring and the breakdown of the group's activities. Moreover, ACRS's work was suspended *before* the election of a Likud government in Israel in May 1996, which created a series of crises in bilateral peace negotiations, suggesting that factors other than the political climate in the bilateral talks influence both the success and failure of multilateral cooperation.

In sum, the multilateral working groups did not always evolve in tandem with the highs and lows of the Israeli-Palestinian track. Despite the important role played by the Israeli-Palestinian negotiations in fostering a positive overall regional environment and enhancing the prospects for cooperation, other forces were also driving the process. To understand the multilaterals, it is necessary to examine these forces. Indeed, the multilaterals offer an excellent opportunity to draw on broader theoretical explanations of why states might engage in regional cooperation, and the forces that both facilitate and impede such cooperation. Such an analysis will allow us to move beyond daily speculations toward long-term thinking about what factors will be most critical in shaping regional relations in the coming decades.

## The Organization and Design of the Book

The book is organized as follows: Chapter 1 establishes the theoretical framework needed to explain regional multilateral cooperation. To illustrate the leverage gained by a process conception of cooperation, I consider several other explanations derived from the general IR literature, broadly characterized as power, interests, domestic politics, and ideas. The power hypothesis focuses on extraregional influence and participation, particularly the role of the United States. The interest explanation focuses on regional players' cost-benefit calculations and institutional efficiency. Domestic politics is limited to the role public opinion and the domestic economic environment plays in the political leadership's calculations of how to stay in power. The ideational hypothesis focuses on shared ideas held by small groups of policy elites.

After evaluating these alternative explanations for multilateral cooperation, the chapter emphasizes the advantages of linking cooperative processes to constructivist notions about how interests come to be defined through interaction. However, this study is about the interactions, not the interests. That is to say, I do not claim that participants' interests, traditionally understood, changed in the process. Rather, I explore how participants' interactions shaped thair perceptions of, and commitment to, the process. The chapter also explains how the origins of cooperative processes are often dependent on leadership and the ideas of leaders representing powerful states. Finally, I offer an explanatory framework for multilateral cooperation which considers the mechanisms that may facilitate or impede such cooperation.

Chapter 2 pauses from the narrative to consider the historical context of the multilaterals, reviewing pre-Madrid efforts to establish Arab-Israeli cooperation in the arms control, economic, water, and environment issue areas. This chapter underscores the dramatic differences between the pre- and post-Madrid Middle East but also foreshadows a number of continuities and difficulties for those engaging in regional cooperation efforts today.

Chapter 3 addresses the origins of the multilaterals, including the negotiations leading to their emergence at the first Moscow organizational session in January 1992, and the creation of the working groups. The chapter addresses both the motivations of various regional actors in attending this forum as well as the desire of the United States to add this track to the Arab-Israeli peace process. To explain the origins of the process, the chapter illustrates how the United States projected its structural power to create such a process, but emphasizes that such power could also have led to alternative outcomes. To comprehend fully why the multilaterals emerged, we must turn to the ideas held by the small group of American elites who projected American power based on a shared set of beliefs about Arab-Israeli peacemaking.

Chapters 4–6 examine the empirical cases that are divided according to issue areas. To assess the value of a theoretical framework centered on process, I apply the framework from chapter 1 across four multilateral working groups (arms control, economic development, water, and the environment).[14] Because these issue areas range from "hard" (arms control) to "easy" (environment) cases according to the conventional wisdom about cooperation in international relations,[15] they not only provide variation on the dependent variable[16] — multilateral cooperation — but also offer an opportunity to assess the extent to which the nature of the issue area affects the prospects for cooperation as compared to other explanatory forces. Each empirical chapter first reviews the development of the working groups and then proceeds to analyze these developments through theoretical perspectives outlined in chapter 1. All chapters illustrate how the process of multilateral interaction shaped the participants' view of the process and perceptions of policy options, with some groups proving more successful than others at reaching common understandings in their respective issue areas.

Chapter 7 concludes by reviewing the central arguments of the study, suggesting implications for how IR theory should address questions of regional multilateral cooperation, and offering policy prescriptions for the future of Arab-Israeli multilateral cooperation.

In the study, I have made particular use of open-ended personal interviews with American, Israeli, and Arab officials involved in the multilateral process and its respective working groups. Because written material is scarce given the sensitivity and contemporary nature of this topic, author interviews were essential to the study and were conducted both in the region and in Washington, D.C. In order to elicit candid responses to my questions, nearly all the interviews (with the exception of those with former Israeli Prime Minister Yitzhak Shamir and former U.S. Secretary of State Baker) were conducted on a confidential, anonymous-source basis. Such exchanges were critical for discerning accurately elite beliefs about the costs, benefits, and purposes of multilateral cooperation, as opposed to rationales that may appear on the public record. Given the centrality of cognitive variables to this study, such interviews were a critical methodological component to the research, in addition to traditional document analysis. In many cases, I reinterviewed officials to determine how the process evolved and the extent to which perceptions shifted over time as a result of new interactions and also in response to environmental changes. The book largely covers developments in the multilateral process from the Madrid Peace Conference in October 1991 to late 1996, the formative years of the multilaterals.[17] As one scholar and practitioner of Arab-Israeli diplomacy, Itamar Rabinovich, has observed, this basic period, "shrouded as it is by both nostalgia and controversy, looms ever more distinctly as a notably significant chapter in the evolution of Arab-Israeli relations."[18]

# Beyond the Handshake

# 1 Explaining Regional Multilateral Cooperation

Arab and Israeli participants in the multilateral peace talks invariably would describe their endeavor as *cooperative*, a novel exercise in cooperation. How else to describe the hundreds of meetings, dozens of projects, tens of activities aimed at solving regional problems? And yet, what formal institutions and policy adjustments have they to show for their work? Have they successfully solved any specific, major regional problem? Indeed, how can one define a process as cooperation if the tangible outcomes are few, the actual adjustments in policy modest? Could it be that, despite the participants' own understanding of their activities, they were not cooperating? Or is it that they were cooperating, but political scientists do not have a vocabulary to explain it?

The emergence and development of the multilateral track of the Arab-Israeli peace process challenge the predominant theories of International Relations (IR). Across the spectrum, IR theory would downplay, ignore, or dismiss the multilaterals. Realists—who often equate the region with balance of power politics[1]—are unlikely to focus on nascent cooperative processes. Liberal Institutionalists might dismiss the theoretical impact of the multilaterals because they do not seem to produce cooperative outcomes (i.e., functioning international institutions or regimes). In fact, IR theorists have spent far more time considering *why* cooperative processes form, endure, and decline than *how* they develop, work, and affect the ideas and policies of those who participate in them. This study will illustrate why the "how" question becomes so critical in understanding interactive forums in international politics, be they formal institutions or informal negotiating processes like the Arab-Israeli multilaterals.

I argue that to explain and appreciate different forums of regional cooperation we need an alternative understanding of cooperation, viewing it not just as an outcome but also as a *process*. Seeing cooperation as a process suggests that we examine how cooperation works. Because IR theorists have generally accepted the definition of cooperation as policy adjustment (an outcome-oriented definition), the literature tends to overlook the process element of cooperation and therefore its implications for how international actors think and behave.

In this book, I draw on certain constructivist lessons to show how participant interactions within multilateral cooperative processes shape their perceptions of, and commitment to, the process itself. At times, such interactions made the participants aware that they shared joint interests and could pursue them through multilateral forums. In other cases, interactions exacerbated preexisting tensions, reinforcing participants' perceptions that they did not share particular interests. I do not (and cannot) claim that participants' interests, traditionally understood, changed within the course of the process studied here. To be sure, over the long term the process may facilitate changes in interests and policy adjustments, but there is little evidence for such changes at this point; indeed, such changes are not the subject of this study. The focus here is on the nature of the participants' interactions within a multilateral setting and the extent to which they were able to reach common understandings about the value of the cooperative process and the issue areas under discussion.

The chapter proceeds as follows: First, I summarize the theoretical argument. Second, I consider the advantages of reconceptualizing cooperation as a process. In particular, I focus on why such a redefinition is critical when considering multilateral cooperation as opposed to other cooperative forums (e.g., bilateral negotiations). Third, I review several alternative approaches that might be employed to explain multilateral cooperation and describe their limitations in explaining cooperative processes like the Arab-Israeli multilaterals. At the same time I argue that different forces may be at work to varying degrees at different stages of the process. Thus, a modification of a structural power argument focused on leadership does provide insight into the origins of the multilaterals. But in the fourth section, to explain the subsequent development stage of the process, I turn to a consideration of constructivism. The final section outlines the study's theoretical framework for explaining both the origins and most significantly the varied development of the multilateral process. This framework draws on constructivist methods to illustrate how interactions can shape how actors view the cooperative process, leading to both successful and unsuccessful multilateral cooperation. In the remainder of the book, I apply this framework to explain the empirical cases of regional multilateral cooperation.

## The Argument in Brief

To explain how the Arab-Israeli multilateral working groups developed in varied ways, I examine how the regional actors themselves viewed the cooperative process and the extent to which this process facilitated common understandings or failed to do so. In all cases, I seek to explain rather than assume regional views of this process. The empirical examples in the following chapters illustrate how this cooperative process affected regional support for multilateral cooperation in both positive and negative directions. All groups struggled with varying degrees of success to depoliticize the "technical" issues on their agendas. In the pursuit of the broader goal of facilitating interactions, they all attempted to use the cooperative process to define otherwise politically charged issues (at least in the Middle East context) as technical. Indeed, the relative ability of the working groups to reconceptualize their issue areas as technical rather than political problems explains a large part of the variation among the more and less successful groups.

I suggest several mechanisms by which cooperative processes can facilitate or impede such transformations from the political to the technical. Not all of these mechanisms are evident in each empirical case, but the list represents the range of forces which can enhance or undermine successful multilateral cooperation. Facilitating mechanisms include the redefinition of problems as integrative—as opposed to distributive—issues; shifting understandings of acceptable policy options; acceptance of new partners and coalitions; the development of new vocabulary and shared beliefs surrounding the issue area; and intensified interactions among regional participants, including smaller and more informal negotiating sessions involving issue area experts. Impeding mechanisms include a polarizing outside political process that infringes on and spotlights the working group's activities; domestic pressure and sensitivity to public opinion opposing the cooperative process; existing national identities that feel threatened by the process; perceptions that the process is inequitable; and changing perceptions about the external environment (security or economic) which challenge the consensual knowledge developed in the working groups.

For example, while ACRS made some progress in redefining the arms control problem and the value of security cooperation in more consensual ways, that group ultimately failed because it could never overcome the politically divisive and publicly explosive issue of Israel's nuclear capabilities, in part because of Egypt's perception that the working group had developed in ways that threatened its traditional regional leadership role. In contrast, the other working groups—while facing numerous obstacles—proved more successful in reaching common understandings about the value of their cooperation and the nature of their issue area because, through their interactions, they were better able to define their issues in technical terms and appreciate the value of multilateral cooperation in serving other regional interests.

The book's focus on the process of cooperation, or the "how" aspect of the workings of international forums, does not preclude "why" questions or suggest they are unimportant. It is often necessary to recognize those forces that create a cooperative process before examining its development. Many scholars have found that the forces driving an institution's formation may not be the same ones that drive its development or decline.[2] The research on the Arab-Israeli multilaterals contained here supports this finding. Chapter 3, which considers the origins of the multilateral peace process, argues that extraregional actors—most prominently, the United States—were responsible for the formation of this process.

To explain why the multilaterals emerged, I argue that we need to understand how significant actors like the United States saw the process, holding views which were more closely tied to nonmaterial, ideational factors than to assumed structural concerns offered by traditional theories like realism or neoliberalism. I draw on modifications of power arguments that focus on the role of leadership, and the ideas of leaders, in creating and shaping new international forums. Specifically, a small group of policy elites within the administration—who were part of a larger community of Middle East experts in Washington, D.C.—shared similar notions about how to resolve the Arab-Israeli conflict and greatly influenced American policy in this region, including the formation of the multilateral peace process track. That said, once the multilaterals were formed, the cooperative process itself and the views of regional participants toward it became the critical forces in determining how the process proceeded.

## Rethinking the Meaning of Cooperation in Multilateral Settings

Most IR literature does not problematize cooperation but rather accepts cooperation as an outcome based on mutual interests which leads to policy adjustment among international actors. Robert O. Keohane best represents this view of international cooperation. Keohane "takes the existence of mutual interests as given and examines the conditions under which they will lead to cooperation" and does not "concentrate on the question of how fundamental common interests can be created among states."[3] Thus, Keohane is interested less in the cooperative process than in cooperative outcomes defined largely as policy adjustment. As Keohane explains, "Cooperation, as compared to harmony, requires active attempts to adjust policies to meet the demand of others."[4] Drawing on Charles E. Lindblom's definition of policy coordination,[5] Keohane argues, "Cooperation occurs when actors adjust their behavior to the actual or anticipated preferences of others, through a process of policy coordination."[6] For cooperation to take place according to Keohane's conception, "patterns of behavior must be altered."[7] This outcome-based notion of cooperation focused on policy adjustment has become generally accepted in IR scholarship, even among those arguing from different theoretical perspectives.[8]

Keohane applied his definition of cooperation to case studies involving economic coordination among advanced industrial powers. But if these were the standards set to examine other parts of the world (e.g., the Middle East) and different issue areas (e.g., security politics), we might conclude that cooperation (defined as policy adjustment) scarcely if ever takes place. Perhaps many IR scholars, particularly from the realist tradition, would have little difficulty with this observation since they tend not to expect much cooperation regardless of what area of the world is under discussion.[9] Yet a major problem arises with this line of thinking. Might we be missing major empirical developments by limiting our conception of cooperation to policy outcomes? What if policymakers themselves believe they are engaging in cooperation? How can we explain the gap between what political scientists call cooperation and what many policymakers believe cooperation to be?

The Middle East multilateral cases suggest a need to reconceptualize cooperation in order to address important processes occurring in a critical area of the world. Such a reconceptualization should enhance studies of other regions and institutions by highlighting dynamics that the current definition of cooperation misses. It also narrows the gap between what participants involved in international negotiations view as cooperation and how IR scholars study the phenomenon. The criteria for success and failure also change because cooperation is not just about producing specific policy outcomes but also about efforts to reach common understandings.

Viewing cooperation as a process rather than an outcome emphasizes actor perceptions of interests, a step that precedes Keohane's outcome-driven definition of cooperation and one which he "black-boxes." The process definition of cooperation therefore does not subsume or substitute itself for Keohane's notion of cooperation. Indeed, the formulation of common understandings may be an important step in the process of producing adjustment of policies, or specific policy outcomes, although this study is not suggesting it is a necessary condition. In other words, I am not arguing that cooperative outcomes do not matter; after all, those involved in cooperative processes would like to see "facts on the ground," concrete results that they might show to their domestic constituents. Still, the Middle East multilaterals demonstrate the value of conceptualizing a different type of cooperation based on process.

But how can we define cooperation as a process rather than an outcome? The anthropologist Stacia E. Zabusky's approach to cooperation in her study of the European Space Agency—which draws on social and cultural forces rather than individual motivations or interests—is useful in understanding cooperation in social institutional settings.[10] Citing Jürgen Habermas, Zabusky observes that participants in cooperative arenas are not just trying to produce something, they are also *trying to reach common understandings*.[11] Zabusky notes how other disciplines, including political science, tend to black-box cooperation (as opposed to examining how it works) and in doing so view cooperation as something you can identify and can compare to other phenomena, like "competition" or "conflict." In contrast, Zabusky opens up the black-box of cooperation to see what it means to participants involved in such processes, arguing that "cooperation is, in essence, a *process* of production."[12] An important aspect of cooperative processes is Margaret Mead's notion of "working together."[13] But cooperation is not easily obtained just by working together. Indeed, conflict and controversy are integral aspects of the cooperative process: "The practice of cooperation . . . consists of the ongoing negotiation of the often irreconcilable differences put into play by the division of labor, a negotiation that proceeds through conflict and ambiguity as much as through solidarity and orderliness."[14] For Zabusky, cooperation and conflict are not separable concepts; they are part of the same interactive process. Such a conception of cooperation is useful for understanding and explaining cases of multilateral cooperation in the Middle East.

I therefore define cooperation in this study as *a process of working together in an effort to achieve common understandings*. "Common understandings" in this study do not suggest that actors have fundamentally altered core beliefs—also referred to as "learning" in some contexts.[15] Actors may reach common understandings for purely instrumental and material reasons (although once these understandings are reached the actors may maintain a normative commitment to maintaining them). Rather, I use "common understandings" in a more limited sense, namely when the actors commonly perceive the value of a cooperative endeavor and the substantive problems on the negotiating agenda. It is also important to note that not all cooperative processes succeed. Many such efforts, including cases in the Arab-Israeli multilaterals, fail in their efforts to achieve common understandings.

Viewed in this way, many international negotiations would constitute elements of cooperation provided the negotiations involve dialogue and efforts to achieve common understandings rather than unilateral initiatives imposed on various actors. Thus, all of the Arab-Israeli multilateral working groups are examples of cooperation. Once we see that the parties are working together, trying to achieve common understandings, the inquiry shifts to the extent to which the working groups were able to reach common understandings as a result of this often contentious process. Shared ideas and agreements are possible, but the question for these cases of Middle East multilateral cooperation is how the participants reach such agreement. This is especially problematic because the participants involved in cooperative processes often assume negative views of the process, and may even resist it. Cooperative processes are full of contention and debate.

Cooperation is not tantamount to success (as an outcome definition might suggest) and does not preclude failure. What determines the level of success is the extent to which the participants reach common understandings of problems on the agenda. Of course, one would expect to find a correlation between successful cooperative processes and the creation of new institutions or policy adjustments among the actors. But the fundamental challenge of the process definition of cooperation is that outcomes are not the only way to judge the value of cooperation—efforts to reach new understandings can be just as critical in changing the nature of regional relations.

Once the definition of cooperation is broadened to include its process elements, we may ask which factors in the process affect how or whether actors can reach common understandings. Most critical is the establishment of a process that allows for interaction among participants. Rather than serving as "teachers,"[16] institutions or cooperative processes can also serve as points of contact for interaction that would not otherwise take place. At certain stages, such interactions will resemble a teaching process—when, for example, participants share previous experiences and lessons with the larger group in a seminar format, a dynamic that Emanuel Adler has labeled "seminar diplomacy."[17] Referring to the experience of the Organization for Security and Cooperation in Europe (OSCE), Adler explains, "Because what matters most is not the outcome but the pedagogical process, not all seminars produce final documents and reports. The expectation is that . . . delegates will later disseminate the ideas raised at the seminar in their respective political systems, thus spreading the seeds of shared understandings across national borders."[18] Indeed, extraregional participants like the United States and the Europeans conducted such seminars in the Arab-Israeli multilateral working groups, particularly at the early stages of the process when the actors were trying to define basic concepts and working agendas but were not yet prepared to engage one another in serious dialogue.

The process of *talking* among participants is another central component of working together both in formal and informal settings, and meetings allow the participants to understand what they are doing and to become "socialized" into the process.[19] Meetings allow participants to make connections, both in terms of understanding the substantive problems on the agenda and in order to build social relationships. Of course, these interactions can also highlight differences among participants, which is why cooperation often fails. In the case of the Arab-Israeli multilaterals, we will see how meetings and the process of talking through problems led to both understandings and divisions on similar issues.

The particular interactive setting in which Arabs and Israelis found themselves—multilateral—presents an interesting dimension to the definition of cooperation as a process. I suggest that multilateral negotiations or forums are more conducive to definitions of cooperation focusing on process rather than outcomes. To understand why this is the case, it is important to understand why multilateral forums are not just quantitatively (involving three or more parties) but *qualitatively* different than bilateral forums.[20] According to Hampson and Hart's study of multilateral negotiations across a variety of issue areas (security, economic, and environmental), multilateral negotiations differ from bilateral interactions because they are more complex, often involve nonstate actors including expert communities who try to shape the agenda, and tend to be more protracted. The protracted nature of multilateral forums suggests more room for actor positions to change over time as perceptions of the process change. Hampson and Hart observe that because firm or "bottom line" preferences are rarely known at the outset in multilateral negotiations, utility maximizing models (such as game theory) are less useful than process models because the latter can better evaluate how preferences change over the course of protracted negotiations. Such a process approach does not view "bargaining outcomes and payoffs as fixed and as a distributive form of negotiation (i.e., zero-sum)" but rather treats "negotiation as an integrative or positive-sum game and as an exercise in value and norm-creation where the evolution of trust and reciprocity and the creation of new values may be more crucial to negotiation success or failure than the way payoffs are arranged and structured."[21]

Another study of multilateral negotiation also contends that multilateral negotiations focus on process more than outcomes because they are often about developing a consensus rather than bargaining over policy adjustments.[22] That is to say, there are often no clear interests at the outset which are bargained over as in many bilateral negotiations. Multilateral forums are useful arenas to explore how actor positions develop in both consensual and conflictual ways, an examination which requires a conception of cooperation that focuses on the process rather than the outcome of such interactions.

Thus, multilateral cooperation is defined in this study as *the process of three or more actors working together in an effort to achieve common understandings*. This definition is limited to multilateral cooperation and distinct from the term "multilateralism." John Ruggie, for example, defines multilateralism as "an institutional form which coordinates relations among three or more states on the basis of 'generalized' principles of conduct."[23] These generalized principles of conduct are expected to extend beyond the particular interests of states that are committed to the norm of multilateralism. Examples of such principles include diffuse reciprocity (as in MFN arrangements in the GATT) or indivisibility (such as collective security principles in NATO). What matters, Ruggie argues, is not the number of states involved in an institution but rather "the *kind of relations* that are instituted among them."[24] Moreover, Ruggie argues prescriptively that multilateralism can enhance peaceful interstate relations through its "adaptive and even reproductive capacities which other institutional forms may lack and which may, therefore, explain the roles that multilateral arrangements play in stabilizing the current international transformation."[25]

While Ruggie's definition is useful for characterizing the nature of political relations in Europe, this definition of multilateralism is closer to an outcome definition because it characterizes a set of relationships to which multilateral cooperation in other regions may or may not lead. In other words, multilateralism as defined by Ruggie is a possible *outcome* of multilateral cooperation processes, but it is not the only possible outcome. Ruggie's multilateralism is an outcome to which regional actors may aspire given its stabilizing implications, but destabilizing outcomes are also possible. The interesting aspect of multilateral cooperation, in my view, is its potential to *create* "generalized principles of conduct" or new common understandings in often conflictual and contentious processes like the Arab-Israeli multilaterals.

## Alternative Explanations for Multilateral Cooperation

Why is a process conception of cooperation most appropriate for explaining the Arab-Israeli multilaterals? To answer this question fully, we must address some of the alternative frameworks in the IR literature and assess the extent to which they can explain either the origins or development of this process. The theories can be grouped into those which assume actor interests and/or base interests on material conditions (structural power, contractual approaches, domestic political determinants, and cognitive rationalists) and those that seek to explain actor interests drawing on social, often nonmaterial factors (constructivists). This review will demonstrate the value of modified power arguments based on leadership for explaining the multilateral's origins and the leverage gained through constructivist approaches for explaining how such processes develop.

*Power Approaches: Hegemons and Leaders*

One explanation for the Arab-Israeli multilaterals focuses on power arguments. These approaches suggest that powerful actors explain how new institutions emerge and how they function once established. I consider two variants of this argument: hegemonic stability and power through leadership. I find the second variant of greater relevance for this study because it best explains the origins of the multilateral talks.

The school of thought most closely associated with the power variable, neorealism, does not tend to focus on questions of institutionalized cooperation, because in an anarchic, self-help environment, states are more concerned about balancing powers or threats to their survival[26] and thus cooperation is usually expressed through short-lived alliances or coalitions. The emergence of more enduring forums for cooperation that do not rest on specified threats (like the multilaterals) poses empirical challenges for this line of thinking. However, a variant of neorealism, hegemonic stability theory, does attempt to explain the apparent anomaly of international institutions in a realist self-help world. Hegemonic stability arguments posit that the presence of a dominant power is necessary for the provision of collective goods that international regimes or institutions offer, such as an open liberal economic system.[27] Hegemons, global or regional, impose institutions or regimes on weaker states and tolerate free riders because these institutions serve their own long-term interests. If hegemonic stability explained the emergence of multilateral cooperation in the Middle East, we would expect the extraregional hegemon, the United States, to have created this process to serve its own general interests over time, regardless of what other players in the process demanded or contributed.

Hegemonic stability theory is not particularly helpful in understanding the multilaterals.[28] First, the multilateral working groups do not provide collective goods (resources are limited and membership is restricted). Second, the incentives to create this process were ambiguous, and the American crafters of the multilaterals did not have a clear idea of where this particular process would lead. Moreover, U.S. Secretary of State Baker was willing to sacrifice the multilaterals if initiating them meant the Syrians would boycott the entire Madrid process, which suggests that the Americans were sensitive to the demands and constraints of regional parties. So why bother expending the energy to create this additional process? Traditional structural power arguments do not answer this question well. The ambiguity and uncertainty of outcomes typical in multilateral forums weakens the argument that such institutions are simply tools for major power players to fulfill their own parochial interests.

The weakness of the hegemonic stability thesis in explaining the multilaterals does not rule out the role of power in different forms. While the leadership of a great power (the United States) might have been necessary to create the multilateral process, leadership is not always practiced for hegemonic purposes. Oran Young has argued that the hegemonic stability thesis, while parsimonious, has obscured the study of different forms of political leadership that may be critical to the creation of international institutions or regimes.[29] Rather than focusing on the presence or absence of a great power, Young shifts attention to individual leaders, who may, but need not, represent the great powers. Leadership by individuals may be particularly important in negotiations to create new institutions because

> regime formation in international society typically involves a large element of integrative (or productive) bargaining in contrast to distributive (or positional) bargaining and proceeds under a (more or less thick) veil of uncertainty. The participants in institutional bargaining do not begin with a clear picture of the locus and shape of a welfare frontier or contract curve, and they ordinarily seek to reach agreement on institutional arrangements encompassing enough issues or expected to remain in place long enough so that it is difficult for those negotiating on behalf of an individual participant to make confident predictions about the impact of particular options on that participant's own welfare.[30]

Indeed, the origins of the Arab-Israeli multilaterals largely followed such logic.

Helpful to our understanding of the role of leadership in the establishment of the multilaterals is Young's distinction between leadership types, two of which are relevant to this study: structural and intellectual. A structural leader represents a powerful state and is able to "translate power resources into bargaining leverage in an effort to bring pressure to bear on others to assent to the terms of proposed constitutional contracts."[31] Thus, it is not just the presence of a great power (hegemon) that brings about new regimes, it is the ability of particular leaders to project the material power they represent to achieve *agreed upon* (not imposed) ends. In general, structural leadership may be utilized more where there is a great asymmetry of power, so that the leader of the powerful state has the tools to influence others' behavior. These tools may include "arm twisting and bribery"[32] or side payments and other rewards to weaker parties agreeing to engage in the new arrangements the structural leader prefers. Yet the structural leader must use these resources skillfully, because, unlike what is assumed in hegemonic theorizing, the weaker parties will always carry some leverage of their own.

In the Middle East case, the structural leaders representing the United States (e.g., Secretary of State Baker) may have engaged in some arm twisting and side payments to get the regional parties to the Madrid peace process, but each of these parties had its own leverage against the United States, raising the threat that the conference might not take place if Baker pushed too hard or failed to utilize American influence skillfully. Often, structural leaders are not exercising power to serve their own (or their country's) material interests. Rather, "their incentives to strive toward agreement . . . are apt to center on more intangible rewards, such as the satisfaction of seeing progress toward goals they espouse, the receipt of accolades from their peers, or the achievement of a place for themselves in history."[33]

Intellectual leaders may also play a significant role in bringing about new institutions, by relying on the "power of ideas" rather than negotiating skills to "shape the thinking of the principals in processes of institutional bargaining."[34] These intellectual leaders may but need not be the same individuals who serve the other leadership roles. For instance, intellectual leadership can emerge from outside governments, from international organizations, think tanks, interest groups, or academia where new ideas and ways of framing problems may be generated and influence decision makers. Sometimes, as with the economic theories of John Maynard Keynes, the ideas produced by an individual can develop into a school of thought that carries significant influence in policy circles.[35] In Middle East peacemaking, many institutes and individuals attempt to influence the policy community, and some leaders within the region have attempted to express intellectual leadership through books and memoirs.[36] In the case of the multilaterals, we need to discern the extent to which intellectual leadership has played a role in forming this process and the way in which it was structured. I draw on these ideas about leadership to explain the origins of the multilaterals, arguing that the exercise of structural and intellectual leadership by the United States was most critical at this beginning stage. Chapter 3 provides empirical support for these arguments.

## Interest-Based Approaches: Functionalism and Interdependence

A second explanation that may potentially account for the multilaterals focuses on the interdependence among regional parties that can produce new forums and institutions to deal with common problems. Once in place, these institutions can provide further incentives for Arab-Israeli cooperation. Accordingly, the multilaterals should be the outcome of a need to solve common problems shared by both Israelis and Arabs and should create institutions that will produce further cooperation, perhaps even in the political realm. A review of the two most important schools associated with this line of thinking—neofunctionalism and neoliberal institutionalism—will underscore their deficiency in explaining either the origins or development of the multilateral process. Still, because neofunctionalism[37] was developed to explain the European integration process in the late 1950s, it can provide useful lessons for other regions establishing new regional institutions.

Neofunctionalists argued that growing levels of interdependence and economic cooperation in Europe would lead to new interactions that would produce greater cooperation, and even "spill over" to the political realm, producing political integration through supranational governance. They believed that solving common problems (beginning with technical issues) would lead to new interactions that would redefine actors' interests, particularly their loyalty to national units. However, given its shortcomings in explaining even the European case,[38] neofunctionalism's generalizability to other regions is questionable. In particular, the notion that actors would over time shift loyalties to a supranational unit is a highly unlikely and farfetched scenario in regions like the Middle East.[39]

That said, neofunctionalists' more limited arguments, particularly those suggesting that ongoing interaction can shape actors' views of the region, will prove important in explaining the development of the multilaterals and their potential to bring about different types of regional relations. Moreover, American policymakers adapted the neofunctional lesson regarding the importance of technical cooperation to the multilateral working groups, although they were under no illusions that this type of technical cooperation would be sufficient to bring about political accommodation. But in limited ways, the interaction within the context of technical cooperation around issue areas of common concern did move the political process forward, both by building relationships among elites who would also negotiate at the political (bilateral) level and by creating proposals that would be integrated into peace treaties. While the core of the neofunctional argument as applied to Europe (the shift from national to supranational identities) is inapplicable to the Arab-Israeli context, its arguments about the ability of interactive forums to facilitate new conceptions of regional relations are useful for understanding other regional cooperation processes like the multilaterals. Indeed, the framework I employ in the study draws on the lessons of this earlier literature.

A more recent liberal variant drawing on functionalist arguments—neoliberalism—pursues a more systemic logic, emphasizing the role of institutions in promoting cooperation and enhancing interdependence. Unlike the neofunctionalists, this approach relies on a contractual conception of interests (which are assumed) and thus is less useful for explaining the Arab-Israeli multilaterals. Rather than explain the supply of international institutions and cooperation, neoliberals focus on the demand for institutions as a solution to market failures that lead to inefficient results because agreements that would benefit all parties are not made. The attributes of the system impose transaction and information costs that create barriers to cooperation. Institutions can reduce transaction and information costs for the realization of joint gains.[40] Therefore, if states have shared interests, they will have the incentive to form and maintain cooperative relations and create institutions if existing forums of cooperation are not satisfying these interests.

Underlying the contractual approach are several basic assumptions, all of which are problematic in the case of the Arab-Israeli multilaterals. First, it assumes that institutionalized cooperation is a response to states' demand for this solution. While demand for solutions to coordination problems[41]—those that respond to common aversions—were certainly present in the Middle East with regard to specific issues in areas such as water (to avoid a depletion of scarce resources) and the environment (to avoid regional catastrophes like oil spills), this demand was present long before the multilateral process began. Earlier efforts to launch cooperative regional efforts on the water problem, for example, failed because the political climate was not ripe or the initiatives lacked the backing of the American government. In other words, the demand for cooperation is not sufficient to bring it about. In such circumstances, structural leadership and international political conditions play a more critical role. Moreover, some issue areas, like arms control and refugees, did not generate a demand for solutions by regional parties, but rather were promoted and included on the agenda by the United States. Finally, some institutions that emerged from the multilaterals—such as a Middle

East development bank—were not created in response to a demand by either the United States or most regional parties, and existing institutions already served many of the functions used to justify the bank's formation.[42]

Another assumption of the contractual approach is the instrumental nature of cooperation, whereby states enter cooperative relations to serve a defined need. As we will see in chapter 3, however, the American originators of the multilaterals did not focus on solving the substantive problems that could bring joint gains to regional parties across issue areas, but rather were concerned with the political utility of the multilaterals in enhancing Israeli normalization. The actual issues eventually included in the process were less important to U.S. policymakers than initiating the process itself. Moreover, many regional players were coaxed into joining the multilaterals by the United States through political and monetary incentives. At the start, the Arabs viewed this process as an American-Israeli initiative and saw little gain from cooperating with Israel in such an unprecedented manner.

Contractual approaches also underscore the efficiency of institutionalized cooperation that can lower transaction costs, or the costs of making agreements that would benefit all parties. Even if power is essential to the formation of international institutions, the functional purpose of institutions in making cooperation cheaper and easier so that states may overcome collective action problems[43] and realize shared interests explains why such institutions persist. Thus, even if the foundations of the Arab-Israeli process were based on power, its continuation after Moscow may be attributable to the functional purpose it served in coordinating cooperative efforts in efficient ways. This assumption carries some explanatory value for the multilateral process, which certainly increased communication, information on substantive issue areas, and regular meetings among regional parties (many of whom had never met Israelis before in official capacities). This functional purpose was particularly useful in the Environment and Water working groups where multilateral solutions facilitate agreements that could not be made on a bilateral basis and increase the sources for information and research on common problems.

However, this explanation is indeterminate, given that for some of the issue areas alternative bilateral and subregional solutions might have proved more efficient. But such alternatives lacked the political and cognitive purpose the multilateral format provided in making Israel a "normal" part of the larger region. Moreover, the actual operations of the multilaterals did not demonstrate an efficient organization: the meetings of each group rotated among different capitals; no overall permanent secretariat was created, and there was little interaction and issue linkage among the working groups and much confusion about where to obtain information that came out of the process (since five different extraregional players chaired the groups, the sources of information were decentralized).

Finally, the instrumental approach suggests more about how to produce cooperative outcomes than about how conflict might emerge even if institutions are serving all the important functions for which they are designed. One gets the impression that once an institution is established, the actors can transcend the politics surrounding the particular issue area because the incentives to cooperate are great and the means for doing so easy. But as discussed earlier, conflict can be an integral component of cooperative processes, as was certainly the case in the Arab-Israeli multilaterals.

### Domestic Politics

One of the major critiques of both power and interest-based approaches like neoliberalism has been these theories' relative neglect of domestic politics.[44] Because these approaches are committed to a rationalist social science methodology, they often adopt the assumption of unitary state actors where the state is black-boxed. States, as unitary actors, enter cooperative relationships when it is to their benefit and they can gain from this interaction. Interests, or rather preferences, are assumed rather than explained by the theorist. Critics of this approach observe that the preferences of states and their decision to enter into or defect from cooperative relations are affected by what occurs within the state as much as by what occurs from without.[45] The solution, these critics argue, is to bring domestic politics into explanations of cooperation to understand why states hold the preferences they do. However, like the previous approaches, domestic explanations do not consider how cooperative processes themselves influence these preferences. Instead, they focus on internal, often material, forces that explain actor preferences. Following this agenda, some scholars drawing on the Middle East consider internal state processes—such as coalition building, political-economic considerations, public opinion, or preferences of institutions like the military—to enhance our understanding of nations' motivations for going to war or for deciding to cooperate.

Michael Barnett argues, for example, that states preparing for war look not only to their external security environment but also to their internal political and economic environment and conduct their security policies within the confines of these domestic constraints.[46] Examining both Egypt and Israel, Barnett finds that each (despite vastly different regime types and cultural, historical experiences) must calculate its war strategies based on domestic political economic considerations, bringing state-society relations into national security calculations. Likewise, Etel Solingen looks at the domestic environment and argues that political coalitions favoring domestic economic reform policies (i.e., liberalizing coalitions) will pursue regional cooperation, particularly if they face "similarly committed regional partners."[47] Steven David argues that in considering alliance formation, Middle East states often are more concerned with balancing internal threats to the governing regime than with external state-based threats, thus explaining apparently anomalous alliance behavior.[48]

While bringing in domestic politics improves the application of international relations theory to Middle Eastern politics, it is not a panacea. Because the multilateral track is a low-profile process receiving little media and public attention and does not threaten the core (borders and sovereignty) interests of the participants, the range of options is greater for the elites driving this process forward (or backward). While the bilateral tracks are greatly influenced by public opinion, domestic coalitions, security, or even regime survival considerations, the multilaterals are much more insulated from these forces. While this insulation is not absolute (e.g., negative public opinion can slow cooperation efforts), the issues under discussion in the multilaterals are further removed from the public's concerns and understanding. While the general Israeli public, for example, can easily grasp the costs and benefits associated with giving up land or serving less military time in the West Bank, the benefits of regional security regimes or specific confidence-building measures are not readily apparent. At a later stage in the process—if and when durable institutions are established that influence national politics—the public may weigh into the process to a greater extent. But at this nascent stage of Arab-Israeli regional cooperation, the process was by and large elite-driven and does not require the inclusion of such domestic politics explanations as might be necessary for other processes and policy outcomes.

At a normative level, one may argue that domestic constituencies *should* be better educated about regional cooperation processes, and that the difficulties in the normalization process are the result of the elite focus of the peace process that neglects the people-to-people requisite for enduring peace. But the central purpose of this chapter is to explain the origins and development of Arab-Israeli multilateral cooperation, not to prescribe solutions to the difficulties. In such an explanation, domestic politics does not weigh heavily.

*Rational Cognitivists*

In response to dissatisfaction with static and structural accounts of international relations, and the failure of these approaches to account for the end of the Cold War,[49] international relations scholars have increasingly turned to ideational variables to enhance explanations of policy choice and change.[50] Even traditionally rationalist literatures, such as regime theory, have considered the role of cognitive forces in bringing about new institutions.[51]

The Goldstein and Keohane volume, *Ideas and Foreign Policy*, best exemplifies the rationalist approach to ideas.[52] While they criticize other rationalist approaches for neglecting ideational forces, Goldstein and Keohane do not cede their rationalist assumptions. Rather, they move to the unit level of analysis (individual beliefs) to determine the causal role of ideas on policy outcomes. As they explain, "we seek to show that ideas matter for policy, even when human beings behave rationally to achieve their ends. . . . Hence this volume criticizes approaches that deny the significance of ideas, but does not challenge the premise that people behave in self-interested and broadly rational ways."[53] Thus, while ideas are more than "hooks" used by powerful players to achieve their goals, they still serve rational purposes to achieve desired ends.

Specifically, Goldstein and Keohane point to three scenarios when ideas can bring about particular policy outcomes: when they "[1] provide road maps that increase actors' clarity about goals or ends-means relationships, [2] when they affect outcomes of strategic situations in which there is no unique equilibrium, and [3] when they become embedded in institutions."[54] They then proceed to structure the empirical cases included in their volume around these three functions in an effort to demonstrate the independent role of ideas in shaping outcomes, in addition to power and interest variables. They argue "that ideas *as well* as interests have causal weight in explanations of human action."[55] Like the approaches discussed above, this methodology assumes interests and thus would not allow for the notion that a cooperative process, and the ideas discussed within it, could alter or shape (not just compete) with interests. One critic, who generally supports cognitive analysis, explains the "theoretical snarl" of such an approach: "The strong case—that the power of the idea itself explains its acceptance—first must demonstrate that interests are interpenetrated by ideas, but then ideas must be shown to exert influence untainted by the interests they have just been shown to interpenetrate. The move is untenable and, in any case, is not required to establish the utility of an ideas-focused approach."[56] Constructivists share this critique and have advanced an alternative method for analyzing the relationship among ideas, culture and norms (nonmaterial forces), and actor interests. While the rational cognitivists attempt to demonstrate the causal effect of ideas on policy, constructivists are more concerned with demonstrating how ideas shape interests—or the source of interests and identity.[57]

## Constructivist Advantages

Despite its diversity, the body of literature under the rubric of constructivism has come to signify a particular approach that is, on the one hand, critical of rational choice approaches (particularly neorealism and neoliberal institutionalism) and, on the other, proscientific (thus distinguishing itself from other interpretive or postmodernist theories).[58] This school of thought also shares some general assumptions that sound familiar themes from the earlier European integration literature.[59] However, constructivism is not yet an alternative theory of international politics but rather an approach or method for explaining international politics.[60] I argue that extensions of this approach can be useful for understanding and explaining Arab-Israeli multilateral cooperation.

The most basic assumption of constructivists is the notion that the international environment is social and ideational, not just material.[61] Constructivists argue that material conditions cannot be divorced from the social foundations and collective sets of ideas about the nature of international politics. Constructivists believe that social, ideational factors can constitute interests and that interests cannot simply be assumed based on material conditions like power and wealth. Because politics are socially constructed, the structure of the international environment and its material possessions cannot be understood apart from the actors (states and the individuals who represent them) of which it is made—agent and structure are mutually constitutive.[62] Social structures in international politics, such as sovereignty, international institutions, or other interactive settings, can affect and shape state identities and interests. The construction of these interests and identities is not a static process because the meaning and significance of collective ideas is related to, and influenced by, time and place.[63] This recognition allows us to see how interactive processes may shape and change interests and identity over time.

Constructivism presents significant advantages when studying processes like the Arab-Israeli multilaterals. First, the constructivist method can explain why such processes originate by showing that even if a powerful player is necessary to create new institutions, one must understand why the power holds particular interests that lead to this outcome. Such interests may be based on ideational as well as material factors. Chapter 3 illustrates empirically, for example, how ideational forces contributed to the construction of American interests in creating the multilateral peace process. Second, a constructivist approach helps explain why the multilateral working groups developed as they did because it allows the explanation to focus on the cooperative process itself. We cannot understand how the activity of these groups progressed without understanding the interactions within this cooperative process.

Constructivism has been applied to a number of empirical studies.[64] Jeffrey T. Checkel argues that constructivist work has largely succeeded in demonstrating that nonmaterial factors like norms and identity matter in the construction of state interests and international structures. What is missing, in his view, are the questions when, why, and how such construction takes place. Moreover, Checkel observes that constructivists tend to look at successes—places where identity and interests *do* change—rather than cases where they do not.[65] Thus, the central critique of constructivism is the problem of scope. Constructivism needs to go beyond showing "social construction matters" to demonstrating when, why, and how social construction occurs and, subsequently, why sometimes it fails to occur.[66]

By focusing on the cooperative process of multilateral interaction, this book seeks to address some of these critiques. The "when question" is answered by deferring to modified power arguments based on leadership. Thus, the possibility for social construction occurs when a powerful actor creates an interactive process. The "how question" is addressed by emphasizing interaction in the cooperative process itself—particularly a multilateral process—as a mechanism by which actor views and positions may change, at times allowing participants to recognize they share joint interests. However, constructivists have been subjected to criticism for appearing to focus on cases where interests have changed (usually for "the better").[67] While I do not focus on a change of interests, this study demonstrates how interactions may *facilitate as well as impede* common understandings.

## A Framework for Analysis of Multilateral Cooperation

The analytic framework for this book consists of three parts. The first explains the origins of regional multilateral processes, in which the predominant forces are distinct from those influencing how such processes develop. The second part presents the dynamics involved in explaining successful multilateral cooperation based on the process conception of cooperation. The third suggests the dynamics by which such processes can fail as a result of a number of impediments to cooperation. Together, these parts explain both the origins and varied development of regional multilateral cooperation in the Middle East, and potentially in other regions engaging in similar cooperative dialogues.

### The Origins of Regional Cooperation

The concept of structural and intellectual leadership as a variant of power explanations is key to understanding why and how an Arab-Israeli multilateral cooperative process emerged. Leaders who represent powerful actors project their power to create, or "supply," new institutions. Often, such leadership is supplied from extraregional actors (in the Arab-Israeli case, by the United States) exercising sources of leverage over regional actors who may not be enthusiastic about new interactive forums. Indeed, Israel and Arab parties expressed serious reservations about engaging in the multilateral talks. Without the structural leadership of the United States, it is unlikely such a process could have emerged.

That said, to understand the particular shape of new cooperative forums we also must examine the source of interests motivating the powerful leader.

As constructivists would expect, the source of these interests is not only material but also ideational. This explains the link between structural and intellectual leadership. The ideas of powerful players matter and affect the nature of new institutions or processes. For example, a small group of American policy elites within the administration—who were part of a larger network, or community, of Middle East experts in Washington, D.C.—shared similar notions about how to resolve the Arab-Israeli conflict and greatly influenced American policy in this region, including the formation of the multilateral peace process track.

To explain the creation of new interactive forums, it is necessary to identify the critical power upon whose leadership the process depends and the ideas motivating the policies of that power. One needs to demonstrate that regional demand alone would not have been sufficient to bring about a new process without the leadership of such a power. Chapter 3 presents empirical support for this dynamic.

## *The Development of Successful Cooperation*

This study defines cooperation as the process of parties working together in an effort to achieve common understandings. Successful cooperation occurs when a particular interactive process leads actors to develop common understandings with respect to a given issue area. I am not saying that it takes a change of broad, national interests to mark the success of multilateral cooperation. Rather, I am referring to the parties' support for cooperative dialogue across issue areas and achievement of common understandings within them. The process can change perceptions about the value of such activity. Thus, parties can come to a consensus about the utility of the cooperative process and reach common understandings even if they do so to serve different strategic interests.

What are the indicators, or mechanisms, by which we can evaluate the extent to which the parties are reaching common understandings, or engaging in successful cooperation? A key component of this transformative process is the ability of various working groups to frame a politically divisive process into a technical problem that may be addressed in a cooperative manner. In the Middle East cases, all issues began as political issues because of the unprecedented involvement of Israel. This explains why the Syrians, for example, chose to boycott the multilateral working groups from the outset. Moreover, the particular working groups were all associated with divisive issues focused on Arab concerns about Israeli military or economic advantages. Arms control, for example, was linked to the question of Israel's nuclear capability and the military balance of power between Israel and the Arab states. Economic development was perceived by many as an Israeli design to impose its hegemony on the region. Water and the environment were viewed from a distribution perspective that touched on charged questions like land and sovereignty. In short, none of the issues on the multilateral agenda were inherently "technical." The parties had to transform these issues into solvable problems conducive to multilateral cooperation.

What are the specific mechanisms that can facilitate cooperation as defined here? I suggest five such mechanisms which operated in the Arab-Israeli multilateral cases and may be generalizable to other cooperative processes: 1) problem identification; 2) shifting understandings of acceptable policy options; 3) acceptance of new partners and coalitions; 4) the development of new vocabulary and shared "myths" surrounding the issue area; and 5) intensified interactions among regional participants, including the participation of technical experts. All of these cooperation facilitators assume the establishment of a process where dialogue, meetings, and continual interactions are taking place.

Defining problems differently as a result of a cooperative process is an important facilitator in the effort to reach common understandings among the participants. The ability to frame problems as integrative ("we all have a stake in solving this") rather than distributive ("who will gain more if we address this problem") is an important component of problem identification. For example, the Water working group was able to make significant progress once the parties understood that the group would only address issues of increasing and improving the region's existing water supply as opposed to deciding how this scarce resource would be distributed among the regional parties. In the arms control group, the Gulf states were more willing to accept the process once they understood that the problem of arms control was not just about restricting the number of arms shipped to the region but also about building confidence among the regional parties to avoid, in part, unintentional conflict.

Shifting understandings of acceptable policy options is also an important dynamic that can facilitate positive cooperation. For example, in the Economic Development working group, actors came to see the establishment of new regional institutions as serving their interests, even though before the multilaterals the creation of such Arab-Israeli forums would have been unthinkable. The discussions to create such institutions, like a regional development bank, fostered common understandings of the economic problems plaguing the region and also intensified elite contacts, another facilitator of cooperation as discussed below.

The ability to view other regional players as acceptable partners for cooperative ventures allows new coalitions to form, again enhancing the prospects for broader agreement on regional problems. In the Middle East cases, the most critical development was the Arab parties' growing acceptance of Israel as a legitimate partner. Some Gulf states, for example, no longer viewed Israel only as the occupier of Palestinian land, but saw it also as a useful partner in creating new water development schemes like desalination centers. Indeed, the slow integration of Israel into regional partnerships is an important ingredient not just for the success of the multilateral working groups but also for the normalization of regional relations more broadly.

All groups also attempted to create a shared set of vocabulary and consensual (though not necessarily scientific) knowledge surrounding their issue area in order to reach common understandings of their problems. For example, the first sessions of the working groups often took on a "seminar diplomacy" format, with extraregional parties lecturing the regional participants about the nature of the issue area and creating a common language for working group activities. Many Arabs and Israelis were not well versed in arms control vocabulary before the multilaterals, and were introduced to important concepts like confidence-building measures (CBMs) which would later constitute a central element of their working group activity. In the economic realm, constant discussions regarding the dynamics of globalization helped frame regional economic problems in common ways.

Finally, increased interactions among regional elites help facilitate more successful cooperation. A good indication of this was the movement of the working group activity from large and more formal plenary sessions to smaller, more informal "intersessional" activities. Often, the intersessional meetings would include nonpolitical specialists in order to address the more technical aspects of a given issue area (a good illustration of moving the issues from the political to the technical realm). Moreover, the more informal sessions allowed regional elites to develop personal relationships and a sense of a common stake in the success of their efforts. Some elites commented in interviews that at times they saw their Arab or Israeli counterparts more often than their own spouses. These personal relationships can play a critical role in developing common understandings that cut across national boundaries.

When assessing empirical cases, it is useful to evaluate how actors view the process and the extent to which the cooperation in the working groups has led to new and more consensual understandings of similar problems and the value of the cooperative process itself based on indicators like those outlined above. Often, the results may be mixed, with some elements of success and failure apparent in all groups. It is critical to keep in mind that all cooperative processes are tenuous and even those issues that are more successful at transforming themselves into "technical" problems still have political salience to the actors involved. Indeed, a number of impediments to successful cooperation are possible at various points in the process.

## The Development of Unsuccessful Cooperation

When actors do not reach common understandings as a result of a cooperative process or when they view the process in negative, conflictual ways, cooperation has failed. The absence of some facilitators like those outlined above can lead to cooperation failures. For example, Egyptians and Israelis could ultimately not define the arms control problem or frame the nuclear issue differently enough to lead to common understandings, leading to a deadlock in the arms control group.

However, the impediments to cooperation extend beyond the mere absence of certain facilitating factors related to the process. Other developments—both within and outside the process—can impede cooperation, slowing or even halting efforts to reach common understandings. By specifying the impediments to cooperation—again derived from the Arab-Israeli cases—we might be better equipped to suggest prescriptions for how to improve such processes. Impeding mechanisms include: 1) a polarizing external political process; 2) domestic pressure and sensitivity to public opinion; 3) a sense of threat to pre-existing national identities; 4) perceptions that the process is inequitable; and 5) changing perceptions about the external environment. Not all of these impediments appeared in each case of Arab-Israeli multilateral cooperation, and some proved to be more critical than others in particular cases. Still, the list suggests the range of forces that may block cooperative efforts. The lack of funding for regional projects is also a critical impediment to cooperation, but this factor affects the prospects for actual projects more than the cooperative process itself.

It is not uncommon for outside political developments to infringe on positive developments within a cooperative process. In the Middle East multilaterals, the most obvious political development affecting the working groups was the Israeli-Palestinian bilateral negotiating track. While the bilateral and multilateral tracks did not move in tandem at all times, negative bilateral developments did make the process of reaching common understandings across multilateral issue areas more difficult. Even if regional elites desired to continue sessions in the aftermath of a political crisis, they were often impeded from doing so because of political sensitivities and the potential for such meetings to be read as insensitivity to the Palestinian track. Another example of an outside political process impeding a working group's activity was the Nuclear Nonproliferation Treaty (NPT) renewal conference in the spring of 1995. This conference was viewed by the Egyptians as a useful opportunity to highlight the issue of Israel's nuclear capability (Israel is not a signatory to the NPT and maintains a policy of nuclear ambiguity), which subsequently led to a stalemate in the multilateral arms control group.

Another potential problem for multilateral cooperation is resistance from domestic constituencies and concern about how the cooperation will play out in public opinion. Certain domestic groups will always have a stake in particular issue areas, such as the agriculture sector in water development schemes, and may object to how elites are defining the problem (e.g., a focus on water use). In certain cases, like the Arab-Israeli multilaterals, general public opinion may not look favorably upon cooperative efforts with states they feel are not legitimate partners. One reason the multilaterals were kept so low profile, for example, was to protect the process from anticipated negative public reactions (particularly in the Arab world) to Arab-Israeli cooperation before the bilateral peace process was resolved. At times, press coverage of multilateral initiatives led to the cancellation of certain activities, such as a joint Arab-Israeli naval exercise in the region sponsored by the arms control group. Sensitivity to negative public reactions among Arab leaders has proved a constraining—though not debilitating—force in moving cooperation forward.

Strong national identities among key participants in multilateral cooperation can also prove an impeding factor if the cooperative process is viewed by these actors as developing in ways that challenge their roles in the region.

Multilateral cooperation often gives smaller states a stronger voice vis-à-vis their larger regional neighbors than they would maintain in a bilateral setting, a possibly disturbing development to powers who view themselves as regional leaders. Egypt, for example, views its leadership position in the Arab world as an important element of its national identity, and does not look favorably upon processes which threaten this sense of self. The arms control case demonstrates how Egypt sought to focus on the divisive nuclear issue because it represented an area in which Egypt has traditionally taken a leadership role and was one which it thought it could use to counter what it viewed as a multilateral process that was diminishing, rather than enhancing, Egypt's leadership status.

Perceptions among regional participants about the equity of the process can also impede progress. If regional parties perceive a cooperative process as benefiting others—particularly regional rivals—more than themselves, they may be less inclined to continue the process of reaching common understandings. For example, Egypt and Jordan often competed to house new regional centers and institutions and, when they failed to secure them, were apt to become reluctant to engage in cooperation. Arab parties also held persistent fears that Israel was gaining more out of multilateral cooperation (particularly political recognition) than they were earning, leading to boycotts of certain multilateral activities like the regional economic summit in Doha in the fall of 1997.

Finally, changing perceptions of the external environment—security or economic—can potentially impede cooperation because the parties may no longer view regional problems in common ways. For example, interactions within the economic working group fostered common understandings about globalization and its relationship to regional relations (namely, that regional cooperation would serve globalization objectives). However, altered understandings of the global economic environment may lead to negative views of the value of a continued cooperative process. Likewise, changing perceptions of the strategic environment as the common dangers of the Gulf War grow more distant may also reduce the incentives for regional parties to engage in cooperation on regional arms control in the future.

In sum, for each empirical case in chapters 4 through 6 we must assess the extent to which the cooperative process succeeded in creating common understandings as well as the types of impediments which disrupted the process. The cases of Arab-Israeli multilateral cooperation illustrate both dynamics. This framework for analyzing multilateral cooperation provides explanatory leverage by reconceptualizing cooperation as a process, not just an outcome. Without such a framework, we would not only have difficulty in explaining and understanding the value of multilateral cooperation in the Middle East, but we also might be precluding analysis of important cooperative processes occurring in other parts of the world.

# 2 The Historical Record: Pre-Madrid Regional Cooperation

The Arab-Israeli multilaterals are not only distinct from the bilateral peace process, but they are also a departure from previous peacemaking efforts focused on the substantive issue areas included in the multilateral talks. Before proceeding to the emergence and development of the multilaterals, it is worth highlighting some of these historical differences in order to understand the unprecedented nature of this process and the extent to which regional relations changed after the Gulf War and the collapse of the Soviet Union. At the same time, these pre-Madrid efforts also foreshadow many of the difficulties the multilateral working groups would face despite the altered global and regional environments. Examples from the arms control, economic development, and water and environment issue areas will illustrate both the contrasts and continuities in addressing regional cooperation in the Arab-Israeli context.

## Arms Control

Pre-Madrid efforts to address regional arms control underscore the difficulty of creating such processes in the polarized security environment that existed during the Cold War. Such efforts can be divided into two types: (1) *supplier restraint initiatives*, or efforts by extraregional powers to limit the supply of arms and technology (conventional and unconventional) to the region; and (2) *regional initiatives*, focused on developing demilitarized zones or limited military deployments in sensitive border areas, or other confidence-building measures (CBMs) between Israel and its Arab neighbors, including proposals to establish regional nuclear and weapons of mass destruction free zones (NWFZ/WMDFZ). The supplier initiatives did not involve coordination among Israel and Arab states, while regional efforts consisted primarily of bilateral arrangements mediated by an outside party or unilateral initiatives presented to international bodies. In this sense, both types of previous arms control initiatives are distinct from the multilateral ACRS process.

This brief review of previous arms control initiatives illustrates the difficulty of establishing a regional arms control process without a conducive global and regional security environment. The historical efforts, while by and large failures, also reveal the extent to which extraregional pressures and leadership were necessary for attempts to establish regional arms control measures. The variety of past initiatives also offered U.S. policymakers several alternatives for promoting regional arms control after the Gulf War, and raises the question of why policymakers favored ACRS over other options, a question which the next chapter will consider.

*Supplier Restraint Initiatives*

Before ACRS, extraregional powers made several attempts to address the arms control problem by restricting the flow of arms and technology to the region. However, none of these efforts succeeded, and the difficulty of establishing a supplier regime led many to emphasize the need for regional initiatives, like ACRS, that could potentially curb the demand for what seemed an endless supply of weapons to the Middle East.

The first supplier initiative to address the problem of the arms race in the region, the Tripartite Declaration of May 25, 1950, was an agreement among the United Kingdom, France, and the United States to regulate the flow of arms to the Middle East.[2] The declaration led to an enforcement mechanism two years later, the Near East Arms Coordinating Committee (NEACC), which monitored arms transfers until the arms race escalated with the Soviet-initiated Egyptian-Czechoslovakian arms deal in 1955. This deal, along with cleavages among the Western powers, undermined the initiative and led to a renewed regional arms race.

Subsequent supplier efforts, including several Soviet initiatives in the

1950s[3] and President Lyndon B. Johnson's proposal for an arms shipment register in the wake of the 1967 Arab-Israeli War,[4] also failed and continued to underscore the difficulty of establishing such regimes and the need for additional arms control strategies. While Johnson's arms register idea eventually resurfaced, albeit over twenty years and several conflicts later,[5] the Cold War environment led the Americans and Soviets to utilize arms sales as a means to balance regional players and enhance superpower influence. The United States, for example, sold over $30 billion in arms to Egypt and Israel alone between 1979 and 1990.[6] Even with détente in the 1970s, renewed efforts to limit conventional weapons to the region, such as the Carter administration's Conventional Arms Transfer Talks (CAT) from 1977 to 1979, deteriorated along with political relations between the U.S. and Soviets.[7]

Finally, even one of the most serious efforts to create supplier restraints in the Middle East—the Bush Arms Control Initiative of May 29, 1991— faced the same fate as all previous efforts in this area.[8] Despite the highly visible efforts by President George Bush and Secretary of State James A. Baker III to promote regional arms control in the wake of the Gulf War,[9] divisions among Western suppliers could not be bridged. Moreover, the end of the Cold War (and the presidential election of 1992) led to increasing pressure from the defense industry for continued, and even increased, arms exports, undermining the rhetoric of supplier restraint.[10] Thus, this high-profile attempt to institutionalize a multilateral supplier restraint regime for the Middle East region among the five permanent members of the UN Security Council (the United States, the Soviet Union, China, Britain, and France) unraveled by the fall of 1992 after a series of unsuccessful follow-up meetings among the permanent five.[11]

## Regional Arms Control Initiatives and Arrangements

Before ACRS, there had been some successful attempts at regional arms control, but most of these examples were limited, bilateral arrangements springing from either bilateral peace treaties or disengagement agreements on disputed borders between Israel and its Arab neighbors. While another set of regional proposals focused on creating a zone free of weapons of mass destruction (including nuclear weapons), the proposals were unrealistic in the absence of an Arab-Israeli political accommodation, particularly since no negotiating forum to discuss them existed before the Madrid process. Still, these limited precursors to ACRS set the stage for a more ambitious multilateral arms control agenda.

Indeed, since the 1948 Arab-Israeli war Israel and its immediate neighbors have engaged in both formal and informal security arrangements to minimize the prospects for conflict. Such arrangements include: armistice agreements between Israel and each of its Arab neighbors (Egypt, Jordan, Syria, and Lebanon) from 1949 to the mid-1950s; Israeli-Egyptian demilitarized zones and zones of limited military deployment on the Golan Heights from 1974; the de facto demilitarization of the Sinai from 1957 to 1967 and the creation of buffer zones through the Sinai I and Sinai II agreements (1974–75); and finally, the establishment of the Multinational Force and Observers (MFO) to verify security arrangements in the Sinai in the wake of the Egyptian-Israeli peace treaty in 1979. An extensive tacit security regime also developed between Israel and Jordan beginning with the Black September crisis in 1970, leading to cooperation to maintain stable borders as well as information and intelligence exchanges and even conventions to regulate aerial activity and maritime commerce from Aqaba and Eilat.[12] Together, these bilateral security arrangements and CBMs contributed to limited stability despite the absence of a comprehensive regional peace.

However, these types of arrangements were largely limited to the military realm, and were always bilaterally based in terms of regional participation. Unlike the ACRS experiment, the purpose of these agreements was well defined: the prevention and limitation of armed conflict on border areas between Israel and its immediate neighbors. In many cases, these agreements were viewed as an alternative to peace agreements rather than as a complement, as was the intention with ACRS.[13] Moreover, with the exception of the Israeli-Egyptian security agreements embodied in their peace treaty and the tacit Israeli-Jordanian security cooperation, these bilateral security arrangements did not require direct Arab-Israeli cooperation, but rather were mediated by outside parties.

A second type of regional arms control initiative is exemplified by proposals for nuclear (NWFZ) or weapons of mass destruction free zones (WMDFZ) that, unlike the limited bilateral security arrangements, were intended to reduce or eliminate dangerous unconventional weaponry from the entire region.[14] Since 1974, Egypt has been the most persistent and vocal advocate for nuclear arms control, offering initiatives for both a Middle Eastern NWFZ and a WMDFZ at the United Nations.[15] For the Egyptians, the preferred arms control sequence is to address the nuclear question first, and the political dimension second—the exact opposite to the Israeli preference. Moreover, Egyptian proposals traditionally called for Israel to sign the Nuclear Nonproliferation Treaty (NPT) and to place its nuclear facilities under the inspection of the International Atomic Energy Agency (IAEA).

However, since the mid-1960s—when Israel is believed to have acquired a nuclear weapons capability—Israel's official position on nuclear weapons has been the simple statement that Israel will not be the first country to introduce nuclear weapons into the region. This policy of ambiguity has served Israeli interests in maintaining an existential deterrent while avoiding conflict with the United States on the proliferation question.[16] Thus, Israel has refused to sign the NPT although it has signed other global conventions on unconventional weapons, such as the Chemical Weapons Convention (CWC) in January 1993. Not surprisingly, Israel tends to stress the need to establish a WMDFZ, which by its definition includes not only nuclear, biological, and chemical weapons, but also destructive conventional weaponry, such as certain missile technology.[17] Neither the Egyptian nor the Israeli initiatives were expected to produce serious discussions because they were largely viewed as attempts to score "points and counter-points in the Arab-Israeli propaganda battle . . . While both sides could claim the moral high ground for their proposals for NWFZ, they knew that the whole exercise was futile, no more than diplomatic posturing."[18]

These previous efforts at regional arms control illustrate both the challenges and the promise for a process like ACRS. The challenges were many, but the most fundamental problem centered on the contrasting approaches to the nuclear issue between the Egyptians and Israelis. Yet in contrast to the past, the Cold War no longer dictated competitive regional security relations and for the first time, regional parties could engage in a dialogue, rather than a debate, on security structures for the region. In the context of the conflictual history of Arab-Israeli security relations, ACRS emerged in an environment that seemed to offer the promise of taking on the tremendous challenge of regional arms control.

### Economic Development

Arab-Israeli economic cooperation efforts before the Madrid conference underscore their limited nature and the economic and political impediments to Arab-Israeli cooperation in this issue area. This background reveals that to the extent that Arab-Israeli economic interaction did occur, it was largely orchestrated from the outside in conscious attempts to impose cooperative relations in the region, particularly in the wake of the Egyptian-Israeli peace treaty of 1979. The limits to such cooperation have been primarily political, but even without political impediments, the economic foundations for cooperation between the developed Israeli economy and the developing Arab region are not conducive to integration proposals or to region-wide free trade areas (although subregional zones, particularly among Israel, Jordan, and a Palestinian entity, are feasible).[19] The past record of Arab-Israeli economic relations serves as a contrast to the post-Madrid environment, where many of the political and economic obstacles of the past were consciously overcome in efforts to foster unprecedented Arab-Israeli economic cooperation.

## *Proposals Under President Eisenhower*

In late November 1954, U.S. Secretary of State John Foster Dulles and British Foreign Secretary Anthony Eden met in Paris informally to discuss proposals to end the Arab-Israeli conflict through a comprehensive peace settlement. These talks led to a secret U.S.-British project, also known as operation ALPHA,[20] the outlines of which were made public by Dulles in an address before the Council on Foreign Relations on August 26, 1955.[21] The plan envisioned Israeli territorial concessions in the Negev and the resettlement of Palestinians in neighboring states, as well as some limited repatriation. These conditions required significant economic aid packages for Israel to compensate the refugees and development schemes to facilitate the refugees' resettlement, including water development. Moreover, the authors of this peace proposal envisioned economic dividends for Israel in terms of new trade opportunities with Arab states and the end of the Arab secondary boycott of Israel. Had the ALPHA plan succeeded, the potential for Arab-Israeli economic cooperation might have been tested. However, with both Israel and Arab states opposed to the plan, ALPHA never materialized, nor did the development plans associated with it.

Yet the Eisenhower administration continued to focus on the lack of economic development in the Middle East as a source for continued regional conflict. To this end, in 1958 the administration offered one of the earliest proposals for a regional development bank, the Middle East Economic Development Fund. As in the case of ALPHA, the proposal sought in part to address the Arab refugee problem resulting from the Arab-Israeli conflict. The basic idea was to transfer funds from the Arab "haves" to the Arab "have nots" in order to create a more stable regional environment.[22] However, due to concerns over how American oil companies might be affected by a regional funding mechanism[23] as well as a belief that bilateral assistance programs would provide the United States with better leverage with which to promote its interests in the region, the proposal was not pursued.[24] Despite the dormancy of this idea for over thirty years, political considerations—namely, further attempts to resolve the Arab-Israeli conflict—again brought the proposal to the attention of American policymakers. Indeed, these early ideas for regional economic development to improve the political climate planted the seeds for future proposals like the Arab-Israeli multilaterals which carried a similar causal premise. However, in the absence of political accommodation, regional schemes involving Israel and Arab states were restricted to limited and often secret channels.

## The Arab Boycott

With no comprehensive Arab-Israeli peace—which seemed increasingly distant after the 1956 Suez war—economic relations were viewed as yet another tool in the regional conflict rather than a means to promote peace. The Arab League economic boycott of Israel, which became institutionalized with the 1951 creation of the Central Office for the Boycott of Israel (CBO) in Damascus, was the clearest expression of the impediments facing Arab-Israeli economic cooperation.[25] The boycott created a taboo on Arab-Israeli commercial contact, which has been difficult to break even in the post-Madrid/post-Oslo period, particularly within the Arab private sector. The boycott worked at several levels to prevent Arab-Israeli economic contact.

The primary boycott prohibited any direct trade or commercial contacts between Arab states and Israel. The secondary boycott prohibited trade with companies that conducted business in Israel, while the tertiary boycott targeted firms (such as suppliers) doing business with companies operating in Israel. The secondary and tertiary boycotts led to a comprehensive "black list" of foreign firms which did not comply with the Arab boycott's terms (which in turn led to comprehensive antiboycott legislation in the United States beginning in 1977 to prevent American firms' compliance with the boycott). Other restrictions also resulted from the boycott that went beyond sanctioning Israel, such as the widespread travel ban on Jews by denying entry visas to Arab states, which prevented both Israeli and Jewish tourism and business contacts within the Arab world. Yet the primary Arab boycott of Israel proved to be far more symbolic than economically painful. While vastly different accounts of the economic impact of the boycott on Israel make it difficult to quantify its effect, most analysts agree that the secondary and tertiary aspects of the boycott (with over 6,300 foreign firms blacklisted by the CBO) proved far more detrimental to the Israeli economy than the lack of direct Arab-Israeli commercial ties.[26]

The threat of losing business in the Arab world discouraged many foreign companies from pursuing commercial interests in Israel, particularly since antiboycott legislation was not enforced and even nonexistent in most of Europe and Asia. In fact, during the growth of the Israeli economy in the years following the Madrid conference, the primary boycott was still technically in place. The central difference during these years—in addition to domestic economic reform policies in Israel—was the growth of foreign direct investment in the Israeli economy and growing exports to areas that were formerly restricted under the secondary boycott, primarily in Asia.[27]

According to an Israeli Ministry of Finance study for 1972–1983, Israeli exports would have been 1 percent higher if the boycott was not in place, costing Israel $6 billion. The Hufbauer, Schott, and Elliott study estimates an annual loss of $258 million from 1951 to 1980, averaging from 2.3 percent of Israel's GNP (1951–60) to 5.9 percent (1973–80).[28] While the figures vary, few doubt the serious economic effects of the secondary and tertiary boycott on Israeli economic growth, and the rather limited effects of the primary boycott. Thus, the history of the Arab boycott underscores the relatively low potential for direct Arab-Israeli commercial relations on *economic grounds* (with the exception of the Israeli-Jordanian-Palestinian triad)[29] and the need to consciously foster these types of contacts to further political ends given the lack of economic incentives to build economic ties even under conditions of peace. Unlike in the security realm where Arabs and Israelis encounter genuine security interdependencies, their economic dependencies on a region-wide basis (as opposed to subregions) are few, and provide a weak foundation for building a wider cooperative economic framework.

## Israeli-Egyptian Economic Cooperation

An excellent example of the impediments to wider Arab-Israeli economic cooperation is the Israeli-Egyptian experience in the wake of their peace accord in 1979. Even at its peak in 1981, Egyptian-Israeli trade relations were minimal, with Egyptian exports totaling $550 million and Israeli exports to Egypt totaling just $115 million.[30] Moreover, the majority of Egyptian exports were in the oil sector, with none of the other export sectors surpassing $1 million.[31] While Israel has repeatedly attempted to expand bilateral economic relations with Egypt and implement other measures included in their peace treaty, the Egyptians have resisted, arguing that normalization is dependent on progress on other political fronts (primarily with the Palestinians).[32] Private sector contact between Egyptians and Israelis before the Madrid process was nearly absent. However, even after the Israeli-Palestinian Oslo agreement, the limited nature of Egyptian-Israeli trade relations did not fundamentally change, raising questions about the potential for comprehensive regional economic cooperation, even under peace conditions, beyond periodic joint ventures.

## Israeli-Palestinian Economic Relations

The Israeli and Palestinian economies are the most interdependent in the Arab-Israeli context. After Israel's occupation of the West Bank and Gaza in the 1967 conflict, the Palestinian economy became inextricably linked to and dependent upon Israel. Many debate the impact of the Israeli domination of the Palestinian economy. Some point to its positive effect in leading to rapid economic growth due to access to the large Israeli market, which had been closed before 1967. Others note the negative socioeconomic effect of dependency on the Israeli market where political crises disrupt its economy (particularly the dependence of the Palestinian labor force on the Israeli market).[33] In fact, both effects have played out on the ground, leading to mixed results. For example, the combined per capita GNP of the territories rose from 13.8 percent of the Israeli GNP in 1970 to 22.7 percent in 1986.[34] By 1987, the combined per capita GNP of the West Bank and Gaza was comparable to middle-income economies (at $1717) according to the World Bank's classification, making it higher than the per capita GNP of both Syria and Jordan.[35] But this growth was the result of extreme dependence on Israel, with over one-third of the combined labor force of the territories employed in Israel in 1986 and the wages earned there accounting for nearly one-fourth of its GNP.[36]

The dependence of Palestinian labor on the Israeli market has created one of the greatest setbacks to Palestinian economic development, particularly during politically unstable periods. Because of lower wages and poor employment opportunity in the territories, Palestinians have had to rely on these volatile external labor markets (often in unreliable labor sectors like construction) despite the devastating economic risks of such dependence. After the intifada (beginning in December 1987) and then the Gulf war, Israeli restrictions on Palestinian labor increased as Israelis, because of security concerns, began substituting foreign workers from Asia and Eastern Europe for Palestinian labor. The lack of indigenous development from either public or private sector foreign investment because of political uncertainty and legal restrictions also created tremendous challenges for future attempts to develop a viable Palestinian economy.[37]

While the Israeli occupation of the West Bank and Gaza left the Palestinians little choice in economic affairs, it is likely that even in the wake of a final status agreement on the nature of the Palestinian entity that the Palestinian economy will remain linked to Israel given its proximity and labor needs, although both sides will want to limit Palestinian labor dependence on Israel for political and security reasons. The protocol governing Israeli-Palestinian economic relations under their interim agreement (signed in April 1994 in Paris) already established a virtual customs union, although its implementation was greatly impeded by the delays in extending Palestinian self-rule and by Israeli closures of the Palestinian territories in the wake of terrorist incidents.[38] Consequently, the Israeli-Palestinian experience is not exemplary of the overall pattern of economic cooperation in the region, which is far more limited, and provides one of the few cases (along with Jordan) of high potential for expanded economic cooperation, albeit by necessity more than by desire.

*Summary*

Before the Madrid and Oslo peace process, Arab-Israeli economic cooperation remained limited and largely theoretical, restricted to academic debates identifying sectors where economic cooperation could one day take place to support peace, often citing areas like water development, tourism, and regional infrastructure projects. Even after the Egyptian-Israeli peace treaty, the potential for regional economic cooperation remained unfulfilled, and the Arab boycott continued to prevent efforts to further regional cooperation through trade and commercial contacts. In fact, one of the few examples of Arab-Israeli economic interaction before Madrid—the Israeli relationship with the Palestinian territories—created a negative image of Israeli domination.

Still, academic conceptualizations and external government efforts (particularly by the United States) outlining the cooperative potential of the region were important in providing many ideas that would later appear as regional projects across various sectors in the Regional Economic Development working group (REDWG), particularly in areas like water development, communications networks, and tourism.[39] Yet before a peace settlement, these plans could not be attempted on the ground, particularly given the absence of any regional economic forum to foster such initiatives. But even with a peace settlement, the above overview of Arab-Israeli economic relations suggests a note of caution for those promoting Arab-Israeli economic cooperation. While the economic basis for Arab-Israeli cooperation—at least on the broad regional level—has always been questionable, political roadblocks proved the most serious impediment for even limited joint ventures. With the removal of some of these political roadblocks at the Madrid conference and the establishment of the multilaterals, the potential of many of these joint economic schemes could be tested on the ground.

## Water and Environmental Cooperation

As was the case in the arms control and economic issue areas, Arab-Israeli water and environmental cooperation faced political obstacles despite the more technical nature of these issue areas where mutual gain from cooperation is perhaps most obvious. Attempts before Madrid to forge cooperative arrangements in these areas either failed or were limited to bilateral agreements, largely between Israel and Egypt and, in secret fashion, Jordan. Any regional multilateral cooperation that did occur (through the United Nations, for example) did not promote direct Arab-Israeli contact as did the Madrid multilaterals. As in the economic case, however, earlier cooperative attempts provided ideas and frameworks that would serve as a basis for many of the later projects which emerged from the Arab-Israeli multilateral talks.

One of the earliest and most prominent attempts to establish an Arab-Israeli regime which would regulate water usage focused on the Jordan River basin and became known as the Johnston Plan. In an effort to alleviate tensions plaguing the region in the aftermath of the 1948 Arab-Israeli war, the Eisenhower administration began to promote a basin-wide project (the Unified Development of the Water Resources of the Jordan Valley Region) that included four riparian states—Israel, Jordan, Syria, and Lebanon. The plan was based on a proposal by Charles T. Main of the Tennessee Valley Authority and suggested a formula for the equitable distribution of waters in the basin.[40] Eric Johnston, President Dwight D. Eisenhower's special envoy, met with technical teams from the four riparian states and Egypt from 1953 to 1956 in an attempt to secure a water sharing agreement. Eventually, the parties agreed that as a technical arrangement the basin-wide project was acceptable, a success largely achieved because the negotiations were limited to technical personnel and avoided publicity.[41] However, despite technical agreement, the political implications of the plan (i.e., Arab recognition of Israel) proved unacceptable for the Arab parties. They could not approve any collaboration with Israel prior to a political settlement of the Arab-Israeli conflict. As Miriam Lowi explains, "the experience of the Johnston mission elucidates the fact that profound geopolitical and security-related concerns, emanating from historical circumstance and the character of relations in the basin, often dominate the seemingly technical issue of allocating water resources."[42] Despite the failure of this agreement, the plan guided Jordanian and Israeli actions with regard to their water supplies and contributed to a tacit water regime between these two adversaries.[43] Still, until Madrid, such cooperative arrangements remained both secret and bilateral.

Despite the failure of the Johnston Plan, the United States government continued to promote water cooperation schemes in the region, largely to serve the political purpose of promoting Arab-Israeli political accommodation. For example, in May 1967 (on the eve of the Arab-Israeli war) the United States sponsored an international water conference and, following the war, former President Eisenhower proposed a "water for peace" program which envisaged the construction of several nuclear reactors (in Egypt, Israel, and Jordan) to provide power and to desalinize seawater for the development of agro-industrial centers.[44] However, these conferences and plans ultimately did not produce direct Arab-Israeli interaction nor tangible projects because of the adverse political climate in the region.

The United States made efforts once again in the 1970s and early 1980s to develop cooperative water plans for the Jordan River basin. At issue was the Jordanian plan to dam the Yarmouk River to enable Jordan to utilize the winter flows that had been running into the Dead Sea. The Carter administration announced it would fund the project if an agreement with Syria and Israel were reached. Over a three-year period Assistant Secretary of State Philip Habib shuttled among the parties but failed to reach an agreement. The Syrians would not respond to any overtures regarding a trilateral water sharing plan and would not agree to a project which involved cooperation with Israel.[45]

One of the only successful programs to promote Arab-Israeli water and environmental cooperation—the Middle East Regional Cooperation Program (MERC)—was established in 1979 in the context of the Egyptian-Israeli peace process, and was thus limited to largely bilateral initiatives. The MERC program was mandated by Congress and given to the Agency for International Development (AID) to administer; its declared purpose was to "reduce political and social tensions in the Middle East by designing, promoting, and executing cooperative technical projects."[46] The program promoted bilateral and trilateral cooperation among Israeli, Egyptian, and American scientists in areas like food, water, and land protection. To the extent that other regional actors were involved (e.g., Jordan and Saudi Arabia), Egypt worked with them on a bilateral basis. Until Madrid, this program was not able to promote broader regional Arab-Israeli cooperation in these issue areas.

The United States was not the only body involved in promoting environmental cooperation in the region. The United Nations Environment Program was responsible for the coordination of a regime—the Mediterranean Action Plan (Med Plan)—aimed at improving the environmental conditions of the Mediterranean Sea and the surrounding countries, including Israel and a number of Arab states.[47] The Med Plan is comprehensive in nature, involving everything from the establishment of regional centers to coordinate oil spill management (an idea later discussed and implemented in the multilateral environmental working group) to the adoption of legal arrangements to preserve endangered marine species. The plan established the Land Based Sources Protocol which sets limits on industrial, municipal, and agricultural emissions into the Mediterranean and controls wastes transmitted by rivers and through the atmosphere. Interestingly, traditional sources of interstate conflict in the Mediterranean region did not derail the agreement, in part because Arab recognition of Israel was avoided in the larger Mediterranean context (e.g., Syria ratified the plan with the qualification that its ratification did not constitute recognition of Israeli sovereignty). While multilateral, this forum did not promote direct Arab-Israeli interaction at the regional level as did the Madrid multilateral process. However, the relative success of the Med Plan suggested fertile ground for such cooperation in substantive terms if political obstacles could be overcome.

## Summary

This chapter's survey of pre-Madrid efforts to establish Arab-Israeli regional cooperation in the arms control, economic, water, and environmental issue areas underscores the difficulty of such efforts in the absence of political accommodation. The conflictual Arab-Israeli environment impeded the progress of many regional cooperation schemes, limiting both the nature (e.g., little if any direct Arab-Israeli contact) and scope (e.g., largely bilateral or U.S.-sponsored trilateral agreements) of such endeavors. Thus, the establishment of the Madrid multilateral working groups marked a serious and unprecedented departure from all previous regional cooperation efforts. Still, these pre-Madrid examples also laid the groundwork and proposed many of the ideas that would later emerge in the multilaterals, from security CBMs to desalination plants to regional oil spill centers. Unlike earlier efforts, however, the multilaterals would establish a process by which Arabs and Israelis would discuss and even implement these ideas in a large regional setting, albeit always in the context of a tense political environment that would continue to pose obstacles for the resolution of these "technical" problems. But with the Madrid conference changing the overall nature of Arab-Israeli relations because of the willingness of Arab parties to recognize Israel as a state and a legitimate regional player, the ability of these adversaries to overcome or at least manage political divisions allowed these issue areas to be considered technical—with varying degrees of success—for the first time in the history of the conflict.

# 3 The Origins of the Arab-Israeli Multilateral Talks

> We live in an age when many of the world's regions, once ravaged by war, are now coming together. We see this above all here in Europe, but we see it too in Asia and in Central and Latin America . . . Increasingly, the Middle East stands out, but not in the way that should make any of us proud. Our challenge—our opportunity—is to begin the process of making the Middle East a region, not just in the geographic sense, but in the political, the economic, and indeed, in the human sense as well.
> —James A. Baker III[1]

Why was a multilateral regional forum made part of the process of Arab-Israeli peacemaking at Madrid? What forces best explain how such an unprecedented cooperative process originated in the polarized context of Arab-Israeli relations? To account for the origins of the multilaterals and its working groups, this chapter first presents an overview of the international and regional context in which this process emerged, including the developments leading up to the Madrid conference of October 1991 and the motivations of key regional parties for agreeing to attend the first multilateral organizational session in Moscow in January 1992. The chapter then turns to alternative arguments—as suggested in chapter 1—to assess the extent to which they can account for the emergence and nature of the process.

Arguments based solely on regional demand and domestic environments cannot adequately explain the origins of Arab-Israeli multilateral cooperation, particularly since these forces often impeded such cooperation. Rather, arguments based on structural leadership and the ideas of leaders representing powerful states (especially the role of American leadership and the belief sets of the U.S. elites responsible for this process) best explain the creation and shape of the Arab-Israeli multilaterals. In particular, a small group of policy elites within the administration—who were part of a larger network, or community, of Middle East experts in Washington, D.C.— shared similar notions about how to resolve the Arab-Israeli conflict and greatly influenced American policy in this region, including the formation of the multilateral peace process track.

The final section of the chapter characterizes the development of this Middle East policy community, which mirrored the larger trend of increasing professionalization of American foreign policymaking.[2] As aspects of foreign policymaking became the domain of specialized "issue networks,"[3] groups of American Middle East policy elites, and the ideas they espoused, strongly influenced the direction of American policy. Without them, it is unlikely that the multilaterals would have emerged.

This chapter also exposes the essential character of the origination stage and its lack of a clear substantive objective in any of the issue areas. At this stage, U.S. policymakers focused explicitly on the multilateral's value in facilitating the bilateral tracks and the normalization of Israel in the region rather than on the substantive results that might emerge from it. In fact, the purposes and prospects for the multilaterals beyond the Moscow organizational session were uncertain and not of great concern to senior U.S. policymakers. According to a senior U.S. official, the process was not based on any conscious model with clear ends in mind but rather was "developed on the run."[4] As another top official noted, the entire multilateral process was established with "little thought to intentions or implications."[5] That the multilaterals generated a cottage industry employing a multitude of professionals, experts, academics, and policymakers both inside and outside the region should not distract from the reality of its origins. The multilaterals' origins demonstrate that its founders had little understanding or interest in what the process could substantively produce across the issue areas ultimately included on its agenda, but very clear ideas about how regional relations needed to be restructured after the Gulf War and the role a multilateral process could play in this effort.

## The Road to Moscow

The developments and negotiations leading to the Moscow organizational session of the multilateral peace process highlight two potential forces at work in its origins: structural change at the international and regional levels and domestic motivations for participating in such a forum among regional actors. In basic theoretical terms, several levels of analysis were at work, including the international and regional balance of power, American hegemony, domestic pressures among regional participants, and significant actions by individual policy elites, particularly U.S. officials.

*The International and Regional Environment*

The final years of the Soviet Union, particularly its economic collapse in the early 1990s, significantly reduced its ability to influence events in the Middle East. As a result, decades of U.S.-Soviet rivalry in the region gave way first to the rollback of the Iraqi invasion of Kuwait and, second, to the promotion of an Arab-Israeli peace settlement. The international environment quickly evolved from an impediment to a facilitator of an Arab-Israeli peace process. As one analyst explains, "The breakup of the Communist regimes and ultimately the disappearance of the Soviet Union caused a de-globalization of the conflict, and its return to regional dimensions. . . . The renewal of diplomatic relations with Israel by Moscow and Moscow's assertion to Syria and the PLO that it would support only a diplomatic solution—all these removed the strategic Soviet umbrella over the Arab cause."[6]

While the end of the Cold War removed the Soviet impediment to a peace settlement, the success of the 1990–91 Persian Gulf War created new opportunities for the initiation of a sustainable peace process. As one analyst of post-Gulf War changes observes, the Gulf War dispelled "two long-standing myths among Arabs: one, that Arab states had the ability to achieve military parity with Israel as a prelude to regaining the occupied territories; and two, that pan-Arab solidarity would inevitably surface when one or more Arab countries engaged in a conflict with a non-Arab power."[7] The shattering of these myths, to the extent that they were still valid on the eve of the Gulf War,[8] enhanced the prospects for Arab-Israeli reconciliation efforts. The strengthening of statist identities among Arab states—and the resultant weakening of Arabist norms such as opposition to Israel—may have provided important enabling conditions for greater Arab-Israeli cooperation after the Gulf War.[9]

Moreover, the Gulf War presented a common threat to Arabs and Israelis and, in turn, an opening for new efforts to revitalize the Arab-Israeli peace process. The unprecedented American show of force in the region, leading to its perception as the guarantor of regional stability, provided the United States with leverage to push forward new initiatives. Although Secretary of State Baker was wary of engaging in a new peace initiative after the failure of his pre-Gulf War efforts to bring the Israelis and Palestinians to the peace table, he recognized the opportunities brought about by the postwar regional environment. Even with the hard-line Likud government still in power in Israel, under the leadership of Yitzhak Shamir, Secretary Baker perceived new opportunities for progress in what seemed only months earlier an intractable conflict:

> I believed the invasion of Kuwait and its liberation by an American-led coalition had established a dramatic new reality in the region. Arab radicalism had been discredited, thus strengthening the hand of moderate Arab nations such as Egypt and Saudi Arabia. In defeating Iraq, the United States had earned the deep gratitude of all of the Gulf Arabs. At the same time, we had also neutralized the gravest threat to Israel's security. The Soviet Union, long a force for trouble in the area, was now a partner of American diplomacy. And American credibility internationally was higher than at any time since the end of World War II. It was apparent to me that the Gulf War had created an unprecedented window of opportunity to pursue the possibility of peace between Israel and her Arab neighbors. As Dennis Ross was fond of observing, 'We've just seen an earthquake. We have to move before the earth resettles, because it will and it never takes long.'[10]

"Window of opportunity" became the new catchphrase in American peace process diplomacy, justifying an activist U.S. approach. In congressional testimony in February 1991, Secretary Baker presented the administration's postwar vision, including as its fourth pillar a revived peace process. As President Bush argued before a Joint Session of Congress on March 6, 1991, "We must work to create new opportunities for peace and stability in the Middle East. On the night I announced Operation Desert Storm, I expressed my hope that out of the horrors of war might come new momentum for peace."[11] A momentum for peace appeared possible in the wake of a conflict that left the Arab world newly divided, American influence at its peak, Israelis recognizing security vulnerabilities in the aftermath of Iraqi Scud missile attacks on its territory, and Yasir Arafat and King Hussein of

Jordan suffering the consequences (politically and economically) of their support for Saddam Hussein.

These two watershed events, the Cold War's conclusion and the Gulf War, led to what one Israeli official called a "regional identity crisis."[12] That is, if superpower rivalry no longer dominated the regional agenda, and if Israel was no longer perceived by the Arab world as the only, or even the most dangerous, threat to the region, then how should regional players organize? The door was opened to new thinking about how to organize regional relations, particularly Israel's role in an evolving regional environment.

From March to October 1991, Secretary of State Baker conducted shuttle diplomacy to negotiate and gain approval for the first Arab-Israeli peace conference that would launch direct negotiations between Israel and the Palestinians and its other Arab neighbors. The United States issued assurance letters to the parties specifying the nature and framework of the negotiations. The process set up two bilateral negotiating tracks, one between the Israelis and Palestinians and the other between Israel and Arab states on its borders (Syria, Lebanon, and Jordan). Aside from the symbolism of bringing Israel together with its immediate neighbors and the larger Arab world (the states of the Gulf and North Africa sent observer delegations), sanctioned by the European Community's presence and observers from the United Nations, the Madrid conference established a negotiating framework that would lay the groundwork for all future peace process advances, including the multilateral talks.

### Madrid and the "Two Track" Concept[13]

The favorable international and regional conditions for a new peace initiative did not make inevitable a multilateral negotiating forum, which would depart from the bilateral approach of encouraging the parties to engage in negotiations to resolve border conflicts and security arrangements. The multilateral track was in fact far from an inevitability. While the idea that regional cooperation could build on common interests to enhance peace was not new, and had been floating among government and academic circles for years,[14] the ultimate inclusion of the multilateral track in the Madrid letter of invitation was not fully thought through.[15] To understand the inclusion of the multilaterals, it is necessary to understand the peace process diplomacy leading up to the Madrid Peace Conference of October 1991, including Arab and Israeli negotiating positions before the Gulf War, when the peace process was at a standstill.

While little progress was made during the Reagan years in moving the peace process forward,[16] the Palestinian intifada beginning in late 1987 created a new reality for peace process diplomacy. The massive unrest in the territories and the resultant growth of grassroots leadership, often spontaneous, in the West Bank and Gaza not only threatened to make the status quo less desirable from the Israeli perspective; it also challenged the Tunis-based leadership of the Palestine Liberation Organization (PLO). The PLO still represented the only widely recognized voice for the Palestinian people, yet the reality on the ground was quite different. The PLO leadership, particularly Yasir Arafat, recognized that the growth of indigenous forces in the territories threatened to marginalize the PLO and undermine its legitimacy among the Palestinians living in the West Bank and Gaza. Secretary of State George Shultz capitalized on this vulnerability at the end of Reagan's second term and established an American-PLO dialogue—after the PLO agreed to recognize United Nations Security Council Resolutions 242 and 338—in the hope that a more moderate PLO would sanction the opening of a dialogue between West Bank Palestinians and Israel.[17]

Despite the U.S.-PLO dialogue, the United States had no illusions that Israeli Prime Minister Shamir would change his position on Palestinian representation in any future negotiations: "no" to the PLO, "no" to diaspora Palestinians (those Palestinians living outside the West Bank and Gaza), and "no" to Palestinians with residences in East Jerusalem. Thus, the prospects for revitalizing the peace process were dim on the eve of the Bush administration. As Secretary Baker conceded, "From day one, the last thing I wanted to do was touch the Middle East peace process. . . . There was no real evidence to believe the climate was ripe for generating any momentum in a conflict that had defied resolution for nearly half a century. . . . It seemed neither side was interested in considering the difficult choices necessary to create a real peace process."[18] Still, the United States left the door open, encouraging the Israelis to share ideas on the future of an Israeli-Palestinian dialogue. The result was Shamir's four-point plan—later lengthened into twenty points—with its cornerstone the proposal for Palestinian elections inside the West Bank and Gaza to choose a Palestinian delegation to negotiate the details of a self-rule agreement (similar to the autonomy plan included in the Likud-supported Israeli-Egyptian Camp David Accords). While the issue of Palestinian representation proved too contentious to bring this plan to fruition, its proposal led to the collapse of the Israeli national unity government.

One of the Shamir points, however, contributed to the formulation of the multilateral track. This point emphasized the need to bring the wider Arab world into the peace process with Israel in bilateral and regional forums: "Israel calls for the establishment of peace relations between it and those Arab states which still maintain a state of war with it, for the purpose of promoting a comprehensive settlement of the Arab-Israeli conflict, including recognition, direct negotiations, ending the boycott, diplomatic relations, cessation of hostile activity in international institutions or forums and regional and bilateral cooperation."[19] While hardly startling or noteworthy at the time, some senior U.S. officials claim that this rather short section of the Shamir plan planted the seeds in their minds for the creation of a multilateral, second track of the peace process.[20] The U.S. officials reasoned that in order to convince Shamir to attend a peace conference that had the appearance of an international conference (thus satisfying Arab preferences for this type of forum), they would add a supplemental multilateral track to Madrid, keeping in mind that Shamir highly valued establishing relations with the wider Arab world with whom he had no fundamental ideological conflict (in contrast to the Palestinian track).[21]

By most accounts (American, Israeli, and Arab), the United States, spurred by an Israeli desire to broaden Arab participation in the peace process, initiated the multilateral track. The U.S. purpose in creating an additional multilateral track was to convince Israel, under the leadership of Yitzhak Shamir, that the risk for peace was worth taking.[22] The United States would sweeten the Madrid deal, which the Likud leadership feared would become what they abhorred, an international peace conference imposing solutions upon Israel, by adding the multilaterals to enhance Israel's legitimacy in the larger Arab world. Israel sought assurance from the United States that it would work to broaden Arab participation, in order to balance what Israel perceived to be the concession it was making by agreeing to such a conference. While most Arab parties were not enthusiastic about the concept (preferring an emphasis on the bilateral tracks), few could say no to an American-sponsored initiative on the heels of the Gulf War. Of course, even if Israeli-inspired, the process was crafted by the Americans to serve U.S. purposes as well. For example, the United States considered the multilaterals an excellent tool for bringing extraregional participants (and their financial contributions) into the peace process without ceding the predominant American role in the political aspects of the process.[23] The multilateral concept also fit well with the worldviews of the key U.S. policymakers seeking a way to normalize Israel's place in the region.

It remained, nonetheless, little more than a concept. Throughout the Madrid conference, the multilateral notion had little content other than the reference line included in the Madrid letter of invitation. At the time, the multilaterals were not considered an independent process but rather were intricately woven into the larger Madrid framework. Most policymakers believed that the bilateral track would always take precedence and did not expect the multilaterals to serve as more than a cover for Shamir and a ceremonial facade for Israel to quietly establish bilateral contacts with Gulf and North African states. Moreover, the United States fostered the belief that the multilaterals were not essential by making attendance at the first multilateral conference optional—a concession to the Syrians in return for Syrian agreement to attend the Madrid conference itself.[24] Consequently, the United States diminished the importance of this track in the minds of the regional players, which led to low expectations for any future success. Even the issue areas to address multilateral problems, though listed in the Madrid invitation, were not finalized or agreed to by all the parties at Madrid. For example, although the refugee issue was listed in the Madrid letter of invitation—largely because Secretary Baker believed it needed to be addressed and expected that this would induce Palestinian participation in the process—neither the Israelis nor the Palestinians were enthusiastic about its inclusion.[25] The Israelis preferred to deal with this issue in the bilateral final status discussions. The Palestinians were concerned that the group would emphasize settling Palestinians in their present locations and thus forfeit the Palestinian quest for the "right of return."[26] Indeed, when the regional and extraregional parties were invited to Washington a month before Moscow to organize the content and procedure of the multilaterals, the sessions were contentious, particularly concerning Palestinian representation in the Refugee group.[27] With many issues left unresolved on the eve of the conference—the Palestinians even boycotted the inaugural Moscow session—many observers questioned whether this process would get off the ground, let alone continue past its first meeting.

## The Moscow Organizational Session

Thirty-six parties—including Israel and eleven Arab states—participated in the Moscow multilateral organizational session in January 1992. They agreed to break into five working groups that would meet separately for the next round of meetings, and they established a steering group[28] to determine the venues, dates, and agendas of the working groups. The working groups, led by various extraregional "gavelholders," would cover five regional issues: Arms Control and Regional Security (U.S. and Russia); Regional Economic Development (the European Community/Union); the Environment (Japan); Water (U.S.); and Refugees (Canada). The groups were intended to create small-scale projects where Israelis and Arabs would cooperate on common regional problems. Decisions in all working groups would be governed by consensus, as is common in multilateral bodies.[29] This kind of cooperation was designed to increase confidence among Arab and Israeli elites (drawing on the confidence-building measures, or CBMs, from other international models, particularly the Conference on Security and Cooperation in Europe, or CSCE) and convince the people in the region that peace would provide tangible benefits. U.S. officials presented the multilaterals as a way to "address functional issues on a region-wide basis. . . . In conceiving the multilaterals, we hoped to create a web of functional interests vaulting political fault lines. . . . Early on, it was evident that for most participants the multilaterals were seen as a 'win-win' situation. All could gain, and all have."[30]

At the early stages, creating this "web" of common interests appeared more attainable in the project-oriented Environment, Economic Development, and Water working groups than in the politically-charged Arms Control and Refugee groups.[31] Indeed, most American policymakers did not harbor great expectations for the durability of the overall process or its ability to produce tangible outcomes. From the outset, for example, the multilaterals excluded Iraq, Iran, and Libya, while Syria and Lebanon chose not to attend the Moscow session or any subsequent multilateral meetings. Yet these states will ultimately have to be included in a regional process given their centrality to many of the issues under discussion, particularly regional security and water. Moreover, controversy over Palestinian representation[32] led to both Palestinian and Israeli boycotts of working group sessions during the first year of the process, undermining the confidence-building nature of the talks and signaling difficulties, even for the less controversial Environment and Economic Development working groups. Funding sources for the working group projects were also not well-defined at the outset, despite regional expectations for multibillion dollar grants, creating a significant obstacle to implementing many regional projects.[33] But most importantly, the American sponsors and the regional participants understood that the bilateral process would always take precedence and believed that the multilaterals could never outpace the progress achieved in the bilaterals.[34] The central concern was the bilateral peace tracks.

Consequently, despite the high-level official participation at Moscow, the senior U.S. Mideast policymakers did not focus on the multilateral track after its inaugural session. They had achieved their primary goal—getting Shamir to join the Madrid process and gaining wide Arab acceptance of Israel as a negotiating partner. As Secretary of State Baker observed in the concluding Moscow session, the multilaterals could "be a complement and can be a catalyst for the bilateral talks and for progress in the bilateral talks" but, "of course, the bilateral talks remain the heart of the peacemaking process."[35] [See appendix A for the full text of Baker's address.] Any benefits from the multilateral track, if it survived, would be what one top official called "gravy."[36] With little attention paid to its potential implications, responsibility for the multilateral track moved—both symbolically and literally—from the seventh floor of the State Department (home to the Secretary's suite of offices) to the working-level officials in the Near East Affairs and other bureaus addressing the functional issues included in the process. In parallel, many of the Arab participants hoped that their attendance at the Moscow session had satisfied the United States, and that the process would not materially progress after its symbolic purpose at Moscow was fulfilled. As one Israeli participant observed, it was not resolved "how much [of the process] was fig leaf and how much was real."[37]

*Why They Came*

Given the centrality of the bilateral tracks and the uncertain purpose of a regional multilateral track, why did regional parties agree to join this additional peacemaking forum? The simple answer is that the United States wanted them to come and encouraged broad regional participation in this process. While this explanation is satisfactory for participants like Saudi Arabia who simply could not refuse a U.S. initiative on the heels of the Gulf War, the calculus of other states was more complex. This is especially true because of the nonparticipation of the Syrians and Lebanese,[38] raising the stakes for those who did participate. Thus, the following review of motivations regarding a multilateral process reveals the ambivalence of regional actors in participating in such a forum.

Israel

Israel was the main promoter of a regional track which could enhance Israel's integration into the life of the region and foster relations with Arab states that did not sit on its borders. Since its birth in 1948, every Israeli government had sought international and regional acceptance of its existence as a sovereign and legitimate state in the international community. This quest for recognition led consecutive Israeli governments to demand that Arab states sit down face to face with Israel in direct, bilateral negotiations and to shun international conferences that would allow Arab states to avoid recognizing the Jewish state while imposing solutions upon it. The Likud party, in control of the government through Madrid and Moscow, was particularly wary of international conferences, especially those that involved the Europeans, who it felt were pro-Arab, and international organizations like the U.N., considered sympathetic to the Palestinians. The Israelis were also concerned about the original U.S. design of the multilaterals, which established two baskets (modeled on the CSCE), one on security and one on "human resources." In the Israeli view, such a structure highlighted the arms control issue (leaving room for Arab pressure on Israel) and limited the points of contact Israel could establish with its Arab counterparts, which was its primary motivation for attending the talks. The Americans were largely responsive to these Israeli concerns, as the final structure of the multilaterals illustrates.[39] Thus, despite some initial concerns, Israel favored the multilateral track, particularly since it was able to influence the structure of the forum. The Moscow conference allowed Israelis to sit down with Arab neighbors for the first time to discuss issues of region-wide concern. They could return to the Israeli people and tell them that the fruits of negotiating with the Arabs were paying off. Finally, they would become a recognized state in the region without, in their opinion, paying too high a price.

## Egypt

Egypt, as the only Arab state at peace with Israel at the time, was expected to participate in the multilaterals. Given its close and critical relationship with the United States (and its annual receipt of over $2 billion in foreign aid), Egypt was especially unlikely to upset the United States by rejecting what then seemed like a harmless initiative. Moreover, the low-key nature of the multilaterals tempered likely domestic resistance to normalization with Israel that was widespread among Egypt's intellectual and professional elite. Some observers believe the Egyptians expected the process to develop not into real multilateral cooperation, but rather into a framework perpetuating an Arab bloc-vs.-Israel mentality. Egypt, it seems likely, expected its leadership position in the Arab world to be enhanced by this process, as it could capitalize on issues like Israel's nuclear weapons to rally other Arab states behind Egyptian leadership.[40] The multilaterals also seemed to provide a forum for the Egyptians to keep actively engaged in Arab-Israeli peacemaking as their role in the bilateral tracks diminished. And finally, there were substantive incentives stemming from regional projects that would involve and benefit Egypt directly—incentives, along with U.S. pressure, that kept them in the process long after they believed it benefited Israel more than themselves.

## Jordan

With few natural resources, a small population, and a developing economy, Jordan favored regional cooperation efforts. Jordan's readiness to make peace with Israel and include it in joint projects to develop the region was no secret. In fact, for many years Jordan had engaged Israel quietly in cooperative ventures both in the security and water realms. Even before Madrid (in March 1991), Crown Prince Hassan proposed a plan for regional cooperation efforts based on the CSCE.[41] Jordan also hoped to use the process to rebuild its strained relations with the Saudis and other Gulf states in the aftermath of its taking a pro-Iraqi position during the Gulf war. The multilateral nature of this track also provided Jordan—and other small regional states—with leverage against larger Arab powers like Egypt. Finally, the Jordanians wanted to ensure that their bilateral interests with Israel were represented at the conference, enjoying the cover of a large number of international participants, which Jordan believed bolstered the Arab position in negotiations with Israel.[42]

## The Palestinians

Because of disagreements over the makeup of their delegation, the Palestinians boycotted the first organizational meeting in Moscow. While the Palestinians accepted restrictions on their participation at Madrid (namely, no diaspora Palestinians or PLO representatives), they insisted that these restrictions did not apply to the multilaterals because of the nature of the issues it covered, particularly the Refugee group.[43] The Palestinians were also concerned that the pace of the multilaterals not surpass gains at the bilateral level, arguing that Israeli normalization should await resolution of the Palestinian-Israeli conflict. In the words of the Palestinian delegation head to the bilateral talks, Dr. Haidar Abdel-Shafi, "I don't see that these multilateral talks are very relevant in the face of no progress in the bilateral."[44] Other Arab states shared this concern and Syria boycotted these talks (along with Lebanon) for this reason.

Despite this rocky start, the Palestinians had several reasons for ultimately joining the multilaterals and playing an active role in several of its working groups. Perhaps the most important objective for the Palestinians was to utilize this forum for gaining recognition from the international community and other regional participants—especially Israel—of their national cause and desire for equal status as a core player in the region. Indeed, the ultimate compromise concerning Palestinian participation allowed for tacit Israeli-PLO contacts[45] and then, after Oslo, to a distinct and active Palestinian delegation with an equal voice in the process's decision-making. Moreover, some Palestinians have noted the qualitative difference in dealing with the Israelis at the multilateral level, where they felt empowered by the extraregional presence, as opposed to at the bilateral one, where they still felt patronized by their Israeli counterparts.

Aside from providing the Palestinians with the intangible benefits of international and regional legitimacy, the multilaterals also offered a practical opportunity for the Palestinians to engage the extraregional participants and make the case for bilateral assistance to the territories. In some cases, as in the Regional Economic Development Working Group (REDWG), the Palestinians were the central item on the agenda. For example, one of the earliest REDWG projects was the commissioning of a World Bank study on the development needs of the Palestinians. This study laid the ground work for the donor conference that took place in Washington, D.C., in the aftermath of Oslo, where the international community pledged $2.4 billion to Palestinian development.[46] Many of the regional projects proposed in the other working groups—particularly Water and the Environment—included Palestinian areas in their development plans. The Refugee group's primary focus was on how to improve the standard of living of Palestinian refugees in the region, although it left the contentious issue of right of return for the bilateral Israeli-Palestinian final status talks.

## The Gulf Cooperation Council (GCC) States

The Persian Gulf War underscored the acute security threats the GCC states (Saudi Arabia, Kuwait, Qatar, Oman, Bahrain, United Arab Emirates) faced and their subsequent inability to confront them without significant foreign, and particularly American, support. The failure to create an Arab security regime drawing on Egyptian and Syrian forces after the war only enhanced the Gulf's dependency on American power to secure stability in their subregion.[47] Therefore, security regimes proposed by the United States were viewed more favorably—even if they involved Israel—especially if they provided an additional security umbrella against "rogue" forces in the region like Iran and Iraq.

However, the Saudis were the least receptive to the idea, which not only was problematic because of the inclusion of Israel, but also because of the status it gave the small Gulf States, whom the Saudis preferred to control within the Saudi-dominated agenda of the GCC. In addition, the Saudis were concerned about pressure for financial assistance, the possibility that human rights would creep on to the agenda, and that the process would move faster than progress on the Israeli-Syrian track, with which they were most concerned.[48]

Yet for the other Gulf states, the process proved far more appealing. The multilaterals gave them equal footing with the Saudis and even a degree of independence, as their hosting of multilateral events that brought Israeli delegations to their countries for the first time demonstrates.[49] The multilaterals not only provided a forum for the smaller Gulf states to gain leverage against the Saudis, it also provided a mechanism of anchoring the United States into the region, which was viewed as an essential inevitability despite domestic costs. Thus, the Gulf states acknowledged that working with Israel in the multilaterals was one way to enhance American involvement in their subregion.

## The Maghreb

The Maghreb states who joined the multilaterals—Algeria, Mauritania, Morocco, and Tunisia—were primarily concerned with the economic agenda of the process, with the possible exception of Tunisia, which played an active role in the ACRS working group. Algeria's principal concern was with ways the multilaterals, particularly development projects, could abate its internal problems, while Morocco focused on the prospects for developing tourism in the region. The Moroccans also used this regional forum to advance their bilateral relations with Israel, with which they had long conducted secret talks; Morocco was among the first of the peripheral Arab states prepared to normalize relations with Israel. While Tunisia proved to be more active generally than the other Maghreb states outside the Economic group, its primary interest in the process was originally economically motivated.

## Explaining the Origins of the Multilaterals and Its Working Groups

### Regional Demand and Domestic Environments

A variety of incentives led regional parties to participate in the initial stage of the Arab-Israeli multilateral talks, but no regional party demanded the multilaterals as a condition of their participation in the Madrid process. Israel presented the greatest demand for such a forum in order to gain widespread Arab recognition as a legitimate state in the region. Arab parties demonstrated a variety of interests in the establishment of such a forum. Some Arab motivations were, in fact, contradictory. For instance, while Egypt saw the process as potentially reputation-enhancing, many smaller Arab states perceived an opportunity to limit the power of their larger neighbors and exert greater influence under the multilateral umbrella than was possible in smaller inter-Arab frameworks.

Regional parties were not, however, uniformly in favor of this process. Saudi Arabia agreed to attend largely because of U.S. pressure. Others were cautious about their participation given Syria's strong opposition to the multilaterals from the outset. Indeed, following the Moscow organizational session, the Syrians criticized the multilaterals and placed continued pressure on other Arab parties to boycott the process. As a government-run daily in Damascus asserted over a year after the multilaterals were established, "Israel is trying to exploit those negotiations to attain its old/new goal of cost-free normalization with the Arabs. We must recognize that the multilateral negotiations were a fatal Arab mistake. These negotiations did great damage to the general Arab position."[50] Other Arab participants, particularly the Palestinians—as their boycott of the Moscow session indicates—were also displeased and cautious about the role of the multilaterals in the context of the wider peace process, and were persistent in their demands that the multilaterals not overshadow the bilaterals. Arab leaders also believed that public opinion opposed normalization with Israel before there was progress on the Palestinian track, and this served as a counterweight against Arab support for a regional process including Israel. Indeed, the multilaterals' low profile was largely a response to Arab sensitivity about engaging in unprecedented cooperative processes with Israel, particularly considering that the working groups were formed well before the Oslo breakthrough in Israeli-Palestinian relations.

And even the Israelis, the primary regional backers of the multilateral proposal, expressed ambivalence about its undefined agenda and open-ended nature in terms of Palestinian and international participation, leading to Israeli boycotts of two of the working groups' (Economics and Refugees) first sessions in the spring of 1992. Shamir himself understood the benefits of a regional forum for Israel but was not deeply committed to the notion of a multilateral track if it jeopardized his more central interest in the makeup of the Palestinian delegation at Madrid. Israeli domestic opinion enthusiastically welcomed Arab recognition of Israel but was not pushing for greater Israeli inclusion in the Arab world through regional forums. The Israeli public, too, was preoccupied with developments in the bilaterals, particularly the bilateral relationship with the Palestinians.

When turning to the formation of particular working groups, we also see that regional demand and domestic political concerns cannot fully account for the origins of the process.

## Arms Control

In the arms control arena, neither Arab nor Israeli participants were enthusiastic about creating a new negotiating forum for regional security issues. The overall Arab view was one of caution, with particular concern that ACRS should not outpace progress on the bilateral tracks. The Gulf states were also concerned about the implications of regional arms control on the flow of arms to their subregion, particularly in the wake of the Gulf War. And while the Israelis were not opposed to ACRS, they sought to downplay its importance as compared to other working groups.

Moreover, the pre-Madrid arms control efforts underscored the considerable gap between Arab and Israeli positions on regional arms control, creating concern and uncertainty for both sides as they entered the ACRS process. Because no party clearly envisioned how ACRS would develop, it is difficult to discern a clear interest in forming such a multilateral forum. No party believed that ACRS would make security cooperation cheaper and easier or that other security alternatives (particularly traditional bilateral security options) were not preferable. In fact, regional behavior indicated a strong preference for bilateral security arrangements and skepticism toward multilateral security forums.[51] So why bother if regional participants perceived better ways to provide for their security?

When turning to the domestic orientations of the regional actors, we find no serious internal political or economic pressures for multilateral security cooperation in either Israel or any Arab state. If anything, we find the opposite. Initially Israel, under the leadership of Yitzhak Shamir, was in fact wary of the ACRS group, fearing it would turn into a forum for Arab pressure on Israel on the nuclear issue with international backing. While a cadre of Israeli elites within the Ministry of Defense began to recognize the need for Israel to engage in regional arms control, the overall Israeli attitude toward arms control forums was one of suspicion and caution. As for the Arab parties, all faced tremendous domestic resistance to cooperating with Israel in the regional context before the Palestinian issue had been resolved. If anything, cooperating with Israel prematurely on regional issues was a source of vulnerability for Arab regimes, not a source of strength.

Furthermore, while both Arabs and Israelis were increasingly concerned about the costs of arms buildups relative to domestic economic development, none viewed even a successful regional arms control process as a replacement for unilateral defense requirements or one that could relieve them of the defense burden. There is little evidence that incentives to scale down military spending in order to channel investment into economic development (the so-called peace dividend) translated into greater demand for regional arms control.[52] Despite economic problems and growing deficits in Arab regimes, including oil-rich Saudi Arabia, major arms sales continued as the search for alternative (and cheaper) global suppliers became an active pursuit.[53] The Gulf states in particular were wary of an arms control process that would threaten their arms purchases by calling for arms reduction, becoming more cooperative in ACRS only when it was clear that arms reduction was not on the agenda. Domestic economic constraints still left alternatives open other than regional arms control, including the search for alternative arms suppliers or less costly defense and deterrence-based strategies, which did not require multilateral coordination.[54] From the perspective of domestic politics focusing either on regime stabilizing considerations or domestic economic conditions within states, the evidence would not suggest the establishment of a regional security process involving Israel.

Economic Cooperation

A similar story emerges in the economic area. Neither the Arab parties nor Israel expected great economic gains from such a forum. In addition, both sides enjoyed many alternatives for economic development that were preferable from efficiency and economic standpoints.

The central economic interests of the Arab states lie outside, rather than within, the region, with the unique exception of the Palestinian case. This holds even without the inclusion of Israel in the intraregional trade equation, with intra-Arab trade among the core peace process parties (Egypt, Jordan, the Palestinians, Syria, and Lebanon) even lower than trade among these parties and Israel.[55] Intraregional goods trade in the Middle East accounts for only a small percentage of total trade conducted by the region's states, a mere 6.2 percent.[56] Intraregional nonmineral-fuel trade is also remarkably low at only 6 percent.[57] And while labor movements among Arab states (primarily to oil-producing states in the Gulf) were substantial in the 1970s and 1980s—18 percent of the labor force of the exporting countries (Egypt, Jordan, Lebanon, Syria, and Yemen) worked in the Gulf in the early 1980s[58]—the combination of falling oil revenue and the Persian Gulf War led Gulf states by the mid-1990s to replace the Arab work force with Southeast Asian labor. Moreover, the labor-exporting (non-oil-producing) states pursued protectionist economic policies during these decades, which limited the prospects for competitive exports that could make their way into the lucrative Gulf markets, further reducing intraregional trade prospects. However, some economists argue that the low level of economic integration in the region, particularly among Arab parties, is not just the result of poor economic policies or external crises, but may be the result of economic causes that do not naturally lead the region into a trading bloc.⁵⁹ While Middle East states (Turkey excluded) may have some limited complementarity (specializing in goods sought by other regional states), overall the regional picture is one of competition, with most regional parties pursuing their economic interests in the large European and North American markets. As an IMF working paper summarizes, "Despite favorable geographical and cultural elements, the MENA [Middle East and North Africa] remains remarkably unintegrated. . . . Intra-regional trade is small, tourist and labor flows are skewed, and private capital transactions remain limited. . . . There has been very little effective regional economic policy coordination."⁶⁰ Considering that Arab parties have had little interest or success in facilitating trade and economic integration even among themselves, we would expect them to have harbored even less interest in fostering economic relations with Israel, especially before all political issues were settled.

The Israelis also had no inherent economic interest in regional cooperation with Arab states, contrary to widespread Arab fears of Israeli hegemonic designs.⁶¹ Israel could gain some limited benefits from increased trade with the Arab world. For example, industrial products like cement could be transported more cheaply to its neighbors than abroad. Services like tourism, computer technology, construction, and water planning are also ripe areas for enhanced cooperation, as the multilaterals demonstrated.⁶² Joint ventures drawing on the cheaper labor market in Arab states such as Jordan, and Israeli access to European and American markets through its Free Trade Agreements are also potential lucrative areas for cooperation.⁶³

Still, Israel's primary markets and economic interests remain in Europe, the United States, and more recently in Asia, not in the developing Middle East. As the former Israeli deputy secretary for economic affairs asserted, "Israel's trade with the EU makes up 50 percent of its overall trade. We also trade with the United States, Japan, and several other countries in the Far East. I do not believe trade between Israel and the Arab countries will rise above 10 percent *even if peace is established in the region.*"⁶⁴ Israeli Deputy Foreign Minister Yossi Beilin also did not hide Israel's limited economic interest in the Arab region, explaining, "Theoretically, we have the option of not getting into the Middle East game. . . . The potential for trade with the Middle East is not great—perhaps several hundred million dollars, but not much more."⁶⁵ Moreover, with Israel quickly becoming a high-tech economy, Europe, the United States, and Asia look far more attractive than the Arab world, and not just because they serve as key export markets. As one economic analysis explains, "The U.S., Europe and Asia provide the strategic alliances, suppliers, merger and acquisitions targets, and financing of Israel's high-tech needs."[66]

Yet despite these limited economic interests, Israel held a political interest in promoting cooperation and viewed REDWG from a political, not an economic, perspective. Beilin understood this dilemma well: "There is a problem with saying, 'OK, if you [Arab states] are afraid of us, we don't see our economic future as traders in the Middle East. If you don't want our business and are afraid of us, then we will go our own way..' . . . During all those years when they argued that we were an alien element . . . we claimed a place in the region. Now that we have made peace, by choosing not to trade with our neighbors we would remain an alien element."[67] Israeli interest in REDWG was thus political from the outset, as was its desire to establish regional economic institutions that would facilitate its political more than its economic integration into the region. Moreover, promoting economic development in Arab states became an Israeli interest because of the widespread belief that development promotes political stability. Thus, from both the Arab and Israeli perspectives, the interest in and prospects for regional economic cooperation in order to serve narrow economic interests were minimal if not entirely absent when REDWG was established, leaving open the question of why and how such a process was initiated.

Finally, an economic explanation implies that the choice for a cooperative forum or institution is the result of its being the most efficient way to satisfy mutual interests in the given issue area. This logic is undermined by the existence of alternative, efficient solutions. Indeed, at the time of REDWG's creation—and during negotiations over establishing the institutions that sprang from this process—several alternatives for regional economic development were available and preferable from an economic efficiency-based calculus. Some of these alternatives—such as bilateral and subregional economic cooperation schemes[68]—were considered and eventually pursued in the wake of the Israeli-Palestinian and Israeli-Jordanian peace accords.

But by far the most preferable alternative for successful regional economic development according to many economists is unilateral economic reform by states in the region. According to an IMF working paper on the scope of regional integration in the Middle East and North Africa region, while increased regional interaction and cooperation can bring some economic gains to the region, these gains are limited and are subordinate to policy changes *within* these states. As the paper observes, "Rather than set as their first economic policy priority the goal of regional integration, MENA countries should focus on domestic policy reforms and the associated process of greater integration into the world economy."[69] A study group of economists from Harvard University and regional participants analyzing economic cooperation in the Middle East came to a similar conclusion.[70] While the group found that Arab-Israeli peace and enhanced regional economic cooperation in projects like tourism, hotels, and joint airports carried many potential economic gains for regional parties, most of the participants stressed the greater need for domestic policy reform if regional states were to truly realize a peace dividend.[71] Recognizing the importance of regional, Arab-Israeli projects for primarily political purposes, many economic observers still prescribe domestic policy reform as the most viable long-term solution to low growth and high unemployment in the region.[72] Thus, fostering regional economic cooperation among Arabs and Israelis was a *choice* rather than an efficient response to economic demands of regional parties whose economic needs might have been better met by alternative policies.[73]

Domestic demand for economic cooperation was also not evident in the region, with both Arabs and Israelis concerned about different aspects of the process. From the Arab perspective, normalizing ties with Israel was a risky proposition. Important Arab participants, like Saudi Arabia, were not enthusiastic about entering this process and made it clear they were not willing to pay its bills. The Syrians continued to apply pressure to other Arab participants to stay away from cooperative ventures with Israel before bilateral disputes had been settled. The Arab private sector was particularly hostile to normalized economic contacts with Israel, and the Arab press also reflected this anti-normalization stance, as the substantial literature on Israeli economic hegemony illustrates.[74] As for Israel, REDWG was established during the tenure of an ideological Likud government (led by Yitzhak Shamir), which boycotted the first session because of the Palestinian representation issue. Israelis were suspicious of European intentions as gavelholder of the working group, fearing European designs to gain a foothold in the peace process rather than foster regional economic development. While Israeli public opinion strongly favored normalization and acceptance by its Arab neighbors, most Israelis, and particularly the Israeli business community, did not demand deep economic relations with the Arab world. Key domestic constituencies had to be coaxed into the economic cooperation process by government officials for the sake of the peace process, a position that the private sector ultimately embraced.[75] And, like the general multilateral process, neither Arab nor Israeli publics were familiar with this process, excluding the possibility that these publics created a pressing demand for it.

## Water and Environment

The primary argument that we would expect to account for the creation of the most "functional" working groups of the multilaterals would be a regional-interest explanation. (I do not consider domestic politics here because they played virtually no role in these particular issue areas). According to such an argument, the regional parties' shared interests in addressing water scarcity and environmental threats should lead to expectations for mutual gain by cooperating in these spheres. Moreover, the creation of a regular forum for regional interaction would have made cooperation on these issues easier and more efficient to maintain, and reduce transaction costs by dealing with these problems regionally as opposed to bilaterally. For example, setting up a regional desalination plant—bringing in more financial resources and expertise—is theoretically a cheaper, more efficient way to develop such technology, which would be more limited and expensive at the bilateral level. Indeed, of all the issue areas, both water and the environment lend themselves to regional solutions that in many ways fit a contractual approach to cooperation. The interests and benefits of cooperating in such a forum are less ambiguous than in the case of either arms control or economic development.

But this argument faces a serious limitation. If interests were so strong in demanding such a regional solution to these issue areas, why didn't a similar type of multilateral forum emerge much earlier? An interest-based approach neglects the political environment and the power brokers who are often necessary to bring about cooperative arrangements. These external forces are critical in understanding why new cooperative forums emerge when they do, and why they might assume a particular shape or format (e.g., multilateral) rather than another (e.g., bilateral or trilateral). Indeed, other alternatives that would have satisfied regional demands and interests in solving common problems more cheaply and more readily through cooperation were possible after the Gulf War. For one, tacit bilateral or trilateral (Israel, Jordan, and the Palestinians) cooperation on water was possible among riparian states, and would have avoided the political problem of cooperating with Israel before the Palestinian track was resolved and perhaps have proved more efficient than the large and unruly multilateral forum that ultimately emerged. Jordan had tacitly cooperated with Israel on sharing the Jordan waters for decades, with the American-sponsored Johnston plan of the early 1950s serving as a guide despite the plan's official failure.[76] Or the regional parties could have opted for more public cooperation on water enhancement projects at the subregional level (just the Jordan River riparians) and in smaller, more technical forums under the cover of existing international conferences or scientific gatherings. For the environment, the region already had an existing forum to discuss and negotiate this issue, the Mediterranean Action Plan (Med Plan),[77] which avoided the problem of direct Arab-Israeli interaction which was still problematic before the Oslo Accord. And, of course, there was always the alternative of an inter-Arab forum or national projects excluding Israel. True, many of the regional water and environment projects would have to include Israel because of practical externalities. But, for the water issue, Israel could have been included in a different fashion and for the environment the region could have waited until all political disputes had been resolved, just as they had already waited over forty years to deal with common environmental concerns other than those covered by the Med Plan. Given that no particular environmental crisis between Israel and Arab parties initiated a sudden demand to solve these threats multilaterally with Israel, what was the rush? From a regional demand perspective, the answer is not clear.

In short, while regional participants displayed a variety of interests in engaging in the multilaterals, neither Arabs nor Israelis demanded their establishment and all were equivocal at best about the value of cooperation in the various issue areas on its agenda, leaving regional demand as an insufficient foundation for explaining its origins. The diffuse regional interests—not to mention the numerous regional forces working against the formation of a multilateral process—were not sufficient to create a regional multilateral forum that included Israel.

## The Altered Strategic Environment

A traditional power argument would point to the external environment, or the altered regional and international balance of power in the early 1990s, as responsible for the emergence of Arab-Israeli cooperation. Indeed, the developments leading to the Moscow conference demonstrate that the altered international and regional environment did make such a forum possible and thinkable in the minds of both American and regional elites. But pre-Moscow negotiations illustrate that *what was possible was not inevitable*, particularly given the variety of choice for American Mideast diplomacy in the wake of the Gulf War.

For example, the Americans could have satisfied regional parties with compromise formulas on the bilateral tracks, which is ultimately what took place (in particular, satisfying Shamir's concerns on Palestinian representation proved to be the greatest potential challenge to convening Madrid). At the time the multilaterals were conceived in the run-up to the Madrid conference, the Arab parties would have been perfectly content had the Americans left the multilaterals out of the Madrid letter of invitation, perceiving them as a political reward for Israel rather than a generator of real solutions to problems facing the Arab participants. While by Moscow Arab parties like the Palestinians recognized the utility of the multilaterals to soften the Madrid rules governing their representation in the peace process, they were originally opposed to the notion that normalization could proceed without progress on the Palestinian track. And, of course, Arab concerns about the multilaterals moving ahead of the bilaterals led to Syrian opposition to the regional forum even before Madrid.

In short, the American team did not *have* to expend the energy to create this additional peace process track, which required lengthy diplomacy by Secretary Baker. And in the end, Secretary Baker was willing to give the whole initiative up if persisting in it meant that Syria would refuse to attend the Madrid conference and the subsequent bilateral negotiations with Israel. This reveals how close the process came to confinement in American policy papers rather than becoming a new regional forum for Arab-Israeli cooperation. External shifts in power balances and strategic conditions may have bid well for some sort of Arab-Israeli cooperation, but it certainly did not dictate the formation of a multilateral process.

Moreover, the altered strategic environment offered the Americans choices other than a multilateral process as created at Moscow or no multilateral process at all. Alternative strategies were available to promote Arab-Israeli cooperation on issues of common concern that may have been more likely to succeed, such as informal subregional working groups where participants had a more substantive basis for cooperation (as in the Gulf of Aqaba area or the Jordan Rift Valley). Or the Americans could have supported quiet discussions, or even secret forums, among regional experts to address these technical problems, without convening a large organizational session and subsequent plenary meetings that included political representatives. But these types of forums would have likely been bilateral, or trilateral, and thus would not have guaranteed the wide regional participation and Arab acceptance of Israel that the Americans sought. These types of concerns about how to organize regional relations (i.e., the importance of normalizing Israel) were prevalent among the American elites who designed this process, and who represented the official side of the Middle East policy community in Washington.

## *Leadership, Ideas and the Middle East Policy Elite*

While traditional power arguments may be insufficient to explain the origins of regional multilateral cooperation, other variants of power do play a role. In particular, U.S. leadership is the primary force explaining the origins of this process. For example, the critical participation of the Saudis was the result of the fact that the Americans were willing to use the capital they generated during the Gulf War to "encourage" reluctant Arab parties to attend a multilateral forum that did not intuitively serve narrow self-interests. As a senior American official put it, the United States carried a lot of "chits" in the wake of the Gulf War that "we wanted to cash in on."[78]

The United States exercised not only its structural leadership (or willingness to exert influence based on its prominent position in the region), but also intellectual leadership, insisting on a multilateral process because of firmly held beliefs about how the region should be shaped. Again, the exertion of power does not tell us as much as the motivations and worldviews of those elites representing the dominant power and their ideas about the goals and objectives that their power can bring about. In this case, these goals were more concerned with intangibles like Arab acceptance of Israel than with maximizing the power position of the United States. Thus, what matters is *who* exercises leadership, and the ideas of those leaders.[79]

This is not to say the Americans served no narrow interests by creating the multilaterals. For example, the multilateral track enabled the United States to get the Europeans "out of the way" in terms of core peace process issues (i.e., the bilaterals), giving them control over the Economic working group from which the United States expected very little. The economic substance of the multilaterals was of minimal concern to top policymakers, who were more concerned with getting Madrid and Moscow off the ground than with the agendas of the working groups. Moreover, bringing the Europeans and Japanese into the process would help pay the peace process bills without sacrificing the prominent U.S. position as mediator in the bilateral talks.

Nonetheless, including these extraregional parties in the peace process entailed some risk that expectations would be raised, leading to more aggressive, and unwanted, intervention by European powers. The Europeans were particularly problematic because of Israel's—particularly Shamir's—strong distrust of their ability to serve as neutral interlocutors given their perceived bias toward the Arab position. It is also questionable whether the Americans needed the multilateral track to draw on European funds and support for the Madrid process, which could have been targeted as bilateral progress necessitated (such as the appeal for European and other international funding for the Palestinians in the wake of the Oslo Accord).

Thus, the normative aspect of American diplomacy cannot be ignored. The American elites who structured the Madrid and Moscow conferences were committed to Israeli normalization into the Arab world and believed it was worth capitalizing on a revived peace process to create a forum that would enhance this goal. But how were these ideas transmitted, and how did they become so influential in shaping American policy? To understand the role of ideas, we must also specify the agents who carried and transmitted them, who in this case were a small group of policy elites responsible for Middle East policy in the executive branch.[80]

The policymakers in the Bush administration who shaped the Madrid and Moscow conferences were not principally partisan political elites but rather foreign policy professionals who had served successive administrations (Democratic and Republican) and had well-developed views about the Arab-Israeli conflict and the requisites for its resolution (namely, the importance of Arab acceptance of Israel in order for Israel to make peace). The nature of this group of elites mirrored larger changes in the American foreign policy establishment that began with the National Security Act of 1947, which substantially increased the size and power of the executive branch, a trend which only accelerated in the wake of the Vietnam War and Watergate. This growth led to a professionalized foreign policy establishment, where intellectual credentials, not social status, were the valued commodity. As Nelson Polsby explains,

What do we mean by professionalization? John Foster Dulles and Dean Acheson came to their concerns about foreign affairs through their families: Acheson's father, born a Canadian, was a bishop in the American branch of the Church of England. Dulles began as secretary to his uncle, Robert Lansing, who was secretary of state in the Wilson administration. These were among the last of an old guard. Today specialists in foreign affairs have Ph.D.s or at least extensive explicit training; even Henry Kissinger, born in Germany, and Zbigniew Brzezinski, born the son of a Polish diplomat, had to do graduate work and write dissertations on their way to participation in foreign policy-making. . . . Foreign policy specialists are being recruited to the entourages of presidential candidates based on brains; the loyalty comes later. That's professionalization.[81]

The subset of this establishment, the Middle East policymaking elite, has evolved in a similar fashion. The old American elites responsible for Middle East policy were largely the same men who dictated other facets of American foreign policy: a group of "wise men" who came from business backgrounds and tended to view the Middle East through the prism of American oil interests.[82] To the extent that Middle East "specialists" were found in the pre-Nixon era, they were located in the Bureau for Near East Affairs at the State Department (representing the so-called "Arabists") and earned their expertise largely from living in the region.[83]

Increasingly, however, the nature of this policy community has changed, as a growing number of Middle East specialists came from Ph.D. programs and from more diverse backgrounds (including American-Jewish officials). Since the 1967 Arab-Israeli war in particular, a new type of policy community emerged which, despite disagreements over tactics and even strategy, shared an intellectual and normative commitment to solve the Arab-Israeli conflict. The ideas these policymakers hold about Arab-Israeli relations stem from shared understandings of the conflict formed both by common interpretations of history and through interactions among these elites in forums and seminars, such as those sponsored by Washington think tanks. While many of the Middle East policymakers are Jewish (explaining in part their initial interest in the peace process), their religion does not dictate their beliefs concerning Arab-Israeli peacemaking, nor do these beliefs stem from individual, cognitive biases. Rather, the ideas held by these elites were formulated through social interaction, education, and experience, leading to their shared intellectual understanding of the region.

Specifically, these policymakers—some of whom were studying in Israel during the 1973 Yom Kippur (or October) War—interpreted the lessons of the conflict in similar ways: namely, that to ensure Israel's security and to end the conflict, a peace deal had to be made with the Arab states, and the United States would play a critical role in such a deal. Moreover, unlike their "Arabist" predecessors, the new set of American Mideast policymakers did not view close relations with Israel as a liability when negotiating with Arab states, nor did they believe that the United States could support Israel at all costs. As one observer of the American Middle East policy community observed: "They [the American Middle East policymakers] all arrived at the same conclusion: A settlement will be achieved not by squeezing Israel, as Arabists advocate, nor by coddling Israel, as the Zionist lobby might like, but by cajoling the Jewish state to take 'baby steps.' . . Or to take an 'incrementalist' approach, a term [Dennis] Ross prefers."[84]

At any given time over the last twenty years, a segment of this community has occupied critical official positions in the U.S. government, particularly the State Department and National Security Council.[85] Consider the following members. Dennis Ross wrote his doctoral dissertation on Soviet decision-making and, before his high profile position in the Clinton administration as special Middle East peace coordinator, held positions at State, Defense, and the NSC in the Reagan and Bush administrations. Ross was particularly influential in forming American policy after the Gulf War, serving as the director of policy planning in the State Department at the time. As a member of Secretary Baker's "inner circle,"[86] Ross was behind many of the administration's foreign policy initiatives, including the Madrid and Moscow conferences. Ross "represents a permanent establishment that influences government while presidents come and go. Less partisan and ideological than many of the appointees who come to town with each new administration, these foreign policy professionals are critical to many decisions but function almost entirely out of the spotlight."[87] Ross's earlier writings reveal his emphasis on establishing Arab-Israeli dialogue as a means to build trust and confidence, ideas which he would later introduce when conceiving the multilateral track of the peace process.[88] Because of Ross's influence in successive administrations, his ideas about Arab-Israeli peacemaking were critical in the formation of American policy in the region.

Others who worked with Ross in the Bush and Clinton administrations shaped the intellectual agenda based on their own expertise and the lessons from previous U.S. experience in the peace process. Assistant Secretary Edward P. Djerejian joined Baker's inner circle when he took over the Near East Affairs Bureau in late 1991, becoming "one of Baker's top peace process strategists, along with Dennis Ross. . . . According to insiders, Djerejian and Ross direct a small cadre of experts assigned to the Middle East peace process."[89] Raised in Queens, New York, by Armenian immigrant parents from Turkey, Djerejian represents the "new breed" of Foreign Service Officers (FSOs): he served in Lebanon, Morocco, Jordan, and Syria, and was also trusted by the Israelis, who viewed his experience in Syria as an asset to the peace process.

Another key player, Daniel Kurtzer, similarly challenged the traditional characteristics of the policy elite with his ability to gain the trust of both Arabs and Israelis, having served in Arab capitals and Israel, speaking Arabic as well as Hebrew. As one of the key architects of Secretary Shultz's policy toward the PLO in the Reagan administration, Kurtzer also brought a good deal of continuity to the Bush team, and continued to serve in the Clinton administration, including as the U.S. ambassador to Egypt. Like the other top Mideast policymakers, Kurtzer studied the Middle East in graduate school, earning a doctorate from Columbia University. Aaron Miller, one of the chief architects of the Madrid peace conference (and a close associate of Dennis Ross in the Bush and Clinton administrations), received a Ph.D. in Middle Eastern studies from the University of Michigan and is the author of numerous books and articles on Palestinian nationalism.

Similarly, Martin Indyk wrote his dissertation on the Camp David peace process and founded the influential Middle East think tank, the Washington Institute for Near East Policy, before his entry into government in the first Clinton administration. Indyk's think tank provided an arena where members of the Middle East policy community, both in and out of government, would convene and conceptualize American policy in the region. Indeed, Dennis Ross authored the Washington Institute's first policy paper. Indyk's think tank also organized study groups comprised of important members of the policy community who would issue influential reports. One such study group included many of the officials who would serve in the Bush and Clinton administrations and provided a blueprint for an Arab-Israeli peace that influenced future peace process diplomacy.[90] Other reports emphasized the importance of confidence-building among Arabs and Israelis and the importance of Arab acceptance of Israel in order to facilitate the bilateral peace process, ideas which became an important rationale for the multilaterals.[91] Indyk subsequently entered government as President Clinton's NSC adviser on the Middle East and then as U.S. ambassador to Israel and assistant secretary of state for Near East affairs.

Thus, a professionalized community of American officials responsible for Middle East policy developed and led to continuity in American policy in this region and commonly held beliefs about how to resolve the Arab-Israeli conflict. This institutional memory also gave these policy elites tremendous influence over U.S. policy regardless of the president or secretary of state in power. The emergence of the multilateral process is a reflection of this group's larger vision about how to reshape regional relations in order to bring about an Arab-Israeli peace. Most critical to this vision was a belief that Israel had to gain acceptance in the Arab world (thus demonstrating to the Israeli public that peace with the Arabs was possible and genuine) in order for Israel to make the concessions necessary for a lasting peace (i.e., concessions on the Palestinian track, including land in the West Bank and Gaza). The idea of creating a multilateral process stemmed from these fundamental conceptions about how to resolve the Arab-Israeli conflict.

Senior U.S. officials responsible for negotiating the Madrid and Moscow conferences perceived the multilaterals less as a forum for solving regional problems than as a "conditioning process" whereby Arab parties would get used to Israel acting as a normal player in the regional landscape, in settings that provided opportunities for direct interaction. According to this logic, just including Israel in a regional multilateral process would "change the climate" in the region.[92] As a senior U.S. official explained, the Americans viewed the process in terms of its "psychological impact" more than by its ability to produce substantive results across various issue areas.[93] The issue areas were *chosen* by the United States to serve larger political interests in efforts to resolve the Arab-Israeli conflict. Thus, the groups were not, initially, intended to solve the substantive problems on the agenda. They were intended to facilitate Arab-Israeli political accommodation. The groups were created because the American sponsors valued their political purpose, and pushed such cooperation forward even against the wishes of some regional players. As another senior official involved in the negotiations explained, the idea of the process was to "make normative" the notion that Arabs and Israelis could talk to one another, legitimizing this interaction by establishing a new negotiating framework.[94]

In this way, American ideas about Israeli political integration into the larger region shaped the structure of this process, creating a broad regional forum where North African and Gulf states would join the core Arab parties in a cooperative process that included Israel. In American minds, only an event on such a broad and unprecedented scale would fulfill their notions of how the region needed to be reshaped in the aftermath of a war that afforded them the opportunity and tools to carry out this vision.

## Summary

The altered international and regional strategic environment in 1991–92 made a cooperative Arab-Israeli process thinkable and more likely, but it in no way necessitated a new multilateral peace track to address regional issues, particularly not one on such a broad scale as that established at the Moscow organizational conference. Nor can regional preferences fully explain the origins of this process; if anything, they should have worked against its establishment both in general and across the specific issue areas included in the process. To understand the origins of the multilaterals, one must search for forces outside the region — namely, in Washington, D.C.

The Americans who created this process were a small group of influential elites responsible for U.S. policy in the Middle East who were part of a professionalized foreign policy establishment that brought significant continuity to American policy in the region. By creating a multilateral peace track, these elites served normative interests, particularly the notion that for Israel to be accepted into the region as a normal player, a process had to be established with the widest possible regional participation, even if more modest subregional arrangements could have produced more substantive results in the issue areas under discussion. The originators of the multilaterals thus were not concerned with the substance of the working groups or what would ultimately emerge from them. In their minds, any tangible cooperative projects in particular issue areas would be "gravy," but certainly not the primary rationale for expending American leadership to launch a new multilateral process.

First and foremost, the process was created to foster Arab acceptance of Israel. In an indirect way, the Americans hoped the multilaterals would facilitate a regional atmosphere where bilateral peace treaties would stand a better chance of success. That the process went beyond this original purpose and produced a multitude of regional forums, some of which endured despite a number of serious crises on the bilateral tracks, was unexpected. The multilaterals would proceed to produce many surprises, both positive and negative, as the following chapters will illustrate. But the subsequent development of the multilaterals should not cloud the fact that the process was initiated by forces and individuals outside the region with particular visions of a future Middle East.

# 4  Regional Security Cooperation

If balance of power, zero-sum politics has an archetype, the Arab-Israeli arena would seem to provide an obvious candidate. For some, even the tremendous changes brought about by the end of the Cold War and the Iraqi invasion of Kuwait did not fundamentally alter the regional security environment. The proliferation of weapons of mass destruction among authoritarian and often internally unstable regimes and the continued flow of conventional weaponry to the Middle East make for an extremely dangerous environment.[1] Middle East countries surpass all other developing regions, and even some industrial states, in both quantity and quality of their military forces and armament capabilities, with increasingly modern inventories producing considerable potential for major destruction.[2] In conjunction with this overwhelming stockpile of destructive weapons, the region is plagued by political instability. Extremists continue to carry out atrocious acts of terrorism, and democratic leadership and institutions are virtually absent in the majority of Mideast states. How, many ask, can one talk about Arab-Israeli regional security cooperation under such conditions? Others may ask, how can one *not* address the prospects for a cooperative regional security process given the stakes?

The emergence and development of the Arms Control and Regional Security working group (ACRS) suggest that these questions are no longer hypothetical. The initiation of ACRS as an unprecedented cooperative security experiment among Israel and a large number of Arab parties—despite its failings—defies the notion that this region can be understood only according to competitive, balance of power paradigms. Certainly, balancing and competitive security relationships continue and in some ways have increased, particularly against "rogue" states like Iran and Iraq, as the threat of terrorism rises. Yet regional states have also begun to contemplate and engage in a complementary strategy of security cooperation, as the ACRS case demonstrates. This chapter will explore the dynamics operating within ACRS that both favored and impeded cooperative security postures in the Arab-Israeli context.

Understanding these dynamics has become more critical as regional elites increasingly recognize the role such arrangements can play in building more stable regional security environments in the absence of Cold War-era superpower domination. Certainly, new cooperative security arrangements will not eliminate the possibility of war, nor will they ensure long-term regional stability on their own. They can, however, serve as an important "pillar" of a more stable regional security architecture.[3]

The ACRS case illustrates the advantages of conceptualizing cooperation as a process because the process itself helps explain both the strengths of ACRS and its shortcomings. ACRS represents a limited failure according to a process conception of cooperation because it ultimately did not lead to common understandings of regional security and even exacerbated regional divisions despite its unexpected early progress. This chapter will illustrate how the cooperative process affected the thinking of its participants in both positive and negative directions. Ultimately, the working group was unable to transform highly charged political issues surrounding the security issue area, particularly Israel's nuclear capabilities, into a technical problem more conducive to a multilateral solution. One cannot understand why this transformation failed to occur without examining how key participants in ACRS viewed the process. In particular, Egypt increasingly viewed ACRS as a threat to its traditional leadership role in the region, leading to initiatives that (in its view) favored Israel and Egypt's traditional Arab rival, Jordan, at its expense. Thus, while the empirical record will reveal impressive progress in moving a regional security agenda forward, the process itself brought to the fore political impediments that proved even more difficult to overcome than the strategic obstacles working against Arab-Israeli security cooperation.

This chapter will demonstrate these points first by surveying ACRS's empirical record. The second section will then analyze and explain ACRS's development by highlighting both the mechanisms favoring successful cooperation, or the ability of the working group to reach common understandings, and the forces working against regional security cooperation which ultimately led to the breakdown of the official ACRS working group in late 1995.

## The ACRS Record

### ACRS Emerges[4]

Before the Israeli-Palestinian Declaration of Principles, signed on September 13, 1993, ACRS's activity was limited to a series of workshops where American, European,[5] Russian, and other extraregional experts shared their own regional experiences with the group.[6] In these first meetings, little regional interaction occurred between Arab parties and Israel, and the United States' attempt to create a working agenda illustrated early on the serious substantive differences between the Israeli and Arab (particularly Egyptian) approaches to arms control and regional security. The empirical record underscores the critical role played by the United States in this early period in an attempt to jump-start a viable regional security dialogue based on Western experiences in arms control.[7] As in other prenegotiation experiences, ACRS's first sessions focused on several major areas that better illustrate the difficulties facing the working group and its reliance on extraregional guidance: problem identification, a search for options, and a commitment to negotiate some substantive arms control (broadly defined) measures.

### Problem Identification

The first challenge for the ACRS process was to reach a common understanding among Arabs and Israelis of the problem the group sought to address. Central to this dispute was the question of which part of the ACRS acronym the group would focus on, arms control or regional security. The parties' positions initially divided along the Arab-Israeli fault line, with the Israelis preferring to deal with regional security issues first through a series of incremental confidence-building measures (CBMs) and confidence- and security-building measures (CSBMs)[8] while the Arab states, particularly Egypt, sought to focus on arms control first (defined as arms reduction measures, including nuclear weapons) as a necessary requisite for larger regional security cooperation. This gap in understanding of the group's central problem explains why the Israelis referred to the process as the RS&AC working group while the Egyptians referred to it as the arms reduction working group. Extraregional participants, especially the United States, exerted much effort in this early stage of the process to bridge the gap, and to reach a common working agenda acceptable to all parties. While some of the Arab parties assumed more flexible views over time and were willing to engage in confidence-building without Israeli concessions on nuclear weapons or other arms reduction measures (the Gulf states were particularly wary of defining arms control as arms reduction given their own security interests), the Israeli and Egyptian positions remained unchanged and contributed to many of the problems ACRS faced at later stages of the process.

Still, all parties became sensitive in this initial stage to the nature of arms control and CBMs and recognized the potential for these measures to foster regional stability even absent a comprehensive peace, albeit with limitations. During the first two ACRS plenaries following the Moscow organizational session in January 1992, the regional parties did not interact much but rather sat and listened to the various experts brought in to educate the players on regional arms control. A number of "track two" initiatives—academic conferences bringing regional officials and academics together for more open, informal discussions of sensitive issues to facilitate progress on the official negotiating track—contributed to identifying the types of problems and issues ACRS could address. Many such efforts took place before the establishment of ACRS, from mid-1991 until the Moscow conference, and included many of the same regional officials that would later form the official delegations to ACRS. Some track two conferences produced publications of the proceedings,[9] and led to a more informed discussion of how arms control lessons from other regions might apply to the Middle East. For example, one of these conferences led to a book that brought together European experts on arms control with Middle East experts to consider what the East-West arms control experience might teach Arabs and Israelis.[10] The conclusions drawn in this project foreshadowed the substance of the seminars that later followed in ACRS during its first two years.

One of the most critical conclusions of this study was the notion that while the European experience was distinct in many ways from the Arab-Israeli context, lessons could be applied to the Middle East. The main lesson was that CBMs and CSBMs could work and help facilitate Arab-Israeli political relations, as was the case in the CSCE and U.S.-Soviet arms control experience. Both these experiences underscored that incremental approaches to arms control, focusing first on CBMs and then CSBMs, tended to precede formal arms control measures, such as the banning of certain military activities or actual force reductions. In the European experience, first generation CBMs focused on transparency of military activity to avoid war by accident or miscalculation, while second generation measures, or CSBMs (beginning in 1986) focused on access rather than transparency (e.g., on-site inspections of military facilities became mandatory and stricter terms were developed for notification of military activity).[11] Thus, the second generation CSBMs emphasized verification measures to ensure the CBMs were being implemented, so that the objective became not only the prevention of war but also the reduction in the possibility for surprise attack. Finally, third generation CSBMs (in the late 1980s, coinciding with the end of the Cold War) went beyond limiting military exercises (through notification procedures) to actually banning certain types of activity and placing various types of military equipment (tanks, artillery) in monitored sites to limit their use. Thus, the European experience demonstrated the utility of an incremental approach to arms control, moving toward more difficult measures as confidence builds among adversarial parties. A consensual knowledge developed among arms controllers regarding the most effective arms control sequence, where "this sequence progresses from 'software' (e.g., doctrines, notification of military exercises) to 'hardware' (e.g., force reductions, elimination of weapons systems) through measures that steadily improve communication and transparency."[12] The central message of the study and the subsequent seminars in ACRS was that just as in the European experience, precursor CBMs were possible and desirable for the Middle East, but grand arms control designs should be avoided.[13]

Another definitional problem ACRS faced in this early period was the question of how to define the Middle East. The Israelis in particular were adamant that the region be broadly defined, to include non-Arab states like Iran, Turkey, and even Pakistan and India. The Israelis argued that they could not compromise on their own unconventional capabilities unless all security threats in the region were addressed, including the unconventional capabilities of the so-called rogue states (Iraq, Iran, and Libya). In the end, the group decided to leave the geographical definition of the region flexible, with the potential for non-ACRS parties to join the process at an acceptable time and after substantive arms control agreements had been negotiated. Moreover, the parties agreed that different security issues affected different regional parties, and thus a flexible geographical definition also addressed this problem. However, all parties recognized that once the more advanced arms control measures were considered (i.e., arms reduction and force limitation measures), the region and its subregions would have to be defined more specifically.[14]

While division in the group between a focus on conventional (the Israeli position) and unconventional (Egypt's position) weapons remained,[15] the early seminar-type plenaries led the ACRS parties to a better understanding of the nature and scope of arms control in their region. Most significantly, the regional parties accepted the broad definition of arms control as not only a means to prevent war but also as a mechanism to build confidence and trust to enhance the political process.[16] Disagreement on the tactics to achieve this trust, though serious, should not obscure the degree of consensual knowledge that emerged as regional parties learned and discussed arms control issues multilaterally for the first time since the onset of the Arab-Israeli conflict.

## Search for Options: An Arms Control Agenda Emerges

While the United States cosponsor and other non-Middle East parties dominated ACRS in this pre-Oslo period—particularly the first two ACRS plenary sessions in May and September 1992—in an attempt to lead the regional parties toward common definitions of the arms control problem, the cosponsors also encouraged the regional parties to develop their own positions. Even before the third ACRS plenary in May 1993, regional academics and diplomats (including non-ACRS members like Iran) were meeting in various international forums to discuss regional security issues, such as a United Nations conference in Cairo in April 1993 to discuss regional arms limits.[17] As one analyst commented, "The Cairo conference ... is not likely to change any minds, but it may mark the beginning of a dialogue."[18] In an effort to foster this dialogue, which had been largely absent from the first two ACRS plenaries, the cosponsors requested from all ACRS participants their long-term "vision" of regional security in their concluding statement of the second ACRS plenary in Moscow in September 1992, an exercise that produced several "vision papers" from regional parties. The cosponsors also requested that the regional parties create lists of acceptable CBMs and CSBMs that could form ACRS's working agenda in future meetings. By the third ACRS plenary in May 1993, these papers and policy formulations played an important role in clarifying regional positions in a search for options that would shape ACRS's work agenda once it was ripe for negotiating specific agreements. This was particularly important given that, except for Egypt with its well-formulated positions on arms control, the other regional parties had not developed and debated serious arms control initiatives within their respective governments. Moreover, the vision statements offered a rare opportunity to understand how various regional parties conceptualized security issues, something that is often difficult to discern because of the generally closed nature of these types of discussions in both Israel and the Arab states.[19] The Israeli vision paper became public when it was published by one of the members of the Israeli delegation to ACRS.[20] This document is particularly significant because it was debated within the Israeli government in late 1992 (on the eve of the Chemical Weapons Convention [CWC] signing conference on January 13, 1993) and approved by the Israeli cabinet, with Prime Minister Yitzhak Rabin taking a special interest as the Israeli defense minister at the time—the ministry responsible for ACRS.

The essential elements of the Israeli vision paper on regional security and arms control were first revealed in Foreign Minister Shimon Peres's address at the signing ceremony of the CWC in January.[21] In the address, Peres outlined a proposal for the construction of "a mutually verifiable zone, free of surface-to-surface missiles and chemical, biological and nuclear weapons."[22] As Shai Feldman observed, in substance the Peres proposal—which was essentially the Israeli long-term security vision—adopted the April 1990 initiative of Egypt's President Hosni Mubarak, except that the Israeli requirement for a WMDFZ was a comprehensive set of regional peace and mutual verification measures.[23] As the vision paper itself stated, "In the spirit of the global pursuit of general and complete disarmament, Israel will endeavor, upon the establishment of relations of peace, that the states of this region should jointly establish a mutually verifiable zone free of ground-to-ground missiles, of chemical weapons, of biological weapons, and of nuclear weapons."[24] The vision paper also underscored Israel's position on the sequencing and substance of the working group's agenda, arguing that "the Middle East RS&AC process can only achieve its practical goals if the process is in step with the peace-making efforts aiming at ridding the region of the conflicts afflicting it."[25] Again, the Israeli position viewed ACRS as a means to build political confidence and establish incremental security measures, not as a means to deal first and foremost with Israel's nuclear capabilities. This explains the paper's focus on "comprehensiveness," both in terms of ACRS's tasks (not just curtailing arms buildups or proliferation but also building confidence) and in relation to weapon types (conventional and unconventional). As the paper explains, "For progress to be made, the RS&AC process has to be pragmatic. . . . Progress must be incremental, through a step-by-step approach. . . . The first steps in the process should be: Establishing of Confidence Building Measures."[26] Finally, the paper stressed Israel's preference for a regional arms control framework and verification process (as opposed to an international framework), with the region broadly defined ("the arms control accords will include *all* states of the region"). In the concluding general remarks of the document, the Israelis underscored the notion that regional security entails broader political accommodation and cooperation by arguing that economic cooperation between Middle East states would support the ACRS process.

Some of the Arab participants also presented their long-term visions for regional security. While these have not been made public, some distinctions and some commonalities are apparent according to discussions with ACRS participants. Egypt's position on arms control—in contrast to the other Arab states—was clear and public, and served as the strongest contrast to the Israeli vision. The most obvious distinction was the sequencing of the process, with the Egyptians in particular stressing the need to focus on the nuclear question at the early stages, which they argue is in itself a CBM.[27] However, while the Jordanians did not deny that Israel would eventually have to compromise on the nuclear issue and sign the Nuclear Nonproliferation Treaty (NPT), they assumed a position closer to the Israelis in terms of stressing the need for CBMs (including political measures) before more formal arms reduction measures.[28] Indeed, the conceptual agreements worked out in ACRS later shaped the security section of the Israel-Jordan peace treaty, which referred to ACRS's work [see appendix B].[29] While the Jordanian position came closest to the Israelis, resistance from other Arab states to the modeling approach (again Egypt in particular) was apparent in their long-term visions. Some Arab parties were especially sensitive to drawing on the Conference on Security and Cooperation in Europe (CSCE) framework which accepted the territorial status quo, clearly a problematic assumption in the Arab-Israeli context.[30] Still, all parties, Israelis and Arabs alike, were united in their papers by including provisions to rid the region of unconventional weapons. The main area of disagreement among the visions was the timing—the question became when and how to undertake certain arms control provisions.[31]

In addition to the long-term vision papers, the parties also agreed at the May 1993 meeting to a series of CBMs that would start the group's working agenda. To this end, they developed the notion of intersessional activities, or smaller workshops that would meet in between larger plenary sessions and focus on specific CBM areas. The parties agreed that various extraregional members would "mentor" these intersessional activities: the United States and Russia would direct the declaratory CBMs, long-term objectives discussions, and a verification workshop; Canada headed the maritime CBM workshops; Turkey took responsibility for the exchange of information and prenotification CBMs; and the Netherlands sponsored the communication-related CBMs. The extraregional mentors encouraged high-level participation in these intersessionals, and particularly the involvement of military representatives from respective governments who could facilitate the technical aspects of these agreements and tended to cooperate better with each other than the political representatives.[32]

Aside from launching intersessional activities, the May 1993 plenary served as an important "icebreaker" meeting between Israeli and Arab participants that allowed future activity to continue. At this meeting, the co-sponsors were able to get the regional parties to talk to one another, rather than just sit in a room and listen to lectures from outside experts. According to one participant, before the May meeting even Arab delegation members were not particularly friendly to one another, creating a tense and terse atmosphere. When the head of the Israeli delegation wanted to shake hands with the Arab delegates, one of the Arab representatives sitting next to the Israelis remarked, "Wait in line. . . . They haven't talked to me yet either."[33] After this meeting, relations became less formal and more friendly among all participants, with delegations addressing each other directly in frank discussion. The Gulf states also became more relaxed at this meeting when a Jordanian representative emphasized the political-military nature of arms control as opposed to a strictly technical definition, a definition which concerned Gulf states sensitive to arms race charges in their subregion.[34]

## Commitment to Negotiate: The Beginning of Intersessionals

The beginning of intersessional activities in the summer of 1993 (on the eve of the Oslo breakthrough) underscored the growing commitment among the regional parties to engage in arms control negotiations as they perceived common benefits from such a process, both in terms of facilitating the bilateral track of the peace process and in order to address common security problems that required multilateral cooperation. The fact that the Labor government in Israel assumed a more flexible approach to the contentious issue of Palestinian representation in the multilaterals, allowing the Palestinians to join the ACRS process by the third ACRS plenary (May 1993), provided political cover for other Arab participants to engage in more serious and substantive discussions and activities.[35] For example, a verification workshop took place in Cairo in mid-July 1993, marking an important precedent of moving multilateral working group meetings to the region itself, rather than limiting venues to European capitals and Washington.[36] During this intersessional, the participants visited the Sinai in order to observe and learn from the example of the Multinational Force and Observers (MFO) which was established to monitor the Sinai peninsula as part of the 1979 peace treaty between Israel and Egypt. At this point, the Egyptians were still quite favorably inclined toward the ACRS process, or what reports from an Egyptian daily termed the "committee on arms limitation," writing of the "importance of Egypt's role in initiating and establishing peace" and observing that "the committee [ACRS] chose Cairo as the venue for the seminar, which is just further evidence that Egypt is the land of peace and security."[37] However, because ACRS, like all the multilateral working groups, was always dependent on the success and pace of the Palestinian peace track, the commitment of regional parties to negotiate substantive arms control and regional security principles and activities would likely not have been able to materialize without the dramatic breakthrough between Israel and the Palestine Liberation Organization (PLO) on September 13, 1993, known as the Oslo Accord. While precursor CBMs might have been possible in limited areas, the Oslo Accord set the stage for an acceleration of regional activity across all the multilateral working groups. ACRS was no exception. As one Arab participant explained, the Israeli-Palestinian breakthrough constituted the beginning, with all preceding activity merely prenegotiation exercises.[38] The time became ripe for Arabs and Israelis to enter into more extensive negotiations on the details of specific security documents, statements, and even the establishment of regional security institutions. While external leadership by extraregional powers may have been necessary to create ACRS and guide its early work, progress on the political track and growing regional awareness about how to proceed with regional arms control led to greater regional initiative as ACRS developed. As we will see in the next section, this initiative sometimes led to positive developments in the working group, but it also ultimately led to the demise of the process despite continued American interest in seeing it continue.

## ACRS's Development After Oslo

On the day of the signing of the Israeli-Palestinian Declaration of Principles (September 13, 1993), the ACRS participants were meeting in Canada for an intersessional activity on maritime measures. According to one account of this meeting, ACRS delegates watched the signing ceremony together, leading to "a celebration that evening at which position papers gave way to embraces, festivities, and what one participant characterized as a 'magical evening.' "[39] Several separate intersessional activities followed throughout the fall of 1993, when movement to more detailed and focused discussions was apparent. The intersessional topics included not only maritime measures but also workshops on communications, prenotification of military activities, long-term objectives, and declaratory statements and information exchanges [see table 4.1]. ACRS parties were also invited to observe a NATO exercise in Denmark during this time. However, it was with the November 1993 ACRS plenary in Moscow that a more defined negotiating agenda emerged. At this meeting, the participants agreed to divide all activity into two "baskets" (based on the 1975 Helsinki terminology), a *conceptual* and an *operational* basket. The conceptual basket would include all declaratory measures and statements, while the operational basket would address more technical CBMs. These two baskets shaped the remainder of ACRS's negotiating history, with future intersessionals constructed around them. Both demonstrate the rather expansive nature of the working group's agenda as well as the increasing polarization between the Israelis and Egyptians as regional relations multilateralized in ways that allowed for greater Israeli interaction with Arab parties, which threatened the traditional role of Egypt in the regional security equation.

### The Conceptual Basket

The Vienna intersessional in October 1993 began to address conceptual issues such as long-term regional security objectives and declaratory measures that would state general principles and norms to guide regional arms

TABLE 4.1 ACRS Working Group Calendar of Meetings, 1992–1995

| Meeting | Date, Place |
| --- | --- |
| Plenary Session | May 1992, Washington, D.C. |
| Plenary Session | September 1992, Moscow |
| Plenary Session | May 1993, Washington, D.C. |
| Intersessional (air base visit) | June 1993, United Kingdom |
| Intersessional (verification seminar) | July 1993, Cairo |
| Intersessional (NATO observation) | September 1993, Denmark |
| Intersessional (maritime measures) | September 1993, Nova Scotia, Canada |
| Intersessional (communications workshop) | September 1993, The Hague |
| Intersessional (prenotification and military information exchange) | October 1993, Antalya, Turkey |
| Intersessional (long-term objectives and declaratory measures) | October 1993, Vienna |
| Plenary Session | November 1993, Moscow |
| Operational Basket (communications) | January 1994, The Hague |
| Conceptual Basket Workshops | January–February 1994, Cairo |
| Operational Basket Workshops | March 1994, Antalya, Turkey |
| Plenary Session | May 1994, Doha |
| Operational Basket (maritime demonstration) | July 1994, Italy |
| Operational Basket (naval officers meeting) | August 1994, Canada |
| Conceptual Basket Workshops | October 1994, Paris |
| Operational Basket Workshops | November 1994, Dead Sea, Jordan |
| Plenary Session | December 1994, Tunis |
| Operational Basket (maritime exercise planning) | January 1995, Tunis |
| Operational Basket (communications network) | March 1995, Cairo |
| Operational Basket Workshops | March–April 1995, Antalya, Turkey |
| Operational Basket (communications network) | May 1995, The Hague |

TABLE 4.1 *(continued)*

| Meeting | Date, Place |
|---|---|
| Conceptual Basket | May 1995, Helsinki |
| Operational Basket (naval officers symposium) | July 1995, Ontario, Canada |
| Conceptual Basket (regional security center) | September 1995, Amman |

Source: Bruce Jentleson, *The Middle East Arms Control and Regional Security (ACRS) Talks: Progress, Problems, and Prospects* (San Diego: Institute on Global Conflict and Cooperation, 1996) and *The Arms Control Reporter* (Cambridge, MA: Institute for Defense and Disarmament Studies, 1994 and 1996 eds.).

control. A cosponsor paper prepared for the November 3–4 plenary in Moscow summarized the understanding reached at the Vienna workshop, explaining that "the goal of the process of arms control could be the increase in the security of all states of the region accompanied by the lowest possible level of arms possession. . . . The parties should agree on the sequence of the development and use of armaments control measures and on regional security. At the same time it is quite obvious that the process will go on a stage-by-stage basis, proceeding from simpler to more intricate measures."[40] Keeping these broad goals in mind, the cosponsors shaped the working agenda of the conceptual basket, which consisted of two key initiatives that were negotiated over the following two years in the context of the general plenaries and during the conceptual basket intersessional meetings in January–February 1994 (Cairo)[41] and October 1994 (Paris).[42]

*The ACRS declaration or statement of principles*
The keystone of ACRS's conceptual basket was a document initially drafted at the February Cairo conceptual intersessional, termed a "Declaration of Principles (DoP) and Statements of Intent on Arms Control and Regional Security." This document was largely modeled on the Helsinki Final Act agreement of 1975, in an effort to define and formulate general principles to guide regional relations in the security realm (broadly defined). Just as in the Helsinki case, this would not be a legally binding agreement but rather a normative statement that might at least guide and

constrain regional action on sensitive security matters by creating norms of acceptable behavior. In this sense, this conceptual exercise sought to influence more directly the political realm, in contrast to the operational basket's focus on more limited, technical, military-related CBMs. Over the year between the creation of the DoP in February 1994 to the last ACRS plenary in December 1994, the ACRS delegations passionately debated the content of this document, with many contentious issues left in brackets at the end of the Cairo meeting to indicate areas of continued disagreement among the parties.[43]

The ACRS DoP (see appendix C) begins with a preamble outlining the role of arms control and regional security in the broader peace process context, stressing not only ACRS's security purpose but also recognizing that ACRS "should continue to complement the bilateral negotiations and help improve the climate for resolving the core issues at the heart of the Middle East peace process." The first section of the DoP proved most controversial. This section addressed the "Fundamental Principles Governing Security Relations Among Regional Participants in the Arms Control and Regional Security Working Group." Some of the less controversial aspects of this section included principles such as refraining from the use of force and acts of terrorism, or respect and acknowledgment of sovereignty, territorial integrity, and political independence. More contentious provisions, however, addressed questions of Israeli withdrawal from Arab territory and how to define self-determination for Palestinians. The second section, "Guidelines for the Middle East Arms Control and Regional Security Process," essentially confirmed many of the lessons from the pre-Oslo stage, including the need for comprehensiveness in arms control and a step-by-step approach to building regional trust and security. This section also reaffirmed the consensus-based nature of the ACRS process, as is common in most multilateral forums. The final section, "Statements of Intent on Objectives for the Arms Control and Regional Security Process," included objectives previously discussed in the working group: by means of CBMs, preventing conflict by misunderstanding or miscalculation; limiting military spending in the region in favor of a social and economic focus; reducing conventional arms stockpiles and races; and finally, establishing a WMDFZ, "including nuclear, chemical and biological weapons and their delivery systems." At the end of the Cairo intersessional, the parties agreed to review the controversial sections of the text and resume the negotiation of the DoP at the next ACRS plenary in May 1994 in Doha.

The Doha meeting (attended by 37 countries, including 14 regional delegations) represented a critical point in ACRS and the overall multilateral process, as it was the first meeting of the working group to meet in the Gulf region (the Water group was the first to enter the Gulf, with a plenary session held in Oman in April 1994). These unprecedented Arab-Israeli multilateral meetings were significant not only because of their symbolic effect—bringing large, public Israeli delegations to Gulf states with whom Israel had no formal diplomatic ties—but also because they provided cover for quiet movement toward establishing bilateral relations between Israel and Arab states in the Gulf and North Africa.[44] They also reflected the enhanced role of the regional participants and greater interaction between Israel and the Arab parties as ACRS developed. Interestingly, this meeting also provided an opportunity for the Egyptians to reintegrate themselves into the regional security agenda after years of isolation in the wake of the Camp David Accords.[45] However, the increasingly independent positions of the smaller GCC states were perceived as a threat to Saudi domination of this subregion. Tensions between Qatar and Saudi Arabia were particularly apparent, with the Saudis challenging "the U.S. representative's contention that not all Arab delegates were opposed to confidence-building measures before progress was made in the bilateral tracks of the peace talks."[46] Reportedly, the heads of the American and Saudi delegation had a "heated argument" on this issue.[47] The result was a rather unproductive meeting in substantive terms, and the plenary failed to produce agreement on the ACRS DoP.[48] While disagreement on the disputed sections in the DoP continued to spark debate and division, the greatest stumbling block to agreement on the DoP at Doha was the Saudi position.

Though the Saudis had never been active participants in ACRS or enthusiastic supporters of arms control efforts that included the Israelis, they had not objected to the group's working agenda before Doha, assuming a "cooperatively inactive" approach.[49] However, the venue of the ACRS plenary in Qatar angered the Saudis, who preferred a much quieter and more conservative Gulf role in the process.[50] The DoP was also a concern for the Saudis and other Arab states sensitive to the pace of the working group (in that it should not surpass or overshadow progress on the bilateral front) because it constituted one of the most serious arms control documents in the history of the Arab-Israeli conflict. As Assistant Secretary of State Robert Pelletreau suggested, "Agreement on this declaration [the ACRS DoP] would provide a road map to achieving specific arms control and the security arrangements in a post-peace-process Middle East."[51] In an unusual sign of seriousness, the Saudis sent a senior representative of the regime to the Doha meeting, in contrast to earlier ACRS sessions where lower-level officials from local embassies often represented the Saudis. The Saudi representative repeatedly objected to moving the DoP forward, on the grounds that the multilateral talks and the various CBMs on the ACRS agenda should only materialize after progress on the bilateral negotiating tracks.[52] According to a U.S. participant in the talks, the Doha meeting proved a step back, or at least a pause, in moving the ACRS agenda, and particularly the DoP, forward.[53] The meeting ended with no agreement on the DoP. The Saudis, in an effort to slow the normalization process begun by the other GCC states, made it clear that they would not host future multilateral meetings, ACRS or otherwise, in their country or attend multilateral sessions in Israel.[54] In the end, the final Doha statement stated the parties' commitment to continue working on the DoP until they could agree on a final text.

By the fall of 1994, the Saudis' position began to soften, particularly since the GCC states were no longer hosting regional plenaries. Quiet high-level Saudi contacts with Israelis were reported, leading the Saudis to address the Israelis directly for the first time in the December 1994 Tunis plenary.[55] A Saudi prince addressed Israeli delegation head David Ivry, and Ivry responded in Arabic, breaking the ice between the two.[56] However, while Saudi objections to ACRS and the DoP lessened and the Tunisian hosts optimistically expressed the hope "of moving our region from one of rival blocs to one of cooperation," new and even more serious obstacles emerged, most significant of which was renewed pressure by the Egyptians for Israel to sign the NPT as the international review conference approached in April.[57] The specific proposal to include NPT language in the DoP led to a deadlock in the group, and a failure to approve the document.[58] Indeed, this issue proved most significant in freezing ACRS's work the following year. Despite the failure to approve the DoP, ACRS delegates still believed some modest progress was possible on other items on ACRS's agenda, particularly some of the more technical CBMs in the operational basket. And while the DoP itself was never approved, the negotiation process surrounding it demonstrated increasing willingness of smaller Arab parties to at least implicitly side with Israel against other Arab states in what potentially could have led to a greater depolarization of Arab-Israeli security relations had the process continued.

*The regional security center*

The proposal to establish a regional security center (RSC), or initially a conflict prevention center (CPC) modeled on the CSCE CPC in Vienna, was first raised in the closing statement of the Doha plenary, when Qatar offered to set up such a center "once peace is achieved."[59] Discussions on establishing a regional conflict prevention or resolution center continued during a conceptual intersessional meeting in Paris in October 1994.[60] By the December Tunis plenary, the parties agreed to establish the center in Amman (with related facilities in Qatar and Tunisia) despite the continued disagreement over the ACRS DoP.[61] However, the purpose of the center remained vague, leaving room for a variety of interpretations of its scope and mandate. The center became a particularly contentious issue between Jordan and Egypt. Jordan (as host of the center) preferred a broad mandate, with the RSC subsuming much of the ACRS working agenda over time as it became the hub for all regional security activity.[62] Egypt, however, wished to limit the RSC mandate to specific conflict prevention activities, and diminish its importance in the overall regional security efforts. Despite Egyptian resistance, the Jordanians chose a location for the RSC and began planning activities for the center, such as a seminar on military doctrine sponsored by the French. Future workshops on verification issues (addressing both unconventional and conventional weapons) were also a possible agenda item for the center, building on work begun on this issue in earlier verification intersessional activities. At a September 1995 intersessional in Amman, all ACRS parties except Egypt agreed to the RSC mandate. Because of the Egyptian objection (again, related to the NPT issue), the RSC could not begin its operations.[63] The U.S. sponsors decided to come out of the meeting with a "clean" document (i.e., no disputed bracketed text) that would only note the Egyptian objection to the overall statement so that once this objection was resolved, the process could move forward without renegotiating the entire text.[64] Should ACRS activities resume, the RSC could be ready for immediate use, having already received funds and equipment for operation from several extraregional sponsors.[65]

## The Operational Basket

In contrast to the conceptual basket, the operational basket activities focused on specific, technical CBMs and CSBMs modeled again on the

U.S.-Soviet and European experience. Because the types of activities covered in this basket—communication networks, prenotification and military information exchange agreements, and maritime measures—were less political in nature, this basket carried the greatest potential for moving an arms control agenda forward under conducive political conditions. While some of this type of activity occurred before Oslo, most of the basket's activities took place after September 13, 1993.

*The communications network*

The communications network proposal, sponsored by the Netherlands, was first discussed in an intersessional seminar in September 1993 in The Hague, with technical discussions among the ACRS parties continuing in January 1994 (also in The Hague). The project was agreed to in principle at the Doha plenary in May 1994, although the parties did not agree to join or turn on the system at the Doha meeting.[66] The purpose of the network was to create an electronic communications system to link foreign ministries in the Middle East in order to enhance crisis management and prevention, as well as to facilitate communication related to ACRS activities. Drawing on lessons of initiatives like the hotline developed between the U.S. and Soviets during the Cold War, the ACRS communication network was similarly designed to avoid misperception of intentions and inadvertent conflict between adversaries, even before a political rapprochement was reached. Like other ACRS activities, joining the network was voluntary. The parties initially agreed to place the system in The Hague (utilizing the existing CSCE network based there), and planned to move it to Cairo on a permanent basis (this location was confirmed at the last ACRS plenary in Tunis). Discussions on setting up the network continued at the November 1994 intersessional at the Dead Sea (in Jordan) in preparation for the December Tunis plenary.[67] At the Tunis plenary, the parties agreed to a start-up date for the communications network, targeting March 1995. At subsequent operational basket intersessionals (in March and April 1995), six ACRS parties agreed to link themselves to the communications system (Egypt, Israel, Jordan, Tunisia, Qatar, and the Palestinians). The system was officially inaugurated and became operational in early April 1995, although only Israel and Egypt had joined the system by that time.[68] However, as with the rest of the ACRS agenda, the overall deterioration of this working group in the spring of 1995 prevented further implementation of the network.

## Prenotification agreement and exchange of military information

Another set of operational CBM and CSBM activity was sponsored by Turkey, and included negotiations on a Prenotification of Certain Military Activities agreement as well as establishing procedures for the exchange of military information among ACRS participants. In the November 1994 intersessional in Jordan,[69] the prenotification agreement was discussed in more detail, and the parties agreed to hold a joint regional military exercise in the future.[70] The Israeli delegation also invited other ACRS parties to visit Israeli military bases, an invitation agreed to by Arab parties at the Tunis plenary in December.[71] By the Tunis plenary,[72] the ACRS parties agreed to a prenotification document calling for advance notification of military exercises involving more than 4000 troops or 110 tanks,[73] and also agreed to an exchange of information on less sensitive military information (such as curriculum vitaes of military officers or technical military manuals). Fourteen regional ACRS parties agreed to these operational CBMs: Egypt, Israel, Jordan, the Palestinians, Morocco, Algeria, Tunisia, Saudi Arabia, Kuwait, Bahrain, Oman, Qatar, the United Arab Emirates, and Yemen.[74] While these types of CBMs were impressive, they would likely not have gone further— even if the ACRS process had continued—until other key parties (the Syrians, Iranians, Iraqis) joined the process. Providing and sharing sensitive military information is more difficult if participation is limited, since parties (particularly the Israelis) feel they are divulging information that might become available to non-ACRS parties without a reciprocal agreement with those states. This lack of reciprocity is more difficult in these types of CBMs than is the case with either the communications network or maritime measures where immediate benefits to the participating parties outweigh potential risks of such involvement.

## Maritime confidence-building measures

Of all the operational CBMs, the maritime area is perhaps the most promising arena for promoting Arab-Israeli security cooperation, as was the case in the East-West experience. As agreed to at the end of the prenegotiation stage, Canada served as the extraregional mentor for maritime-related projects. Maritime CBMs are considered "easier" than other technical military confidence-building because they present clear benefits to the regional parties committed to such measures. As Peter Jones, a Canadian diplomat who worked on ACRS's maritime measures, explains, "Of all spheres of military rivalry in the Middle East, the maritime sphere is generally regarded as the least contentious. . . . There are relatively few Middle East disputes of a purely maritime or naval character."[75] That said, Jones and others note that serious maritime incidents have occurred in the region (among regional navies and between regional and extraregional navies as well as with terrorist organizations), providing incentives for regional parties to address this problem in cooperative ways.[76]

These incidents underscored the potential for cooperative projects to prevent such disturbances, which could escalate into more serious conflict. However, in order to move toward the negotiation of concrete measures as quickly as possible, the Canadian mentors proposed that the ACRS parties focus first on the least controversial types of maritime measures: Search and Rescue (SAR) and the Prevention of Incidents at Sea (INCSEA) agreements. Jones explains the benefits of these particular maritime CBMs in moving the regional security agenda forward: "Search and Rescue is first and foremost a humanitarian activity and no state could object to steps designed to enhance the ability of the region to respond to humanitarian tragedies. With respect to INCSEA, no state wants to see an unplanned incident escalate into a tense situation. . . . Both require naval officers to work cooperatively toward the establishment and realization of agreed operational goals."[77] Beginning with the first maritime intersessional meeting in Nova Scotia, Canada, on September 13, 1993 (the day of the Oslo DoP signing), ACRS's negotiations in this operational area centered on establishing these two agreements.

The Nova Scotia intersessional constituted a prenegotiation exercise, with its format largely seminar style in an effort to educate the regional parties on general issues of maritime confidence-building. However, this meeting set the stage for the subsequent detailed discussions within the operational basket on SAR and INCSEA agreements for the ACRS parties. The main lesson from the INCSEA discussions for the regional participants was that early communication of intentions between ships is the best precaution against misunderstanding, and can be arranged by establishing special signals known in advance to all parties who sign the INCSEA agreement.[78] The SAR talks emphasized the need to pool resources to respond to humanitarian disasters and to standardize procedures for these responses among the regional participants. In preparation for the negotiation phase of the maritime measures, regional participants asked Canada to draft an INCSEA agreement text for the Middle East, which would constitute the first multilateral INCSEA agreement in any region.[79] This text served as the working draft for the agreement negotiated by ACRS parties in the next maritime intersessional in Antalya, Turkey, in March 1994.

At the Antalya meeting, modest progress was made in the SAR area, with the parties envisioning the future ACRS communications network as a mechanism to share information about various states' SAR procedures and to facilitate SAR coordination. Some parties offered to host a regional Rescue Coordination Center at a later stage of the process.[80] The parties also agreed to accept the Canadian INCSEA text as the ACRS draft document. Much disagreement occurred over how operationally constraining the ACRS INCSEA agreement should be in relation to existing bilateral regimes, such as the question of whether certain technology aboard a ship had to be banned outright, or whether it simply could not be used in the proximity of another regional ship.[81] However, as Jones explains, INCSEA agreements do not intend to prevent surveillance activity, they just seek to make these types of activities safer by building on regional parties' mutual interests in avoiding unwanted incidents.[82] Other problems specific to the Middle East context emerged, such as the problem of areas where there is no international water (i.e., the Red Sea) and thus where INCSEA agreements are not applicable but are most needed. However, despite these areas of disagreement at the Antalya meeting, the parties accepted over seventy percent of the draft ACRS INCSEA agreement.[83]

The practical nature of the INCSEA and SAR agreements was reinforced by a naval demonstration for ACRS parties at an intersessional meeting on July 15, 1994, off the coast of Venice, Italy. The demonstration involved a Canadian frigate and a U.S. ammunition ship (as well as an Italian maritime patrol aircraft) simulating a contact at sea under an INCSEA agreement, including a response to a SAR distress call.[84] This demonstration led to consideration of conducting a similar demonstration in the region drawing on regional participation and equipment. In conjunction with this exercise, a second maritime intersessional, the Senior Naval Officer's Symposium, was held that summer from August 29 to September 1 in Halifax, Canada. Attended by ten regional delegations, the ACRS representatives toured Canadian maritime facilities, observed another SAR demonstration, and discussed future maritime CBMs in the ACRS context. The naval officers also clarified some of the details in the ACRS INCSEA text, which paved the way for further negotiations on the agreement in the operational basket meeting the following November in Jordan. At the November meeting, after three days of negotiation on the text, the INCSEA document was agreed to by all

ACRS parties, except for agreement on its title (or the type of agreement it constituted) and final article.[85] Regional parties at the November meeting first considered the SAR text as well.

At the larger ACRS plenary session in Tunis the following month (December 1994), both the INCSEA text and SAR framework were agreed to. Despite the general deterioration of ACRS after the Tunis plenary, particularly during the NPT review conference in April 1995, the maritime intersessionals continued to meet and make progress on both the INCSEA[86] and SAR agreements at sessions in April and July, 1995, in Antalya and Ontario respectively. While the parties agreed to the proposed regional naval demonstration at the Tunis plenary (scheduled to take place off the Tunisian coast), the exercise never occurred because of an Israeli leak publicizing the activity during a fairly sensitive time in the political process.[87]

Despite the promise in this area of confidence-building, the general demise of ACRS over political issues—most notably the NPT dispute between Egypt and Israel in April—precluded further activity even in this rather cooperative basket. Still, a network of naval contacts among regional parties was established along with some technical agreements to enhance regional stability. Indeed, the extensive work conducted within the operational basket and the regional interest and involvement in its activities made ACRS's failings more disturbing.

## The Breakdown of ACRS

Any multilateral negotiation, but especially one dealing with sensitive matters of security, is likely to face obstacles to moving a working agenda forward. In the ACRS case, some of these challenges did not just slow ACRS down, but actually brought the process to a halt. As mentioned above, ACRS faced many limitations from the outset, the most significant of which was the sensitivity to developments in the bilateral peace tracks, which led key regional players like Syria and Lebanon to boycott the talks. And, of course, other key parties critical to a regional security dialogue were not invited because of their support for international terrorism and other "rogue-type" activities—Iraq, Iran, and Libya. Another Middle East-specific problem related to the balancing of the ACRS agenda among various subregional interests, particularly the subregional concerns of the Levant as opposed to the Gulf and North African regions.

Other, more generic problems in the process also became apparent, such as the failure to maintain consistent delegations to the talks in order to build an institutional memory and a community of experts on arms control issues, a problem which is common to protracted multilateral negotiating forums.[88] Still, ACRS was able to overcome these limitations and challenges—as did the other multilateral working groups—during its first three years and even achieved some substantive progress. In other words, these obstacles, whether general or specific to the Middle East, were not insurmountable. Yet one problem that was apparent in ACRS from the start became insurmountable by the spring of 1995 and led to the breakdown of the group's activities and freezing of the ACRS process.

The problem was the continued dispute between Egypt and Israel over the nuclear issue,[89] particularly the Egyptian demand that Israel sign the NPT and adhere to IAEA inspections of its nuclear facilities as required by the global treaty.[90] While the Egyptian delegation had consistently pressed the Israelis on this issue from the start of the ACRS process, it was not until the last ACRS plenary in December 1994 that this issue prevented the ACRS agenda from moving forward, at that time blocking the approval of the ACRS DoP. The context for the increased conflict and deadlock resulting from the NPT dispute between Egypt and Israel was the upcoming international conference in April 1995 to renew the global nuclear nonproliferation regime indefinitely. The global conference again focused the limelight on this contentious issue, although the conference in itself does not entirely explain the Egyptian decision to link the NPT extension to ACRS's activities. Leaving motivations aside at this point, the breakdown of ACRS is directly linked to the NPT dispute,[91] with the aftermath of the NPT conference leading to several contentious ACRS intersessionals and ultimately to the final ACRS meeting in September 1995. Despite high-level meetings among Israeli officials—including an April 1995 meeting called by Prime Minister Rabin and attended by Foreign Minister Peres and ACRS delegation head David Ivry—and between the Israeli and Egyptian foreign ministers Peres and Moussa following the NPT conference, differences on the arms control and NPT issues were left unresolved, and continued to prevent further progress in ACRS.[92] In fact, the continued dispute between Israel and Egypt on the nuclear issue led to an overall deterioration in bilateral Egyptian-Israeli relations.[93]

With the Egyptians failing to gain Israeli nuclear concessions at the global level or the Israeli signature of the NPT, the nuclear fallout subsequently descended on ACRS's territory with negative results. According to ACRS participants, the ACRS intersessional meeting in Helsinki in May 1995, following the NPT conference, was particularly tense and dominated by heated, personal exchanges between the Egyptian and Israeli delegations.[94] By this time, most of ACRS's conceptual activities were stalled, although as noted some operational intersessional activities continued. At the last ACRS intersessional meeting on the regional security center (RSC) in Amman in September 1995, all parties agreed to the center's mandate by consensus except Egypt. While other Arab parties were sympathetic to Egypt's position on the NPT, they did not share the desire to stop all ACRS activities until the issue was resolved. However, because ACRS decisions were based on the consensus rule, the objection of one party—particularly one as significant as Egypt—was enough to freeze the entire process. The American sponsors recognized they could not hold an ACRS plenary (which was initially planned for September 1995) that was intended to approve a number of ACRS projects, including the RSC, if the Egyptians continued to object. ACRS ceased to officially operate once this dispute came to the fore. A process offering some promise of novel Arab-Israeli security cooperation, surprising in itself, came to a halt.

## Explaining ACRS: The Promise and Limits of a Cooperative Security Process

### *A Limited Cooperation Success*

Despite its setbacks and its ultimate breakdown, ACRS established a cooperative process that in many ways generated common understandings that would not have been possible absent such a process. The ACRS working record demonstrates how a cooperative process can facilitate common understandings by 1) redefining problems in consensual terms; 2) creating a shared vocabulary and knowledge base; 3) making new policy options and negotiating partners acceptable; and 4) increasing interactions among participants. Over time, however, these facilitative mechanisms were overshadowed by the impeding mechanisms identified in chapter 1, particularly the perceived threat ACRS posed to the regional identity of a key participant.

The ACRS process, particularly its early seminar-style sessions, helped shape regional participants' understandings of arms control by offering a broader definition which included CBMs and CSBMs. Before the ACRS exercise, many regional participants viewed arms control in the more narrow sense of arms reduction and elimination. Thus, without an ACRS process even this fundamental understanding of what arms control means may not have emerged. Related to this redefinition of arms control was the introduction of new vocabulary and shared knowledge among regional participants, largely disseminated by external actors experienced in arms control negotiations. Again, the objective of early ACRS plenaries was to create common understandings of arms control by sharing other regional experiences, such as the CSCE negotiations and the U.S.-Soviet talks. In particular, the conventional wisdom among arms controllers based on these previous experiences focused on an incremental approach to arms control, whereby sequencing the "software" issues (various CBMs) before the "hardware" (verification measures and actual troop and arms reductions) enhances the likelihood of successful negotiations. While Egypt and Israel continued to disagree over the timing of the working group's activities and even the definition of confidence-building (e.g., the Egyptians viewed Israel's willingness to sign the NPT as a CBM while Israel insisted this issue could only be addressed at the end of an arms control process), the regional participants did reach broad agreement on the usefulness of CBMs and the integral role they play in regional arms control talks. Indeed, much of the ACRS working record was based on a variety of CBMs, both at the conceptual and operational level.

New policy options also became acceptable as a result of ACRS, such as the creation of regional security institutions and the beginning of joint security exercises, particularly in the maritime area. Joint military exercises and discussions became legitimate and acceptable to regional participants, although not to the extent that they could withstand public scrutiny, as demonstrated by the cancellation of a joint naval exercise scheduled to take place off the Tunisian coast. Still, the arms control education process within ACRS created documents, like the ACRS DoP, which would have been unthinkable several years before. ACRS produced the foundations for a future regional security agenda if such a dialogue resumes. The working group also produced several nascent arms control agreements and institutions. Army and navy contacts among Israeli and Arab officials produced a prenotification agreement, Search and Rescue (SAR) and Incidents at Sea (INCSEA) arrangements, and a regional security center, among other projects. Despite the tremendous political and substantive obstacles faced by the working group and despite its eventual breakdown, ACRS demonstrated that regional security cooperation was at least possible in the Arab-Israeli context.

Moreover, new partners and coalitions emerged as a consequence of ACRS. Indeed, one of the objectives of the ACRS process was to depolarize the nature of Arab-Israeli relations by underscoring common security interests and building cooperative projects and institutions around them. In order to do this, however, real multilateral negotiation was necessary, where shifting coalitions with multiple interests (not just an Arab versus an Israeli interest) could emerge. Despite the continued polarized nature of the Egyptian-Israeli conflict over the nuclear issue, the ACRS record demonstrates that genuine multilateral cooperation took place. Arab bloc behavior vis-à-vis Israel was more apparent at the initial stages of the process, but it gradually receded as common security concepts and practical projects benefiting all sides developed. According to an Israeli participant in the talks, one could no longer discern an "Arab view" on security, particularly since subregional threat perceptions varied and were accentuated in the aftermath of the Gulf War.[95] The Jordanians in particular often assumed a middle-ground position between the Israelis and Egyptians, and other players like Qatar perceived cooperation with Israel as a means to curb Saudi influence and voice a more independent position under the GCC umbrella. Even the Palestinians, the most sensitive to keeping the pace of ACRS behind bilateral progress in their negotiations, assumed different security priorities than other Arab parties, particularly on the nuclear threat question which, given their proximity to Israel, was not a central concern to them in a military sense.[96] While ACRS parties debated a variety of arms control and regional security measures, these debates did not always fall along the Arab-Israeli fault line, and thus contributed to one of the Americans' overall peace process purposes of normalizing Israel. As is common in multilateral forums, negotiations are less zero-sum, leaving room for creative coalitions and mediation based on complex interests.

Finally, ACRS allowed interactions among regional participants to intensify as the working group met more frequently in intersessional meetings and regional parties became more active. ACRS facilitated military contacts among Arab and Israeli representatives that were not previously possible (at least publicly) at the regional level. The military-to-military contacts were especially valued because military representatives were believed to focus on common threats rather than divisive political or ideological issues, thus increasing the prospects for successful cooperation. For example, the regional naval officers who participated in ACRS intersessional activities made more rapid progress in moving the working agenda forward by means of concrete proposals in the maritime area. Many of the Arab and Israeli military participants in ACRS developed close personal ties and similar understandings of regional security issues through their contacts at both the official and unofficial (track two) sessions.[97] The military resistance to verification measures in arms control processes, for instance, weakened as a result of increased contacts with military counterparts, allowing some flexibility on mutual inspection measures, a concept with which regional participants were unfamiliar before ACRS.[98]

As continued military contacts developed among ACRS delegations, bureaucratic support for ACRS activities broadened at home, creating or assigning specific departments to oversee ACRS-related activities. For example, before ACRS, the Israelis had very little arms control expertise in their Defense Ministry, but as ACRS developed, a cadre of high-level specialists responsible for the working group legitimized arms control activity, particularly since the Israeli delegation was headed by the esteemed director general of the Ministry, David Ivry.[99] The U.S. government also promoted training among regional experts in arms control and multilateral negotiation, such as a two week arms control training seminar in January 1996 for Israeli officials from a wide range of government ministries.[100] The United States intended to plan further seminars of this type for other regional delegations, including the Syrians, in order to institutionalize arms control expertise across bureaucracies in the Middle East.[101] Indeed, a variety of track two forums continued after the official ACRS process broke down, suggesting the value of intensifying interactions among regional elites in order to create a stronger and more permanent constituency for regional arms control.

## Why ACRS Failed: Impediments Within the Cooperative Process

Why, despite progress in moving a multilateral regional security process forward and an increasingly favorable political environment in the wake of the Oslo Accord, did ACRS break down by the fall of 1995? To be sure, ACRS's record reveals a reliance on outside powers in establishing this process and serious gaps between Arab parties and Israel on security perceptions and negotiation positions. Yet ACRS's development after Oslo suggests that despite the difficulties facing the process from the outset (including the continued absence of key regional players like Syria, Iran, and Iraq), ACRS overcame some of these obstacles and established a negotiating agenda for security cooperation. In fact, the group accomplished more than its originators had anticipated and raised questions about the traditional view that regional security cooperation was impossible in the Arab-Israeli arena. Given ACRS's progress up to 1995, why did it ultimately collapse?

The first section of the chapter set the stage for this puzzle by documenting the extensive work agenda developed by the ACRS participants. As they adopted more consensual views about the purpose and nature of regional arms control, some limited progress was possible on both conceptual and operational levels and accelerated after the Israeli-Palestinian Declaration of Principles in September 1993. However, the empirical review also signals the intensification of division between Israel and Egypt on the nuclear issue as the Egyptians assumed an increasingly negative view of the working group and its goals, leading to a final breakdown stage in ACRS's short history. This breakdown occurred *before* the general freeze in the bilateral peace process after the 1996 Israeli elections, which suggests that outside political forces were not the central impediment. The process itself helps explain the ACRS breakdown—more specifically, the way that actors viewed the cooperative process as it developed, together with their inability to transform the political aspects of the arms control problem into less politically charged technical problems. Because the Egyptians developed a negative view of security cooperation as they perceived a challenge from ACRS to Egypt's regional identity (i.e., its regional role), their support for the process diminished. Regional identity concerns proved the major impediment to ACRS's success and ultimately stalemated the working group and led to its breakdown.

As illustrated by ACRS's problems, a state's support for security cooperation cannot always be assumed from either the external "objective" strategic environment or from internal forces constraining national security policy. Whatever it might have gained in strict security terms, Egypt feared losing status in several respects.[102] First, Egypt's championing of the nuclear issue provided it with a bona fide claim to Arab leadership. Second, Egypt drew heavily on the nuclear issue in global fora for status as a leader of the "nonaligned nations." Third, a genuinely robust ACRS and development of a regional multilateral security regime would contribute to the broader normalization of Arab-Israeli relations, and this would make less relevant Egypt's position as the key Arab interlocutor with Israel and the United States. Fourth, normalization also heightened Egyptian concerns about Israel as a rival for status and influence in the region.

While the regional environment remained constant in objective terms, the Egyptian perception of ACRS changed as the process developed in ways contrary to its self-identity in the evolving regional environment. In order to explain ACRS's development and eventual demise, one must understand the forces shaping Egyptian perceptions and behavior.

Identity is always a relational concept, and regional political identity stems from the way policy elites perceive their nation's role in relation to others in the region and globally. For my purpose here, I am not examining the cultural or historical conditions that formed the Egyptian political identity,[103] but rather I seek to discern the main characteristics of this identity — or national self-concept — in order to determine how this force influenced Egyptian support for the ACRS process. Egyptian foreign policy elites perceive their nation as a regional leader and an important player in the international community, a perception that has spanned different leaderships and ideological orientations. As one account of Egyptian foreign policy explains, "One factor on which a high degree of consensus has been maintained throughout the leaderships of Nasser, Sadat and Mubarak has been the Egyptian elite's perception of their country's leading role in the Arab world."[104] Another Mideast scholar observes a similar pattern: "This jolt to the mental geography and sense of self must be seen against the background of a deeply held Egyptian belief in Egypt's centrality to the region around it. Nasser had given the Egyptian claims a radical thrust, but the material with which he worked predated him — Egypt's belief in its supremacy and its urge to pursue its destiny in places such as the Sudan, Syria, and the Arabian peninsula."[105] This quest for regional leadership and prestige is widely noted in scholarship on Egyptian foreign policy. As another observer of Egypt writes, "In the case of Egypt, it is certain that the almost fanatical emphasis on the prestige of Egypt as a value of Egyptian policy-making related directly to the obsession of Egypt's decision-makers with 'dignity.'"[106]

While Egyptian elites certainly must take into account domestic pressures and unrest in the formation of their policies (particularly the Islamic fundamentalist threat to the government), they are generally an outward looking group proud of their perceived status as a great nation both historically and today, a perception which also provides domestic legitimacy. Egyptian elites are not only looking outward at the objective security environment but also inward at their subjective view of their role in regional developments. The nuclear debate is in part an expression of the Egyptian political identity and worldview shared by important elites responsible for national security policy. Indeed, Egypt's position on Israel's nuclear capabilities follows a pattern of Egyptian security policy, where concerns for regional and international status have contributed to its positions on other important issues, such as the Suez crisis and its intervention in Yemen.[107]

Since 1973, the Egyptians have been among the leaders in raising the nuclear issue in the international community, introducing annual resolutions at the United Nations urging the establishment of a nuclear weapon free zone in the Middle East based on the NPT and IAEA inspections (the Egyptians signed the NPT in 1981).[108] After the Gulf War, Egypt renewed efforts to establish a nuclear-free Middle East and continued lobbying all parties in the region to sign the NPT, leading to the spring 1995 standoff.[109] The heavy push on the nuclear issue in ACRS thus was not totally new, although to a greater extent than ever before there was a trade-off in terms of an achievable regional security agenda. However, also to a greater extent than before Egypt's status interests as served by this issue were being threatened by another Arab state, Jordan, delineating and seeking to legitimize an alternative Arab position. Particularly disturbing to Egypt was Jordan's perceived enthusiasm for moving the ACRS agenda forward with the terms on the nuclear issue as laid out in the Israeli-Jordanian peace treaty sufficing, well short of the Egyptian position. The multilateral nature of ACRS allowed Jordan to exert more influence vis-à-vis Egypt than was possible in bilateral relations with its larger Arab neighbor. In fact, Jordanian-Israeli military cooperation grew faster than anticipated, as Jordan took the lead in implementing the proposed ACRS regional security center (which would be established in Amman). This became an additional impetus for Egypt to link virtually all of the ACRS agenda to the nuclear issue, as the very multilateral nature of the ACRS process was providing other Arab states a venue and vehicle for voicing independent positions; i.e., for genuinely multilateralizing the process in a manner that threatened the position and status of Egypt as bloc leader and primary interlocutor.

Egypt's identity as a pivotal regional and international power led to status concerns resulting from a process that was perceived to threaten Egypt's position. Identity and status concerns arising from an ACRS process offer a more compelling explanation for the Egyptian focus on Israel's nuclear capabilities than the traditional security perspective emphasizing military balances of power.[110] Traditional security conditions actually favored the progress that ACRS made in its first three years (e.g., the profound shift in the global and regional systemic structure of strategic alliances), and these conditions did not significantly change.[111] Moreover, on the specific issue of the nuclear threat, the political and identity-harming effects of this issue appear to be as great as or greater than the actual military threat posed by the Israeli capability, despite some genuine fears of Israel (in the military and economic realms) prevalent in the Arab world.[112] Arab elites understand Israel's deterrent purpose, with many acknowledging that, between the reality of nuclear fallout and the international political condemnation that offensive use would engender, Israel's nuclear capability does not pose a realistic strategic threat to Arab states, in contrast to Israel's formidable conventional capabilities. As a senior Egyptian official conceded, "Israel has nuclear weapons but will not use them unless she finds herself being strangled."[113] A top foreign policy adviser to President Mubarak, Osama El-Baz, asserted, "It would be an act of total lunacy for any Israeli regime to venture and launch an [nuclear] attack, or threaten an Arab country that is living in peace with Israel."[114] While some of Egypt's fears are well taken, particularly its concern over nuclear accidents, these concerns do not point to an immediate nuclear threat to Egypt in the military sense.

The problem is less the nuclear threat than the political threat Israel poses to Egypt's perception of itself in the region, and Egypt's subsequent use of the nuclear issue to assert its regional status. In responding to questions concerning regional security activity that included Israel, Egyptian Foreign Minister 'Amr Moussa spoke not of a military threat, but of a political challenge to Arab identity, noting that "preserving this [Arab] identity is one of the main factors for consolidating stability in the region while living in peace with Israel."[115] After Oslo, Israel's increasing acceptance in the Arab world diminished Egypt's central role as the bridge between Israel and Arab parties. As one Middle East analyst observed, Egypt was bypassed as Israel dealt directly with Yasir Arafat and "signed a treaty with Jordan without either country consulting Egypt (which drove the Egyptians crazy).... Israel has been forging economic ties with the likes of Oman, Bahrain, Morocco and Tunisia without anyone dialing Cairo.... So Egypt struck back. It initiated an Arab crusade to pressure Israel to sign the Nuclear Nonproliferation Treaty, which meant Israel either had to reveal its bombs in the basement or risk alienation from its new neighbors."[116] Fouad Ajami similarly observed in the months following the NPT dispute, a "disquiet over the country's place in the region" and "a belief that the United States is somehow engaged with Israel in an attempt to diminish and hem in the power and influence of Egypt."[117] Consequently, Ajami attributes Egypt's NPT campaign to "Egypt's panic about its place in the region, the need to demonstrate some distance from American power, and the desire to reassert Egypt's primacy in Arab politics."[118] After interviews in the Gulf concerning the NPT dispute, an Israeli journalist observed, "the dispute between Egypt and Israel over the question of Israel's joining the NPT is seen in the smaller Gulf states more as a sign of Egypt's concern over losing regional influence and as a struggle for prestige."[119]

Moreover, key Egyptian elites—in their private and public statements when discussing regional security issues—reveal their concern over identity questions. Before a visit to the United States by President Mubarak in late February 1997, an Egyptian official explained the Egyptian role in Mideast peacemaking:

> We take account of the importance of the U.S. as a superpower, and it has to take account of the importance of Egypt as a regional power which has a role which it will never abandon. . . . Egypt has to exercise its regional role, which . . . no one has the power to negate. . . . Egypt is determined to achieve internal stability and economic progress while continuing to act politically in the region and affirm and develop Egypt's historic and future role in an area stretching from the Horn of Africa to the northern Mediterranean via the Middle East.[120]

Another key Mubarak adviser asserted: "Egypt is not and will never be a small or vassal state, nor can it be subjected to pressure. . . . As the biggest country in the Middle East, Egypt wields major influence and leads in a number of areas, and that ought to be acknowledged. . . . [Egypt] does not seek hegemony or control [of the region] but stability, peace and equitable security for all."[121] Because regional processes like ACRS were perceived by Egyptian elites as threatening this predominant role in regional affairs, and even enhancing the role of Egypt's traditional rivals like Jordan and Israel, it is not surprising that they assessed regional security cooperation as of limited and even negative value.

Such a national self-concept leads to policy positions that may appear to contradict assumptions of narrow concerns based on "objective" security interests in maintaining stability. As William Quandt observes, Egyptian foreign policy searches for a role

> that goes beyond merely reflecting or protecting its own interests as defined in narrow terms. Egyptians, by and large, see for their country a significant role in the Middle East, in the Arab world, in the Islamic world, in Africa, and in the Third World. They were proud of the fact that their country, along with India, Yugoslavia, Indonesia, and China, was instrumental in forging the nonaligned movement. They take pride in the fact that Egypt counts for something in world affairs. They are reluctant to see Egypt reduced to the stature of just another overpopulated, impoverished Third-World country. They fear that if they have no larger role in the region, they will not be accorded the respect and the assistance to which they feel entitled.[122]

The Egyptian interest in preserving its status and affirming its identity as the key regional power broker was less well served by continued progress in Arab-Israeli multilateral regional security cooperation than by sharpening and raising the salience of conflict on the nuclear issue, even if—indeed, to a degree precisely because—it meant the breakdown of ACRS.

## Summary

In the conflictual context of the Middle East, the establishment and development of ACRS marked considerable progress in creating an unprecedented regional security process and even moved in the direction of creating common understandings among regional participants about the nature and purpose of regional arms control. Had we limited our understanding of cooperation to one based on outcomes, the ACRS process and its impact on regional security thinking might have been ignored or dismissed as unimportant. This chapter, however, has demonstrated that the ACRS process facilitated cooperation by redefining security problems, creating a shared security vocabulary and knowledge base among regional elites, making new policy options and partners acceptable, and increasing interactions among Arab and Israeli military officials.

While ACRS faced serious limitations in its ability to move Arab-Israeli relations into more cooperative security patterns, its creation and short working record underscored that Middle East adversaries could participate in a regional security cooperation process. This empirical reality broke some major cognitive barriers and taboos in what the parties believed could ultimately be achieved in this region, even if the process remained arduous and fragile. Needless to say, ACRS faced an uphill battle from the outset, but its development highlighted both the new possibilities for creating more cooperative security relations as well as the continuing and unanticipated impediments to such cooperation, including those that were unrelated to traditional security concerns.

ACRS ultimately failed, even when cooperation is viewed more broadly, because the working group proved unable to turn the political issues surrounding the arms control area—particularly the politicized issue of Israel's nuclear capabilities—into technical problems more conducive to successful multilateral cooperation. In this case, the process developed in ways that proved threatening to the regional role and identity of one of its most important participants, Egypt. This impediment led to the politicization of the working group and the inability to make progress in the more consensual areas on its agenda. Despite surprising progress within ACRS's short lifetime and despite continuing track two efforts to forge common understandings of arms control among regional elites, political obstacles—particularly the nuclear issue—are likely to remain and make further progress in regional arms control and security cooperation difficult.

# 5 Regional Economic Cooperation

The Regional Economic Development working group (REDWG) and the parallel Arab-Israeli cooperative economic forums that developed in the aftermath of the Israeli-Palestinian Oslo Accord constitute something of a success story for the multilaterals. To be sure, measuring success in this process requires different criteria than for many other regional forums, where tangible outcomes like economic growth and development are standard indicators. While a narrowing of the economic disparities in the Middle East may ultimately be required for durable peace and regional stability, the REDWG process cannot be judged solely according to these long-term economic needs and goals. Although the American sponsors of the process believed that REDWG could facilitate economic development generally,[1] their primary objective was to facilitate political ties and cooperation between Arabs and Israelis. According to the process conception of cooperation, the working group made progress in its efforts to achieve common understandings among its participants concerning the value of regional cooperation in this issue area.

This story of REDWG's evolution is thus not about the prospects and impediments to economic development in the Middle East and North Africa region. Rather, it is about the development of an unprecedented forum for Arab-Israeli economic cooperation where weak economic foundations exist upon which to build such cooperation. The political intentions of this process were present at its outset and persisted throughout its development. Despite setbacks and stalls that occasionally brought the process close to breakdown, REDWG surpassed expectations about what Arabs and Israelis could achieve. And unlike ACRS, this process did not collapse.

While REDWG faced problems similar to those of other multilateral working groups, such as setbacks in the bilateral peace process and the lack of sufficient funding to implement many of the larger regional projects, the group was able to survive and expand. Yet to do this, REDWG had to reinvent itself to the point where the most significant economic cooperative activity occurred outside the formal REDWG context. The spin-off parallel processes that emerged from and remained associated with REDWG—such as the Middle East and North Africa (MENA) economic summits—proved resilient, if battered, forums for Arab-Israeli cooperation. Indeed, few outsiders are aware of the extent to which Arab-Israeli regional economic cooperation flourished after Oslo, producing regularized contacts, abundant meetings (in the hundreds) and nascent institutions even in the darkest hours of the bilateral peace process. In the context of the Arab-Israeli conflict, this was a remarkable accomplishment.

What accounts for the nature of REDWG's development and the proliferation of related forums of Arab-Israeli multilateral economic cooperation? Most importantly, REDWG participants made progress in depoliticizing the process, enabling them to see economic issues as "technical" ones amenable to regional, multilateral cooperation. While political divisions inevitably created problems for the group, participants sought and reached common understandings about the purpose and utility of economic cooperation, in large part because of their changing conceptions about the nature of economic development and the impact of globalization on regional relations. Specifically, regional participants developed common conceptions about the role of Arab-Israeli economic cooperation in attracting foreign investment in a globalized economy.

Because regional parties can serve their economic interests in a variety of ways (e.g., domestic structural reform, continued centralized planning, or bilateral economic arrangements), understanding why regional elites choose to believe a particular path serves their interest becomes important in explaining outcomes that may appear anomalous in the abstract. Both Arabs and Israelis—while generally rejecting the notion of a "New Middle East"[2]—increasingly perceived a shared value to continuing economic cooperation in order to foster the region's integration into the global economy, creating a business-friendly environment by reducing the political risks of economic investment in the region. Shared beliefs among key regional elites about the fact and role of globalization provided common incentives for continued cooperation even if intraregional economic ventures were limited and at times viewed negatively, especially during periods of high tension in Israeli-Palestinian relations. An additional incentive to continue cooperative ventures stemmed from regional parties' desire to enhance their regional roles by housing the new institutions that were expected to emerge from the process.

As in the case of arms control, the parties' view of the process cannot be assumed. Economic incentives reveal less of the REDWG process than an understanding of the way in which elites gradually supported economic cooperation based on shared beliefs developed in part through their interactions in the multilateral context. Shared interpretations of globalization also explain the variation among the different economic projects that emerged from Arab-Israeli cooperation, with some projects proving more vulnerable to bilateral setbacks than others. According to the perceived globalization logic, we would expect projects oriented outside the region to attract greater support than those focused primarily on improving intraregional cooperation, as the former reflects the shared understandings of regional parties in the economic issue area. Consequently, the relative durability of the MENA economic summits (established to garner extraregional private sector investment) should not be surprising (as, conversely, it was not surprising when the higher political profile of the summit process, presented by some as an integrative mechanism, led to setbacks in REDWG generally). Likewise, projects that were less directly outward-looking and more explicitly focused on creating intraregional projects, like the proposed Regional Business Council (RBC), proved more vulnerable to bilateral setbacks. After reviewing the empirical story of REDWG, the chapter will explain its complex development by exploring both the facilitators and impediments to successful cooperation in this issue area.

## The Development of REDWG: The Empirical Record

### REDWG Emerges

Despite expectations about the relative ease of economic as opposed to security cooperation, controversy and deadlock marked REDWG's pre-Oslo record, although some important progress was made on planning for Palestinian economic development. The central reasons for this deadlock proved to be the question of Palestinian representation and the style of the European Union's leadership (as REDWG gavelholder).[3]

Noneconomic controversies surrounding REDWG had to be overcome before the group could focus on the issues within its bailiwick. The question of Palestinian representation in the working group was the most significant obstacle. This dispute led the Israelis to boycott the first REDWG plenary (after the January 1992 Moscow conference) on May 11–12, 1992, in Brussels. The Israelis insisted that Palestinians from outside the West Bank and Gaza Strip (the diaspora Palestinians) could not attend any multilateral meetings, following the restrictions initially laid out in the Madrid letter of invitation. This concern arose from the Israeli perception that participation by diaspora Palestinians would imply tacit acceptance of the PLO and broaden the Israeli-Palestinian dispute to outside the territories.[4] Attempts by Israeli Foreign Minister David Levy to find a compromise that would enable the Israelis to attend were reportedly rebuffed by the European sponsors.[5] Israeli suggestions that diaspora Palestinians could attend as members of other Arab delegations were also rejected by the Palestinians, particularly since they had gained the support of Secretary of State Baker on this issue.[6] Moreover, the extraregional sponsors were prepared to proceed with the May meeting even without Israeli participation.[7] The inclusion of diaspora Palestinians led some Israeli commentators to call for an Israeli reassessment of the value of the multilateral talks,[8] despite a recognition of the benefits Israel received from such a forum. Moreover, the Israelis were particularly cautious about the aims of a European-controlled REDWG, given the historical mistrust by Israelis of European designs in the Arab-Israeli peace process and the perception of a European bias toward the Arab side.

Thus, while thirty-eight regional and extraregional delegations attended the May meeting in Brussels (in the seminar-style format used in the first rounds of all the multilateral working groups), the absence of the Israeli delegation limited the group's progress in terms of proposals to generate regional projects and ventures. Still, the Europeans and Americans were determined to go forward with the session because of their belief that economic cooperation could facilitate the peace process.

Following the Brussels plenary, a new Israeli Labor government was elected, under the leadership of Prime Minister Yitzhak Rabin and Foreign Minister Shimon Peres. The election not only led to a more flexible Israeli position on the issue of Palestinian participation, but it also signaled greater attention to the economic development area given Peres's (and his key aides') long-standing beliefs about the importance of economic cooperation to regional peace and stability.[9] Organizational changes in the Foreign Ministry, such as the establishment of a new Peace Department and Policy Planning Division, also signified more emphasis on cooperation and economics, with the new Director-General, Uri Savir (the future architect of the Oslo channel), suggesting that "the criteria for diplomats abroad will be measured more in terms of enhancing trade than winning debating points on the history of the Arab-Israeli conflict."[10] Not surprisingly, a compromise was quickly found to enable Israeli participation in the second REDWG plenary in Paris on October 29–30. This entailed the new government's accepting an Egyptian compromise that allowed for diaspora Palestinian participation, but only if they were not members of the Palestine National Council (PNC) or residents of East Jerusalem.[11] In Peres's words, "We [Israel] are not going to ask the chief rabbinate for its 'kosher' stamp for Palestinian negotiators."[12] Peres also assumed a more favorable position on a larger European role in the multilateral process and, even before the October REDWG plenary, suggested several ideas for cooperative economic activities in REDWG during a visit by Secretary of State Baker to the region in July.[13] The Israelis also intended to press for more definitive areas of economic cooperation at the Paris meeting, including the establishment of subcommittees of experts to negotiate practical economic proposals in areas like tourism, agriculture, transportation, energy, finance, and Red Sea development.[14] In a briefing to the Israeli cabinet on the eve of the Paris plenary, Peres argued that while multilateral progress was contingent on the bilaterals, "there is no need to wait" before engaging in multilateral projects.[15] The fact that the Israeli delegation was co-headed by the governor of the Bank of Israel, Jacob Frenkel, suggested a serious intent under the new Israeli government to attack substantive common problems, rather than focus solely on divisive political disputes.

Yet this enthusiasm to join REDWG in the second Paris plenary led to a perception (and fear) among Arab states that Israel sought to dominate these discussions. For example, one American official present at the Paris meeting noted how the Israelis entered the process too ambitiously, presenting a proposal for a Middle East development bank without first gaining the support of the United States.[16] Arab participants, who argued that such ideas were not feasible before further bilateral progress was made in the peace process, rejected the proposal.[17] At this early stage, little contact occurred between Arab parties and Israel and the sessions were primarily a forum for extraregional participants to present lists of potential projects. Most of the early proposals were quite modest, and stressed less contentious cooperative areas like tourism, university exchanges, communications, and job training.

While these laundry lists of ideas for regional cooperation proved critical once the bilateral process allowed more serious and direct Arab-Israeli negotiations, the pre-Oslo period was limited because of Arab parties' reluctance to move ahead before bilateral progress had been made. As the head of the joint Jordanian-Palestinian delegation to REDWG, Dr. Fayez Tarawneh, explained at the Paris meeting, "We cannot make any contact with the Israelis with Arab lands occupied and their people under siege.... The Israelis would like to cooperate right now but... we cannot accept this as it would indicate normalization before peace."[18] According to Tarawneh, the Arab states coordinated their positions before the Paris meeting in a separate session and reached an agreement to link multilateral progress with the bilateral talks.[19] Still, the Jordanian delegation head expressed optimism over the potential of these talks, arguing that "the multilateral talks are an important forum attended by several states as representatives of the world nations, and the Arabs should not waste the chance to affirm their positions and principled stands and should prepare for a better future for the region after the Middle East problem is resolved."[20]

Because of the limitations in fostering Arab-Israeli projects in the pre-Oslo period, the European sponsors shifted the focus of the group toward extraregional studies of development needs of the region, particularly of the West Bank and Gaza. Extraregional participants played a major role in structuring the work agenda, with such items as commissioned feasibility studies. By the Paris plenary, extraregional REDWG members assumed the role of "shepherds" (or managers) for specific initiatives in different sector areas: tourism (Japan); transportation and communications (France); vocational training (the United States); data bank for regional specialists on economic development, or bibliography (Canada); energy and networks (EU); agriculture (Spain); financial markets (United Kingdom); trade (Germany); institutions, sectors, and principles (Egypt).[21]

Yet it was at the third REDWG plenary in Rome on May 4–5, 1993, that more serious work began. The parties by that time not only understood how REDWG worked but demonstrated some willingness to begin projects by agreeing to engage in intersessional, technical workshops between the larger plenary sessions. Perhaps the most significant development at Rome was the tasking of the World Bank to conduct feasibility studies and recommendations for development, primarily of the West Bank and Gaza Strip. The World Bank sent teams of experts to the region to study the development needs of the Palestinian economy and infrastructure, and produced a report (with input from the key regional parties—Israel, Jordan, and the Palestinians) detailing its conclusions. The report was presented at the fourth REDWG plenary in Copenhagen in November 1994.[22] While the Israelis hoped REDWG would also focus on wider Arab-Israeli regional projects, they were supportive of the World Bank study because they recognized the significance of improving economic conditions in the territories for a political settlement and greater security for Israel itself.

This World Bank study later served as the framework for future extra-regional assistance to the West Bank and Gaza after the Oslo Accord, when a donor conference pledged over $2 billion in assistance to the Palestinians over a five-year period. In this sense, REDWG served its original mandate of facilitating the bilateral peace process despite its lack of progress in advancing wider regional development projects. The Rome meeting also reflected greater seriousness than the previous plenaries in that the extra-regional shepherds began committing funding for the regional proposals. These included a pledge of $14 million from the United States for training, $3 million from Italy for energy projects, $400,000 from Spain for agriculture studies, and $6 million from the EU for feasibility studies for projects such as roads, electricity grids, and commerce.

In the wake of the plenary, the regional parties also expressed greater willingness to work with the shepherds in moving these projects forward. A sign of greater regional willingness to cooperate in this process was the announcement by Israeli Deputy Foreign Minister Yossi Beilin after the Rome plenary (in the beginning of June 1993, still *before* Oslo) that several of the multilateral working groups would meet in the region itself in the next round (Fall 1993) of plenary sessions. As one Western diplomat involved in the process observed, the Arab and Israeli participants were "getting used to seeing each other in seminars. There is regular contact. Nobody would have thought that the multilateral sessions would be more successful than the bilateral ones."[23] Thus, despite the rough start, a substantive working agenda for REDWG had been defined and had gained the commitment of regional parties on the eve of Oslo.

While the Oslo political breakthrough in Israeli-Palestinian relations allowed REDWG to engage in more significant economic planning and for Arabs and Israelis to interact more directly than in the previous period, the working group also faced some serious difficulties that limited its ability to implement many of its projects. And yet, rather than lead to the demise of Arab-Israeli multilateral economic cooperation, these problems led to the diffusion of cooperation into parallel processes that produced nascent Arab-Israeli economic institutions. This unique evolution of multilateral economic cooperation raises important themes that the subsequent sections will address; namely, the growing regional forces both impeding and facilitating cooperation and the increased role of perceived globalization pressures in shaping the nature and prospects for such cooperation to continue.

## Post-Oslo Activity (November 1993–October 1994)

### Progress

The first plenary after Oslo took place in Copenhagen on November 8–9, 1993. This session was the first plenary in which regional parties agreed by consensus to a plan that specified a list of substantive economic projects, termed the Copenhagen Action Plan (CAP).[24] As Uri Savir explained in his concluding remarks at the Copenhagen plenary, "For this first time the working group on Regional Economic Development is engaging in substance abandoning the academic discussions which characterized its work in the past."[25] In contrast to earlier REDWG meetings, the regional parties expressed an interest in taking more concrete actions, in coordination with the extraregional sponsors, to enhance regional economic development and private sector interest in the region.

To that end, the regional endorsement of the CAP signified a readiness to engage in region-wide cooperative efforts that went well beyond the development needs of the West Bank and Gaza. The Plan covered ten sectors and proposed thirty-five regional projects.[26] In a REDWG intersessional workshop in Cairo the month following the Copenhagen plenary, the group continued its work on the CAP, approving several agricultural projects, a pollution cleanup of the Gulf of Aqaba, the preservation of marine life and coral, as well as a joint tourism project involving the Palestinians, Israelis, and Egyptians.[27]

The breadth of the action plan led the group to establish a smaller monitoring committee (MC) in its next plenary in Rabat in June 1994. The MC would oversee the implementation of the various projects on behalf of the plenary members and encourage greater regional initiative. While the MC's full membership still included regional parties from the Gulf and Maghreb, the four "core" regional parties (Israel, the Palestinians, Egypt, and Jordan) took the lead and established four subcommittees (infrastructure, trade, tourism, and finance). The goal of the subcommittees was to better coordinate the work carried out in the intersessionals and bring the projects to fruition.

At its first meeting on December 5, 1994, in Cairo, the MC clarified the membership and organization of the group, deciding that it would be co-chaired by the core regional participants (rotating the chair between them every six months) and the European Union. It was agreed that senior officials representing the core parties would chair the sectoral committees and that its meetings would normally take place in the region approximately every six months, again highlighting enhanced regional initiative and interaction.[28] The MC also established a small secretariat in the region—a proposal initially discussed at the June REDWG plenary in Rabat and endorsed by the steering group of the multilaterals in a meeting in Tabarka in July 1994—comprised of representatives from each of the four core parties. The secretariat began operating in Amman in March 1995.[29] At the Amman Summit in October 1995, the participants decided to transform the MC into "a permanent regional economic institution to be based in Amman."[30]

The creation of the MC secretariat began to signal a shift in REDWG away from centralized economic cooperation under the European umbrella toward more diffuse, and often smaller, forums headed by different extra-regional parties. Yet, despite the beginnings of negotiations over specific economic projects in the year following Oslo, REDWG faced several serious impediments to progress that ultimately restricted its work. This led to various spin-offs that owe their existence to REDWG but ultimately were better able to implement REDWG's agenda than the original working group.

Problems

A variety of forces contributed to REDWG's problems, including its large size, the discontinuity of leadership because of the rotating nature of the European Union gavelholder, the inherent limitations of economic integration schemes in the region, and bilateral peace process setbacks. However, two developments were most significant in diminishing REDWG's impact: 1) the increased competition between the United States and the Europeans over leadership in the economic cooperation sphere; and 2) the lack of funding for the large-scale public sector projects necessary to implement the group's working agenda. Thus, rather than serving as a facilitating force in multilateral economic cooperation, extraregional parties began creating impediments to moving the regional agenda forward.

From the outset of the multilaterals, the United States was negative toward European intervention in the peace process, particularly because the Israelis did not trust the major European powers. However, the United States also recognized the need to involve the Europeans at least at the financial level to support regional development initiatives that could buttress the political process. The American solution was to give the Europeans control over REDWG as its gavelholder in order to reap the economic benefits of European involvement without ceding control over the more central bilateral peace tracks, which remained firmly under the leadership of the United States.

Before the Oslo Accord, the Americans were satisfied with this arrangement, since most of REDWG's work remained conceptual at that stage. However, after Oslo, when the demand and potential for more serious and substantive economic development plans arose, the United States preferred to reassert its leadership role, although it still hoped the Europeans could financially support the process. Needless to say, the Europeans resented the expectation that they would foot the bills while the Americans received all the political credit for progress in Arab-Israeli cooperation.

The U.S.-European tug-of-war began as early as September 1993, when discussions began in the wake of Oslo on organizing an international donors conference for economic assistance to the Palestinians. While REDWG had sponsored the World Bank study on Palestinian economic development needs, the Americans took the initiative and proceeded to organize and sponsor the donors conference in Washington on October 1, 1993, outside of REDWG. This U.S. initiative angered the Europeans, as a struggle began over the relationship of the donors conference to REDWG's work, and over who controlled economic activity in the Arab-Israeli peace process. According to one official involved in this dispute, the discussions "got ugly" as both the Americans and Europeans tried to gain the upper hand.[31]

In a week of arguments before the conference, the EU agreed that the conference could take place in Washington, but demanded that the follow-up work would occur within REDWG. The United States preferred the follow-up work to take place within the multilateral steering committee, which the United States co-chaired with Russia. Ultimately, the parties agreed to a compromise whereby the conference would establish a separate ad-hoc liaison committee (AHLC) for Palestinian assistance (including both the Americans and the Europeans) which would report to the steering group. The parties decided that the Norwegians would serve as the first chair of the AHLC, which was expected to rotate. However, the Norwegians became the de facto chair since the parties could never agree on the next chair, reflecting the continued tensions between the United States and Europeans over leadership of the process.

The story of the AHLC was the first of several similar episodes in which the U.S. preference for implementing the economic dimensions of peace agreements outside the European-controlled REDWG became clear. The establishment of the Israel-Jordan-U.S. trilaterals followed a similar pattern, with the United States resisting REDWG in operationalizing the economic components of the Israel-Jordan peace treaty. While the largest split occurred with the establishment of the economic summits, these leadership battles beginning in the aftermath of Oslo posed significant setbacks for REDWG, at least from the European perspective. Indeed, the European launching of the Barcelona process with a ministerial level conference including fifteen European and twelve Mediterranean participants[32] in November 1995 — and the Euro-Mediterranean partnership to which it has led — was viewed by many as a direct response to the American effort to maintain control over regional economic affairs.[33]

In addition to the U.S.-European leadership rivalry, the more fundamental problem of funding limited REDWG's ability to implement its agenda and contributed to the spin-off pattern that emerged after Oslo. When the multilaterals began, many believed that the participation of the oil-rich Gulf states, particularly the Saudis, would contribute to the financing of regional development projects, especially those affecting the Palestinian areas. However, with the Saudis facing unprecedented economic pressures and expressing reluctance to support regional initiatives before the bilaterals had been resolved, they made it clear that others should not "look to us to pay the bills" for multilateral economic projects.[34] Moreover, the Europeans and Japanese were also slow to channel public funds into multilateral development projects, with most funding remaining in the hundreds of millions rather than the multibillion dollar range necessary for some of the more ambitious initiatives, such as regional canals.[35] According to an Israeli Foreign Ministry official, while the Europeans and Japanese were expected to contribute large investments into regional development, there was, instead, a "lack of political will among wealthy countries outside the region . . . [who] have not made development of the Middle East a domestic priority."[36]

Rather than small sums of money devoted toward a number of feasibility studies of various initiatives included in the CAP, the regional parties preferred funding for concrete projects that would be visible to the public at large (e.g., hotels, airports, new roads). To that end, many of REDWG's participants—regional and extraregional—began to recognize that the public sector orientation of the group was not realistic during times of government budget cuts and greater reliance on private sector growth. These forces created an impetus for a new type of regional forum—the MENA summit process—that could attract private sector funding. Because REDWG was not designed to promote private sector investment, the United States responded to the regional parties' desire to create a parallel economic process that would satisfy these goals and that would also be in accord with its own self-interest in retaining influence in the economic realm.[37]

*The Diffusion of Economic Activity*

After its June 1994 plenary in Rabat, REDWG's plenaries became briefing opportunities for activities occurring outside the full working group, primarily within the new MENA summit process and in the subcommittee work of REDWG's MC.[38] Indeed, the economic cooperation spawned by REDWG both within its MC secretariat[39] and in the related MENA summit process generated a tremendous amount of regional economic activity, including over one hundred meetings and workshops among regional participants from mid-1994 (when the MC's subcommittees and MENA summits were launched) to early 1997 [see table 5.1]. Much of the substance of this activity relied on REDWG's initial work, but the operationalization of the projects and institutions largely occurred outside the formal REDWG framework. The MENA process produced three institutions: the Bank for Economic Cooperation and Development in the Middle East and North Africa (MENABANK), the Regional Business Council (RBC), and the Middle East and Mediterranean Travel and Tourism Association (MEMTTA). However, as plans for these institutions progressed at the economic summits, the sub-

TABLE 5.1 REDWG and Related Regional Economic Cooperation Calendar of Plenaries and Sample Intersessionals, 1992–1997

| Meeting | Date, Place |
| --- | --- |
| *Plenary Sessions* | |
| First Plenary | May 1992, Brussels |
| Second Plenary | October 1992, Paris |
| Third Plenary | May 1993, Rome |
| Fourth Plenary | November 1993, Copenhagen |
| Fifth Plenary | June 1994, Rabat |
| Sixth Plenary | January 1995, Bonn |
| Seventh Plenary | April/May 1996, Amman |
| *REDWG Monitoring Committee* | |
| Joint Meeting of the Sectoral Committees | December 1994, Cairo |
| Monitoring Committee Meeting | January 1995, Bonn |
| Monitoring Committee Meeting | June 1995, Cairo |
| Core Party Meeting | October 1995, Amman |
| Core Party Meeting | November 1995, Cairo |
| Monitoring Committee Meeting | December 1995, Brussels |
| Core Party Meeting | January 1996, Amman |
| Core Party Meeting | May 1996, Amman |
| Core Party Meeting | June 1996, Cairo |
| Core Party Meeting | August 1996, Cairo |
| Monitoring Committee Meeting | February 1997, Amman |
| *Finance* | |
| Financial Markets and Stock Exchange Cooperation | April 1994, London |
| Finance Committee Meeting | December 1994, Cairo |
| Meeting on Financing Institutions | January 1995, Washington, D.C. |
| Finance Committee Meeting | January 1995, Bonn |
| First Meeting of the Task Force on Financing Institutions | March 1995, Washington, D.C. |
| Finance Committee Meeting | April 1995, Amman |
| Task Force on Financing Institutions | April 1995, Amman |

TABLE 5.1 *(continued)*

| Meeting | Date, Place |
|---|---|
| Finance Committee Meeting | May 1995, Cairo |
| Task Force on Financing Institutions | May 1995, Cairo |
| Finance Committee Consultations with the Europeans | June 1995, Bonn, Paris, and London |
| Task Force on Financing Institutions | June 1995, Paris |
| Task Force on Financing Institutions | July 1995, Moscow |
| Finance Committee Meeting | August 1995, Amman |
| Task Force on Financing Institutions | September 1995, Cairo |
| Task Force on Financing Institutions | September 1995, Rome |
| Task Force on Financing Institutions | October 1995, Washington, D.C. |
| Task Force on Financing Institutions | November 1995, Cairo |
| Task Force on Financing Institutions [MEDB Charter Deposited with the United Nations for Signatures and Ratification by Prospective Members] | February 1996, Cairo [August 1996, New York] |
| Informal MEDB Transition Team Meeting | September 1996, Washington, D.C. |
| Informal Task Force Meeting | November 1996, Cairo |
| MEDB Transition Team Meeting | January–February 1997, Cairo |
| MEDB Meeting: Committee of Prospective Bank Members | May 1997, Washington, D.C. |
| *Trade* | |
| Trade Committee Meeting | December 1994, Cairo |
| Trade Committee Meeting | January 1995, Bonn |
| Trade Committee Meeting | April 1995, Cairo |
| Trade Committee Meeting | June 1995, Cairo |
| Trade Committee Meeting | July 1995, Cairo |
| Trade Committee Meeting | September 1995, Amman |
| Trade Committee Meeting | December 1995, Geneva |
| Trade Round Table | December 1995, Geneva |
| Trade Committee Meeting | February 1996, Amman |
| RBC Steering Committee | March 1996, Amman |

TABLE 5.1 (*continued*)

| Meeting | Date, Place |
|---|---|
| *Tourism* | |
| Private Sector Cooperation Workshop | February 1994, Cairo |
| Common Regional Priorities Meeting | June 1994, Rabat |
| Tourist Agents Meeting | October 1994, Cairo |
| Tourist Agents Meeting | December 1994, Cairo |
| Tourism Committee Meeting | December 1994, Cairo |
| Tourism Committee Meeting | January 1995, Bonn |
| Tourism Seminar | January 1995, Cairo |
| Tourism Workshop | January 1995, Bonn |
| Aqaba Tourism Workshop | January 1995, Aqaba |
| Tourism Committee Meeting | March 1995, Cairo |
| Tourism Workshop | March 1995, Amman |
| Tourism Workshop | May 1995, Eilat |
| Tourism Workshop | June 1995, Cairo |
| Tourism Committee Meeting | July 1995, Haifa |
| Tourism Workshop | July 1995, Amman |
| Private Sector Workshop | September 1995, Tel Aviv |
| Tourism Workshop | September 1995, Casablanca |
| Tourism Task Force | October 1995, Cairo |
| Tourism Workshop | December 1995, Tunis |
| MEMTTA Interim Board of Governors and Executive Council Meeting | January 1996, Bethlehem |
| MEMTTA Interim Board of Governors and Executive Council Meeting | February 1996, Alexandria |
| MEMTTA Americas Division Meeting | May 1996, New York |
| MEMTTA Executive Council Meeting | September 1996, Tunis |
| MEMTTA Executive Council Meeting | November 1996, Cairo |
| MEMTTA Executive Council Meeting | October 1997, Orlando |

TABLE 5.1 (*continued*)

| Meeting | Date, Place |
|---|---|
| MEMTTA Americas Division Executive Committee | Five Meetings, Dec. 1996–Nov. 1997 |
| MEMTTA European Division Meeting | November 1997, London |
| *Infrastructure/Agriculture* | |
| Agricultural Workshop | March 1994, Cordoba |
| Veterinary Services Workshop | April 1994, Sharm al-Sheikh |
| Infrastructure Committee Meeting | December 1994, Cairo |
| Electricity Grids Interconnection Workshop | December 1994, Aqaba |
| Infrastructure Committee Meeting | January 1995, Bonn |
| Regional Navigation Workshop | January 1995, Washington |
| Civil Aviation Workshop | April 1995, Toulouse |
| Ports Workshop | April 1995, Marseilles |
| Railways Workshop | May 1995, Paris |
| TEAM Meeting | June 1995, Amman |
| Infrastructure Committee Meeting | June 1995, Amman |
| JRV, Joint Steering Committee | June 1995, Ein-Gedi |
| Regional Transport Study Workshop | July 1995, Amman |
| TEAM Steering Committee | September 1995, Cairo |
| SEMED Workshop | September 1995, Cairo |
| Electricity Grids Interconnection Meeting | September 1995, Haifa |
| TEAM and SEMED, Joint Meeting | November 1995, Amman |
| Telecommunications Workshop | December 1995, Tel Aviv |
| Electricity Grids Interconnection Meeting | January 1996, Cairo |
| Transport Workshop | January 1996, Amman |
| JRV, Joint Steering Committee | March 1996, Tiberias |
| Fast Track Transport Projects, Expert Meeting | April 1996, Cairo |

TABLE 5.1 (*continued*)

| Meeting | Date, Place |
| --- | --- |
| Transport Strategy Group | April 1996, Cairo |
| Regional Transport Study, Steering Committee | May 1996, Amman |
| TEAM and SEMED Steering Committees | May 1996, Amman |
| Infrastructure Committee Meeting | May 1996, Amman |
| Telecommunications Strategy Group | June 1996, Cairo |
| Transport Committee Meeting | June 1996, Amman |
| Transport Sector Coordination Meeting | July 1996, Brussels |
| Integration of Electricity Grids | September 1996, Amman |
| JRV Steering Committee | September 1996, Tel Aviv |
| Transport Committee Meeting | October 1996, Amman |
| Regional Transport Study Meeting | October 1996, Amman |
| TEAM and SEMED Steering Committee Meetings | October 1996, Cairo |
| Interconnection of Electricity Grids Meeting (with consultants) | November 1996, Amman |
| JRV Trilateral Economic Committee Meeting | January 1997, Jordan |
| Regional Transport Study Meeting | April 1997, Amman |
| *The First MENA Summit* | *October–November 1994, Casablanca* |
| Amman Summit Steering Committee | April 1995, Amman |
| Amman Summit Steering Committee | September 1995, Madrid |
| Ad Hoc Project Meeting: Core Party Ministers | September 1995, Amman |
| Ad Hoc Project Meeting: Core Party Officials | October 1995, Amman |
| Amman Summit Steering Committee | October 1995, Washington, D.C. |
| REDWG Preparatory Meeting | October 1995, Amman |
| *The Second MENA Summit* | *October 1995, Amman* |
| Cairo Summit Steering Committee | April 1996, Rome |
| Cairo Summit Steering Committee | July 1996, Rabat |

Regional Economic Cooperation                    127

TABLE 5.1 *(continued)*

| Meeting | Date, Place |
|---|---|
| Cairo Summit Steering Committee | September 1996, New York |
| Cairo Summit Steering Committee | November 1996, Cairo |
| *The Third MENA Summit* | *November 1996, Cairo* |
| Doha Summit Steering Committee | May 1997, Washington, D.C. |
| Doha Summit Steering Committee | October 1997, Washington, D.C. |
| Doha Summit Steering Committee | November 1997, Doha |
| *The Fourth MENA Summit* | *November 1997, Doha* |

Sources: REDWG Monitoring Committee Secretariat, *Annual Report: December 1994–May 1996* (Amman, May 1996); Tim Sheehy, *Report on the REDWG Committee Secretariat* (Oxford, 1997); Bureau of Near Eastern Affairs, *Middle East Peace Process: Meetings Following the Madrid Conference* (Washington, D.C., November 8, 1996); *REDWG Update* (issues 1–6); and author interviews with U.S. officials, May 15, 1997, Washington, D.C. Because many technical meetings, or intersessionals, convene with no public record, the list of meetings represents a significant but still incomplete account of all regional economic activity related to REDWG.

stantive work to create them was "given back" to REDWG through its MC secretariat and the subcommittees responsible for each institution.[40]

*The MENA Summits*

The origins of the MENA summits are difficult to trace, although many attribute the idea to Shimon Peres.[41] By the summer of 1994, many of the regional parties felt that REDWG had completed most of its studies, and the time had come to package REDWG's ideas and projects for the international business community. The model for MENA was Davos, an esteemed annual international business conference in Switzerland organized by the privately-funded World Economic Forum (WEF), where leading figures in the world's business and political community meet to network and forge deals.[42] In conjunction with the Council on Foreign Relations (CFR), the WEF organized the MENA summits in an attempt to create a regional version of Davos and generate private sector business interest in the Middle East. While the MENA process got off to a rough start and continued to face serious political impediments, the economic summit experiment proved a relative success in fostering Arab-Israeli cooperation.

## The Casablanca Summit, October 30–November 1, 1994

The Casablanca Summit launched the new MENA process, bringing together representatives of sixty-one countries, including heads of state, ministers, and high-level delegations. The event was co-chaired by U.S. President Bill Clinton and Russian President Boris Yeltsin. Arab participants mirrored those who participated in REDWG activities. Just as with REDWG, the Syrians and Lebanese boycotted the conference (as well as those that followed) because of their insistence on holding regional cooperation hostage to bilateral progress in their negotiations with Israel. In addition to the high-level political representation, 1,114 prominent business representatives attended the event (including representatives from nearly 150 American firms). As Secretary of State Christopher explained:

> We must transform the peace being made between governments into a peace between peoples. . . . Only the people of the private sector can marshall the resources necessary for sustained economic growth and development. Only the private sector can produce a peace that will endure. . . . Now . . . we must form a public sector-private sector partnership for government and business to bring their political and economic power jointly to bear.[43]

The lifting of the secondary and tertiary Arab boycott by the Gulf Cooperation Council (GCC) a month prior to Casablanca paved the way for new opportunities for international business to invest in regional initiatives that included Israeli participation [see appendix D].[44]

The conference agenda included panel discussions focusing on economic needs and investment opportunities by sectors similar to those developed in REDWG (infrastructure, trade, finance, and tourism). National representatives and international financial organizations (like the World Bank) conducted presentations outlining regional project proposals and the necessary financing to implement them.[45] The financing requirements for many of these projects reached the multibillion dollar range, far surpassing the levels of funding committed to REDWG projects from governmental sources.[46]

However, the title of the Israeli background paper on the Summit, "From Peace-making to Peace-Strengthening," and its assertion that the conference "illustrates the region's intent to maintain and promote this framework for the advancement of regional cooperation,"[47] revealed the Israeli view of MENA as another means to further its political acceptance into the region as much as a forum to further economic development.[48] This might explain the Israeli enthusiasm in Casablanca, exemplified by its unusually large delegation, comprised of high-level political representation, including eight government ministers (led by Foreign Minister Peres), along with 130 Israeli businessmen.[49] The large Israeli presence, however, backfired, fostering Arab fears of Israeli economic hegemony and turning the summit into much more of a high-profile event than Arab regimes had anticipated.[50] Still, despite the political tensions and sensitivities, the official speeches and final Casablanca Declaration [see appendix E] reflected a cautious optimism about the potential for regional economic cooperation as a foundation for peace. As Prime Minister Rabin observed:

> The Casablanca meeting could be a landmark in peace development. . . . The mere fact that this unique, large conference, was convened, is the expression of a new opening. It will create, not immediate results, but people will meet one another. I don't remember any conference where so many representatives of Arab countries, Europeans, Americans, from all religions—the mere fact that they are convened, talk to one another, get to know one another, creates a better basis for whatever resolution, creates new realities in the economic life, more readiness to do it and more likely to sign a peace treaty.[51]

In this sense, Casablanca was a continuation of the original purpose of the establishment of the Arab-Israeli multilaterals.

Thus, despite the negative reactions among Arabs to the aggressive Israeli participation at the summit, Casablanca emerged as another event in the chain of icebreakers between Arabs and Israelis. As Oded Eran, who served as Israeli Deputy Director General for Economics in the Foreign Ministry, explained, "To say that the Casablanca Conference was a negative milestone in the Israeli-Arab relations is simplistic. Not that there is not truth behind this, but it is neither precise nor correct. . . . The Casablanca Conference was a breakthrough, and following it, a process started, that—like any process—has its ups and downs, but the overall direction is positive."[52]

In order to enhance the prospects for continued regional cooperation and private sector involvement in regional development, the final Casablanca Declaration laid out a blueprint for future economic cooperation activity. Recognizing that "there must be an ongoing process to translate the deliberations at Casablanca into concrete steps," the Declaration called for the establishment of three regional institutions (a bank, a tourism board, and a regional business council) as developed in the REDWG's MC.[53] The Declaration also called for the creation of a Summit steering committee to follow up on Casablanca's agenda and to coordinate the Summit's activities with "existing multilateral structures such as the REDWG and other multilateral working groups."[54] An executive secretariat was subsequently established in Morocco to assist the steering committee and to help implement the regional initiatives and institutions called for by the conference.[55] And most significantly, the parties agreed to convene a similar summit the following year in Amman.

## The Amman Summit, October 29–31, 1995

The Amman Summit convened with the participation of representatives from over sixty nations and more than a thousand regional and international businesses.[56] The overwhelming Israeli presence at Casablanca led to greater sensitivity at the Amman meeting, where Israel reduced the political representation of its delegation and placed more emphasis on private sector participation.[57] Moreover, the summit took place in a considerably more positive political environment, convening on the heels of the signing of "Oslo II," the Israeli-Palestinian agreement outlining interim steps for Palestinian self-rule and Israeli withdrawal from parts of the West Bank and Gaza.

However, general Arab discomfort with accepting Israel as a fully legitimate political and economic partner continued.[58] Formidable opposition, particularly from the private sector, emerged in the Arab world as Arab-Israeli economic and political ties strengthened. Many Arab parties argued that normalization was moving too quickly, and should await full resolution of the political conflicts between Israel and its neighbors, particularly the Palestinians. In Jordan, strong voices of opposition to normalization and the growth of business contacts—particularly among leftist and Islamist forces—posed a significant problem for the Jordanian government as it struggled to encourage private sector participation at the summit. Twelve of Jordan's professional associations, for example (with a total membership of 80,000) adopted anti-normalization resolutions even before the Israel-Jordan peace treaty,[59] and continued to discourage their members from engaging in the types of economic cooperation efforts taking place within the MENA context.

In order to minimize the political opposition to normalization and the perception of Israeli political domination, the Amman Summit organizers attempted to shift the focus from the political symbolism of Casablanca to a more narrow focus on business interests and economic development schemes.[60] The business emphasis would underscore the economic benefits of such summits for the Arab participants rather than showcase the increased political acceptance of Israel in the region. As a Jordanian overview of the Amman Summit explained, "While the Casablanca summit turned out be largely a political event . . . the Amman gathering will focus more on specific projects, investments, joint ventures, infrastructure proposals, financing arrangements, and other nuts and bolts of regional economic development."[61] Similarly, an Egyptian businessman observed the shift in focus from Casablanca to Amman, noting that "Casablanca gave political legitimacy to regional cooperation. . . . The Amman summit, meanwhile, is about promoting public-private partnership in the region. . . . Casablanca was more of a show for grandiose projects than a springboard for regional cooperation."[62]

The Jordanian sponsors of the summit therefore sought to balance the peace process demands of encouraging regional projects that included Israel with economic priorities for Arab states that had little to do with Israel or the peace process. In its briefing book for the summit, Jordan emphasized the theme of regional prosperity, explaining the primary objective of the MENA conference as the need to "examine the regional structures and policies needed to effectively develop the region's potential, with a view to integrating the region into the global economy."[63]

While Israel continued to stress the summit's peacemaking purpose,[64] Arab parties recognized the potential of these summits to attract international financial interest in their countries and the Arab world more generally. Jordan offered twenty-seven "priority proposals," estimated to total $3.5 billion, including regional initiatives from REDWG's agenda as well as national development plans that were targeted to both government and private sector financing.[65] Following the Israeli model at Casablanca, Jordan also distributed sophisticated background booklets on a variety of economic sectors in Jordan and the potential for economic development, capitalizing on the opportunity to showcase its economic reforms and political developments for the international investment community, something that would not have been possible without the convening of such a conference.[66]

Many of the speeches emphasized the need to focus on practical economic projects with increased private sector financing. As Prime Minister Rabin stated, "No one will come here because of our winning smiles; they all want to make money."[67] Rabin continued by stressing the need for Amman to produce "concrete" results that would improve the daily lives of the region's peoples, a theme repeated throughout the conference by Israelis and Arabs alike. The need to improve the economic plight of the Palestinian territories, both through bilateral agreements with Israel and through regional economic projects included in the multilateral agenda, received particular attention given its importance to overall political progress.[68]

Yet, despite the general desire to get down to business at Amman and further the regional economic agenda, politics inevitably intruded. This time, however, the central political conflicts emerged between Arab states. The most publicized dispute of the summit began with Egyptian Foreign Minister Moussa's address, when he accused other Arab states (i.e., Jordan) of "rushing" into peace and normalization with Israel.[69] King Hussein responded angrily to the accusation by asserting that if Jordan's actions constituted "rushing in," then Egypt was similarly guilty when it made peace with Israel seventeen years before.[70] Moussa also raised the nuclear issue in his address, reflecting Egypt's negative position toward regional cooperation absent significant Israeli concessions on the bilateral tracks and on the nuclear issue in particular. It is important to note that this Egyptian attitude emerged *before* the assassination of Yitzhak Rabin and before the election of the Likud government and Prime Minister Netanyahu in Israel.

This suggests that political impediments to regional cooperation—most strongly voiced from Egyptian quarters—were not specific to contentious regional security issues, but surfaced in even mutually beneficial areas such as economic development. However, while Egypt expressed concerns about "rushing" toward cooperation with Israel, its interest in the continuation of a regional economic forum outweighed its political reservations, since Egypt perceived the process as enhancing its regional position (it would host the following summit in Cairo) and contributing to larger globalization objectives. Behind the scenes, the Egyptians were actively engaged in facilitating economic institutions emerging from the process, particularly the development bank. Egypt fought with Jordan for the bank, insisting it be placed in Cairo, not Amman. The Egyptians also contended with Qatar to host the next MENA summit.[71] On a more visible level, Egypt sent a high-level delegation to the Amman Summit, including seven ministers and 150 representatives.

Thus, the Amman summit proved a relative success in moving the MENA process forward beyond political symbolism toward more practical Arab-Israeli economic cooperation. While this cooperation did not lead to enormous financial dealings between Israelis and Arabs (which few expected in any case), it did facilitate the establishment of the three multilateral institutions (the MENABANK, the RBC, and MEMTTA) and thus routinized Arab-Israeli economic cooperation. As a senior U.S. administration official explained, "What you hear [at Amman] is the business of doing business taking hold. . . . As a result of that success, it's having an impact on the political dynamic itself."[72] A number of deals were also cut or conceived at the Amman meeting.[73] And finally, the summit generated related cooperative forums among the core regional parties, such as ministerial level economic planning talks in The Hague.[74]

However, the seriousness of the summit's outcomes also led to intense Arab opposition to normalization with Israel, reflecting domestic environments that limited the pace of many cooperative efforts. Thus, Amman's outcome illustrated two simultaneous yet conflictual trends: the institutionalization of Arab-Israeli economic cooperation and increased opposition to these developments within vulnerable Arab regimes.[75] As one analysis put it, "The summit looks like a car with the driver pressing both the accelerator and the brakes at the same time."[76]

## The Cairo Conference, November 12–14, 1996

Between Amman and Cairo, Israeli Prime Minister Yitzhak Rabin was assassinated by an Israeli extremist, an unprecedented wave of terrorism struck Israeli cities during February and March of 1996, and early elections called for by Prime Minister Shimon Peres led to the Labor government's defeat, bringing a right-wing coalition led by Likud's Benjamin Netanyahu to power by May. Yet this political climate was coupled with growing economic incentives to convene MENA-type summits, illustrating the tension between competing pressures.

On the political side, Egypt (both at the government and private sector level) began to signal uneasiness about convening an Arab-Israeli economic conference in the midst of bilateral deadlock and uncertainty over Prime Minister Netanyahu's intentions on implementing the Oslo Accords. In late August 1996, President Mubarak suggested the conference would not take place if the new Israeli government did not uphold its commitments to the Palestinians,[77] creating a highly publicized debate in both Israel and the Arab world about the value of these conferences.[78] However, as one analysis correctly observed:

> Egypt will not lightly abandon the Cairo conference, an event which sits well with its new self-image as an increasingly dynamic, open and liberal economy, at least by Middle East standards. It has much to gain from hosting the meeting.... A high-profile event of this kind should be a magnet for foreign business people just as Egypt's rapid privatization programme is making it a darling of international investors.[79]

Indeed, within weeks, Mubarak announced that Egypt would host the summit as planned, although it attempted to lower the level of the meeting, calling it a conference rather than a summit as in Casablanca and Amman.[80]

Likewise, Palestinian and Jordanian private sector representatives were hesitant to attend the conference. The Palestinians argued that they had little incentive to engage in regional projects when their internal economic situation was in crisis, particularly given the difficulty in attracting foreign investment when borders were closed due to Israeli security concerns.[81] Jordanian business representatives viewed the conference as evolving into a political forum offering little to business interests and were also hesitant to show support for such a meeting while the Palestinian track was deteriorating.[82] Given the Jordanian private sector's resistance to the Amman Summit when the political climate was measurably better, its negative response to Cairo—even though over forty Jordanian businesses were ultimately represented—was not surprising.[83]

Yet, in conjunction with this rather polarized political climate was a growing regional consensus on the need to attract foreign investment by improving regional cooperation and to showcase domestic economic reforms in order to facilitate the region's integration into the global economy. On the eve of the conference, for example, President Mubarak addressed the Egyptian Parliament in a long, detailed speech outlining the demands and nature

Regional Economic Cooperation                                                                                     135

of globalization and the need for Egypt to adapt itself to this new economic environment.[84] The intense focus on presenting the MENA region to the outside international community (as opposed to emphasizing intraregional cooperation between Israel and Arab states as in the previous conferences) largely reflects efforts to balance political pressures to "postpone" an Arab-Israeli summit and international economic pressures that underlined the benefits of such a conference. This tension and shift in focus was demonstrated by the nature of the projects presented at Cairo and the tone of the conference itself.

Most of the regional projects presented at Cairo were recycled from the Amman Summit and were the products of the work carried out by the REDWG MC's subcommittees, particularly those focusing on regional infrastructure and transportation.[85] Many of the proposals were targeted to the international business community rather than to governments, and thus large projects like regional canals were dropped from the agenda. In contrast to the other core parties, Israel's project presentation focused only on cross-regional projects (reflecting its continued views of economic cooperation as a peacebuilding mechanism) while other regional presentations included both regional and national project proposals.[86] However, the decision by the Israeli Minister of National Infrastructure, Ariel Sharon, and the Agriculture Minister, Rafael Eitan, not to attend the Cairo conference raised some doubts about the new government's level of interest in promoting regional economic cooperation as compared to the previous government. As one analysis of the conference noted, "the high-level political encouragement that was clear during the period of the Labour administration in Israel is now conspicuous by its absence."[87]

The shift in focus from regional to national development reflected the altered political environment and the Egyptian desire to sanction Israeli actions without jeopardizing business interest in a conference that served Egyptian economic interests and enhanced its regional status. Egyptian Deputy Foreign Minister Raouf Saad (who was also the Egyptian contact point for the REDWG MC Secretariat) explained one of the central differences between Cairo and the previous two MENA summits:

> The concept of regional cooperation is changing and acquiring a larger dimension. Casablanca was a very special conference in that it was the first time an international conference encompassed Arabs and Israelis meeting in an Arab country. It was a signal that under peace,

Israel was being accepted not only as a political entity, but also as an economic partner in the region. Here, peace would mean that parties are all equal, that there would be no exception, and no special treatment for any party and that the peace process is not a hostage to this or that party. In this respect, Israel does not necessarily have to be part of all regional cooperation plans, and the summit process does not hinge upon the political situation in Israel. . . . Regional cooperation is acquiring a wider definition, opening new horizons for inter-Arab cooperation.[88]

While Arab-Israeli economic cooperation was not completely rejected, the political tension in the region led the Egyptians to deemphasize this component of the summit process in favor of a broader economic development theme stressing domestic reform and inter-Arab cooperation. According to one American official present at Cairo, the Egyptian sponsors "played around" with the program to reflect these new priorities, frustrating the Americans and nearly leading Secretary Christopher to stay away from the conference.[89] Yet, given that the Cairo conference was proving to be the only game in town in terms of Arab-Israeli cooperation, the Americans decided the absence of the secretary would send the wrong message to the region and to international investors. This goal was made somewhat easier because of Egypt's primary interest in ensuring that the conference would prove to be a business success, a tacit concession that "Egypt cannot live off the Arab-Israel conflict any longer."[90] President Mubarak demonstrated his understanding of the altered international environment when he addressed the conference with a speech that focused almost entirely on the global economy, with only short references to the peace process in his introductory and concluding remarks.[91]

Indeed, the general interest both among government and business representatives in capitalizing on the conference to further national economic reforms and attract private sector investment in domestic and regional infrastructure led to some surprising positive developments despite the tense political climate. Over ninety countries were represented at Cairo, including more than two thousand business people. A lunch hosted by Israeli Finance Minister Dan Meridor and Industry and Trade Minister Natan Sharansky on the second day of the conference drew an unexpected number of Arab business representatives, including those from Tunisia, Saudi Arabia, Oman, and Egypt. Some sideline political meetings even took place between Israeli

Foreign Minister David Levy and his Qatari counterpart, Hamed Bin Jassem, who invited Israel to attend the next MENA summit in Doha.[92]

Not surprisingly, the outcome of the conference reflected the ambiguity of interest between furthering economic cooperation and investment in the region and reluctance to move too quickly absent bilateral progress. Such ambiguity was expressed by Egyptian Prime Minister Kamal Ganzouri in the closing session, where on the one hand he asked, "How can you ask Egypt and the Arab states to go ahead with regional cooperation in this situation now?" and on the other suggested "There may be problems now but we still look forward to cooperation to put ourselves on the world map."[93] While Israeli business representatives (whom the Egyptians perceived as a potential peace lobby) initially expressed optimism over their reception at the Cairo conference), Egypt continued policies that restricted the development of business contacts with Israelis as it sought to "cut Israel down to size."[94] The proposed gas deal between Egypt and Israel was put aside in favor of an Egyptian-Turkish gas agreement (estimated to cost from $2 to $4 billion) primarily because of the slow pace of Israeli-Egyptian negotiations on the deal,[95] but the failure of this highly publicized project only contributed to the perception that regional cooperation with Israel faced serious setbacks. Foreign Minister Moussa made the new emphasis clear at the conference's closing, arguing that "Arab-Arab cooperation is the backbone. That doesn't exclude cooperation with others under the right conditions but we don't want any one country to be the center."[96] No one had any doubt as to the country to which he was referring.

While the final Cairo Declaration [see appendix G] differed little from the previous summit declarations and pledged to continue the establishment of the three regional institutions decided on at Amman, the veneer of continued Arab-Israeli regional economic cooperation was tarnished by the tone and emphasis of the conference.[97] Still, Arab-Israeli economic cooperation had not been completely removed from the regional agenda. Even the convening of the conference during such a politically sensitive time suggested that the economic cooperation process that began in REDWG and Casablanca was more durable than most expected. This durability was reflected by the decision of the parties to continue the process and convene the next summit in the Gulf region in the fall of 1997.[98] Although no large-scale summit convened in 1998 or 1999, Arab and Israeli business representatives continued to attend smaller meetings seeking to encourage private sector investment in the region.[99]

*Nascent Arab-Israeli Multilateral Institutions*

The work of REDWG's subcommittees and the MENA summits led to the formation of three nascent Arab-Israeli institutions. The following review of the negotiations to establish these institutions reveals their varied success and the forces that both facilitated and impeded their development, which I explore in greater detail later in the chapter.

## The Regional Business Council (RBC)

The RBC was originally discussed and conceptualized within the REDWG's MC trade committee, but was operationalized within the MENA summit context.[100] Out of the three institutions created by the MENA process, the RBC faced the greatest setbacks, and proved to be the institution most vulnerable to negative peace process developments. Because the RBC depended on the active participation of regional private sector representatives, Israeli closures of the Palestinian territories posed particular problems for the group in that Palestinian business representatives found it difficult to attend meetings and were much less willing to discuss cooperative trade relations in such an environment.

The RBC's origins date to the 1994 Casablanca Summit, when the parties agreed on the need for a mechanism to build links between private sector entrepreneurs to encourage intraregional trade and investment. To this end, the Casablanca Declaration encouraged "the establishment of a private sector Regional Chamber of Commerce and Business Council to facilitate intra-regional trade relations."[101] Meanwhile, the region's trade ministers initiated a related process that became known as the "Taba Trade Leaders Group," a series of ministerial level meetings among the core parties—led by the United States—to foster economic cooperation and investment.[102] Following discussions in April and July of 1995,[103] Egypt, Israel, Jordan, and the Palestinian Authority signed an agreement to establish the RBC at the Amman Summit on October 29, 1995, and urged REDWG's trade committee to work with the private sector to operationalize the institution over the next six months.

An RBC steering committee was established to finalize the draft RBC charter and bylaws. The committee's first meeting took place in Amman on March 3–4, 1996, during which time the parties reviewed a draft of the RBC charter and its work agenda. The core parties also agreed to each contribute

$25,000 towards the costs of establishing the RBC and the United States offered to provide an adviser to help establish the institution and finalize the charter.[104] However, since the steering committee was unable to agree to reconvene after the March 1996 meeting, substantive progress could not be made on approving the charter, deciding the RBC's venue (which was de facto in Amman), and dissolving the committee in order to turn its work over to the new institution. The next steering committee meeting was originally scheduled to take place in Israel in either late May (after the REDWG plenary) or June 1996. However, the Israeli election contributed yet another impediment to getting this meeting off the ground, with political sensitivities significantly increased.

For example, the Israelis insisted on keeping the meeting's venue in Tel Aviv, but the Palestinians responded negatively, arguing it was difficult for them to attend a meeting in Israel for both practical and political reasons. Another attempt to arrange a meeting in July 1996 was also scuttled and reflected the altered political mood. At this time, the Swiss had launched an initiative on the rights of the child (under the REDWG umbrella), and the Palestinians wanted to host a reception related to this initiative in East Jerusalem. But Israel refused to attend such a reception, and the event was canceled. In response, the Palestinians announced they would not attend the scheduled RBC meeting in Tel Aviv. Again, the RBC meeting was postponed. By May 1997, no less than nine meetings had been scheduled and "postponed."[105]

Still, despite the apparent failure of the RBC, some limited progress was made in other related forums and on an ad hoc basis, as business contacts in the region became commonplace even without a formal institution. On a practical level, the United States encouraged training of regional parties (particularly the Palestinians) to improve their marketing skills, helping to develop Palestinian competitiveness and lay the groundwork for future cooperation. Similarly, the Swiss Government promoted regional trade through the Swiss Trade Initiative Middle East North Africa (STIMENA). STIMENA conducted studies on trade agreements within the region, including bilateral agreements among the core parties and agreements with third parties, in order to identify areas of inconsistency and make recommendations for trade harmonization.[106] While the facilitation of intraregional trade is an uphill battle, because of both economic asymmetries and political sensitivities, these more limited training and research exercises could contribute to increased regional cooperation at a later stage.

## The Middle East-Mediterranean Travel and Tourism Association (MEMTTA)

The least controversial of the regional institutions was MEMTTA. Because of its importance for regional economic development and growth, tourism offers visible and immediate rewards to regional parties. Moreover, while MEMTTA addressed intraregional tourism cooperation, its central focus was on increasing the region's share of the global tourism market, and this provided a more outward-oriented institution than the RBC.[107]

Most of the substantive planning for MEMTTA took place within REDWG's tourism committee shepherded by Japan, but was promoted through the MENA economic summits. The Casablanca Declaration called for the establishment of "a regional Tourist Board to facilitate tourism and promote the Middle East and North Africa as a unique and attractive tourist destination."[108] Over the next year, REDWG's tourism committee developed the MEMTTA charter in preparation for the Amman summit. The United States also participated in these meetings, and provided technical assistance to create the association by funding a facilitator, who also established its Americas division. On September 29, 1995, representatives from Cyprus, Egypt, Jordan, Israel, Morocco, the Palestinian Authority, Tunisia, and Turkey initialed a charter to establish MEMTTA, formally signing the charter at the Amman Summit.[109]

The charter established a board of governors comprised of public sector officials to serve as the overall policy body of the association, as well as an executive council of private sector representatives who were responsible for the daily operations of MEMTTA. The parties agreed to place MEMTTA's headquarters in Tunisia. Despite the government participation in MEMTTA, the institution was designed to be run primarily by the private sector. For example, the Americas division included a core group of companies (airlines, hotel chains, cruise lines, tourist offices and operators) all focused on increasing tourism interest in the MENA region. According to the head of MEMTTA's marketing committee, the association needed "to create an image of the Middle East-Mediterranean region that does not now exist in the minds of travelers in order to be able to market the tourism potential hiding under our common umbrella."[110]

Meetings of the interim board of governors and executive council were held in Bethlehem in January 1996 and in Alexandria in February

1996. These meetings further defined the structure of the institution and worked on creating extraregional divisions. In the wake of the Israeli elections, further MEMTTA meetings were postponed to September 1996, when the executive council met in Tunis. However, because of the outbreak of violence following the Jerusalem tunnel incident, the board of governors was not able to conduct a regular session, and instead held an informal meeting in a hotel lobby where they made a strong statement condemning the Israeli action. While the political tensions slowed the board of governors' work, the executive council of private sector representatives continued to meet, with their next sessions taking place on the sidelines of the Cairo economic conference on November 13, 1996, and in Orlando, Florida, in October 1997. MEMTTA's Americas division also met at least five times between the Cairo and Doha economic summits, and its European division met in London in November 1997.

However, because of the political setbacks on the Palestinian track, Egypt refrained from ratifying the MEMTTA charter. MEMTTA could not be formally established until all four core parties approved the charter, and thus, the public sector dimension of MEMTTA was suspended. Without an approved charter, the association could not raise funds from membership dues and could not recruit an executive director, a position that was initially supposed to be filled by March 1997. Still, even without a formal charter, MEMTTA members continued efforts in the marketing and training areas. For example, in the last week of January 1997, the tourism ministries of Israel, Jordan, and the Palestinian Authority cooperated to produce a highly publicized advertisement (appearing in major U.S. and Canadian newspapers) promoting tourism to their subregion. MEMTTA members also worked on a data base and homepage on the Internet to enhance their marketing outreach and participated in a working-level tourism training project in Cairo.[111]

## The Middle East Development Bank (MENABANK)[112]

The negotiations leading to the formation of the MENABANK reveal not only greater regional initiative as multilateral economic cooperation developed, but also the clear political purpose behind its establishment. Despite these political foundations, the bank evolved into another regional tool to promote international business interest in the region, which is why it was able to endure numerous setbacks in the bilateral process. Unlike the RBC, the failings of the MENABANK had more to do with American funding, at least initially, than with regional impediments.

While proposals for a new Middle East development bank were discussed in academic and policy circles even before the 1991 Gulf War,[113] it was only after the Persian Gulf conflict that high-level U.S. officials began to focus on economic development schemes to rebuild the region. In his testimony to the Senate Foreign Relations Committee in February 1991, Secretary of State Baker proposed the creation of a Middle East development bank. However, Baker did not receive approval for the proposal from the Treasury Department, leaving the bank as a "classic case of planting a very good and farsighted idea before it was ready."[114]

Baker was not the only early advocate for a Middle East bank. Crown Prince Hassan of Jordan proposed the creation of a regional development fund as part of cooperation efforts in a CSCE-type structure that would include "non-Arab states."[115] Shimon Peres was perhaps the most vocal and enthusiastic supporter of a regional bank as part of his vision of an integrated "New Middle East" modeled on European cooperation efforts. Speaking to those who were skeptical of such a proposal, Peres argued:

> There is no doubt that it would be possible to get assistance from existing sources, such as the World Bank, the European Investment Bank, and private banks. I believe, however, it is preferable to concentrate all investment money for Middle Eastern development in a bank set up exclusively for that purpose. . . . From a sociopsychological standpoint, the bank will encourage people living in the Middle East to see the regional framework as an entity in its own right. Every child knows the concept of a bank; Israelis often say "Better banks than tanks."[116]

The bank proposal carried a primarily political rather than economic purpose, although some economists suggested various economic rationales for a new Middle East development fund, particularly the need for wider membership and for a financial intermediary between international capital markets and regional investment opportunities.[117] But to become a reality, the idea needed a regional process that could provide its foundations. The REDWG MC's finance subcommittee and the MENA summits served this function.

However, the bank idea faced formidable opposition early on, including from key officials in the Clinton administration. A month before the Casablanca Summit, senior Treasury Department officials expressed skepticism toward the initiative.[118] A senior Clinton administration official said at the time, "It is the unified view of the U.S. government that we do not think the establishment of a Middle East regional bank would be right. . . . We have had mixed experiences with such banks in Europe and Asia, and our Treasury officials feel very strongly on this issue of a banking mechanism."[119] In addition to U.S. reservations, European Union members made no secret of their opposition to a formal development bank for the Middle East. Even in Israel—the principal bank proponent—voices from the Finance Ministry expressed concern about funding such a bank.[120]

Despite the work of the MC's finance committee advocating the creation of the bank, the resistance of the major European powers and the U.S. Department of Treasury posed a major roadblock to the initiative. When a senior Israeli official presented plans for a bank to senior State and Treasury Department officials in Washington in September 1994, the officials informed him that while the U.S. opposed the initiative, if Israel came back with a united position among the core regional parties favoring the bank, the U.S. would "give them their bank."[121] When the core players expressed a shared desire for the bank (albeit for different reasons),[122] the U.S. recognized, for political reasons, that it must support the initiative. Such unprecedented regional coordination was, in the view of senior State Department officials, exactly the type of interaction for which they had hoped when launching the Madrid process and matched their central beliefs about how to organize the region. They could not reject regional cooperation on economic grounds given the political significance of the initiative.

President Clinton boosted the prospects of the bank when he expressed his support on route to the Arava Israel-Jordan peace treaty signing in October 1994.[123] In an address to the Jordanian Parliament, President Clinton publicly endorsed the bank. This endorsement paved the way for a provision in the final Casablanca Declaration calling "for a group of experts to examine the different options for funding mechanisms including the creation of a Middle East and North Africa Development Bank.."[124] In his address at Casablanca, U.S. Treasury Under Secretary Lawrence Summers voiced unequivocal American support for the bank proposal, arguing for the importance of building new regional institutions: "Europe has benefited, and benefited quickly, from its own regional development institution [EBRD]. . . .

Why not the Middle East? ... Development banks can be to the new world order what security organizations were to the old—a banding together of nations with shared vision and a commitment to address their greatest challenges."[125]

While the Americans by this point strongly favored the bank, the Europeans continued to oppose the initiative and preferred existing funding mechanisms for development projects (such as the World Bank or the European Investment Fund).[126] Yet the Europeans harbored political doubts that went beyond the economics of the bank. The Europeans felt the Americans had usurped their only role in the peace process by taking the initiative out of REDWG in order to create a parallel and, in their view, competitive economic process based on new regional institutions dominated by the Americans. The Europeans complained that the United States could not continue to control the political agenda of the region while insisting the Europeans foot the bill. At Casablanca, German and French officials (speaking for the EU) objected to the bank, arguing it would amount "to American control over European money."[127]

Between the announcement of a possible bank at Casablanca and the call to establish the bank at the Amman Summit in October 1995, the EU member-states, the United States, and the core regional players established a special task force to consider alternative funding mechanisms for the region, which met on a nearly monthly basis. Despite these contentious negotiations and continued European resistance, the parties formally agreed to establish the bank at the Amman Summit and finalized its charter in the following months.

At a November 1995 meeting in Cairo, the task force allocated 75.25 percent of the bank's capital, leaving the remaining capital unallocated for other regional (Syria and Lebanon in particular) and extraregional (the Europeans) parties to join at a future date. The United States, as one would expect, received the bulk of the shares (21 percent), while each of the core parties received an equal 4 percent share [see table 5.2]. The bank charter was circulated among prospective members for approval at the end of April 1996 through a "no objection" procedure. A multinational transition team began work in Cairo to lay the groundwork for operationalizing the bank, and within the year was provided office space in Cairo by the Egyptian government. On August 28, 1996, the United States and Russia deposited the bank charter at the United Nations Headquarters for signatures and ratification among the prospective members.

TABLE 5.2 Middle East Development Bank Share Allocation

| Nonregional Members | | Regional Members | |
|---|---|---|---|
| Austria | 1% | Algeria | 2% |
| Canada | 2.5% | Egypt | 4% |
| Cyprus | 0.25% | Israel | 4% |
| Greece | 2% | Jordan | 4% |
| Italy | 5% | Morocco | 2% |
| Japan | 9.5% | P.A. | 4% |
| Korea | 1.25% | Tunisia | 2% |
| Malta | 0.25% | | |
| Netherlands | 3.5% | | |
| Russia | 6% | | |
| Turkey | 1% | | |
| U.S. | 21% | | |

*Total Capital Subscription* 75.25%*
*Total Capital* $5 billion of which only $1.25 billion is paid-in
*The remainder of the capital was reserved for countries expected to join the bank (e.g., Western European states and China).
Source: Agreement Establishing the Bank for Economic Cooperation and Development in the Middle East and North Africa, schedule A, article 1, subscription.

While not all members signed and ratified the charter, in part because the United States had not contributed its portion of the funds needed to start the bank's operations, the transition team continued its work throughout 1997–98, drafting the bank's by-laws, addressing treasury-related issues, finalizing its organizational structure and personnel policy, and completing a headquarters agreement with the Egyptian government. The team also developed a pipeline of projects for consideration once the bank began operations.[128]

However, the setbacks in the bilateral peace process slowed the pace and enthusiasm of regional support for the bank, with only a handful of parties signing the bank charter by May 1997: the United States, Russia, Jordan, the Netherlands, Italy, and Cyprus. The Israelis refused to sign the charter until the Egyptians also agreed to sign. Some reports also suggested that Prime Minister Netanyahu was not as enthusiastic about the bank as his predecessor,[129] but high-level Israeli officials denied this, pointing out that Netanyahu lobbied for the bank in a meeting with members of a congressional subcommittee during a visit to Washington.[130] Although the core parties still supported the bank publicly (such as at the Cairo economic summit),[131] their participation was increasingly linked to the bilateral peace process.

While negative peace process developments certainly damaged the positive cooperation among the core parties in the bank negotiation process, the most serious impediment to getting the bank off the ground was the inability of the U.S. administration to receive congressional funding for the initiative even though the funding requests were quite modest (a $52.5 million annual commitment over five years).[132] In the 1997 budget, Congress authorized funding but did not include the funds in its appropriation. Congress also failed to fund the bank in fiscal years 1998 and 1999. While initially the congressional reluctance to fund the bank stemmed from fiscal concerns and general suspicion of multilateral development banks, increasingly Congress became concerned about the regional commitment to support such an institution given the deteriorating condition of the peace process after Israel's 1996 election. But without funding from the United States—the bank's primary shareholder—the bank's prospects were bleak regardless of peace process developments.

## Explaining REDWG: Progress Amidst Setbacks

What explanatory forces can best capture the complex evolution of REDWG from an externally imposed political forum focused on building cooperation within the region to a relatively durable regional framework (with its many parallel processes and institutions) looking outside the region? What does this evolution tell us about the types of Arab-Israeli multilateral economic frameworks that are most likely to succeed, even in the midst of political turmoil? The following analysis argues that the development of regional multilateral economic cooperation had more to do with developing a consensus concerning the region's place in a global economy than with external powers imposing a structure on the region or with a functional approach to regional economic development. The cooperation process itself and the nature of interactions among participants in the working group better explain the continued development of REDWG despite the obstacles standing in the way of regional cooperation in this issue area. Of the facilitative mechanisms identified in chapter 1, the redefinition of economic problems and the intensified interactions between Arab and Israeli elites were most in evidence and enhanced the working group's ability to move from the political to the technical realm. Impeding factors such as the bilateral peace process and domestic opposition to normalization across the Arab world tended to decrease in importance relative to these facilitators.

The question for ACRS was why, despite progress, did it face insurmountable problems and ultimately fail? The question here is the opposite: Why, despite problems, did the process prove a relative success? My explanation again suggests the need to look at how regional players viewed the process. A review first of the problems facing the working group reveals that they were not insurmountable because the regional players, even in the midst of bilateral setbacks, viewed it as enhancing, not undermining, their economic and political interests. The following section explains why this was the case by outlining the forces that facilitated the working group's ability greatly (though never completely) to depoliticize this issue area and reach common understandings about its value.

*Impediments to Economic Cooperation*

The empirical record reveals a number of major impediments facing REDWG and its related economic activity, impediments which stemmed from both outside the region and from domestic forces within the Arab world. For example, the U.S.-European competition for influence in this issue area and weak extraregional commitment to the establishment of new regional institutions like the MENABANK slowed cooperative efforts, as did the problem of the lack of extraregional funding for working group projects. Moreover, as activity in the working group became more public through the MENA summits, domestic resistance in Arab states emerged because normalization before the resolution of the Israeli-Palestinian conflict was still considered taboo among the public at large. Sensitive to such sentiment, the Arab private sector was reluctant to attend such conferences during tense periods in the bilateral tracks. The anti-cooperation forces within the Arab world only strengthened as political developments worsened after the May 1996 Israeli elections. This anti-cooperation position was clearly demonstrated in the debates in the Arab press over whether Egypt should proceed with the Cairo MENA conference in the wake of the Israeli-Palestinian clashes in September 1996 and the general lack of progress in moving the Oslo process forward.[133] Many editorials in the Arab papers opposed convening the conference, arguing that such cooperation could not continue without progress on the Palestinian track.[134]

However, such obstacles did not prove fatal to the group's activities (e.g., the Cairo conference went ahead as planned) and were less critical to the development of REDWG than the role regional perceptions of the process played in shaping the nature of the working group. For example, even if extraregional management and funding for REDWG and commitment to regional cooperation and institutions could have been maintained, this influence would not have been sufficient to sustain the process in the absence of regional acceptance or if regional parties believed the process was undermining their national interests (including identity-based interests). As demonstrated by the ACRS case in chapter 4, Egypt was willing to withstand American pressure and sacrifice the process once it perceived that cooperation was undermining critical interests, including its perception of its role in the region. In the REDWG case, while friction existed between Egypt and Jordan—as evidenced at the Amman economic summit—Egypt did not feel its regional role being undermined by the process, a perception enhanced by the housing of new institutions like the MENABANK in Cairo, not Amman.

Moreover, none of the multilateral working groups was so critical from a material standpoint that regional parties could not afford to reject participation in them if they perceived them as working against their interests, regardless of extraregional designs or influence. For example, despite continued American efforts to jump-start the RBC, regional resistance impeded its progress. Thus, given the important but working-level involvement of the Americans and the relative lack of interest in the multilaterals at high levels of government after the Madrid and Moscow conferences, regional parties could have stopped the economic cooperation process early on and certainly in the wake of the political difficulties following the Netanyahu election. But this is not what happened. The process faced severe difficulties and produced ambiguous results, but it did not break down. What factors within the cooperative process facilitated the relative success of this working group?

*Shared Support for Regional Economic Cooperation, with Limits*

Understanding the dynamics within the economic cooperation process helps us understand why REDWG developed as it did and even endured some serious setbacks in the bilateral track. To a greater extent than ACRS, the group succeeded in turning politically charged conceptions of economics in the region (such as concerns about Israeli political and economic dominance) into a more technical problem where cooperation with Israel was viewed as beneficial for attracting foreign investment into the region. Thus, unlike the security case, the actors in this instance reached common understandings about the value of regional cooperation in this issue area. To understand why, we must evaluate the factors facilitating this transformation, including the redefinition of economic problems with a private sector focus, the growing acceptance of the "imperatives" of globalization, the development of new partners and policy options to institutionalize these common views, and the increased interaction among regional elites leading to like-minded understandings of regional economic issues.

Before doing so, however, I should clarify my use of the globalization concept to avoid confusions about the purpose of this argument. To focus on regional perceptions of globalization pressures is not to pass judgment on whether these perceptions are accurate or serve the national interests of developing regional states. That debate is beyond the scope of this study. What concerns me here is not whether the particular perception of globalization and free market economic ideology is right or wrong from an economic growth standpoint, but rather the fact that this perception became so widespread, and the way this perception influenced the prospects for multilateral regional cooperation among Arabs and Israelis.

Redefining Problems About Economic Development

A review of the successes and failures of multilateral economic cooperation in the Arab-Israeli peace process demonstrates the relative resilience of those aspects of the process that sought to deemphasize conflict and present a more stable picture to the outside world. By contrast, efforts to promote intraregional trade and financial transactions appeared less durable and more susceptible to shocks in the bilateral peace process. This differential progress points to a key explanatory factor of the economic component of the multilaterals, namely growing perceptions about how regional cooperation furthers globalization objectives.

The Middle Eastern and North African economies have been in a dismal state since the mid-1980s. Not only did oil revenues decrease,[135] but the 1991 Gulf War also destroyed the pattern of labor flows and the resulting remittances that sustained many of the non-oil-producing states in the region.[136] The boom years of the 1970s—largely driven by inflated oil revenue and public investment—had created the facade of prosperity, but this facade crumbled in the face of external shocks and the drying up of public sector funds that had driven development until the mid-1980s. To make matters worse, foreign direct investment has been extremely low in the Middle East at a time when such investment is considered critical to economic growth.[137] Given that large public sector investment is no longer an affordable option for most Middle Eastern economies (a point well underscored by the failure of REDWG's larger projects to secure public sector investment), regional leaders began to take the liberalization alternative more seriously (at least rhetorically), despite ideological resistance and domestic risks.

The rapid growth of the global economy over the past two decades—with unprecedented levels of world trade, information flows (thanks to the electronic revolution), services trade, and foreign direct investment—changed the way elites viewed their ability to foster growth and development. Popularly called globalization, it suggested to elites that for states to compete for a share of global capital flows, they must open up domestic markets to foreign investment.[138] Many economists noted the failure of the Middle East to join the global economy, arguing that with the world economy "moving with the speed of a bullet train," countries can no longer get on or off the train: "If you are not at the station, the chances are the world economy is simply going to pass you by. . . . The Middle East has not even gotten to the station."[139] Middle Eastern leaders became increasingly sensitive to such critiques and began shifting rhetoric and policies, albeit slowly and erratically.

The question for Middle East leaders has been how to compete with other states for international investment. One option is domestic structural economic reform (promoted by the International Monetary Fund) with each state chasing investment alone on the basis of its own economic portfolio.

Structural reform may prove a necessary element of each state's effort to attract foreign investment. At the same time, however, Middle East elites increasingly believed that a stable political climate, fostered by the perception that the Arab-Israeli conflict was moving toward a resolution, would contribute to each state's efforts to improve its economic standing. The REDWG process fostered such beliefs and created a process by which such cooperation could occur. Thus, interpretations of globalization suggested that cooperative relations could change the regional profile from one of terminal conflict to one of relative stability, and subsequently attract foreign investment. While Middle East elites increasingly perceived an interest in attracting foreign investment, they concomitantly began to converge on the idea that the region as a whole could help each state individually in global capital markets.

Developments since the Gulf War strongly suggest regional movement toward common understandings of globalization pressures. From Madrid to Oslo, the economic dimensions of the peace process were given higher priority by both the external parties and regional participants than in previous peacemaking efforts. The key peace process parties—Egypt, Israel, Jordan, and the Palestinians—best demonstrate the perceived pressures of globalization. For example, Israeli Prime Minister Benjamin Netanyahu, Palestinian leader Yasir Arafat and Egyptian President Hosni Mubarak put peace process differences aside to attend the World Economic Forum's annual Davos meeting in 1997. It is not that these leaders were unequivocal proponents and implementers of free-market policies, but they believed in the power—and money—behind these forces (the companies represented at the 1997 Davos meeting conduct an estimated $4.5 trillion a year in business).[140]

In January 1996, for instance, President Mubarak appointed a new prime minister, Kamal el-Ganzouri (an economist educated in the United States), to address the pressing problems of economic growth, poverty, and unemployment in Egypt. One analysis noted Ganzouri's reputed conversion from "central planning to free market policies," mirroring "Egypt's own progress down this path.... El-Ganzouri has made plain his commitment to encouraging investment.... He lamented that Egypt is getting only about $400 million a year in foreign direct investment, considerably less than other countries in a similar phase of development."[141] President Mubarak has himself spoken about the changing nature of the global economy, and the new pressures it creates for regional development. At the Cairo economic summit, he argued:

> In the course of human history, there comes a time when at a fork in the road we have to make a choice. . . . We can choose to let our past be the guide and our future the victim. . . . We can also stare back and choose to mold our destiny. . . . In Madrid, in 1994 in Casablanca, in 1995 in Amman, in 1996 in Cairo, we took a stand and we dared look beyond the horizon. . . . Today our countries are part of the global structure. There are no longer island economies, isolated blocs, and a closed system. The principles of globalization govern the order of our planet. All economic and financial decisions are made on a planetary scale. Direct investments are global. Capital flows react to global variables. Production and distribution respond to global trends. This is the charter of the 21st Century. It is a charter that knows no exception and dares few deviations; one that evolves day by day based on principles of free trade, free market, and the free flow of capital and investments worldwide. . . . Globalization has imposed on all those countries that must belong to the world economy an order of strict rules and conduct, rules by which economies address each other. . . . This process has started in the Middle East. It needs to be sustained. . . . Today, more than ever before, we can look for a core of countries in this region that share their values, their vision, their policies, and are willing to share their future. With time, this core will expand, attract others, and gradually become the power source for the well-being of the peoples of the region.[142]

Importantly, this core of countries subscribing to globalization includes Israel and underscores the extent to which regional challenges and goals fall beyond the Arab-Israeli fault line. Though divided in the past, the two major Israeli parties—Labor and Likud—both converted to a similar, free-market economic ideology.[143] And while Palestinian economic policies are uncertain given their political situation and their domestic economic crisis, the Palestinians also recognized the need for increased private foreign investment to improve their infrastructure and increase employment.

Jordan also demonstrated the shifting regional priority from state-centric economic polices to growing liberalization in attempts to join the global economy. Amman capitalized on its sponsorship of the 1995 MENA summit to showcase its reforming economy and gain international interest in investing in the country. The opening of a McDonald's in Amman was viewed by some Jordanians as an event "with historic significance, whether we like it or not. . . . It represents the official beginning of the new era of nationhood and development in which economic forces and values may prove to be more important than political and cultural ones. . . . For Jordan to seek, welcome and promote this sort of investment is to indicate the future direction of our place in the world, and also of our understanding of that world."[144] While the jury is still out on how far globalization will reach and change national and regional priorities, particularly given the strong domestic resistance to such forces across the Middle East, a core group of players began to display common understandings of globalization pressures.

The multilateral economic cooperation processes since Madrid and particularly Oslo have served to reinforce these common understandings of global economic trends, even for a region like the Middle East. Regional parties increasingly learned that state-financed projects were less likely to materialize and were far more limited than those proposals that could attract private sector investment. The emergence of the MENA summits with their focus on attracting investment from the international business community reflected these new understandings, as did the nascent institutions which emerged from the process.

These cooperative forums allowed regional players to consider new policy options and partners that would have been unthinkable in the past, such as regional multilateral institutions which included Israel as an integral player. Who would have imagined that Israel would be lobbying the United States for a regional bank alongside Egypt, Jordan, and the Palestinian Authority? Indeed, the cooperation process fostered the notion that Israel was among the region's "core" parties, a term that was consistently used to organize multilateral economic activity. The regional parties were able to reach common understandings about the utility of regional multilateral cooperation in furthering globalization objectives because the process allowed Israel to become a "normal" actor in the region and legitimate partner in regional coalitions. The increased interaction among Israeli and Arab elites as REDWG engaged in numerous intersessional activities also enhanced the success of the cooperative process, as did the development of smaller cooperative forums and institutions among the core parties (such as the REDWG monitoring committee). Moreover, the MENA summits served as regional icebreakers and began to create links between the Israeli and Arab business communities that were not previously possible.[145]

Yet, even if key regional parties increasingly shared a common understanding of global economic trends, how did this consensus view affect the prospects for regional economic cooperation? After all, if the economic basis for such cooperation is limited and faces significant political obstacles, why should common beliefs about globalization influence the prospects for intraregional economic cooperation processes involving Israel? Globalization trends encouraged greater regional cooperation (within political limits) not because regional parties believed they could become an integrated regional bloc that could compete globally (the European model), but rather because they believed that greater regional cooperation (or the appearance of cooperation) attracted foreign investors. REDWG and its related activities reinforced such views by encouraging Arab-Israeli cooperation as a means to attract greater international private sector interest in the region.

Regional cooperation through forums like REDWG and the MENA summits evolved in ways that contributed to transforming the Middle East from one of Arab-Israeli polarization to one where Israel operated as an equal regional member with similar economic goals, and where outside investors could feel comfortable doing business. While foreign investors might demonstrate some tolerance for political risks and uncertainty if money can be made, they have much less tolerance for investing in regions plagued by violent, ideological conflict with time-consuming regional travel and bureaucratic tangles. Regional leaders understood the benefits of enhanced regional cooperation in elevating their prospects for competing in the global economy, which explains why events like the Cairo economic conference proceeded even in the midst of regional political crises. Regional parties—particularly Egypt and Jordan—also held political interests in housing new regional institutions which emerged from this process, and often competed with one another for these institutions. These political interests reinforced the globalization incentives and enhanced the prospects for continued cooperation. Yet while the forces of globalization provided strong incentives for greater regional cooperation, these incentives still faced significant political limitations, allowing for variation among different multilateral economic projects and institutions.

The Limits of Economic Cooperation: Explaining Variation

The previous section helps explain why the idea of a "New Middle East" distracts from the possibility that regional parties might engage in multilateral economic cooperation far short of integration. In fact, cooperation survived and expanded *in spite* of such rhetoric, which only strengthened anti-cooperation forces. Rather, because of changed understandings within the region about the effects and pressures of globalization, and a belief that regional cooperation could boost the prospects of the region's integration into the global economy, multilateral economic processes continued in the face of severe bilateral setbacks. However, the record also reveals that some of the nascent institutions emerging from REDWG and the MENA summits proved more vulnerable to negative bilateral developments than others. Why?

Some of the variation among the multilateral economic institutions had little to do with forces within the region. For example, the MENABANK's primary difficulties arose from resistance from outside the region, first by the Europeans and then by a U.S. Congress reluctant to support any multilateral development if it required an increased foreign aid budget. But the principal explanation for the variation among the three central multilateral institutions is the extent to which these institutions reflected regional perceptions of how regional cooperation served globalization objectives. Consequently, those institutions that were created primarily to enhance intraregional trade and cooperation (which rested on weak political and economic foundations), such as the RBC, were less likely to materialize than those that were established with an external focus to increase international interest in the region, such as MEMTTA or the MENABANK.

The purpose of multilateral development banks, for example, is often informational rather than financial (particularly in the case of the MENABANK with its small capital base and numerous alternative financing options)—improving knowledge about regional performance and opportunities for foreign investors.[146] Thus, while the United States supported and promoted the bank for political objectives (mainly, to integrate Israel into the regional fold), the regional parties—particularly the Arab members—valued the bank as a means to improve the regional profile for investment purposes, which explains why they continued to support the bank. Similarly, while MEMTTA included in its objectives greater intraregional trade and cooperation, its central goal was to increase international tourism to the region overall (through its different extraregional divisions). This goal explains why just a week after the contentious Hebron agreement was signed in January 1997, Israelis, Palestinians, and Jordanians collaborated in a public relations effort that placed full-page ads in major American newspapers to promote tourism.[147] To be sure, the complete collapse of all peace process activity precluded the continuation and development of even these outward-oriented regional institutions. But absent greater regional willingness to promote intraregional cooperation solely for political purposes, those regional institutions and political processes that focused on integrating the region with the world rather than the region itself stood the better chance to survive.

## Summary

Arab-Israeli multilateral economic cooperation was relatively successful because the regional parties were able to move beyond the politicized aspects of the process and reach common understandings about the value of cooperation in this issue area. They were able to do so because increased interactions within multilateral settings led to the consideration of new policy options and partners, including new Arab-Israeli institutions, and to shared conceptions (i.e., problem identification) about the role of regional cooperation in a globalized economy. The growing consensus among Arabs and Israelis on the connection between regional cooperation and globalization provided incentives for the parties to continue cooperative processes, albeit within limits as the bilateral track faltered. While regional parties rejected a new "Middle Eastern" identity, multilateral economic cooperation continued because of emerging consensual views among a large number of regional parties about the changing nature of the global economy and the role of regional cooperation within the altered international economic context. Regional cooperation was favored not because the parties desired a "New Middle East," but rather because they viewed such cooperation as enhancing the prospects for the region's integration into the global economy and private sector investment. Several key parties also perceived these cooperative processes as a means to gain greater regional status by sponsoring and housing the new regional institutions that emerged from them.

As political support for peace process-inspired projects diminished with the worsening of Israeli-Palestinian relations after 1996, those cooperative efforts that served globalization goals with outward-oriented agendas proved more resilient to bilateral setbacks. Those initiatives which focused almost exclusively on intraregional projects were more vulnerable to political friction in the bilateral track. That said, this case suggests that even if a positive peace process climate prevails, successful multilateral economic cooperation will ultimately hinge on the extent to which the regional parties see such a process as serving their economic and political interests. If, for example, regional parties change their views about the nature of globalization (i.e., if they no longer value the region's integration into the global economy) and subsequently see less value in regional economic cooperation, or if they perceive such cooperation as undermining regional political roles (i.e., regional identity), such cooperation will be difficult to sustain even with significant extraregional support and substantial bilateral peace progress. Thus, despite past successes, regional multilateral economic cooperation faces significant obstacles from within the region, though cooperative processes like REDWG have made such obstacles more surmountable than they have been in the past.

# 6  Water and Environmental Cooperation

Project-oriented and intended to demonstrate positive, concrete returns on peacemaking efforts, the Water and Environment working groups, of all the multilateral working groups, held out the highest expectations for tangible progress. Water and environmental cooperation focused on projects that could potentially improve the living conditions of millions of people—sewage treatment plants, desalination to increase regional water supplies, oil spill centers to prevent and respond to crises affecting common waters, and a wide variety of regional infrastructure projects. Moreover, both topics—but particularly the problem of water scarcity—posed readily understood threats to Arabs and Israelis and thus provided fertile ground for the parties to address long-term regional challenges.[1] Given the "technical" nature of these issue areas, we would expect such types of functional cooperation to stand the best chance of success even according to outcome rather than process criteria.

However, while both working groups made considerable accomplishments, including influencing sections of the Israel-Jordan peace treaty and the Israeli-Palestinian peace agreements, their development does not drastically depart from the patterns that emerged in REDWG and even ACRS. An analysis of the basis of the groups' relative success underscores the exaggerated distinction between technical versus political issues. The parties' willingness to cooperate in these issue areas cannot be assumed based on their desire to make cooperation cheaper and easier by joining a multilateral forum to address these "consensual" technical topics. Rather, a consensus had to be developed among the regional parties that such types of regional cooperation served their broader interests and political goals. In other words, a political decision had to be made to treat these issues as technical problems.

While consensual knowledge about how to address these regional problems led the parties to support multilateral cooperation—even during difficult periods on the bilateral front—this was not the unproblematic result of a Middle East epistemic community[2] of scientists and experts who illustrated indisputable facts about the water crisis and environmental degradation in the region. Instead, the consensual knowledge developed among the *political* elite, who allowed the experts to enter the process once they were agreed that regional cooperation could be defined in ways that served or at least did not undermine perceived national goals. Specifically, political elites increasingly perceived both the water and the environment issue areas as regional problems that required multilateral cooperation but that could also advance political objectives. They also recognized that these solutions did not have to come at the expense of bilateral solutions that were more politically sensitive, such as the question of water-sharing in the Jordan River basin. Once these common understandings developed at the political level, the technical aspects of the problems could be addressed, and progress could be made on specific projects in a variety of sectors.

Yet regional support for cooperation does not fully explain why particular regional parties were eager to see such cooperation continue even under extremely adverse peace process conditions. Again, the political basis for cooperation predominated, with many of the regional parties viewing such cooperation not only as a way to address water and environment issues, but also as a means to exert political influence vis-à-vis other regional players and gain a place at the regional table. This political value, particularly apparent among the smaller Arab states, became a potential impediment to working group progress given the challenge it posed to the larger regional players. In short, even in the issue areas where regional support for cooperation should be unproblematic, we find that the source of commitment to the process is not self-evident and its politically constructed nature can lead to outcomes we would not fully expect from a functional analysis.

While the Water and Environment working groups developed separate trajectories after the 1992 Moscow organizational session and were chaired by different gavelholders (the U.S. chaired the Water group; Japan, the Environment), this chapter treats the groups together because of their commonalities within the multilateral framework and the overlapping nature of these issue areas in practical terms. Indeed, many of the individuals representing regional parties served in both working groups; at the June 1995 plenary in Amman, for example, the working groups held parallel plenaries in recognition of the close connection between the two. The overall purpose of this chapter is to examine the broader trends of these issue areas in promoting Arab-Israeli multilateral cooperation and the forces driving this process forward and, at times, backward. This chapter, like the earlier ones, does not treat in great detail the substantive problems (water scarcity and environmental degradation) that the groups address. Indeed, the problem of water scarcity in the Middle East has already spawned a considerable literature.[3] Rather, this chapter discusses why and how Arabs and Israelis sat down in a multilateral forum to cooperate on these issues; it is a story of process, not outcomes.

The chapter demonstrates that to understand the development of these working groups, we must examine how regional players themselves viewed the process rather than looking to explanations centered on external actors or the constraints of domestic politics. Indeed, external actors would not have been sufficient to sustain the process—particularly during difficult periods in Israeli-Palestinian bilateral relations—if regional parties viewed cooperation negatively. And even after Oslo, the domestic environments did not alter radically in terms of a greater demand for broader regional cooperation, especially amid diminishing expectations about the ability of these working groups to produce tangible projects that could benefit the public. Rather, the objectives of regional participants drove this process forward, but, as discussed above, these objectives were not as self-evident as we would expect from the nature of these issue areas, which, at least in the case of the environment but even in the case of water after Oslo, should have been obvious candidates for mutual gain.[4] As in the case of security and economic cooperation, the process had to depoliticize these issues in order for the working groups to progress successfully.

The first section reviews the empirical record according to the working groups' pre- and post-Oslo stages in order to document the changing nature of the groups' activities and interaction within the process. The second section proceeds to analyze these developments by considering both the facilitators and the impediments to Arab-Israeli cooperation in these issue areas. This analysis demonstrates the value of examining the process of cooperation to understand the development of these groups, as compared to alternative explanations for multilateral cooperation.

## The Development of the Water and Environment Working Groups

### The Pre-Oslo Record

Before Oslo, the gaps between the Water and Environment working groups were pronounced. The Water group was burdened with the contentious issue of water rights, with its territorial implications for the Israeli-Palestinian track, while the Environment group was propelled by a relatively consensual agenda. Moreover, the absence of the Syrians and Lebanese from the multilaterals adversely affected the prospects for regional cooperation among the riparian states of the Jordan River basin more than was the case with environmental cooperation. Still, despite these differences, the basis for the establishment of both groups was similar, as were the attempts to define a working agenda that satisfied a wide array of regional interests. This overview of the empirical record of both groups before Oslo illustrates the role played by the United States and other extraregional parties, particularly Japan in the Environment case, in shaping the agenda and goals of the working groups in the face of regional indifference and even resistance, underscoring that success in these areas was not a foregone conclusion.

### Water

As was typical of all the multilateral working groups, the early plenary sessions in the Water group were tense and polarized, with little regional interaction and mostly extraregional presentations and seminars about the nature and potential solutions that could form a working agenda. Moreover, as in the case of ACRS, an initial division emerged among Israel and the Arab parties about the sequence of the group's work, with the Arab parties (particularly the Palestinians and Jordanians) interested in dealing with issues of water rights and sharing, while the Israelis preferred addressing technical projects that would improve and increase existing water supplies and promote broad regional cooperation that would enhance progress on the bilateral tracks. Thus, the mutual-sum nature of this issue area was not evident to the parties at the outset, and the leadership of the United States proved critical in shaping a working agenda that did not initially match the expectations of many Arab parties, particularly the Palestinians.

Essentially, while in the first several rounds the Palestinians were pushing the water rights issue, the United States backed Israel's preference for addressing the technical aspects of the water problem and facilitating regional cooperation even before bilateral progress. As gavelholder of the working group, the United States carried great influence with all regional parties, many of whom were more interested in currying favor with the gavelholder than in defending the Palestinian position. Thus, the working agenda that emerged from the first meetings focused on four main areas that largely matched the American desire to facilitate regional cooperation by focusing on sectors that avoided issues of territory and sovereignty.[5]

Four central areas for cooperation emerged early on, and defined all future work for the Water group:

1) Enhancing water data availability;
2) Water management and conservation;
3) Enhancing water supplies; and
4) Concepts of regional cooperation and management on water.

However, while several regional parties expressed an interest in moving ahead with regional projects even before Oslo, it was not until after the signing of the Israeli-Palestinian Declaration of Principles (DoP) in September 1993 that most of the projects under the four sectors were developed and, in some cases, implemented. Indeed, unlike the case with the Environment group, the Water group did not conduct any extensive intersessional activities (or more technically oriented workshops consisting primarily of regional experts rather than political representatives) before the Israeli-Palestinian DoP, particularly because the water rights issue proved too divisive before the parties agreed to deal with this issue bilaterally shortly before the Oslo signing.[6]

Still, signs that some Arab parties were prepared—with U.S. backing—to engage in cooperation with Israel began to emerge before Oslo. While the Gulf states were not initially active in the multilateral sessions, Oman emerged as the first Gulf state to speak in the Water forum and to propose a regional project (at their own initiative) when they gave a presentation on desalination to the full working group at their April 1993 plenary session in

Geneva.[7] This presentation provided the basis for one of the major projects of the working group—a desalination center in Muscat—that developed after Oslo and was ultimately established. Jordan also proposed a number of projects in a position paper as early as the first plenary meeting in Vienna in May 1992, including a regional water charter (that eventually evolved into a Declaration of Water Principles), and other areas that matched the Israeli preference, such as increasing and improving water supplies and the efficiency of existing water resources.

But generally, while some Arab parties (particularly those interested in acquiring a more pronounced regional role in this new multilateral context and gaining the favor and financial support of its American sponsor) were prepared to begin defining and negotiating a common work agenda even before Oslo, little progress was possible as long as the water rights issue clouded the negotiations. Consequently, the primary purpose and character of these early sessions was a limited familiarization exercise, where workshops and seminars were promoted by the Americans in order to "get people together for its own sake" rather than to tackle the substantive items emerging on the agenda.[8] The process remained highly centralized (with large plenary sessions serving as the group's focus rather than project-focused intersessionals) with the United States serving as the intermediary for regional interaction.

The Environment

Unlike the early sessions of the Water group, politically divisive issues did not burden the Environment talks. To the contrary, most of the regional participants were like-minded environmentalists with common understandings of international and regional environmental threats. As the Jordanian position paper for the May 1992 Tokyo plenary observed, "This meeting comes coincidentally only a couple weeks before the greatest environmental conference that man has known [the Rio Summit in Brazil]. But the fact that both these discussions are concerned with the environment is no coincidence. There is a growing realization by all of us who share this planet that we must work hard, and work together, at reversing systemic damage that we have been doing to our environment."[9] The Palestinian participants also found the talks constructive, despite continued concern that the multilateral groups not outpace the bilateral negotiations with the Israelis.[10] Still, the Palestinians were pushing—even in this issue area—for discussion of more politically charged issues, such as Israeli tree cutting, water allocation, and Palestinian control over natural resources in the West Bank and Gaza.[11]

Left to their own devices, it is questionable how far regional parties would have moved without extraregional guidance and direction, in this case from Japan (with American support).[12] Moreover, given that environmental threats did not suddenly emerge with the creation of this working group, we must also ask why such a forum did not appear earlier in the Arab-Israeli context, even on a tacit level as occurred with water cooperation. The Japanese sponsors were particularly eager to avoid contentious issues that would slow or even disrupt the working group's progress—and their only opportunity to assume a leadership role in the American-dominated peace process—and hence supported the Israeli position to leave political issues aside in favor of less controversial environmental projects.

Topics that emerged early in the group's agenda included:

1) Environmental management and education (to raise environmental consciousness in the region);
2) Maritime pollution in the Gulf of Eilat/Aqaba and the Mediterranean Sea;
3) Oil spill emergency planning;
4) Waste management;
5) The re-use of treated water; and
6) Protection of wildlife.

Moreover, in contrast to all other working groups at that time, the Environment group—at the initiative of the Japanese chair and in coordination with the United States—moved to a smaller, technical workshop format by its second plenary meeting in The Hague in October 1992, allowing for direct Arab-Israeli contact much earlier than any other working group.[13] At The Hague, the Israeli delegation proposed a project to combat desertification—which received support from the World Bank representative, who offered to find financing for the project—and was endorsed by a majority of participating states, remaining a central project of the working group in its future meetings.[14] The Japanese delegation proposed a regional environmental code at the May 1993 plenary in Tokyo, which later became the Bahrain Environmental Code of Conduct that was approved unanimously by the full working group in October 1994.[15] Also at the 1993 Tokyo plenary Canada proposed to dispatch a mission to review environmental impact assessment

(EIA) needs in Jordan, Israel, Egypt, and the West Bank and Gaza, a mission which they conducted after the plenary and which produced a report with recommendations for the regional parties.[16] And several intersessional activities, including a U.S. sponsored workshop on hazardous material accidents in February 1993 and a Japanese-led seminar on maritime emergency preparedness in June 1993, illustrated the quick pace of this group and its willingness to proceed with practical projects. This trend only accelerated with the Oslo signing [see table 6.1], when many of the group's projects began to move toward the implementation stage, although international funding and political rivalries posed increasing obstacles to moving these projects from concepts to reality.

### Developments After Oslo

Once the Water and Environment groups were established and had initiated working agendas, and particularly after the Oslo signing accelerated the pace of activity for all the multilateral talks, regional participants increasingly shaped the direction and substance of the process. Regional parties increasingly perceived multilateral cooperation in these issue areas as serving national interests, but these interests had less to do with the substance of the issue than with political interests in enhancing one's regional role and status and gaining external support (both political and financial), particularly from the United States. In this sense, the development of these working groups is not remarkably distinct from that of the other multilateral working groups. If cooperation were based solely on interests in solving the substantive problems under discussion, then regional parties would have been much quicker to halt the process when bilateral negotiations stumbled, given the secondary importance of these issues relative to the core peace process issues of territory and sovereignty.

Instead, regional parties looked for excuses to sustain multilateral cooperation because it served interests distinct from peace process objectives and the substantive issues on the agenda. Thus, only extreme periods of deterioration in Israeli-Palestinian relations slowed the pace of cooperative efforts. The development of these working groups raises questions about the value of making sharp distinctions between the prospects for cooperation across different issue areas.

TABLE 6.1 Water and Environment Working Groups Calendar of Plenary Meetings and Sample Intersessionals, 1992–1996

| Meeting | Date, Place [where available] |
| --- | --- |
| First Water Plenary | May 1992, Vienna |
| First Environment Plenary | May 1992, Tokyo |
| Second Water Plenary | September 1992, Washington, D.C. |
| Second Environment Plenary | September 1992, The Hague |
| Third Water Plenary | April 1993, Geneva |
| Third Environment Plenary | May 1993, Tokyo |
| Fourth Water Plenary | October 1993, Beijing |
| Fourth Environment Plenary | November 1993, Cairo |
| Fifth Water Plenary | April 1994, Muscat, Oman |
| Fifth Environment Plenary | April 1994, The Hague |
| Sixth Water Plenary | November 1994, Athens |
| Sixth Environment Plenary | October 1994, Manama, Bahrain |
| Seventh Plenary (Joint Water and Environment Session) | June 1995, Amman |
| Eighth Water Plenary | May 1996, Hammamet, Tunisia |
| Intersessional Meetings/Workshops | |
| Maritime emergency preparedness seminar | June 1993, Japan |
| Hazardous material accidents workshop | February 1993 |
| Several Water Seminars (including weather forecasting, data base standardization, and study tour of river basins) | October 1993–April 1994 |
| Environment Impact Assessment (EIA) Workshop | June 1994, Canada |
| EIA Training Course | November 1994, Cairo |
| Pesticide Management Workshop | December 1994, Cairo |
| Water Meeting with U.S. Gavelholder | March 1995 |
| Water Meeting | March 1995, Oslo |
| Oil Spill Project Intersessional | March 1995, Eilat |

TABLE 6.1 (*continued*)

| Meeting | Date, Place |
|---|---|
| Sanitation Workshop | March 1995, Washington, D.C. |
| Rain Enhancement Workshop | April 1995, Australia |
| Oil Spill and Environmental Center Meeting | April 1995, Bahrain |
| Gulf of Aqaba Environmental Projects Intersessional | April 1995, Amman |
| Radioactive Waste Workshop | May 1995, Washington, D.C. |
| Water Working Visit to Gaza and Israel | May 1995 (sponsored by Luxembourg) |
| Water Courses | May 1995, Oman and Denmark |
| Water Courses | June 1995, Sweden |
| Water Steering Committee | July 1995, Germany |
| Dutch Aquifer Workshop | August 1995, The Netherlands |
| Coast Cleaning Workshop | September 1995, Eilat |
| Environmental Waste Meeting | September 1995, Amman |
| Water Courses | November 1995, Canada and the U.S. |
| German Study Meeting | November 1995, Tel Aviv |
| Water Data Meeting | November 1995, Aqaba |
| Environment Meeting | November 1995, Beit Shean Valley |
| Environment Workshop | November 1995, Cairo |
| Desalination Center Meeting | December 1995, Washington, D.C. |
| Norwegian Water Meeting | December 1995, Oslo |
| German Water Meeting | December 1995 |
| Water Course | December 1995, England |
| German Water Meeting | January 1996 |
| Water Meeting (agriculture) | February 1996, Luxembourg |
| Israeli Water Course | February 1996 |
| German Water Meeting | February 1996 |
| Water Steering Meeting | February–March 1996, Germany |
| Chemical and Toxic Waste Workshop | March 1996, Switzerland |
| Rehabilitation of Municipal Water Systems | March 1996, Israel |

TABLE 6.1 (*continued*)

| Meeting | Date, Place |
|---|---|
| Desalination Center Training Session | March 1996, Tokyo |
| Desalination Center Training Session | April 1996, Oman |
| Water Data Bank Meeting | May 1996 |
| Environment Steering Meeting | June 1996, Oman |
| Regional Environmental Centers Intersessional | December 1996, Amman |

Source: Bureau of Near Eastern Affairs, *Middle East Peace Process: Meetings Following the Madrid Conference* (Washington, D.C., November 8, 1996); Background paper prepared by the Israeli Foreign Ministry, Jerusalem (no date), in Hebrew. Again, because dozens of technical workshops convene with no record, this list represents only a sampling of intersessional-type activities.

Water

At the first multilateral Water group meeting in the wake of Oslo, in October 1993 in Beijing, one of the key American officials involved in the talks observed a "dramatically different attitude" among regional participants, particularly the Palestinians.[17] Because the water rights issue was subsumed by the bilateral negotiations, and Palestinian control over water resources was addressed in the DoP itself with the creation of a Palestinian Water Authority, the multilateral agenda was able to move ahead on specific regional projects. The working group's efforts also received a boost by convening its next plenary session in Muscat, Oman, in April 1994; the holding of the session in a Gulf capital was a first in the history of Arab-Israeli peacemaking. For a Gulf state with whom Israel had no diplomatic relations to receive an official Israeli delegation—headed by senior officials including Deputy Foreign Minister Yossi Beilin—was a historical and psychological breakthrough for the Israelis, and was viewed favorably back home.[18] Much was made of the working group's acceptance of an Israeli project proposal to prevent water leakage in small communities, the first Israeli proposal to gain acceptance in any of the multilateral talks.

Indeed, while substantive progress was made on the working group's central projects, which were now inching toward implementation stages, the

Oman plenary[19] represented the fundamental purpose and nature of these talks: political acceptance of Israel, accompanied by political maneuvering by the small Arab states for greater international attention and financial support. While the following overview of the four central areas for regional cooperation reveals significant promise and incentives for Arab-Israeli cooperation on technical aspects of water supply and use that could produce mutual-sum results, it is unlikely this type of cooperation could endure if it was not supported by political interests, particularly as the bilateral peace process deteriorated after the election of Benjamin Netanyahu in Israel in May 1996.

Before assessing the motivations for regional actors to engage in multilateral water cooperation as the working group evolved away from an extraregional focus toward greater regional initiative, this section reviews the main areas of its working agenda and the flagship projects of the talks that dominated all working group sessions—both plenaries and intersessionals—after Oslo. The review demonstrates that while the working group's activity slowed considerably in the aftermath of the 1996 Israeli elections, it did not come to a halt, with a variety of smaller-scale meetings taking place and several projects moving ahead as had been planned before the elections. The absence of a full working group plenary is not evidence of the collapse of multilateral water cooperation, especially because such sessions were increasingly viewed as less critical in fostering regional cooperation than smaller forums focused on particular projects.[20] Because of funding limitations, most of these projects were small (in the $2–15 million range),[21] leaving the larger regional infrastructure proposals, such as the much publicized Red-Dead and Med-Dead canal projects,[22] for the MENA summits where they could potentially attract the private sector investment. After Oslo, projects developed around the four main areas presented early in the talks: 1) the enhancement of water data availability; 2) water management practices and conservation; 3) enhancing water supplies; and 4) concepts of regional cooperation and management.[23]

*The enhancement of water data availability*
Water planning and management requires a reliable source of common data available to all regional parties so that a consensus can emerge about the water needs of the region when formulating potential solutions. To this end, the U.S. and EU initiated a data banks project, with its first stage focusing on establishing a Palestinian data bank (largely financed by the Nor-

wegian government) and the second phase linking this data bank to Israel and Jordan to create a common data bank for the subregion. While some of the data consisted simply of identifying the experts and papers specializing in water resource management, much of the data was of a highly technical nature designed for specialists who would be implementing projects on the ground. Because of Egypt's ongoing concern about protecting its water rights in the Nile Valley, Egypt declined to join this project and most of the other working group proposals. But the other core parties in the peace process demonstrated increasing interest and activism, and in the water data sphere established an executive action team (EXACT) at the November 1994 plenary in Athens to implement the data banks project. By the summer of 1996, the project was in the implementation stage, acting on several of the ninety recommendations suggested by the EXACT in a "Terms of Reference" document.

*Water management and conservation*

Several projects emerged in the water management and conservation area, which formed the focus for dozens of intersessional activities from 1993 to 1996. The Norwegians conducted a study on comparative water laws and institutions among the regional parties. The Israelis pursued their project on the rehabilitation of municipal water systems, with experts meeting at intersessional workshops (including in Israel in March 1996) to implement the project by focusing on specific sites for rehabilitation. Work on wastewater treatment also progressed as the group focused on establishing a demonstration facility in the West Bank village of Taffouh. Other projects focused on water usage for agriculture purposes (where much of the region's water supply is depleted) and domestic water consumption in the region. At the May 1996 plenary in Tunis, the United States proposed an initiative to increase public awareness on water and promote water conservation through public outreach activities, a proposal which the working group endorsed. This initiative—the Public Awareness and Water Conservation Project—led to the production of a video shown at youth-oriented events to underscore the regional importance of water.

*Enhancing water supplies*

Two major projects emerged that focused on enhancing regional water supplies. The first was a German study on regional water supply and demand,[24] which produced a book that accumulated reports from the three central regional participants (Israel, Jordan, and the Palestinian Authority) in an effort to arrive at a figure that accurately reflected the water gap in usage between regional parties (an extremely sensitive issue for the Israelis)[25] and the amount of water the region needs in the coming decades to meet regional demand. The German supply and demand study represented the first phase of the project, with the group moving on to its second phase, which was the consideration of alternative means to increase the regional water supply. Four main methods were topics for various regional parties to study and present to the full working group: desalination; importing water by sea; importing water by land (water pipelines); and water management and saving (to reduce water loss from existing pipelines). The final phase of the project was the implementation of the working group's recommendations, which had in some cases begun by the summer of 1996.

The second major project in the water supply sphere, the Middle East Desalination Research Center, was established even in the wake of the 1996 Israeli election and in the aftermath of the September 1996 armed violence between the Israelis and Palestinians. The Omanis officially presented the proposal in the April 1994 plenary in Muscat, training sessions took place in Tokyo and Oman (March and April 1996 respectively), and a director was appointed to the Center in May 1996.[26] An agreement to establish the Center was signed on December 22, 1996, in Muscat by its founding members: Oman, Israel, the U.S., Japan, and Korea. The U.S., Japan, Oman, and Israel committed $3 million to the Center's operations, while the EU committed $3.5 million, providing the Center with a total of $15.5 million in pledged financial contributions, with $7 million available for its first year of operations.[27] The Omanis and other Gulf states were particularly interested in the development of cheaper desalination methods given that their subregion produces approximately half of the world's desalinated water (amounting to millions of cubic meters a year). While some Gulf states, particularly the Saudis, were made wary by their concern that the Center would compete with existing desalination plants in the Gulf (and their ongoing political concern that multilateral projects with Israel await bilateral progress), the Center was created as planned, with the expectation that other regional parties would view it more favorably in the future. Still, despite the clear functional utility of cooperation in this area, the political intentions of this project were apparent. In his statement at the signing of the establishment agreement for the Center in Muscat, the American Ambassador present explained, "It [the Center] is not designed for the benefit of any single state or group within the Middle East region. . . . It is for the benefit for all who are committed to the cause of peace and progress in the entire region. . . . We must recommit ourselves to areas of common ground—such as the Center being established today—and build upon them for the larger goal of a region, at last, living in peace."[28]

*Concepts of regional cooperation and management*
While training programs guided by the European Union were conducted in the context of promoting regional cooperation and management (with 275 regional experts having participated in twelve training courses that had been completed by the May 1996 plenary in Tunisia), the central project emerging in this area was what evolved into a Declaration of Principles for Cooperation on Water-Related Matters and New and Additional Water Resources [see appendix H]. The Declaration—initialed by representatives of Israel, Jordan and the Palestinian Authority (PA) on February 13, 1996, in Oslo—represented the first regional multilateral agreement on water-related issues.[29] Following the mandate of the Water working group, the agreement did not address water distribution or sharing issues, but rather focused on the development of new water resources. Building on work from other sectors of the Water group, the Declaration included sections related to coordination among water institutions and national legislation pertaining to water, as well as proposed areas for water cooperation discussed previously in numerous plenary and intersessional workshops. Given the importance of Syria and Lebanon for progress in such coordination, the regional parties called on these states to join the Declaration. Again Egypt, concerned that such a document would set a precedent for water sharing in the Nile, declined to join. Parts of the Declaration were implemented with the Waternet Project, intended to develop a common electronic water information system and a research center for regional cooperation on water-related matters (scheduled to begin operations in Amman, Jordan, in 2000).

Environment

Despite its relatively active agenda before the Oslo Accord, the Environment group was not immune to political sensitivities and obstacles to moving working group projects forward toward implementation. While the parties agreed at its first meeting after Oslo in Cairo (November 1993) to focus on implementing the variety of projects emerging on its agenda, a dispute led by Egypt arose concerning Israeli nuclear waste. Unlike in the ACRS case, this dispute was ultimately resolved a year later when nuclear waste was dropped from the agenda in favor of a compromise between the Egyptians and Israelis to discuss the issue within the context of a broader subgroup focused on hazardous materials, including chemical and toxic waste.[30] But the dispute revealed that even in "easy" issue areas like the environment, political concerns can both facilitate and impede cooperative processes.

The most visible development of the working group was the plenary session in Manama, Bahrain, in late October 1994.[31] While other multilateral working groups had already met in the Gulf region (Water met in Oman and ACRS met in Qatar the previous spring), this session facilitated the Environment group's momentum in moving its projects from their conceptual to implementation stages. The high-level Israeli representation (including the attendance of Israeli Environment Minister Yossi Sarid)[32] revealed political motivations in capitalizing on the conference to further political ties and normalization between Israel and the Gulf states. The smaller Gulf states also held a political interest in participating in these talks—and even in hosting working group sessions in their capitals—because of the leverage it gave them vis-à-vis Saudi Arabia and the international attention such forums promised.

While the bilateral negotiations always influenced the pace and atmosphere of the Environment group, regional commitment to seeing this process go forward stemmed from forces unrelated to the bilateral peace process. Prime Minister Netanyahu's election in Israel negatively impacted all multilateral working groups, but technical sessions continued even after the Israeli election despite the failure of the working group to meet in a full plenary session originally scheduled for Valencia, Spain, in October and then December 1996.[33] Shortly after the Israeli elections an intersessional meeting took place in Muscat on June 26–27, 1996, primarily to discuss implementation of the Bahrain Environmental Code of Conduct, including the creation of a regional environmental center, which the parties agreed would be established in Amman, Jordan.[34] The intersessional also considered an Egyptian proposal to establish a Coordinating Regional Center for Oil Spill Combating as part of the group's larger oil spill contingency planning project.[35] And despite Egyptian concern about convening a technical intersessional meeting in December 1996 because of slow movement on the Israeli-Palestinian track (the agreement for Israeli redeployment in Hebron had not yet been signed), the Jordanians went forward with the meeting as planned, which not surprisingly took place in Amman and was considering the proposal for the regional environmental center which was expected to be established in Jordan. But increasingly, the deterioration of the Israeli-Palestinian track slowed the working group's activities, as did the lack of sufficient funding, which pushed many of the larger regional schemes into the agenda of the MENA economic summits which sought private rather than public sector funds (see chapter 5 for more details on the MENA summits).

But again, the problems emerging in the working group were not unlike those that emerged in the other multilateral talks in that they had less to do with substantive difference in the technicalities of the issue area (which were few in the Environment case) than with political competition among the Arab parties and ongoing concerns among larger Arab parties (particularly Egypt) about Israel's role in an evolving region. Before expanding on the forces facilitating and impeding cooperation in this issue area, this section will conclude with a brief review of the central projects that emerged from the working group and their development after Oslo.

### Environmental cooperation in the Gulf of Aqaba/Eilat

The Gulf of Aqaba was targeted as a fruitful area for environmental cooperation because the subregion includes key peace process parties (Israel, Egypt, Jordan, and Saudi Arabia) who all share a stake in promoting the area for tourism and shipping while maintaining its renowned coral reefs and marine ecology.[36] Given the high volume of industrial activity in the Aqaba/Eilat region (Aqaba is Jordan's only sea outlet) and the nature of the materials handled in the area (gasoline, phosphates, and other chemicals), the risk of an environmental catastrophe that would damage both the marine ecology and the tourism industry is significant.[37]

At the November 1993 plenary in Cairo, the working group supported a proposal for marine disaster and emergency preparedness and agreed to establish joint Israeli-Jordanian-Egyptian[38] emergency response facilities in the northern half of the Gulf of Aqaba to address common threats like oil spills.[39] The European Union offered funding for the project[40] and was later joined by the Japanese government in financing the facilities.[41] According to a State Department official involved in the working group, the total budget for the oil spill centers was approximately $8–9 million.[42] In March 1995, Israel hosted an intersessional meeting in Eilat focused on the technical aspects of the oil spill contingency project, including discussions of the type of equipment required and personnel training.[43] Another intersessional focusing on other environmental projects and economic development in the Aqaba Gulf convened in Amman in April 1995.[44] The oil spill project led to the creation by the June 1995 plenary in Amman of regional centers equipped to combat oil spills of up to 200 tons and coordinate responses for accidents where oil spreads across national borders. The parties agreed after the plenary to send joint teams from Israel, Egypt, and Jordan to Norway for intensive training as part of the implementation of the project.[45] By the summer of 1996, the centers were operational, and had already been put to the test with an actual oil spill in the Aqaba region in September 1995 which generated a coordinated regional response based on the working group's plans.[46] A similar cooperative project among Israel, Egypt, and Cyprus was established under the umbrella of the Mediterranean Action Plan (Med Plan) in June 1995 to combat pollution and oil spills in the eastern Mediterranean, termed the Agreement on the Subregional Contingency Plan for Preparedness and Responses to Major Marine Pollution Incidents in the Mediterranean.[47]

*Desertification*

In the November 1993 plenary, the World Bank proposed a project to control natural resource degradation in arid and semiarid areas of the Middle East, and Japan announced that it would contribute $530,000 to the proposal.[48] At the April 1994 working group meeting in The Hague, an operational program for the project was adopted with the participation of the Israelis, Egyptians, Tunisians, Palestinians, and Jordanians. The project included the establishment of grazing lands, wildlife, forestation and orchards planting, vegetation for arid regions, and the purification of brackish water. The implementation of the plan would take place through five regional centers which would each address a different aspect of the desertification program: Egypt (vegetation development for desert conditions); Tunisia (the use of brackish and waste water for irrigation); Jordan (livestock and grazing); Israel (forestation and exploitation of runoff water sources); and the Palestinians (professional training for all the above mentioned areas). According to an Israeli participant in the working group, the purpose of the regional centers was to "strive to create a network for the exchange of information, the transfer of technology, and the establishment of pioneer projects by any of the parties."[49] The total budget for the centers was estimated at $12 million.[50]

## The Bahrain Environmental Code of Conduct

The Code of Conduct project was distinct from other working group proposals focused on specific, concrete projects that could be implemented quickly on the ground, and in this sense resembled the Declaration of Water Principles in the Water working group. Both of these documents attempted to define general principles to govern regional cooperation, and called for the establishment of regional institutions to promote cooperative Arab-Israeli relations and forums for long-term development of the region. Because the Code of Conduct was not a project-oriented proposal, it did not require immediate funding from international donors to materialize, and thus became an increasingly important focus for the working group as it became clear that public sector funding would not be readily available for many of the projects originally envisioned. Creating institutions is a cheap way to facilitate cooperation and an easy way to satisfy political interests of various participants who would receive prestige and potential international investment by hosting the institution. After Oslo, all the multilateral working groups increasingly turned toward an institution-building focus, and the so-called project-oriented groups like Water and the Environment were no exception.

The idea for an environmental code of conduct emerged well before Oslo, with the Japanese gavelholder presenting the project at the first working group meeting in Tokyo in 1992. A group of "wise men" (or regional environmentalists from the major participants), also known as the Cairo Consultative Group, was established to negotiate and draft the code. The group met twice and prepared a document for the larger working group, although Japanese officials prepared the first draft based on comments from regional parties at the first meeting.[51] The most active participants were the Egyptians, Israelis, Palestinians, Jordanians, Bahrainis, and Americans.[52] Because the parties agreed the code would be morally rather than legally binding, the group was more easily able to achieve a consensus in favor of the document. The final code [see appendix I] was agreed to at the October plenary in Bahrain (hence its name, which was very important to the Bahrainis who were eager that the code be agreed to at this particular meeting) with forty-one delegations in attendance.[53] The code calls for cooperation in two main areas: joint action in five specific areas of environmental concern (water, marine and coastal environment, air, waste management, and desertification) and a regional framework for environmental cooperation. While the initial purpose of the document was simply to demonstrate that regional parties could agree on principles related to issues of common concern, the participants were less clear on how to move the code from abstract language into specific projects that could be implemented on the ground in practical ways.

## Explaining the Record: The Construction of Technical Cooperation

What drove Arab-Israeli multilateral cooperation on the water and environment issue areas after Oslo, even in the wake of bilateral crises in the Israeli-Palestinian negotiations? While extraregional power via leadership was essential for establishing such cooperation, regional support for the processes largely explains why such cooperation continued and evolved the way it did. Although it is tempting to assume this support on the basis of contractual approaches to cooperation, we must search for the source of regional support for cooperation based on political and ideational forces, which can only be understood upon examination of the process of interaction which occurred in these working groups. The groups achieved relative success in reaching common understandings because the regional parties saw the value of multilateral cooperation both for solving substantive regional problems and for serving broader political interests. Despite a number of impediments, including several outlined in chapter 1, a number of mechanisms facilitated progress in these groups. Most significant among these mechanisms were the increased interactions among regional participants—including the participation of technical experts—which fostered common understandings about the nature of these regional problems and the value of multilateral cooperation in these issue areas for furthering other regional objectives, such as the enhancement of regional status.

### *Growing Support for "Technical" Cooperation*

The demand to solve functional problems of common concern like water scarcity and environmental degradation does not necessarily lead to unproblematic positions among regional parties to engage in cooperative forums—particularly an unprecedented and ambiguous multilateral process—that address these issues in efficient ways. Nor do epistemic communities of regional scientific experts simply "reveal" the parties' need for regional cooperation based on consensual knowledge about effective methods to solve these problems, a consensus that in any case would be questioned even among a self-selected scientific community.[54] Rather, political elites make decisions about whether to engage in functional cooperation and the political value of such cooperation.

Indeed, both working groups faced impediments to successful cooperation despite their more "technical" nature. Early politicization of the issues, influenced by the bilateral peace process, often slowed these groups' ability to identify the problems to be addressed and hindered them from reaching common understandings about the nature and utility of cooperating in these areas. For example, the issue of water rights complicated the early sessions of the Water group, since regional parties still defined the issue in distributive rather than integrative terms. Moreover, minimal regional interaction occurred in both groups as extraregional actors dominated the early seminar-style meetings. Other high profile and politically charged issues, like Israeli nuclear waste, also presented some obstacles in the Environment group despite the relatively positive-sum nature of this issue area. Moreover, the Water group was never able to redefine the water problem in ways that did not threaten Egypt's concern over its control of the Nile River, leading Egypt to refrain from some major working group projects. Progress in both groups was also sensitive to negative domestic publicity in the Arab world because of concerns that normalization await resolution of the Israeli-Palestinian conflict. Still, despite these impediments, both working groups made considerable progress because regional parties developed support for the process.

Some of this support had very little, if anything, to do with the technical knowledge of the working groups or the substantive problems on their agenda. The nature of regional support for the process at times arose from political and ideational concerns about a nation's role in an evolving regional environment and maximizing one's status and prestige vis-à-vis other regional parties. Oman and Bahrain, for example, have substantive reasons to engage in technical cooperation with Israel in areas where Israeli expertise and Western financial assistance can solve problems like desalination and desertification. But these functional interests in cooperation cannot sufficiently explain these small states' persistent support for multilateral cooperation (even in the face of serious political crises) when they have other alternatives for dealing with these functional problems (e.g., through existing forums that do not include Israel, such as national desalination centers or cooperation with the European Union) that would not pose the same political risks as cooperating with Israel before the Israeli-Palestinian dispute has been resolved. These small states were favorable toward such functional cooperation because it also served political interests by giving them more leverage and attention relative to Saudi Arabia, its larger Gulf neighbor and the dominant force within the GCC. Hosting plenary sessions and regional centers also provided legitimacy and could attract funding from international donors. Jordan held similar political interests vis-à-vis Egypt, as demonstrated by the various who-will-host-what debates across all multilateral working groups.

Several officials involved in both the Water and Environment working groups have observed that while cooperation within these project-oriented groups may appear easier from the outside, the types of impediments that emerge in bringing projects from conceptual to operational stages (i.e., to actually solving the problems the groups were in theory supposed to address) were not significantly different from those faced by other working groups.[55] Indeed, the common complaint that both of these project-oriented groups moved away from a project mandate toward more abstract institution-building is revealing, and not just the result of the fact that funding was wanting across the board. Just as in the case of the other working groups, new regional institutions served political interests distinct from the substantive issues on the working agenda. All working groups addressed similar questions, which cut across the uniqueness of the issue area: Where is this new institution going to be? Who is going to run it? What is the mandate and whom does it benefit? These types of questions are difficult problems but they are not Arab-Israeli problems. They are not issues of recognition and existence, which the initial creation of the working groups was intended to address based on American conceptualizations about normalizing Israel into the region.

These problems are related to issues of prestige and influence in a region no longer defined by U.S.-Soviet rivalry where legitimacy derived in great measure from the outside patron. Common understandings about the value of these working groups was based in part on a growing comprehension of the role such a multilateral process could play at the political level. Regional parties developed support for the *process* of multilateral cooperation as much as, if not more than, a desire to solve the substansive problems on the agenda.

That said, increased interactions among regional participants and the proliferation of intersessional activities involving technical experts (approximately 400 water professionals have participated in multilateral activities) fostered common understandings about the nature of these regional problems and their potential solutions. Interactions within the multilateral process allowed regional participants to redefine these issue areas as mutual-sum rather than zero-sum problems. For example, the question of how to divide water resources became a bilateral problem as regional participants began to focus on how to improve the overall supply of water to the region. Moreover, projects like the Declaration of Principles in the Water group and the Bahrain Environmental Code of Conduct in the Environment group reflected the growing consensus among Arabs and Israelis about the nature of these problems and allowed the parties to tackle them, using a technical vernacular, outside the politically charged context of the bilateral track. Projects like the regional water supply and demand study also sought to develop consensual understandings among regional participants about the nature and scope of the water problem in a depoliticized manner. The multilateral process allowed Israel to become a partner in addressing these common problems and produced new policy options—such as Arab-Israeli institutions—that would have been unthinkable before Madrid. It seems clear that deduced assumptions about self-interest among unitary actors acting in a politically neutral environment could not lead us to understand the basis for regional support for pursuing such cooperation without examining the process of multilateral cooperation.

*Alternative Explanations*

The value of a process framework, centered on how regional parties viewed these two working groups, is underscored by the weaknesses of alternative explanations which focus on external actors or domestic politics. For example, once both groups had been established and had defined working agendas, extraregional leadership and involvement in the process, once a critical component, became secondary. Increasingly, the role of the extraregional parties was that of a facilitator and financial donor for operational projects. Regional parties participated more actively in the process after Oslo, and even sponsored plenary sessions and supported new regional initiatives, as illustrated by the more visible role of Oman and Bahrain in the Water and Environment groups respectively. The core peace process parties (Israel, Jordan, Egypt, and the PA) often initiated and promoted many of the working groups' activities, with the notable exception of Egypt's absence from several water projects because of ongoing sensitivity over their water rights to the Nile.

Given that the central extraregional's (the U.S.) political objectives had been met with the establishment of these groups and their positive influence on the bilateral peace treaties and agreements between Israel, Jordan, and the Palestinians, the external parties could have been content with allowing bilateral and trilateral arrangements to subsume the multilateral's agenda. Moreover, none of the extraregional participants, including the United States, could have forced the regional parties to continue multilateral cooperation in the face of bilateral crises because, as the working groups moved toward the implementation of practical projects, voluntary regional participation in the projects was essential. Moreover, just as in the case of the other multilateral groups, none of the issues under discussion was of such fundamental importance that the regional parties could not have afforded to forego such cooperation if the risk in engaging in such cooperation became politically unacceptable.

Likewise, domestic forces in the region do not appear to have been a critical factor in shaping the development of multilateral cooperation, and again, over time they should have worked against such cooperation as the Israeli-Palestinian negotiations faced major crises beginning with the assassination of Yitzhak Rabin in November 1995. True, as working group sessions moved to the region, particularly to the Gulf, the Israeli public positively responded to this recognition of Israel by the larger Arab world. But the public was far more interested in concrete commitments, through either bilateral peace treaties or normalization at the bilateral level (with individual Gulf states), than with regional processes about which they knew little. And once widespread terrorism began in the aftermath of the Rabin assassination, the public again focused on the fate of the bilateral tracks, with normalization moving onto the back burner.

As for the Arab public, these working groups were not producing major dividends that the average citizen could see on the ground (after all, most of the projects were highly technical, involved small levels of funding, and were slow to move toward implementation). And when the political environment deteriorated after the 1996 Israeli elections, Arab political elites were not inclined to promote normalization with Israel, and the Palestinians in particular were pressing for boycotts of the multilateral working groups until the political climate improved.[56] In sum, domestic forces were at best neutral, and at worst hindrances (but not barriers) to proceeding with Arab-Israeli multilateral cooperation in both issue areas.

## Summary

Because the Water and Environment issue areas involve substantive interdependencies between Arabs and Israelis and are often considered the least contentious along the continuum of cooperation case studies, these groups should present the "easy" cases for multilateral cooperation. If Arab-Israeli multilateral cooperation were to result in successful outcomes at all, it should be in these areas. After all, regional interests in avoiding common environmental disasters and in increasing a much-needed scarce resource were more apparent than was the case with either ACRS or REDWG, where extra-regional actors consciously promoted the notion that regional cooperation in these issues was in every player's self-interest. And yet, while both the Water and Environment working groups made considerable progress and were able, as in the REDWG case, to sustain cooperation during periods of significant setbacks in the Palestinian track, these groups also faced problems that often slowed and limited the progress that could be made. While technical experts played a critical role in both groups and increasingly dominated the workshops and intersessional activities after Oslo (and in some cases even before), the political decision-makers shaped and constrained the groups' development, not the reverse.

Consequently, to explain the development of both these working groups, an understanding of regional views of the process is critical. However, these views cannot be assumed based on the functional need of the parties to cooperate on these technical issues to most efficiently solve common problems. Rather, regional commitment to technical cooperation had to be *developed*. The source of this commitment to cooperation was often political, and was based on shared beliefs about the value of the multilateral process in enhancing various players' role in the evolving regional system, and the extent to which they perceived multilateral cooperation (with Israel included) as a legitimate and beneficial enterprise from this perspective.

Thus, these cases not only raise questions about the so-called technical-political distinction, but they also suggest that distinctions among issue areas may be overplayed because the prospects for cooperation are often unrelated to the substantive issues under discussion. That said, the projects that emerged under the working agendas of both groups—some of which even reached implementation stages—were increasingly viewed as beneficial to all players in the region, allowing regional parties to view cooperation as a mutual-sum exercise rather than a source for political division. But we should also recognize the reality of cooperation even in the "easy" areas. Technical cooperation can be as political as any other type of cooperation. These working groups had to make similar efforts to define political problems as technical ones, and were able to do so because they ultimately perceived these cooperative processes as substantively and politically useful.

# 7  Conclusion

The cooperative processes described in this study would have been unthinkable before the 1990s. While these cases of regional multilateral cooperation produced mixed results, they challenge traditional conceptions about the nature of Arab-Israeli relations and how international relations theories are to explain cooperation in such regions. The Arab-Israeli multilateral peace process demonstrated the ability of regional actors to move toward cooperative postures in part because of the altered strategic environment which emerged in the aftermath of the collapse of the Soviet Union and the Persian Gulf War. The multilaterals produced new forums for Arab-Israeli interaction that would have been impossible absent such a process. These interactions led to new understandings of regional problems among Arab and Israeli elites which affected not only bilateral peace treaties but also broader regional relations. Arabs and Israelis began discussing security, economic, water and environmental problems with increasing frequency and in a variety of settings, including sessions which brought Israeli delegations to Arab capitals throughout the region. Numerous cooperative projects and even nascent Arab-Israeli institutions were created. Such cooperation broke taboos and changed conceptions about what was possible in the Arab-Israeli context. Despite serious obstacles which slowed progress in all multilateral working groups, the emergence and development of such novel cooperation marks a major watershed in the history of the Arab-Israeli conflict.

Such cooperative efforts might be dismissed if we limit our understanding of cooperation to definitions based on outcomes, or the making of major policy adjustments. Such an understanding of cooperation prevails in the IR literature and has been primarily applied to developed regions and issue areas like economic development. But if evidence of policy adjustment became the standard set to examine regions like the Middle East or issue areas like security politics, we might conclude that cooperation scarcely if ever takes place. What are we to conclude, then, if members of the region themselves think they are engaging in cooperation? How can we explain the gap between what political scientists call cooperation and what many practitioners believe cooperation to be? Might we be missing major empirical developments by limiting our conception of cooperation to policy outcomes? Indeed, the American elites who crafted the multilateral peace process were far more concerned with the importance of establishing a cooperative *process* to normalize Arab-Israeli relations than with the potential to create cooperative *outcomes*, few of which were expected to take place initially. A different view of cooperation can add valuable insights into international behavior that might otherwise be overlooked or not fully understood.

Cooperation in this study is a process of interactions, interactions which may themselves be quite conflictual. But these interactions can also lead to new understandings which may prove as important to explaining regional developments as more tangible outcomes. In order to capture the process of interaction and its effects on regional relations, this book defined cooperation as the process of working together in an effort to achieve common understandings.

Viewed this way, all of the multilateral working groups provided examples of cooperation, although some proved more successful than others in reaching common understandings about the nature and value of the process in which they were engaged. While all working groups struggled to turn politically divisive issues—divisive, at least, in the Middle East context—into "technical" problems more conducive to multilateral solutions, some groups were better able to depoliticize their working agendas and reach common understandings about the value of their interactions. Various factors impeded or facilitated the transformation of politically divisive issues into technically defined problems. Facilitating forces included the ability of the working groups to redefine their problems in mutual-sum rather than zero-sum terms, the development of new vocabulary and shared understandings about the nature of the problem, shifting understandings about acceptable policy options and negotiating partners, and intensified interaction among regional participants. In addition to the absence of some of these factors, impediments to successful cooperation included the influence of polarizing political processes like the bilateral track, domestic pressure and negative public opinion about the process, perceived threats to key actors' national identity and traditional regional roles, and the perception of an inequitable process. The case studies illustrated a number of these forces at work and may prove suggestive for other regions engaging in similar types of multilateral regional cooperation.

I conclude by reviewing the book's arguments for explaining both the origins and the varied development of the Arab-Israeli multilaterals. I then consider the implications of these explanations for the study of regional cooperation more generally. Finally, I suggest several policy lessons that follow from these theoretical arguments for the task of building Arab-Israeli multilateral cooperation in the coming decades.

## Explaining the Arab-Israeli Multilaterals

This book began with two central questions. First, why did such an unprecedented regional cooperation process emerge? And second, what forces can account for the varied levels of success across its working groups? After examining the empirical evidence, these questions became even more puzzling than they first appeared. For instance, given the limited regional interest in, even resistance to, forming an Arab-Israeli multilateral process, why and how did such a process emerge? Once the multilaterals were established, why did some aspects of the process survive despite its failure to serve conventional understandings of instrumental interests (e.g., wealth maximization and efficient cooperation for mutual gains)? And why did other aspects of the process fail when the favorable external conditions leading to its creation were still in place and when the process was beginning to reveal the benefits that could be gained from such cooperation?

### The Multilaterals' Origins

The origins of the multilateral peace process were the result of an external power (i.e., the United States) projecting its leadership in the region to create a process that matched central beliefs among its key policymakers. The origins of the particular working groups likewise illustrated the role of the leadership variant of power and the ideas of those projecting leadership in forming and shaping the nature of this process, and explains the choice of these cooperative forums and their particular structures. While the altered international and regional environment in the aftermath of the Cold War and Gulf conflict produced favorable conditions for greater Arab-Israeli cooperation, these environmental changes were not sufficient in themselves to bring about a new multilateral process.

The Americans did not *have* to expend the energy to create this additional peace process track, which required lengthy diplomacy by Secretary of State Baker and a good degree of arm twisting. And in the end, Secretary Baker was willing to sacrifice the initiative if it meant that Syria would refuse to attend the Madrid conference and the subsequent bilateral negotiations with Israel. This reveals how close the multilateral process came to remaining in the confines of American policy papers rather than a new regional forum for Arab-Israeli cooperation. External shifts in power balances and strategic conditions may have set the stage for some sort of Arab-Israeli cooperation, but it certainly did not dictate the formation of a novel multilateral process.

Moreover, explanations based solely on regional demand and domestic environments cannot satisfactorily explain the origins of Arab-Israeli multilateral cooperation, particularly as these forces often impeded rather than facilitated such cooperation. Many regional actors were uneasy about cooperating with Israel in a large regional forum before the resolution of the bilateral tracks, a concern that provided Syria's rationale for boycotting the talks. Indeed, Arab regimes were sensitive to negative public views about such cooperation before Israel made compromises on the Palestinian track. While a number of Arab parties were interested in a multilateral forum in order to foster better bilateral relations with the United States and other extraregional participants, a strong regional demand for such a process was not apparent. The diffuse regional interests—not to mention the numerous regional forces working against the formation of a multilateral process—were not sufficient to create a regional multilateral forum that included Israel. Rather, to understand the origins of the multilateral working groups, we must turn to actors *outside* the region.

A small group of policy elites within the Bush administration—who were part of a larger community of Middle East experts in Washington, D.C.—

shared similar notions about how to resolve the Arab-Israeli conflict and greatly influenced American policy in this area, including the formation of the multilateral track of the peace process. Without the ideas and leadership of this group of elites, it is unlikely the multilaterals would have emerged. Because these policymakers believed Israel had to be politically accepted by (normalized in) the broader region for an enduring peace, they preferred to establish cooperative processes with wide regional participation—including the Gulf and North African states—even though smaller, subregional forums might have more efficiently and successfully dealt with the issue areas under discussion.

The normative aspect of American diplomacy cannot be ignored. The American elites who structured the Madrid and Moscow conferences were committed to Israeli normalization in the Middle East and believed it was worth capitalizing on a revived peace process to create a forum that would enhance this goal. These U.S. policymakers focused more on the process itself and its value in facilitating the bilateral tracks than on the substantive results that might emerge from it. In fact, the purpose and prospects for the multilaterals beyond the Moscow organizational session were uncertain and not of great concern to senior U.S. policymakers. The multilateral's origins demonstrate that its founders had little understanding of or interest in what the process could substantively produce across the issue areas ultimately included on its agenda, but very clear ideas about how regional relations needed to be restructured and the role a multilateral process could play in this effort.

## The Multilaterals' Development

Although each working group developed its own pace, and while the particular dynamics driving or impeding regional cooperation varied from one group to the next, a common pattern of development emerged across all issue areas. The leadership of the United States and other key extra-regional parties continued to play an important role in facilitating the agendas of the working groups, but it was no longer the most important factor. Moreover, Arabs and most Israelis alike decidedly rejected the vision of a "New Middle East," with Israel integrated into the larger Arab region much as states were integrated in Europe. The continuation and development of Arab-Israeli multilateral cooperation continued *in spite* of this idea and en-

## Conclusion

dured significant setbacks in the bilateral peace track because other regional interests were at stake.

The focus of the explanation shifts from external to regional parties as the process develops. The way in which regional parties perceived the process was most critical in shaping the nature and outcomes of the working groups. The groups better able to overcome politically divisive issues and turn their issue areas into "technical" problems, where multilateral cooperation was valued for both substantive (i.e., its ability to address the problems on its agenda) and political (i.e., its ability to enhance the status of regional participants) reasons, proved more successful. The case studies demonstrated that the REDWG, Environment, and Water working groups were more successful at reaching common understandings about the value of a multilateral cooperative process than was the ACRS group. But in all cases, the assumption of interests based on power position or efficiency concerns was not as revealing as understanding how particular states viewed a new multilateral process and how sometimes, as in the case of arms control, the parties developed negative positions toward such cooperation. A brief review of each issue area will demonstrate the value of examining the process of interaction and its impact on the perceptions of the participants in order to understand the varied development of the multilateral working groups.

ACRS, for example, represents a limited failure according to a process conception of cooperation because the ACRS process did not ultimately lead to common understandings of regional security, and in fact even exacerbated regional divisions. ACRS did make unexpected progress in forwarding a regional security agenda. A multilateral negotiating process was established, a working agenda defined, substantive negotiations took place and an initial series of agreements on confidence-building measures (CBMs), confidence- and security-building measures (CSBMs), and other regional security initiatives were negotiated. Indeed, compared to other regional security processes, such as the European Conference on Security and Cooperation (CSCE) in its early stages, ACRS's progress was noteworthy. But ultimately, the working group was unable to transform highly charged political issues surrounding the security issue area, particularly Israel's nuclear capabilities, into a technical problem more conducive to a multilateral solution. One cannot understand why this transformation failed to occur without examining how key participants in ACRS viewed the process. In particular, one of the most critical members of ACRS, Egypt, increasingly viewed ACRS in a negative light because it began to threaten Egypt's traditional leadership role in the region and, in Egypt's view, was leading to initiatives that favored Israel and Egypt's traditional Arab rival, Jordan, at Egypt's expense. Thus, the process itself created political impediments that proved even more difficult to overcome than the strategic obstacles working against Arab-Israeli security cooperation.

In contrast, REDWG and its related cooperative forums proved more successful, and aspects of the process even endured a number of serious setbacks in the bilateral track. This is not to say that activity in this issue area did not face obstacles; indeed, many of the economic cooperative efforts slowed after the 1996 Israeli election, particularly those projects and institutions that depended on public sector support. Yet many aspects of this process continued, albeit in varied fashion, even during the bleakest moments in Israeli-Palestinian relations. Unlike ACRS, REDWG was better able to depoliticize the process so that the participants saw the value of cooperating in a regional, multilateral fashion. Participants reached common understandings about the purpose and utility of economic cooperation, in large part because of changing conceptions about the nature of economic development and the impact of globalization on regional relations. Specifically, regional participants developed common conceptions about the role of Arab-Israeli economic cooperation in attracting foreign investment in a globalized economy. Regional cooperation was favored not because the parties desired an integrated region but rather because they viewed such cooperation as enhancing the prospects for the region's integration into the global economy and for private sector investment. This explains why cooperative efforts and institutions that served globalization goals with outward-oriented agendas (such as initiatives to create a regional tourism association and a regional development bank) proved more resilient to bilateral setbacks than those initiatives which focused almost exclusively on intraregional projects (such as a regional business council). And in contrast to ACRS, key regional participants like Egypt viewed the process as enhancing rather than undermining its regional role and status with the creation of new institutions and cooperative forums that brought international attention and potential investment.

Similarly, the Water and Environment groups were able to develop common understandings about the value of the multilateral process (for both political and substantive reasons), allowing cooperative ventures to continue—albeit more slowly and erratically—in the midst of a slowed and even frozen bilateral peace process. Yet even these more inherently technical issues—where gains from regional cooperation were most obvious—faced political impediments, forcing the participants to reach understandings about the value of making these problems areas for mutual gain. Consequently, to explain the development of both these working groups, an understanding of regional support for the process is critical. However, this support cannot be assumed based on the functional need of the parties to cooperate on these issues to most efficiently solve these common problems. Rather, regional support for technical cooperation had to be *developed*. At times this support had very little, if anything, to do with the technical knowledge or substantive problem on the agenda. Rather, it was based on concerns about gaining political leverage vis-à-vis regional rivals and enhancing one's regional role. For example, small Gulf states were interested in seeing multilateral cooperation continue not just because it helped solve regional problems that could not be addressed at the bilateral level, but also because it served their political interests in gaining more leverage and attention relative to Saudi Arabia, its larger Gulf neighbor and the dominant force within the GCC. Hosting regional centers and institutions which emerged from the process provided legitimacy and attracted potential funding from international donors. As in the case of security and economic cooperation, these working groups had to make efforts to turn political problems into technical ones and were able to do so because they ultimately perceived these cooperative processes as substantively and politically valuable.

## Implications for the Study of Regional Cooperation

What do the arguments laid out in this book suggest about the study of regional cooperation processes more generally? First, the book's focus on the process by which cooperation takes place underscores the need to pay attention to nascent cooperative efforts, including those that do not produce major policy initiatives. Indeed, with the end of the Cold War the study of regional relations has re-emerged as an important area for theoretical and empirical inquiry, in both the economic and security realms.[1] Many regional forums have emerged or developed over the last decade in ways that provide interesting areas of inquiry for international relations scholars. However, this study suggests that the process of interaction which takes place within these forums should not be neglected in favor of examining only the outcomes to which they lead. The cooperative process of regional forums and institutions should be given as much attention as the results which they seek to produce. Such an approach will also alter the criteria by which we judge the value of such efforts, which otherwise might be dismissed as insignificant.

Second, power explanations focused on the role of global or regional hegemons cannot fully explain the emergence and development of regional cooperation. Power variables may shed light on why such forums emerge, especially when we move beyond deduced structural power explanations to those based on the role of leadership in the projection of power. But the cases of Arab-Israeli multilateral cooperation demonstrate growing regional initiative as these forums developed. Thus, we must move beyond Cold War paradigms focusing on a handful of great powers and shift attention to regional actors to explain both the prospects and limits of regional cooperation.

Third, both the origins and development of Arab-Israeli multilateral cooperation demonstrate the limits of assuming interests based on either the structural position of actors in the regional environment or material economic interests based on maximizing wealth and efficiency. Rather, these cases highlight the advantages of examining actor perceptions, particularly how the actors themselves view the cooperative process. The basis of actor perceptions may, but need not be, materially motivated. Other nonmaterial factors, such as political identity and status concerns, can play as important a role in determining the fate of such efforts. Thus, the value of regional cooperation lies not only in how it solves substantive problems like economic development or water scarcity but also in how it furthers perceived political interests among its participants.

Consequently, this study also suggests that we scrutinize the conventional wisdom in the IR literature that some issues are "easier" areas for cooperation than others. True, the economic, water, and environmental aspects of the Arab-Israeli process did prove more successful than the security aspects. But if we examine the cooperative process itself, we see that the dynamics operating across all groups were fairly similar. All groups were politicized and competitive to a certain extent. But the particularly competitive nature of security issues does not preclude cooperation from taking place, just as successful cooperation is not a foregone conclusion in other issue areas. While we may still find conceptual advantages to making such distinctions among issue areas, it is not clear that empirical evidence would support these distinctions in all cases.

Finally, to understand the forces that both facilitate and impede cooperation, one must look at the nature of the interaction itself. Studies of regional cooperation thus might ask the following types of questions: Are actors changing the way in which they define problems and developing new understandings and common vocabulary? Are they shifting their understandings of acceptable policy options and partners? Has interaction intensified among the participants to allow them to reach such common understandings? On the other hand, does one observe polarizing political forces impeding the cooperation process? Is domestic pressure or negative public opinion infringing on the ability of actors to make progress? Do the actors perceive cooperation as a threat to their regional roles? Do they perceive it as producing inequitable results favoring one party at another's expense? Have perceptions changed about the value of cooperation based on new understandings of the external environment and its "imperatives"? These are the types of questions one can begin to ask when evaluating the level of success among different regional processes, or the extent to which regional actors are able to reach common understandings through the process of working together.

## Building Arab-Israeli Multilateral Cooperation: Policy Lessons

Taken together, the forces underlying the origins and development of the Arab-Israeli multilateral process offer instructive lessons about how to build such cooperation in the future. To be sure, the bilateral peace track, particularly the Israeli-Palestinian negotiations, must be on the road to resolution before ambitious regional cooperation can be realized. However, the study also demonstrates that these bilateral relationships are not the *only* force facilitating or impeding broader regional cooperation. We need to begin thinking about these other forces so that, if and when the bilateral conflicts are resolved, we do not find ourselves surprised that regional cooperation does not instantly flourish. We need to ask what other factors, beyond the requisite progress in the Israeli-Palestinian negotiating track, have played and will most likely continue to play a role in both facilitating and impeding regional multilateral cooperation. What problems can we expect, and what policies can best address these obstacles to Arab-Israeli regional cooperation? I focus on four central lessons for future policy:

*Recognize the importance and limits of American leadership.*
The analysis demonstrated that while American leadership may be necessary for the formation of new Arab-Israeli multilateral institutions, it is not sufficient to sustain such cooperation if regional parties perceive the process as undermining core interests. That said, by recognizing the limitations of American leadership, leadership can be employed skillfully to enhance cooperative outcomes. Rather than promoting the multilaterals principally as an effort toward the normalization of Israel in the region, American policymakers should adapt their regional agenda to evolving regional conceptions of interests. American policymakers should also promote the multilaterals and their related institutions not as a bilateral peace process tool, but rather as a means for regional parties to satisfy other objectives, such as economic interests, status aspirations, or a desire to strengthen bilateral ties with the United States and other key Western powers. The difficulties faced by the fourth MENA economic summit in Doha in November 1997 illustrated the drawback of the former approach—promoting the multilateral process largely as a tool for the bilateral process.[2] The original intent to use the economic summits as a tool for Israeli economic normalization backfired on efforts to promote regional cooperation, with the summits becoming a convenient medium for Arab states to express displeasure with peace process developments rather than an economic event to increase international interest in the region. The political profile of such events must be lowered in the future and the Israeli aspect of the conference deemphasized to match increasing regional interests in furthering globalization objectives through such forums.

As important as Israeli inclusion within the region is to the creation of a stable Middle East, the evolution of the multilateral economic process away from Israeli integration and toward Middle East integration globally might prove a healthy development. In many ways, forcing Israel's integration into the region through a focus on intraregional schemes can undermine support for the peace process, contrary to intentions. Naturally, American and other extraregional support for Arab-Israeli cooperative projects, particularly in more promising areas like tourism and joint ventures among the Israeli-Jordanian-Palestinian triad, should continue. But attention should be paid to sustaining forums where Israel is not the focus nor intraregional cooperation the sole aim. Routinizing, rather than highlighting, Israeli participation in regional forums best enhances Israeli normalization.

In the security realm, proposals either to jump-start ACRS or create other types of regional security frameworks must acknowledge the limits of American power and the need to build a regional consensus on security issues. While American leadership can play an important role in bridging some of the conceptual gaps between the parties by designing creative solutions that might depoliticize the nuclear debate, ultimately the regional parties will decide the fate of future multilateral security frameworks. Consequently, any proposal must be sensitive to the ideational foundations of security cooperation, particularly how regional players perceive such cooperation in terms of preserving their political identity or at least not undermining other core political interests. More attention thus must be paid to the Egyptian role in multilateral security cooperation. Allowing the Egyptians to host new regional security institutions, for instance, may entice more cooperative positions from Cairo, particularly if the nuclear question is addressed more explicitly in the group.

***Build consensual regional interests even if they are not directly related to the American peace process agenda. Avoid enhancing one regional player's role at the expense of another. Utilize track two initiatives to facilitate a regional security dialogue in ACRS's absence.***
The more that regional parties can reach a consensus on regional problems—even if this consensus has little if anything to do with the peace process itself—the greater the prospects for cooperative relations generally. This has proved to be the case in the development of multilateral economic cooperation, where consensual understandings about the role of globalization and the pressures it creates for a more stable regional environment enhanced the prospects for positive cooperation, albeit with political limits. Political interests in utilizing a multilateral forum to facilitate unrelated agendas of regional parties (such as enhancing one's regional role and status) can also play well into building enduring regional frameworks. The more these types of consensual interests can be fostered by deemphasizing the peace process motivations that led to the creation of the multilaterals, the more likely it is that regional cooperation can withstand the inevitable setbacks at the bilateral level.

Moreover, the framework employed in the study suggests that negative positions toward regional cooperation need not be permanent, even in the contentious security realm. Egyptian positions, for example, may change in ways that could enhance, rather than undermine, regional security cooperation if policy elites believe the process does not threaten Egypt's political identity and possibly enhances it. Israel must make an effort to help sustain Egypt's privileged position within the multilateral framework and clearly express the limited nature of its economic interests in the region. Housing new regional institutions in Cairo, such as a Middle East development bank, will enhance the incentives for Egypt to continue to value rather than fear regional cooperation. While even a durable ACRS process will leave serious regional security threats in the region—particularly from non-ACRS participants like Syria, Iran, Iraq, and Libya as well as from internal threats to many regional regimes—bringing the Egyptians into more cooperative regional security institutions and frameworks is an essential ingredient for regional stability.

And finally, the effort to build common understandings can be strengthened by the continuation of track two dialogues among regional parties. Track two diplomacy brings regional officials and experts together in unofficial settings where more candid discussion of regional security issues can take place. Several track two exercises facilitated the creation and early success of ACRS's work agenda, particularly as it brought many of the same officials involved in the formal process together to discuss similar issues in a much less formal atmosphere. After ACRS's breakdown, many of these efforts continued, and some new ones emerged to fill the vacuum left by the freezing of the official ACRS process.[3] Track two dialogues allow key military officials to continue interacting even at low points in the political process and enhance the prospects for the resumption of a regional security dialogue in the future. Moreover, because some of the track two projects do not receive U.S. government funding, they can include Iranians and nongovernmental Iraqis in an unusual setting where Israelis are also present. The inclusion of these parties in regional security discussions is particularly important for building future understandings about regional security given the significance of these states to both the Arab-Israeli and Gulf security contexts.

*Avoid an overarching regional security regime before bilateral disputes have been resolved and multilateral cooperation regularized.*
Several ideas for new regional security frameworks and institutions have been discussed with greater intensity since the end of the Gulf War within both the unofficial and official peace process tracks. However, the proposal which received the highest profile was the initiative to establish a Confer-

ence (or Organization) for Security and Cooperation in the Middle East (CSCME/OSCME), of which there are several regional versions.[4] Indeed, such a proposal was even included in the Israel-Jordan peace treaty in Article 4 (Security), Section 1b, which called for the creation of a CSCME.

Lessons learned from the successful aspects of the multilaterals suggest that proposals to establish an OSCE-type structure are too broad at this juncture in Arab-Israeli relations, despite the continued need to build regional processes and institutions that go beyond bilateral relationships. But this need can be addressed differently than as suggested by ambitious schemes like a single Arab-Israeli institution modeled on the CSCE, where the security and economic (and possibly the human rights) "baskets" would be embedded within one overarching structure.

On the one hand, a CSCE-type structure seems appropriate for the Arab-Israeli context. For example, the CSCE's basket structure works well to categorize common regional problems in the Middle East. The bipolar nature of the CSCE between the East and West blocs is similar to the original bipolar nature of Arab-Israeli relations at the outset of the multilateral process. The CSCE process increased contacts between East and West, particularly among its scientific communities. This type of interaction between Arabs and Israelis proved useful in the multilaterals as experts shared knowledge in an effort to solve practical problems of common concern. Moreover, the incremental CBM and CSBM approach in the CSCE has worked well in the Middle East context—particularly before ACRS's breakdown—in building trust and personal relations among former adversaries. Finally, the Arab-Israeli multilaterals adopted the CSCE's consensus rule, easing fears over sovereignty and domination by the more powerful players in the process.

Yet it took fifteen years for the CSCE to move to an institutionalized stage, which was only possible with the decline of the Soviet Union and the end of the Cold War. While time is probably less a factor than the appropriate political climate in the case of the Middle East, a CSCE process in the Arab-Israeli arena is too broad and ambitious at this stage of Arab-Israeli relations. A single overarching structure for Arab-Israeli cooperation risks dangerous linkages among the baskets, where the setbacks of arms control, for instance, could also slow economic development progress—linkages that have been avoided by keeping the multilateral working groups distinct. During difficult periods in the bilateral negotiating tracks, regional cooperation is best promoted by as many interactive processes as possible, in a decentralized and low-profile manner. Institutions (plural) are positive outcomes of working group activities, but an institution (singular) could cause unnecessary polarization and would likely be held captive to setbacks in the political process. After a comprehensive peace in the region has been reached, consideration of proposals like an OSCME would be more appropriate as the need for a coordinating body to direct and consolidate regional norms and cooperation would increase. At present, these ideas are premature and even counterproductive.

*Create and facilitate greater decentralization of the multilaterals and related processes.*
The empirical cases demonstrated that decentralizing cooperative processes enhanced the prospects that such cooperation would continue. In the economic, water, and environment cases, the smaller subgroups that operationalized the working groups' agendas were far more successful than the large, centralized plenary forum. ACRS could benefit from following a similar pattern of smaller spin-off forums for cooperative activity. Decentralizing cooperation and turning to smaller, minilateral settings is not a guarantee for success, but it can improve the prospects for a more resilient process in the expectation that bilateral relations will continue to generate regional crises that will make regional cooperation difficult.

# Appendix A

Concluding Remarks by
Secretary of State James A. Baker III
Before the Organizational Meeting
for Multilateral Negotiations on
the Middle East (January 28, 1992)

As we approach the end of our first day, let me start my concluding remarks by saying, quite simply, that I am encouraged that this organizational meeting is taking place, because I think that the launching of these multilateral talks is another important milestone in what I referred to earlier as the historic road that we began in Madrid.

Many here have demonstrated real creativity and vision in the ideas that have been suggested here today and the comments that have been made here. It was heartening to hear some of my colleagues from the Middle East talk about the rich potential of regional cooperation. And, it is also heartening to hear of the readiness of many countries around this table from outside the region to pitch in and help realize that potential.

It should be surprising to no one that we heard today of difficulties as well as possibilities and that we spoke today candidly of problems as well as hopes. It is obvious that enduring regional cooperation will not be possible without progress toward resolving core political disputes that are involved in the multilateral negotiations, and many speakers today have made mention of that. It is obvious that many of the questions discussed today, like arms control and regional security or water, are inherently complex subjects.

But it is equally obvious to me, as I mentioned this morning, that systematic consideration of those kinds of issues can be a complement and can be a catalyst for the bilateral talks and for progress in the bilateral talks, and, of course, the bilateral talks remain the heart of the peace-making process.

We regret that three of the regional parties invited to attend—Syria, Lebanon, and the Palestinians—are not here today. We continue to believe that these three parties could make a significant contribution to the work of these multilateral negotiations, and we encourage them to participate as this process evolves. At the same time, we believe this process can work to their benefit.

Palestinians, in particular, we think, have much to gain from such participation. As Minister Kozyrev and I made clear earlier today—publicly and to the Palestinians—we would be supportive of Palestinian requests to include diaspora representatives in appropriate working groups, such as refugees and economic development, after the Moscow meeting. However, the terms of reference for this meeting, as reflected in the original invitations, call for Palestinian representation based on the Madrid formula, and they should not be changed at the last minute if this entire process is to continue to have credibility with all of us. We regret that the Palestinians are not here. They have chosen not to come, and, in my view, they have once again passed up an important opportunity.

We also regret that the United Nations, which was invited to attend, is not here. We hope for full UN participation in the working groups as the process moves ahead. UN specialized agencies could play an important role in supporting this process.

Now, with the active participation of those here today and with the potential future involvement of others, I think it is time to get to work. And, I think that we have before us a reasonable framework for collective and constructive action.

Tomorrow morning at 10:00, we will begin to discuss five initial working groups—working groups in arms control and regional security, economic development, water, environment, and refugees.

These discussions will be followed this spring by a range of specific follow-up steps, from missions to the region to seminars and perhaps further meetings.

—The European Community has indicated its willingness to play a leading role in promoting regional economic development.

—Japan is considering a mission to the region to explore possibilities for environmental cooperation in the Gulf of Aqaba. It has also made clear its readiness to help regional parties address some broader environmental challenges.

—The water group will be discussing timing, venue, and possible agenda for a first seminar on regional water cooperation.

—I am pleased to confirm that the United States is prepared to host a seminar on arms control and regional security.

—The refugee group will consider practical ways of improving the lot of people throughout the region who have been displaced from their homes. I am particularly pleased that Canada has indicated its readiness to play a leading role in promoting regional cooperation in this area.

In addition, we think consideration should be given to forming an ad hoc steering group. The purposes of such a group would be to provide continuity, to monitor the efforts of the five initial working groups as and when they are formed, and to consider the formation of additional groups.

As we prepare for tomorrow's meetings, I think there are several things we should keep in mind.

First, I think we ought to all remember, because we've all spoken about it up here, the opportunity created by these multilateral discussions. They offer a real and valuable chance to address issues of major importance that do not lend themselves to discussion of the bilateral framework.

Secondly, we should not forget the potential for the multilateral talks to help create a political environment in which the bilateral talks are more likely to accomplish what we all want in the areas of peace, territory, and security.

Third, we should take full advantage of the experience, the expertise, and resources of others, both inside and outside the region.

Fourth, while keeping our horizons and ambitions broad, it might be best if we were to focus initially on some small, practical steps that provide a foundation on which we can build.

Fifth, we should recognize that consensus among all the parties directly concerned is the only sensible way to move ahead in the working groups. Peace is not going to be imposed from the outside; neither can various forms of regional cooperation be imposed. Progress on regional issues requires effort and commitment, particularly by regional parties themselves.

No one should expect immediate breakthroughs toward multilateral cooperation in the Middle East, but neither should we neglect the possibilities for cooperation which exist at this unique moment in the history of the region and at this unique moment in the history of the world.

Look around you, ladies and gentlemen, at the parties gathered at this table. Who would have imagined 50 years ago that the nations of Europe, many of whom were for centuries the fiercest of enemies, would find lasting common purpose in a vibrant European Community? And, who would have imagined even 5 years ago that the United States would launch a new partnership with a democratizing Russia? Who really knows what kinds of cooperation, however improbable it might seem today, might be possible in the Middle East over the rest of this decade?

So, in closing, let me again thank Andrei Kozyrev and his government for their gracious hospitality and for undertaking the logistical difficulties of putting on a conference such as this on short notice. And, my friends, let us all press ahead with renewed determination and renewed energy to make multilateral cooperation a reality in a region which has already known far more than its share of conflict.

# Appendix B

Article 4: Security.
Treaty of Peace Between the State of Israel and the Hashemite Kingdom of Jordan (October 26, 1994)

### Article 4 — Security

1. a. Both Parties, acknowledging that mutual understanding and co-operation in security-related matters will form a significant part of their relations and will further enhance the security of the region, take upon themselves to base their security relations on mutual trust, advancement of joint interests and co-operation, and to aim towards a regional framework of partnership in peace.

b. Towards that goal the Parties recognize the achievements of the European Community and European Union in the development of the Conference on Security and Co-operation in Europe (CSCE) and commit themselves to the creation, in the Middle East, of a CSCME (Conference on Security and Co-operation in the Middle East). This commitment entails the adoption of regional models of security successfully implemented in the post World War era (along the lines of the Helsinki process) culminating in a regional zone of security and stability.

2. The obligations referred to in this Article are without prejudice to the inherent right of self-defence in accordance with the United Nations Charter.

3. The Parties undertake, in accordance with the provisions of this Article, the following:

a. to refrain from the threat or use of force or weapons, conventional, non-conventional or of any other kind, against each other, or of other actions or activities that adversely affect the security of the other Party;

b. to refrain from organising, instigating, inciting, assisting or participating in acts or threats of belligerency, hostility, subversion or violence against the other Party;

c. to take necessary and effective measures to ensure that acts or threats of belligerency, hostility, subversion or violence against the other Party do not originate from, and are not committed within, through or over their territory (hereinafter the term "territory" includes the airspace and territorial waters).

4. Consistent with the era of peace and with the efforts to build regional security and to avoid and prevent aggression and violence, the Parties further agree to refrain from the following:

a. joining or in any way assisting, promoting or co-operating with any coalition, organization or alliance with a military or security character with a third party, the objectives or activities of which include launching aggression or other acts of military hostility against the other Party, in contravention of the provisions of the present Treaty.

b. allowing the entry, stationing and operating on their territory, or through it, of military forces, personnel or materiel of a third party, in circumstances which may adversely prejudice the security of the other Party.

5. Both Parties will take necessary and effective measures, and will co-operate in combating terrorism of all kinds. The Parties undertake:

a. to take necessary and effective measures to prevent acts of terrorism, subversion or violence from being carried out from their territory or through it and to take necessary and effective measures to combat such activities and all their perpetrators.

b. without prejudice to the basic rights of freedom of expression and association, to take necessary and effective measures to prevent the entry, presence and co-operation in their territory of any group or organisation, and their infrastructure, which threatens the security of the other Party by the use of or incitement to the use of, violent means.

c. to co-operate in preventing and combating cross-boundary infiltrations.

6. Any question as to the implementation of this Article will be dealt with through a mechanism of consultations which will include a liaison system, verification, supervision, and where necessary, other mechanisms, and higher level consultation. The details of the mechanism of consultations will be contained in an agreement to be concluded by the Parties within 3 months of the exchange of the instruments of ratification of this Treaty.

7. The Parties undertake to work as a matter of priority, and as soon as possible in the context of the Multilateral Working Group on Arms Control and Regional Security, and jointly, towards the following:

a. the creation in the Middle East of a region free from hostile alliances and coalitions;

b. the creation of a Middle East free from weapons of mass destruction, both conventional and non-conventional, in the context of a comprehensive, lasting and stable peace, characterised by the renunciation of the use of force, reconciliation and goodwill.

# Appendix C

## Declaration of Principles and Statements of Intent on Arms Control and Regional Security[1]

### Preamble

The regional participants in the Arms Control and Regional Security working group,

Reaffirming their respect for the UN Charter,

Bearing in mind the urgent necessity of achieving a just, lasting and comprehensive peace settlement in the Middle East based on U.N. Resolutions 242 and 338, and conscious of the historic breakthroughs since the 1991 Madrid Middle East Peace Conference, particularly the Israeli-Palestinian Declaration of Principles and the Common Agenda between Jordan and Israel,

Recognizing that the multilateral working groups, including the Arms Control and Regional Security working group, should continue to complement the bilateral negotiations and help improve the climate for resolving the core issues at the heart of the Middle East peace process, and that the Madrid Conference also created the opportunity to cooperate in addressing additional issues of region-wide concern,

Agreeing that all regional parties should pursue the common purpose of achieving full and lasting relations of peace, openness, mutual confidence, security, stability and cooperation throughout the region,

Embarking in this context on a process through the Arms Control and Regional Security working group to establish arms control and regional security arrangements aimed at achieving equal security for all at the lowest possible level of armaments and military forces, safeguarding the region from the dangers and ominous consequences of future wars and the horrors of mass destruction, and enabling all possible resources to be devoted to the welfare of the peoples of the region, including such areas as economic and social development,

Recognizing the importance of preventing the proliferation of nuclear, chemical, and biological weapons and of preventing the excessive accumulation of conventional arms in enhancing international and regional peace and security,

Aware that military means, while needed to fulfill the inherent right of self-defense and to discourage aggression, cannot by themselves provide security and that enduring security requires the peaceful resolution of conflicts in the region and the promotion of common interests,

Conscious that the arms control and regional security process seeks to achieve a stable balance among military capabilities in the region that takes into account quantitative, qualitative and structural factors, and that provides for equal security for all,

Welcoming the special role of the United States and Russia as active co-sponsors of the Middle East peace process, and calling on them and other extra-regional states to provide continuing support for the objectives and arrangements of the arms control and regional security process,

Recognizing that the full realization of the objectives contained in this Declaration would be facilitated by the involvement in the arms control and regional security process of all regional parties, and calling on all such parties to support the principles contained in this Declaration and, in this connection, to join the arms control and regional security process at an early date,

Have adopted the following:

## Guidelines for the Middle East Arms Control and Regional Security Process

The participants recognize the following as guidelines for the arms control and regional security process:

—The arms control and regional security process, as an integral part of the Middle East peace process, should create a favorable climate for progress in the bilateral negotiations and complement them by preparing and implementing measures in parallel with progress in the bilateral talks.

—The arms control and regional security process should strive to enhance security and general stability on a region-wide basis, even beyond the scope of the Arab-Israeli conflict, by pursuing regional security and arms control measures that reduce tension or the risk of war.

—The scope of the process must be comprehensive, covering a broad range of regional security, confidence and security building, and arms control measures that address all threats to security and all categories of arms, conventional and non-conventional.

—The basic framework of the process is to pursue a determined, step-by-step approach which sets ambitious goals and proceeds toward them in a realistic way.

—At no stage should the arms control and regional security process diminish the security of any individual state or give a state a military advantage over any other.

—The basis for decision-making on each issue in the arms control and regional security process should be consensus by the regional participants directly concerned.

## Statements of Intent on Objectives for the Arms Control and Regional Security Process

In the context of achieving a just, secure, comprehensive and lasting peace and reconciliation, the participants agree to pursue, inter alia, the following arms control and regional security objectives:

—preventing conflict from occurring through misunderstanding or miscalculation by adopting confidence and security building measures that increase transparency and openness and reduce the risk of surprise attack and by developing regional institutional arrangements that enhance security and the process of arms control;

—limiting military spending in the region so that additional resources can be made available to other areas such as economic and social development;

—reducing stockpiles of conventional arms and preventing a conventional arms race in the region as part of an effort to provide enhanced security at lower levels of armaments and militarization, to reduce the threat of large-scale destruction posed by such weapons, and to move towards force structures that do not exceed legitimate defensive requirements; and

—establishing a zone free of all weapons of mass destruction, including nuclear, chemical, and biological weapons and their delivery systems.

# Appendix D

## Statement by the Cooperation Council of the Arab States of the Gulf on the Cancellation by the GCC of the Secondary/Tertiary Arab Boycott of Israel (October 1, 1994)

The Cooperation Council of the Arab States of the Gulf, having actively supported the Middle East Peace Process ever since the launching of the Madrid Conference, and being fully aware of the important breakthroughs realized so far, particularly in the Palestinian and Jordanian tracks which comprise agreements covering economic cooperation between the Israelis and both the Jordanians and the Palestinians, seriously recognize the importance of a review of the provisions of the Arab boycott of Israel so as to take into consideration progress achieved and substantive future requirements of the peace process.

The GCC member states have constantly reiterated their determination to enhance cooperation with their trading partners in various spheres. Concerning the application of the Arab boycott of Israel, necessary measures have been taken with a view to protecting the mutual interests of the GCC and its trading partners. As a result of these measures and for all practical purposes, the secondary and tertiary boycott are no longer a threat to the interests of these partners.

Whereas the Arab boycott of Israel was enacted by the League of the Arab States, and its review to take into consideration developments and requirements of the Middle East peace process must take place, the GCC member states will support all or any initiative for such review presented in the League of Arab States. Further, the GCC believe that a sponsorship of such initiative by Arab parties directly involved in the bilateral negotiations, whether selectively or individually, shall facilitate the required review and ensure a greater chance of success.

# Appendix E

Casablanca Declaration
Middle East/North Africa Economic Summit
(October 30–November 1, 1994)

1. At the invitation of His Majesty King Hassan II of Morocco and with the support and endorsement of Presidents Bill Clinton of the United Sates and Boris Yeltsin of the Russian Federation, the representatives of 61 countries and 1,114 business leaders from all regions of the world, gathered for a Middle East/North Africa Economic Summit in Casablanca from October 30 to November 1, 1994. The participants paid tribute to His Majesty, King Hassan II, in his capacity as President and Host of the Conference and praised his role in promoting dialogue and understanding between the parties in the Middle East conflict. They also expressed their appreciation to the Government and people of Morocco for their hospitality and efforts to ensure the success of the Summit.

2. The Summit leaders feel united behind the vision that brought them to Casablanca, that of a comprehensive peace and a new partnership of business and government dedicated to furthering peace between Arabs and Israelis.

3. Government and business leaders entered into this new partnership with a deeper understanding of their mutual dependence and common goals. Business leaders recognized that governments should continue to forge peace agreements and create foundations and incentives for trade and investment. They further recognize the responsibility of the private sector to apply its new international influence to advance the diplomacy of peace in

the Middle East and beyond. Governments affirmed the indispensability of the private sector in marshalling, quickly, adequate resources to demonstrate the tangible benefits of peace. Together, they pledged to show that business can do business and contribute to peace as well; indeed, to prove that profitability contributes mightily to the economic scaffolding for a durable peace.

4. The Summit commended the historic political transformation of the region as a consequence of significant steps towards a just, lasting and comprehensive peace, based on U.N. Security Council Resolutions 242 and 338, a process that began with the 1979 Treaty of Peace between Egypt and Israel and enlarged dramatically by the Madrid Peace conference, three years ago. That process has born fruit in the Israel-Palestine Liberation Organization Declaration of Principles. The recent signing of the Treaty of Peace between Israel and Jordan gave a new dimension to the process. The decisions of Morocco and Tunisia to establish, respectively, liaison offices and liaison channels with Israel, constituted another new positive development. These accomplishments and the next stages of rapid movement toward a comprehensive peace in the region, including Syria and Lebanon, need to be powerfully reinforced by solid economic growth and palpable improvement of the life and security of the peoples of this region. The Summit stressed that Syria and Lebanon have an important role to play in the development of the region. The Summit expressed a strong hope that they will soon be able to join the regional economic effort.

5. In this connection, the participants noted that the urgent need for economic development of the West Bank and Gaza Strip requires special attention from the international community, both public and private, in order to support the Israel-Palestine Liberation Organization Declaration of Principles and subsequent implementing agreements to enable the Palestinian people to participate on equal bases in the regional development and cooperation. They stressed the equal importance of moving ahead on Jordanian-Israeli projects as well as on cooperative projects between Israel and Jordan in order to advance the Jordanian-Israeli Treaty of Peace.

6. The participants recognized the economic potential of the Middle East and North Africa and explored how best to accelerate the development of the region and overcome, as soon as possible, obstacles, including boycotts and all barriers to trade and investment. All agreed that there is a need to

promote increased investment from inside and outside the region. They noted that such investment requires free movement of goods, capital and labour across borders in accordance with market forces, technical cooperation based on mutual interest, openness to the international economy and appropriate institutions to promote economic interaction. They also noted that the free flow of ideas and increased dialogue, especially among the business communities in the region, will strengthen economic activity. In this context, the participants noted favourably the decision of the Council for Cooperation of the Gulf States regarding the lifting of the secondary and the tertiary aspects of the boycott of Israel.

7. Based on the agreements between Israel and the PLO, it is important that the borders of the Palestinian Territories be kept open for labour, tourism and trade to allow the Palestinian Authority, in partnership with its neighbours, the opportunity to build a viable economy in peace.

8. The participants paid tribute to the multilateral negotiations initiated in Moscow in 1992 which have significantly advanced the objectives of the peace process. The governments represented at Casablanca will examine ways to enhance the role and activities of the multilateral negotiations, including examining regional institutions which address economic, humanitarian and security issues. The participants noted that the progresses made in the peace process should go along with a serious consideration of the socio-economic disparities in the region and require to address the idea of security in the region in all its dimensions: social, economic and political. In this context, they agreed that these issues need to be addressed within the framework of a global approach encompassing socio-economic dimensions, safety and welfare of individuals and nations of the region.

9. The participants recognized that there must be an ongoing process to translate the deliberations of Casablanca into concrete steps to advance the twin goals of peace and economic development and to institutionalize the new partnership between governments and the business community. To this end:

  a. The governments represented at Casablanca and private sector representatives stated their intention to take the following steps:

  — Build the foundations for a Middle East and North Africa Economic Community which involves, at a determined stage, the free flow of goods, capital and labour throughout the region.

—Taking into account the recommendations of the regional parties during the meeting of the sub-committee on finances of the REDWG monitoring committee, the Casablanca Summit calls for a group of experts to examine the different options for funding mechanisms including the creation of a Middle East and North Africa Development Bank. This group of experts will report on its progress and conclusions within six months in the light of the follow on Summit to the Casablanca Conference. The funding mechanism would include appropriate bodies to promote dialogue on economic reform, regional cooperation, technical assistance and long-term development planning.

—Establish a regional Tourist Board to facilitate tourism and promote the Middle East and North Africa as a unique and attractive tourist destination.

—Encourage the establishment of a private sector Regional Chamber of Commerce and Business Council to facilitate intra-regional trade relations. Such organizations will be instrumental in solidifying ties between the private and public sectors of the various economies.

b. The participants also intend to create the following mechanisms to implement these understandings and embody the new public-private collaboration:

—A Steering Committee, comprised of government representatives, including those represented in the Steering Committee of the multilateral group of the peace process, will be entrusted with the task of following up all issues arising out of the Summit and coordinating with existing multilateral structures such as the REDWG and other multilateral working groups. The Steering Committee will meet within one month following the Casablanca Summit to consider follow on mechanisms. The Committee will consult widely and regularly with the private sector.

—An executive Secretariat to assist the Steering Committee, located in Morocco, will work for the enhancement of the new economic development pattern, thus contributing to the consolidation of the global security in the region. The Secretariat will assist in the organization of a Regional Chamber of Commerce and a Business Council. It will work to advance the public-private partnership by promoting projects, sharing data, promoting contacts and fostering private sector investment in the region. The Secretariat will assist in the implementation of the various bodies referred to in the present Declaration. The Steering Committee will be responsible for the funding arrangements, with the support of the private sector.

10. The participants welcomed the establishment of a Middle East/North Africa Economic Strategy group by the Council on Foreign Relations. This private sector group will recommend strategies for regional economic cooperation and ways to overcome obstacles to trade and private investment. It will operate in close association with the Secretariat and submit its recommendations to the Steering Committee.

11. The participants also welcomed the intention of the World Economic Forum to form a business interaction group that will foster increased contacts and exchanges among business communities and submit its recommendations to the Steering Committee.

12. The participants in the Casablanca Summit pledged to transform this event into lasting institutional and individual ties that will provide a better life for the peoples of the Middle East and North Africa. They resolved that the collaboration of the public and private sectors that constituted the singularity of the Casablanca Summit will serve as a milestone in the historic destiny that is now playing itself out in the Middle East/North Africa region.

13. The participants expressed their appreciation to the Council on Foreign Relations and to the World Economic Forum for their substantive contribution to the organization of the Casablanca Summit.

14. The participants expressed their intention to meet again in Amman, Jordan, in the first half of 1995 for a second Middle East/North Africa Economic Summit, to be hosted by His Majesty King Hussein.

# Appendix F

Amman Declaration
Middle East/North Africa Economic
Summit (October 29–31, 1995)

On October 29–31, 1995, the second Middle East/North Africa Economic Summit was held in Amman, Jordan under the patronage of His Majesty King Hussein bin Talal. The Summit, co-sponsored by the United States and the Russian Federation, with the support of the European Union, Canada, and Japan, brought together government and business leaders from the Middle East and North Africa, Europe, the Americas, and Asia.

Summit participants thank His Majesty King Hussein for his able leadership and for the extraordinary efforts by the Hashemite Kingdom of Jordan to make this Summit a success. The participants also expressed their appreciation for the partnership of the World Economic Forum, which assisted so ably in organizing this event.

The goals of the Summit were to facilitate the expansion of private sector investment in the region, to cement a public-private partnership which will ensure that end, and to work to enhance regional cooperation and development.

In this spirit, business leaders from the Middle East, North Africa and other regions were able to conclude a number of significant commercial and business transactions at the Summit that will help augment the productive capacity of the region and contribute to its broad-based economic development. These ventures involved projects in the fields of tourism, telecommunications, and transportation. Reflecting this public-private partnership, a number of these ventures will benefit from government guarantees, technical assistance, and other support from the international community.

Government representatives conducted a series of negotiations over the past year on institutional arrangements as called for in the Casablanca Declaration which would help underpin the peace process. In this respect, the following agreements have been reached:

—A Bank for Economic Cooperation and Development in the Middle East and North Africa will be established in Cairo. The Bank—as described in its draft articles—will be structured to promote development of the private sector, support regional infrastructure projects, and provide a Forum to promote regional economic cooperation. The Task Force will finalize its negotiations by December 31, 1995 and will continue to explore proposals for the creation of a project preparation and financial intermediation facility. Those wishing to join the Bank will begin their national ratification processes thereafter. Others wish to leave open the option of joining the Bank at a later date, in light of the evolution of institutional arrangements and other developments. The Economic Summit will review this issue at its next meeting.

—The establishment of a Regional Tourism Board, the Middle East-Mediterranean Travel and Tourism Association, to facilitate tourism and promote the region as a unique and attractive tourist destination. The Board will include both public and private representatives.

—The establishment of a Regional Business Council to promote cooperation and trade among the private sectors of the countries of the region.

—The formal inauguration of the Economic Summit Executive Secretariat, which is located in Rabat and works to advance the public-private partnership, promoting contacts, sharing data, and fostering private sector investment in the region. The participants expressed their appreciation to the Moroccan Government for its contribution to this effort, and confirmed their support for its ongoing activities.

As a complement to the regional institutions called for at Casablanca, the Steering Group of the Multilateral Peace Negotiations has decided to establish the REDWG Monitoring Committee Secretariat as a permanent regional economic institution to be based in Amman. All participating parties have agreed that this institution will promote and strengthen regional economic cooperation in the Middle East and North Africa. The regional parties strongly recommend that the Secretariat's activities will cover the range of sectors within the REDWG Monitoring Committee's work, i.e., infrastructure, tourism, trade, finance, and areas within the Copenhagen Plan of Action. The core parties in close consultation with the European Union and other members of the Monitoring Committee undertake to finalize the appropriate document on the structure and operational functions of this institution, which will be submitted to the next meeting of the REDWG plenary, with a view to the commencement of the institution's activities in the first half of 1996. This REDWG plenary will consider the matter, take appropriate action, and report to the upcoming meeting of the Multilateral Steering Group.

The participants at the Summit expressed their strong support for continued progress in the peace process begun at Madrid exactly four years ago, and the importance of achieving a comprehensive peace. Participants took particular note of the advances made in the past year. Summit participants welcomed the signing of the Israeli-Palestinian Interim Agreement in the West Bank and Gaza Strip, and took favorable note of the significant progress made in implementing the Treaty of Peace between Israel and Jordan. The Summit welcomed the decision to organize in Paris, in December 1995, the Ministerial Conference on Economic Assistance for the Palestinians. The Summit also took note of the positive contribution made towards peace by multilateral working groups. While welcoming an increasingly positive atmosphere of openness in the region, the Summit recognized that the circle of peace needs to be widened. Participants expressed the hope that peace agreements between Israel and Syria and Israel and Lebanon would be concluded as soon as possible. The Summit welcomed significant steps taken by regional parties to the Taba Declaration and by the GCC with regard to lifting the boycott on Israel, and expressed its support for additional efforts to end the boycott.

The participants at the Summit declared their intent to implement as soon as possible the understandings reached in Amman. With respect to commercial activities, the business representatives reaffirmed their intention to follow through on the commercial ventures reached here and to explore new opportunities to expand trade and investment in the region. On the part of government, the officials attending the Summit declared their intention to support the activities of the private sector, most particularly by getting the new institutions established in Amman up and running as soon as possible. The participants also welcomed the measures taken by regional parties to open their economies and join the global economy.

To continue such a process whose blueprint and institutions have been established here, in Amman today, two brotherly countries announced their interest to host the next session of the MENA Summit. They are Qatar and Egypt.

His Majesty King Hussein conducted the necessary consultations with the distinguished representatives of the two brotherly states, as well as with other interested parties. He gladly announced that Qatar has graciously conceded its offer to host the next summit in favor of Egypt, who will host it. And it has been agreed by all, including Jordan, the present host, as well as Egypt and others, that Qatar will be the venue of the Middle East/North Africa Economic Summit in 1997.

# Appendix G

Cairo Declaration
Middle East/North Africa Economic
Conference (November 12–14, 1996)

On November 12–14, 1996, the Middle East and North Africa Economic Conference was held in Cairo, Egypt under the presidency of His Excellency Hosni Mubarak. The Conference, co-sponsored by the United States and the Russian Federation, with the support of Canada, the European Union and Japan, brought together senior government and private sector leaders from the Middle East and North Africa, as well as from other parts of the world.

Conference participants thank President Mubarak and the Government of Egypt for hosting this event, and for the excellent organization and generous hospitality provided. The participants expressed their appreciation for Egypt's leadership in the quest for a comprehensive, just and lasting peace in the Middle East.

Participants of the Cairo Economic Conference expressed their unwavering commitment to the achievement of a just, lasting and comprehensive peace in the Middle East, on the basis of the terms of reference of the Madrid Peace Conference, established by U. N Security Council resolutions 242 and 338. In this vein, they reaffirmed their determination to build upon the agreements reached among the parties and underlined the utmost importance of the faithful and expeditious implementation of those agreements by all parties, in particular on the Israeli-Palestinian track. They further recommitted themselves to broadening and deepening peace and achieving further progress on all outstanding issues on all the Arab-Israeli negotiating tracks of the peace process. They urged all parties to pursue measures and policies which would help build confidence between the people of the region.

The theme for the Cairo Economic Conference was: "Building for the Future, Creating an Investor Friendly Environment." The Conference provided an opportunity to encourage international and regional investment in the Middle East and North Africa. The region's economic, commercial and trade potential was highlighted, which is being greatly enhanced by important economic reform programmes currently being undertaken by many states in the region. These reforms which include privatization, structural reform, and removing trade barriers have provided for a more business-friendly economic climate throughout the region.

International private sector representatives were given the opportunity to investigate in detail the increased economic and commercial opportunities in the region. Individual countries presented their investment and development programs, and cross-border opportunities were highlighted as well. Constructive and fruitful discussions were held on topics of particular relevance to both the countries of the region and the international business community.

The participants stressed the crucial importance of the development of the Palestinian economy. They noted with concern that the already weak Palestinian economy is suffering from restrictions and closures which hinder the daily movement of Palestinian labor and trade. They recognized the need of all parties in the region to live in peace, prosperity and security, the improvement of which will enhance the economic viability of the region as a whole. They reiterated that removing restrictive measures and closures will prevent the decline of, and contribute positively to the performance of the Palestinian economy, as well as the political atmosphere surrounding the peace process in its entirety.

The status of the economic institutions called for by the MENA conferences previously held at Casablanca and Amman was reviewed during the conference. The significant progress made on establishing the Middle East-Mediterranean Travel and Tourism Association in Tunis was welcomed by the participants. They underscored the importance of the Bank for Economic Cooperation and Development in the Middle East and North Africa in Cairo and its potential contribution to the promotion of capital flow to the region, to building infrastructure projects and to the development of the private sector in the region. The conclusion of the drafting of the Agreement establishing the Bank was welcomed. Countries were encouraged to sign the Agreement and complete their funding and ratification procedures promptly in order to enable the Bank to begin operations in 1997. Work on establishing a Regional Business Council was also reviewed, and the relevant parties recommitted themselves to moving this important initiative forward.

The Executive Secretariat of the MENA Conferences in Rabat has continued to develop successfully its programmes and activities in fostering public/private partnership in the region between conferences.

The activities of the REDWG Monitoring Committee Secretariat established in Amman pursuant to the Amman Declaration, and formally inaugurated and institutionalized in May 1996, were reviewed. The activities of REDWG and the work of its Monitoring Committee in areas covered by the Copenhagen Action Plan, i.e., infrastructure, tourism, trade and finance were also reviewed. Participants expressed their appreciation for the work done by the Committee.

Government and private sector participants at the conference reaffirmed their commitment to continue to work as partners for peace and prosperity in the Middle East and North Africa. They underscored the importance of the economic underpinnings of peace. Nevertheless, they reaffirmed the urgency of achieving concrete progress in the political dimension of the Middle East peace process.

The participants expressed their appreciation for the unique role played by the World Economic Forum, whose tireless efforts were critical to the success of the conference. They also expressed their gratitude to the Council on Foreign Relations in New York, for its important contribution to a number of Conference sessions.

The participants decided to meet again in late 1997 in Doha, Qatar for the fourth Middle East/North Africa Economic Conference.

# Appendix H

## Declaration on Principles for Cooperation Among the Core Parties on Water-Related Matters and New and Additional Water Resources
## The Multilateral Working Group on Water Resources Oslo (February 13, 1996)

As part of the Program adopted by the Multilateral Working Group on Water Resources (MWGWR) of the Middle East Peace Process, the Government of Norway has sponsored certain activities of the agenda.

Within this context comparative studies on Water Legislation, Institutions and Pricing of the Core Parties were commissioned and executed.

As an outcome of these studies the Parties, facilitated by the Government of Norway and the Office of Gavelholder, have identified common denominators in their water resources management systems and proclaimed this Declaration on Principles for Cooperation Among the Core Parties on Water-related Matters and New and Additional Water Resources. Although the Core Parties in the Middle East Peace Process are considered to be Jordan, Syria, Israel, Lebanon, and the PLO for the benefit of the Palestinian Authority, for the purposes of this Declaration, the term the Core Parties are those who are signatories to this Declaration.

The Core Parties agree that this Declaration and the cooperation thereunder will not affect or alter in any form or manner any of the bilateral or other agreements or undertakings among them, nor does it prohibit or constrain any bilateral arrangements, understandings or agreements aimed at enhancing cooperation in water-related matters.

The Core Parties view this Declaration as an expression of:

The role of the multilateral talks in promoting cooperation and confidence-building in the field of water resources and in the importance of cooperation for the promotion of matters of mutual interest.

A joint resolve to cooperate among them in the development of New and Additional Water Resources.

The importance of water resources management on the basis of locally compatible legal, economic and institutional frameworks and principles.

The recognition that cooperative efforts among them will facilitate the development of New and Additional Water Resources for their joint benefit.

The ability to cooperate on the basis of the common denominators identified within their respective water management systems.

The Core Parties proclaim as objectives of their cooperation:

- identifying the needs of New and Additional Water Resources;
- identifying potential New and Additional Water Resources and the development thereof;
- combining their cooperative efforts in the development of New and Additional Water Resources; and
- enhancing their water supply, and increasing the efficiency of its use.

The Declaration consists of three parts, namely; Common Denominators, Principles of Cooperation on New and Additional Water Resources, and Cooperation on Other Water-Related Matters.

## Common Denominators

The Core Parties identified and agreed to the following common denominators in their water legislation as a basis for cooperation among themselves:

1. Water Resources in Legislation

Their respective water legislations apply to all types of water resources including wastewater and desalinated water.

## 2. Ownership and Administration of Water Resources

All water resources of each party are publicly owned and/or centrally controlled. They are used for the benefit of their respective societies. The Core Parties promote public participation in water resources management. Well drilling, water production and supply are allowed only by permit or license. A Central Water Authority/Government Agency exists in each of the Core Parties, and exercises effective control over water resources.

## 3. Allocation

Domestic uses occupy the first priority in the allocation of water resources.

## 4. Drought Measures

The Core Parties will take appropriate measures in periods of drought and water scarcity.

## 5. Water Quality and Protection

Water quality standards for various water uses have been adopted by each of the Core Parties; water preservation is an overriding concern, and enforcement powers exist in the hands of competent authorities to prevent water pollution, and to mitigate any negative environmental impacts on them at the expense of the polluters.

## 6. Data and Record Keeping

Obligations exist, pursuant to the legislation of each Core Party, to measure, monitor and keep proper record of all water production, supplies and consumption.

## 7. Compliance and Enforcement

Proper sanctions against non-compliance are explicit in the respective legislation of each of the Core Parties. Enforcement of the water legislation is the norm.

## 8. Water Charges

Water is not supplied free of charge in any of the Core Parties. Tariff structures, taking into account different extents of cost recovery, apply to domestic, industrial and agricultural sectors. These tariffs are periodically reviewed and adjusted.

# Principles of Cooperation on New and Additional Water Resources

1. Definitions

For the purpose of this Declaration:

1.1. New and Additional Water Resources are only those potential water resources which are not Existing Water Resources, and which are not part of new and additional water resources developed pursuant to bilateral agreements.

1.2. Existing Water Resources are the individual resources of each of the respective parties' renewable, non-renewable and waste water resources.

1.3. Cooperating Parties are those of the Core Parties, signatories to this Declaration, which actively participate in the development of any specific Project relating to new and additional water resources.

1.4. A New and Additional Water Resources Project, hereinafter the Project, means a project among Cooperating Parties to develop New and Additional Water Resources by specific agreement.

2. General Principles

2.1. The development of New and Additional Water Resources will not adversely affect the development or utilization of Existing Water Resources.

2.2. All arrangements with respect to New and Additional Water Resources will be limited in time and subject to periodic mutual review.

3. Mechanisms of Cooperation

3.1. Cooperation among the Core Parties will be carried out by their respective water institutions through joint bodies on a ministerial and managerial level to be established, as appropriate, for each respective Party.

3.2. Each Project requires the consensus of all the Cooperating Parties for implementation.

4. Ownership and Utilization

4.1. New and Additional Water Resources, developed in joint effort by the Core Parties for the benefit of some or all of them, will be considered as part of their own water resources only to the extent of the share allocated to them.

4.2. Details concerning the utilization and ownership will be the subject of separate agreements for each Project.

4.3. Each Core Party can apply its legislation, within its respective jurisdiction, on the share allocated to it by each Project.

5. Technical, Economic and Financial Issues

5.1. Projects will be technically, economically, and financially sustainable.

5.2. The Cooperating Parties will carry their respective share of the project financing including the costs of operation, maintenance, and amortization of the Project. Due regard will be given to less developed Cooperating Parties and joint efforts will be made to assist in the obtaining of financing on favorable terms, provided that no such efforts affect any of the bilateral donor/recipients arrangements or protocols.

5.3. The Cooperating Parties agree to participate jointly in the raising of the funds needed for the Project implementation, and to secure the funds needed for the operation and maintenance of the new water system.

5.4. The cost to each of the Cooperating Parties of water derived from New and Additional Resources will be based upon the cost of production, operation, maintenance and amortization.

5.5. Water derived from the New and Additional Resources will not be subject to levies on account of conveyance, storage, treatment, or protection in excess of levies which the owner of the project would normally incur.

5.6. Cooperating Parties may, by mutual consent, trade the use of their respective shares of the waters from New and Additional Resources, provided that such trading does not cause harm to the shares allocated to any other Cooperating Parties.

6. Environmental Management

6.1. All Projects will be based on environmentally sound principles.

6.2. The Cooperating Parties give preference to those Projects which utilize advanced technological water usage methods.

6.3. Each Cooperating Party is responsible for the protection of the Project against environmental pollution originating within its jurisdiction.

7. Water Protection

7.1. Each Cooperating Party is responsible for the prevention of harm to those parts of the Projects under its jurisdiction.

7.2. Such responsibility includes inter alia the preservation of water quality and the prevention of unauthorized withdrawals.

8. Operation and Maintenance

The Cooperating Parties will set the standards for the operation and maintenance of the Projects.

9. Areas of Cooperation

It is understood that the following potential areas of cooperation in the development of New and Additional Water Resources for the Cooperating Parties will be further studied in order to determine their feasibility:

9.1. acquisition and import of water including the possibility of carrying such waters through existing or new supply systems (wheeling);

9.2. development of desalination plants;

9.3. rainfall enhancement; and

9.4. any other relevant area of cooperation.

## Cooperation on Other Water-Related Matters

Cooperation on other water-related matters, although originating among the Core Parties, will be open to regional and extra-regional parties of the Multilateral Working Group on Water Resources.

1. Cooperation on Specific Sectors

The Parties express their desire to cooperate among themselves and with other interested Parties on the following Other Water-related Matters:

1.1. weather forecasting, climatology, weather modification, and meteorology;

1.2. environmental conservation;

1.3. sustainable water-related natural resources management and desertification control;

1.4. enhancement of public awareness and participation; and

1.5. human resources development

2. Proposed Areas of Cooperation

The Core Parties will in due time explore possible cooperation among themselves and with other interested parties in the following areas:

2.1. collection, filing, processing, transmission and exchange of water data and related information.

2.2. preparation of plans for flood-protection and utilization; with emphasis on development of Early Warning Systems;

2.3. development of norms, standards and specifications for water devices, equipment and infrastructure;

2.4. transfer and adoption of advanced technology throughout the chains of water storage, conveyance and application, including automation and controls of water systems; particularly related to reduction of crop water requirements;

2.5. water-energy interactions, with emphasis on desalinization;

2.6. establishment of a Regional Center; and

2.7. identification of ways to achieve optimal use of water in the agricultural sector.

3. Mechanism of Cooperation

3.1. The Cooperating Parties will decide on the mechanism of their cooperation on other water-related matters set out in this section.

3.2. All decisions with respect to cooperation on Other Water-related Matters will be adopted by consensus.

4. Specific Cooperation

4.1. The Core Parties agree to hold Regional Seminars on various water-related matters;

4.2. The Core Parties agree to publish the results of their cooperation in a Regional Publication.

5. Extended Cooperation

The Cooperating Parties may by consensus agree to include additional water-related matters in their cooperation.

# Appendix I

## The Bahrain Environmental Code of Conduct for the Middle East (October 25, 1994)

The Multilateral Working Group on the Environment of the Middle East peace process initiated at Madrid in October 1991.

Based upon the discussions which have taken place in the Cairo Consultative Group,

Reaffirming the role of the multilateral talks in promoting confidence-building and cooperation among the regional parties in the field of the environment,

Noting relevant international Declarations and instruments on the environment and sustainable development; and recognizing, in particular, the Rio Declaration on Environment and Development and Agenda 21 adopted in 1992,

Recognizing that, in view of the inseparable relationship between humans and their environment, all aspects of the human environment, be they natural or man-made, are essential to the well-being and the enjoyment of basic human life,

Convinced of the need for the protection and conservation of the environment and natural resources in the region,

Recognizing that in view of transboundary effects of many environmental problems, each party needs to take into consideration effects upon other parties in pursuing its own developmental and environmental policy,

Also recognizing the need for passing on to the future generations of the region a safe, sound and healthy environment as well as the fruits of economic development,

Recognizing the unique environmental characteristics to the Middle East,

Declares as follows:

## Principles

I. The regional parties proclaim the following principles:

1. Natural resources of the region should be utilized on a sustainable basis, and unique environmental resources to the region should be preserved.

2. The parties will strive for a fair and just utilization and coordinated management policies of the shared natural resources in the region.

3. The parties have the right to exploit their own resources pursuant to their own environmental and developmental policies, and the responsibility to ensure that activities within their jurisdiction or control do not cause damage to the environment of other parties.

4. The parties have the responsibility to avoid activities of adverse effect and risks to the environmental security in the region.

5. Economic development should be in harmony with the protection and conservation of the environment, including preservation of ecological balance and safety of human health and well being. The parties will promote cooperation in the protection and conservation of the environment.

6. A comprehensive, just and lasting peace in the region, development and environmental protection are interdependent and indivisible.

7. Regional parties will cooperate and seek the cooperation of other parties in the essential task of eradicating poverty as an indispensable requirement for sustainable development, in order to decrease the disparities in standards of living and better meet the needs of the people in the region.

8. Environmental issues are best handled with the participation of all concerned citizens and social sectors, at the relevant level. The parties shall facilitate and encourage public awareness and participation by making information widely available.

## Guidelines

II. In order to pursue policies in accordance with the Principles, the regional parties should:

a. enact effective environmental legislation. Environmental standards, management objectives and priorities should reflect the state of the environment in the Middle East, paying due consideration to geographical, topographical, and meteorological conditions as well as regional environmental problems such as water, air and marine pollution, waste management, desertification and nature conservation.

b. develop and use environmental management tools such as environmental impact assessment, environmental risk management and monitoring systems, for domestic as well as transboundary impacts; in case of projects with possible transboundary effects, all regional parties involved should endeavor to cooperate on an environment impact assessment.

c. strive for capacity building and human resource development, through environmental training and education.

d. facilitate and encourage public awareness to broaden the basis for enlightened opinions and responsible conduct by individuals, enterprises and communities in protecting and improving the environment.

e. coordinate their environmental policies with one another and cooperate in protecting the over-all environment in the region in good faith and in a spirit of partnership.

f. cooperate in promoting appropriate technology and capability to tackle environmental issues by joint projects, joint research and other activities where appropriate; facilitate the transfer of technology, know-how, and information; notify one another of environmental situations that have regional or transboundary impacts.

g. endeavor to promote the internalization of environmental costs and the use of economic instruments, taking into account the approach that the polluter should, in principle, bear the cost of pollution, with due regard to the public interest and without distorting international trade and investment.

h. resolve all their environmental disputes peacefully and by appropriate means in accordance with the UN Charter and in conformity with relevant provisions of international law and declarations.

## Joint Actions

III. The regional parties will join forces for the environmental protection and conservation and begin to work in the following fields:

## The Bahrain Environmental Code of Conduct for the Middle East 233

### Water

Protection of water quality should be given a top priority. Low precipitation in the region makes it extremely important to maintain the quality of surface and ground water for both economic activities and human consumption.

### Marine and Coastal Environment

The sea surfaces of the Middle East are both economic and environmental assets for the regional parties. They are most vulnerable to pollution, from land base sources and maritime activities in particular. It is essential to apply advanced standards to eliminate these sources of pollution, and to cooperate in all possible ways to assure protection of coasts and biodiversity in waters.

### Air

Economic activities particularly in the industrial, energy and transport sectors are main sources for air pollution in the Middle East. Measures to prevent the degradation of air quality need to be taken.

### Waste Management

With rising living standards and increasing economic activity, the regional parties may have to dispose of increasing amounts of waste in the future. The parties will need to: minimize waste, enact effective regulation for proper treatment, recycling and protection measures, and ensure safe waste disposal within agreed safety measures and emergency preparedness arrangements in the region. Sewage, as a potential important resource, should be collected and treated to be reused for various purposes.

### Desertification

The Middle East region is among those threatened by land degradation including desertification and preventive measures are urgently needed. To combat desertification and mitigate the effects of drought in particular, effective cooperative actions are indispensable.

## A Regional Framework

IV. The parties recognize the need for regional cooperation in the field of environment in the Middle East. The parties will work towards the development of an appropriate framework for regional cooperation in the environmental area. Toward this end, it is important that the regional parties provide timely and early notification and relevant information on environmental situations that have regional impacts on potentially affected parties.

## Extra-Regional Assistance

V. The extra-regional parties, including international organizations, are invited to assist the regional parties in their endeavors to achieve the goals and objectives of the Code.

## Periodic Review

VI. This Code should be brought to the attention of all concerned parties so that they assume their share of responsibility, individually or jointly to ensure that the objectives of the Code are met. The Parties will periodically assess the effectiveness of the Code of Conduct and revise it as appropriate.

# Notes

*Introduction*

1. Address by Uri Savir, former director-general of the Israeli Ministry of Foreign Affairs, at the Seminar in Memory of General Aharon Yariv, Tel Aviv University Dayan Center, May 24, 1995. Reproduced in *Israel Information Service* <gopher://israel-info.gov.il:70/00/speech/sta/950524s.sta>.
2. Remarks by Secretary of State James A. Baker III at the Madrid Peace Conference, November 1, 1991, in *US Department of State Dispatch*, 2, no. 44 (November 4, 1991): 807.
3. Address by U.S. President George Bush at the opening session of the Madrid Peace Conference, October 30, 1991. The full address appears in *US Department of State Dispatch*, 2, no. 44 (November 4, 1991): 803–4.
4. Because regional cooperation before the completion of bilateral peace treaties between Israel and its Arab neighbors is extremely sensitive, the multilateral talks evolved in a low-profile manner. To date, very little has been published about how this process works or the activities undertaken by its working groups. While documentation from the process is not classified, it also is not public, making it difficult for researchers to learn about its proceedings absent interviews with officials who are familiar with the detailed proceedings of the groups. My extensive reliance on personal interviews in this study is the result of this constraint. Existing publications discussing the overall process include: Joel Peters, *Pathways to Peace: The Multilateral Arab-Israeli Peace Talks* (London: Royal Institute of International Affairs, 1996); Dalia Dassa Kaye, "Madrid's Forgotten Forum: The Middle East Multilaterals," *Washington Quarterly*, 20, no. 1 (Winter 1997): 167–86; and Robert J. Bookmiller and Kirsten Nakjavani Bookmiller, "Behind the Headlines: The Multilateral Middle East Talks," *Current History*, 597 (January 1996): 33–37.

5. The full text of the Madrid letter of invitation appears in "Recent Developments in the Middle East Peace Process," *US Department of State Dispatch Supplement*, 4, supplement no. 4 (September 1993): 25–26.
6. Although the process does not include all regional parties (notably Syria and Lebanon), it nonetheless constitutes the only official Arab-Israeli forum to date that expressly addresses regional issues distinct from the bilateral negotiating tracks and includes Arab parties from the Gulf and North Africa who had never before taken part in a public cooperative forum with Israel. Previous attempts to create a "multilateral" negotiating framework between Arabs and Israelis had been both temporary and intended as a forum for bilateral settlements. A notable example was the Geneva peace conference of December 21, 1973, sponsored by the United States and the Soviet Union to accelerate disengagement agreements between Israel and its neighbors (Egypt, Jordan, and Syria) in the wake of the 1973 war. As Secretary of State Henry Kissinger explained, "We strove to assemble a multilateral conference, but our purpose was to use it as a framework for an essentially bilateral diplomacy." See Kissinger, *Years of Upheaval* (Boston: Little, Brown & Company, 1982), p. 755.
7. For more details on the origins of the multilaterals, see remarks by Assistant Secretary of State for Near Eastern Affairs Edward P. Djerejian, "The Multilateral Talks in the Arab-Israeli Peace Process," in *US Department of State Dispatch*, 4, no. 41 (October 11, 1993): 696.
8. The Gulf Cooperation Council (GCC) states participating in the multilateral talks include Saudi Arabia, Kuwait, Oman, Qatar, Bahrain, and the United Arab Emirates (UAE). The North African (Maghreb) states represented are Morocco, Tunisia, Algeria, and Mauritania. The "core" Arab participants are the Egyptians, Jordanians, and Palestinians. Turkey and Yemen also participate in the process. The absence of Syria and Lebanon is discussed in chapter 3.
9. Djerejian, "Multilateral Talks."
10. Concluding remarks by Secretary of State James A. Baker, Moscow, January 28, 1992 in *US Department of State Dispatch Supplement*, 3, supplement no. 2 (February 1992): 27–28.
11. See Louise Fawcett, "Regionalism in Historical Perspective," in Louise Fawcett and Andrew Hurell, eds., *Regionalism in World Politics* (Oxford: Oxford University Press, 1995), pp. 9–36. For the impact of regionalism on security studies, see David Lake and Patrick Morgan, eds., *Regional Orders: Building Security in a New World* (University Park: Pennsylvania State University Press, 1997).
12. See Janne E. Nolan, ed., *Global Engagement: Cooperation and Security in the 21st Century* (Washington, D.C.: The Brookings Institution, 1994).
13. This breakthrough included the first official contacts between Israel and the Palestine Liberation Organization (PLO), leading to a declaration of principles

(DoP) on Palestinian self-rule in 1993. This agreement was followed by a more substantive accord (Oslo II) signed in 1995, which led to Israeli troop withdrawals and redeployments from major Palestinian urban areas and the extension of the Palestinian Authority's (PA) rule beyond Gaza to parts of the West Bank territory. The final status of these territories is still subject to negotiation between Israel and the PA. For more on the Oslo Accords, see David Makovsky, *Making Peace with the PLO: The Rabin Government's Road to the Oslo Accord* (Boulder, Colo.: Westview Press, 1996).

14. My empirical cases include four of the five multilateral working groups. I do not include the Refugee working group, although I discuss this group to some extent in chapter 3, largely because the Refugee group, unlike the other four, depends primarily on a bilateral Israeli-Palestinian resolution, even though the ultimate solution to this problem will require multilateral agreement. In fact, the refugee issue is specified as a "final status" issue in the Israeli-Palestinian peace talks. For overviews of the refugee problem and the multilateral working group, see: George F. Kossaifi, *The Palestinian Refugees and the Right of Return*, Information Paper No. 7 (Washington, D.C.: The Center for Policy Analysis on Palestine, September 1996); Government of Israel, *The Refugee Issue: A Background Paper* (Israel: Government Press Office, October 1994); Salim Tamari, *Palestinian Refugee Negotiations: From Madrid to Oslo II* (Washington, D.C.: Institute for Palestine Studies, 1997); Rex Brynen, "Much Ado About Nothing? The Refugee Working Group and the Perils of Multilateral Quasi-negotiation," *International Negotiation*, 2, no. 2 (November 1997): 279–302; and the Canadian (the group's gavelholder) web site: <http://www.arts.mcgill.ca/mepp/mepp.html>.

15. See Robert Jervis, "Security Regimes," in Stephen D. Krasner, ed., *International Regimes* (Ithaca, N.Y.: Cornell University Press, 1983), pp. 173–94 and Charles Lipson, "International Cooperation in Economic and Security Affairs," in David A. Baldwin, ed., *Neorealism and Neoliberalism* (New York: Columbia University Press, 1993), pp. 60–84.

16. On the importance of dependent variable variation in social science research design, see Gary King, Robert O. Keohane, Sidney Verba, *Designing Social Inquiry* (Princeton, New Jersey: Princeton University Press, 1994), esp. pp. 129–137.

17. The formal aspects of the multilaterals were suspended after 1996, although many informal activities and intersessional meetings continued, particularly in the Water group. In February 2000 the multilaterals resumed at the official level with a meeting of the Steering Committee in Moscow.

18. Itamar Rabinovich, *Waging Peace: Israel and the Arabs at the End of the Century* (New York: Farrar, Straus and Giroux, 1999), p. 41.

*Chapter 1*

1. The Middle East is widely associated with the balance of power paradigm, even by scholars challenging the realist paradigm generally. See Stephen Walt, *The Origins of Alliances* (Ithaca, N.Y.: Cornell University Press, 1987); Shibley Telhami, *Power and Leadership in International Bargaining* (New York: Columbia University Press, 1990); Richard Rosecrance, *The Rise of the Trading State* (New York: Basic Books, 1986); and John Gerard Ruggie, ed., *Multilateralism Matters: The Theory and Praxis of an Institutional Form* (New York: Columbia University Press, 1993).
2. See, for example, Ernst B. Haas, "The Study of Regional Integration: Reflections on the Joy and Anguish of Pretheorizing," *International Organization*, 24, no. 4 (Autumn 1970): 607–46 and Robert O. Keohane, *After Hegemony: Cooperation and Discord in the World Political Economy* (Princeton, N.J.: Princeton University Press, 1984).
3. Keohane, *After Hegemony*, p. 6.
4. Ibid., p. 12.
5. According to Lindblom, "A set of decisions is coordinated if adjustments have been made in them, such that adverse consequences of any one decision for other decisions are to a degree and in some frequency avoided, reduced, or counterbalanced or overweighed." Cited in Keohane, *After Hegemony*, p. 51.
6. Ibid., p. 51.
7. Ibid., p. 53.
8. For example, Wayne Sandholtz's study of cooperation in Europe challenges functional accounts by focusing on cognitive variables, but he still maintains the policy adjustment definition of cooperation. For him, cognitive change occurs *before* decision-makers decide to cooperate, not while they are engaged in the cooperative process itself. See Wayne Sandholtz, *High-Tech Europe: The Politics of International Cooperation* (Berkeley: University of California Press, 1992).
9. For a realist attempt to address questions of cooperation, see Charles L. Glaser, "Realists as Optimists: Cooperation as Self-Help," *International Security*, 19, no. 3 (Winter 1994–95): 50–90 and Robert Jervis, "Realism, Neoliberalism, and Cooperation: Understanding the Debate," *International Security*, 24, no. 1 (Summer 1999): 42–63. For an explanation of why security cooperation is more difficult, though not impossible, see Robert Jervis, "Security Regimes," *International Organization*, 36, no. 2 (Spring 1982): 357–78.
10. See Stacia E. Zabusky, *Launching Europe: An Ethnography of European Cooperation in Space Science* (Princeton, N.J.: Princeton University Press, 1995).
11. Ibid., p. 13.
12. Ibid., p. 19, emphasis added.

13. See Zabusky, p. 18. She is drawing on Mead's *Cooperation and Competition among Primitive Peoples* [1937] (Boston: Beacon Press, 1961).
14. Ibid., p. 22.
15. On different types of learning, see Ernst B. Haas, *When Knowledge Is Power: Three Models of Change in International Organizations* (Berkeley: University of California Press, 1990) and Joseph S. Nye, Jr., "Nuclear Learning and U.S.-Soviet Security Regimes," *International Organization*, 41 (Summer 1987): 371–402. For a review of the learning literature in the organizational context, see James H. Lebovic, "How Organizations Learn: U.S. Government Estimates of Foreign Military Spending," *American Journal of Political Science*, 39, no. 4 (November 1995): 835–63.
16. See Martha Finnemore, *National Interests in International Society* (Ithaca, N.Y.: Cornell University Press, 1996).
17. See Emanuel Adler, "Seeds of peaceful change: the OSCE's security community-building model," in Emanuel Adler and Michael Barnett, eds., *Security Communities* (Cambridge: Cambridge University Press, 1998), pp. 119–60.
18. Ibid., p. 139.
19. See Zabusky, *Launching Europe*, p. 122.
20. See Ruggie, ed., *Multilateralism Matters*, and Fen Osler Hampson with Michael Hart, *Multilateral Negotiations: Lessons from Arms Control, Trade, and the Environment* (Baltimore: The Johns Hopkins University Press, 1995). In contrast, Robert O. Keohane offers a nominal definition of multilateralism as "the practice of co-ordinating national policies in groups of three or more states, through ad hoc arrangements or by means of institutions." in "Multilateralism: An Agenda for Research," *International Journal*, 45, no. 4 (Fall 1990): 731–64.
21. Hampson and Hart, *Multilateral Negotiations*, p. 15.
22. See Jeffrey Z. Rubin and Walter C. Swap, "Small Group Theory: Forming a Consensus through Group Processes," in I. William Zartman, ed., *International Multilateral Negotiation: Approaches to the Management of Complexity* (San Francisco: Jossey-Bass Publishers, 1994), pp. 132–47.
23. John Gerard Ruggie, "Multilateralism: The Anatomy of an Institution," in Ruggie, ed., *Multilateralism Matters*, pp. 3–47.
24. Ibid., p. 6.
25. Ibid., p. 8.
26. See Kenneth N. Waltz, *Theory of International Politics* (Reading, Mass.: Addison-Wesley, 1979) and Walt, *Origins of Alliances*.
27. See Robert Gilpin, *The Political Economy of International Relations* (Princeton: Princeton University Press, 1987); Charles P. Kindleberger, *The World In Depression, 1929–39* (Berkeley: University of California Press, 1973); and Stephen D. Krasner, "State Power and the Structure of International Trade," *World Politics*, 28, no. 3 (April 1976): 317–45.

28. The general applicability of hegemonic stability theory has already suffered sharp criticism, both on a theoretical and empirical basis. See Stephan Haggard and Beth A. Simmons, "Theories of International Regimes," *International Organization*, 41, no. 3 (Summer 1987): 491–517; Duncan Snidal, "The Limits of Hegemonic Stability Theory," *International Organization*, 39, no. 4 (Autumn 1985): 579–614. For empirical critiques, see Oran Young and Gail Osherenko, "The Formation of International Regimes: Hypotheses and Cases, " in Young and Osherenko, eds., *Polar Politics: Creating International Environmental Regimes* (Ithaca, N.Y.: Cornell University Press, 1993), pp. 1–21 and Volker Rittberger and Michael Zürn, "Regime Theory: Findings from the Study of 'East-West' Regimes," *Cooperation and Conflict*, 26, no. 4 (1991): 165–83.
29. Oran R. Young, "Political leadership and regime formation: on the development of institutions in international society," *International Organization*, 45, no. 3 (Summer 1991): 281–308.
30. Ibid., p. 283.
31. Ibid., p. 307.
32. Ibid., p. 289 (Young quote of Kindleberger).
33. Ibid., p. 293.
34. Ibid., p. 307.
35. See Peter Hall, ed., *The Political Power of Economic Ideas: Keynesianism Across Nations* (Princeton, N.J.: Princeton University Press, 1989).
36. Shimon Peres is the most visible example. His ideas, particularly the "New Middle East" concept, have generated a tremendous amount of controversy in both the Arab and Israeli press. See Shimon Peres, *The New Middle East* (New York: Henry Holt, 1993).
37. Most closely associated with forming this school are: Ernst B. Haas, *The Uniting of Europe: Political, Social and Economic Forces, 1950–1957* (Stanford: Stanford University Press, 1958) and Leon N. Lindberg, *The Political Dynamics of European Economic Integration* (Stanford: Stanford University Press, 1963).
38. Ernst B. Haas, *The Obsolescence of Regional Integration Theory* (Berkeley, Calif.: Institute of International Studies, 1975).
39. If anything, loyalties are likely to shift to smaller units, such as ethnic or religious groupings, which have posed significant obstacles to nation-building in the Middle East.
40. See Robert O. Keohane, "The Demand for International Regimes," in Stephen D. Krasner, ed., *International Regimes* (Ithaca, N.Y.: Cornell University Press, 1983), pp. 141–71; Keohane, *After Hegemony*; and Keohane, "International Institutions: Two Approaches," *International Studies Quarterly*, 32 (December 1988): 379–96.
41. For the distinction between collaboration and coordination problems, see

Arthur A. Stein, "Coordination and collaboration: regimes in an anarchic world," in Krasner, *International Regimes*, pp. 115-40.
42. See Dalia Dassa Kaye, *Banking on Peace: Lessons from the Middle East Development Bank*, Policy Paper No. 43 (San Diego, Calif.: Institute on Global Conflict and Cooperation, October 1998).
43. For the classic discussion of the collective action dilemma, see Mancur Olsen, *The Logic of Collective Action: Public Goods and the Theory of Groups* (Cambridge: Harvard University Press, 1965).
44. For a critique of regime theory's neglect of domestic politics, see Haggard and Simmons, "Theories of International Regimes" and Helen Milner, "International Theories of Cooperation Among Nations: Strengths and Weaknesses," *World Politics*, 44, no. 3 (April 1992): 466-96.
45. Robert Putnam, "Diplomacy and Domestic Politics," *International Organization*, 42, no. 3 (Summer 1988): 422-60.
46. Michael N. Barnett, *Confronting the Costs of War: Military Power, State and Society in Egypt and Israel* (Princeton, N.J.: Princeton University Press, 1992). For a domestic-based analysis of Egyptian alliance behavior, see Michael N. Barnett and Jack S. Levy, "Domestic Sources of Alliances and Alignments: the Case of Egypt, 1962-1973," *International Organization*, 45, no. 3 (Summer 1991): 369-95.
47. Etel Solingen, "Economic Liberalization, Political Coalitions, and Emerging Regional Orders," in David A. Lake and Patrick M. Morgan, eds., *Regional Orders: Building Security in a New World* (University Park: Pennsylvania State University Press, 1997), p. 68. For further elaboration of her theoretical framework, see Solingen, *Regional Orders at Century's Dawn: Global and Domestic Influences on Grand Strategy* (Princeton, N.J.: Princeton University Press, 1998).
48. See Steven R. David, "Explaining Third World Alignment," *World Politics*, 43, no. 2 (January 1991): 233-56.
49. See Richard Ned Lebow and Thomas Risse-Kappen, eds., *International Relations Theory and the End of the Cold War* (New York: Columbia University Press, 1995).
50. See Judith Goldstein and Robert Keohane, eds., *Ideas and Foreign Policy* (Ithaca, N.Y.: Cornell University Press, 1993). For further ideational work in political economy, see Peter A. Hall, ed., *The Political Power of Economic Ideas*; Henry R. Nau, *The Myth of America's Decline: Leading the World Economy Into the 1990s* (Oxford: Oxford University Press, 1990); Judith Goldstein, "The Impact of Ideas on Trade Policy," *International Organization*, 43, no. 1 (Winter 1989): 31-71; and Kathryn Sikkink, *Ideas and Institutions: Developmentalism in Brazil and Argentina* (Princeton, N.J.: Princeton University Press,

1991). In the national security realm, see Emanuel Adler, "The Emergence of Cooperation: National Epistemic Communities and the International Evolution of the Idea of Nuclear Arms Control," *International Organization*, 46, no. 1 (Winter 1992): 101–45, and Thomas Risse-Kappen, "Ideas Do Not Float Freely: Transnational Relations, Domestic Structures, and the End of the Cold War," *International Organization*, 48, no. 2 (Spring 1994): 185–214.

51. See Christer Jönsson, "Cognitive Factors in Explaining Regime Dynamics," in Volker Rittberger, ed., *Regime Theory and International Relations* (Oxford: Oxford University Press, 1993), pp. 202–22. Ernst B. Haas previously considered this variable in regime processes in "Is There a Hole in the Whole? Knowledge, Technology, Interdependence, and the Construction of International Regimes," *International Organization*, 29, no. 3 (Summer 1975): 827–76 and "Why Collaborate: Issue-Linkage and International Regimes," *World Politics*, 32, no. 3 (April 1980): 357–405.

52. See especially Goldstein and Keohane, "Ideas and Foreign Policy: Analytical Framework," pp. 3–30, in Goldstein and Keohane, *Ideas and Foreign Policy*. Not all of the contributors to this edited volume, however, fall into this category, despite Goldstein and Keohane's advocacy for a rationalist method in the study of ideas.

53. Ibid., p. 5.

54. Ibid., p. 3.

55. Ibid., p. 4.

56. John Kurt Jacobsen, "Much Ado about Ideas: The Cognitive Factor in Economic Policy," *World Politics*, 47, no. 2 (January 1995), p. 286. For another critique of the Goldstein and Keohane approach to ideas, see John Ruggie, "What Makes the World Hang Together? Neo-utilitarianism and the Social Constructivist Challenge," *International Organization*, 52, no. 4 (Autumn 1998): 855–885.

57. For more on this distinction, see Albert Yee, "The Causal Effects of Ideas on Policies," *International Organization*, 50, no. 1 (Winter 1996): 69–108.

58. See Emanuel Adler, "Seizing the Middle Ground: Constructivism in World Politics," *European Journal of International Relations*, 3, no. 3 (1997): 319–63 and Alexander Wendt, "Constructing International Politics," *International Security*, 20, no. 1 (Summer 1995): 71–81. For a sympathetic review of constructivism from a critical theory perspective, see Richard Price and Christian Reus-Smit, "Dangerous Liaisons? Critical International Theory and Constructivism," *European Journal of International Relations*, 4, no. 3 (1998): 259–94.

59. Early integration theorists noted the critical role of intersubjective beliefs in shaping international outcomes. See Ernst B. Haas, *Beyond the Nation-State: Functionalism and International Organization* (Stanford: Stanford University Press, 1964) or his later work focused on the role of knowledge in international

organizations, *When Knowledge is Power*. Also see Karl Deutsch's work on security communities, including Deutsch et al., *Political Community and the North Atlantic Area* (Princeton, N.J.: Princeton University Press, 1957) and Deutsch, *Nationalism and Social Communication* (Cambridge, Mass.: MIT Press, 1953). For a revival and modification of Deutsch's work in this area, see Adler and Barnett, *Security Communities*.

60. See Jeffrey T. Checkel, "The Constructivist Turn In International Relations Theory," *World Politics*, 50, no. 2 (January 1998): 324–48 and Ruggie, "What Makes the World Hang Together?"

61. Ibid.

62. See Alexander E. Wendt, "The Agent-Structure Problem in International Relations Theory," *International Organization*, 41, no. 3 (Summer 1987): 335–70. Also see Wendt, *Social Theory of International Politics* (Cambridge: Cambridge University Press, 1999).

63. See Ruggie, "What Makes the World Hang Together?"

64. Examples of empirical constructivist works include: Michael N. Barnett, *Dialogues in Arab Politics: Negotiations in Regional Order* (New York: Columbia University Press, 1998); Martha Finnemore, *National Interests in International Society*; Finnemore, "Constructing Norms of Humanitarian Intervention," in Peter J. Katzenstein, ed., *The Culture of National Security* (New York: Columbia University Press, 1996), pp. 153–85; Audi Klotz, *Norms in International Relations: the Struggle against Apartheid* (Ithaca, N.Y.: Cornell University Press, 1995); Thomas Risse-Kappen, "Collective Identity in a Democratic Community: The Case of NATO," in Katzenstein, *The Culture of National Security*, pp. 357–99; Richard Price and Nina Tannenwald, "Norms and Deterrence: The Nuclear and Chemical Weapons Taboos," in Katzenstein, *The Culture of National Security*, 114–52; and Marc Lynch, *State Interests and Public Spheres: The International Politics of Jordanian Identity* (New York: Columbia University Press, 1999).

65. Checkel, "Constructivist Turn," p. 339.

66. To be fair, much constructivist work has focused on why and how questions, particularly those constructivists working with norms. See, for example: Martha Finnemore, *National Interests in International Society*; Klotz, *Norms in International Relations: the Struggle against Apartheid*; Margaret E. Keck and Kathryn Sikkink, *Activists Beyond Borders: Advocacy Networks in International Politics* (Ithaca, N.Y.: Cornell University Press, 1998); Jeffrey W. Legro, "Which Norms Matter? Revisiting the 'failure' of Internationalism," *International Organization*, 51, no. 1 (Winter 1997): 31–63; Martha Finnemore and Kathryn Sikkink, "International Norm Dynamics and Political Change," *International Organization*, 52, no. 4 (Autumn 1998): 887–917; and Thomas Risse, Stephen C. Ropp, and Kathryn Sikkink, *The Power of Human Rights: International*

*Norms and Domestic Change* (Cambridge: Cambridge University Press, 1999).
67. See John J. Mearsheimer, "A Realist Reply," *International Security*, 20, no. 1 (Summer 1995): 82–93.

*Chapter 2*

1. This review does not consider unilateral embargoes initiated by a single power, such as during an armed conflict.
2. Tripartite Declaration, in *Department of State Bulletin*, June 5, 1950, p. 886; and in John Norton Moore, ed., *The Arab-Israeli Conflict: Readings and Documents* (Princeton, N.J.: Princeton University Press, 1977), pp. 988–89.
3. See Yair Evron, *The Role of Arms Control in the Middle East* (London: International Institute for Strategic Studies, 1977), pp. 4–6.
4. Excerpts from Address by President Lyndon B. Johnson, June 19, 1967, in *The Arab-Israeli Peace Process Briefing Book* (Washington, D.C.: Washington Institute for Near East Policy, 1991), p. 9.4. Also see *Department of State Bulletin*, July 10, 1967.
5. In the wake of the Gulf War, a conventional arms transfers register was established under the aegis of the UN Secretary General. UN General Assembly Resolution 46/36 L, December 9, 1991 established the registry. For a review of the work of the UN Register of Conventional Arms in its first three years, see appendix 14D, "The 1994 review of the UN Register of Conventional Arms," in *SIPRI Yearbook 1995: Armaments, Disarmament and International Security* (Oxford: Oxford University Press, 1995), pp. 556–68. The review notes the low participation of Middle East states in the arms registry, suggesting the need for a regional approach. Egypt, in particular, was displeased with the process (see p. 567), in part because its focus was limited to conventional weaponry.
6. Cited in Christopher D. Carr, "False Promises and Prospects: The Middle East Arms Control Initiative," in Jeffrey A. Larsen and Gregory J. Rattray, eds., *Arms Control Toward the 21st Century* (Boulder, Colo.: Lynne Rienner, 1996), p. 256.
7. See Janne E. Nolan, "The U.S.-Soviet Conventional Arms Transfer Negotiations," in Alexander L. George, Philip J. Farley, and Alexander Dallin, eds., *U.S.-Soviet Security Cooperation: Achievements, Failures, Lessons* (Oxford: Oxford University Press, 1988), pp. 510–23. According to Nolan, "reducing the global arms trade was a matter of personal commitment for President Carter, a commitment shared by a number of his most senior advisors" (p. 510). This commitment was formally embodied in Presidential Directive 13 in 1977,

calling for arms transfer limitations to all countries outside of NATO, ANZUS, and Japan.
8. For details on the Bush initiative, see "Fact Sheet: Middle East Arms Control Initiative," *US Department of State Dispatch*, 2, no. 22 (June 3, 1991): 393. For a critique of the Bush initiative and an alternative multilateral conventional arms limitation proposal, see the Congressional Budget Office, *Limiting Conventional Arms Exports to the Middle East* (Washington, D.C.: Congressional Budget Office, 1992).
9. In his testimony before the House Foreign Affairs Committee on February 6, 1991, for example, Secretary Baker put the challenge of regional arms proliferation high on his agenda. See *US Department of State Dispatch*, 2, no. 6 (February 11, 1991): 81–85. Echoing similar themes one month later, on March 6, 1991, President Bush addressed a joint session of Congress and again emphasized the need to end the Middle East arms race; by May 1991, President Bush announced his arms control initiative. For President Bush's speech to Congress, see "The World After the Persian Gulf War," *US Department of State Dispatch*, 2, no. 10 (March 11, 1991): 161.
10. By the time President Bush was promoting his arms control initiative, the United States had became the number one arms supplier to the Third World. See Richard Grimmet, *Conventional Arms Transfers to the Third World, 1984–1991* (Washington, D.C.: Congressional Research Service, July 1992).
11. For detailed accounts of these meetings, see: "Statement Issued After the Meeting of the Five on Arms Transfers and Non-Proliferation," *US Department of State Dispatch*, 2, no. 28 (July 15, 1991): 508; "Progress in Middle East Arms Control," Statement by Reginald Bartholomew, Under Secretary for International Security Affairs, before the Subcommittee on Arms Control, International Organizations, and Science of the House Foreign Affairs Committee, Washington, D.C., March 24, 1992, in *US Department of State Dispatch*, 3, no. 13, (March 30, 1992): 242; "Third Round of Arms Sales Talks Fails to Resolve Notification Issue," *Arms Control Today*, 22, no. 5 (June 1992): 21. For more details on the sticking points of the permanent five negotiations, see "President Bush's Middle East Arms Control Initiative: One Year Later," *Arms Control Today*, 22, no. 5 (June 1992): 11–16.
12. See Aharon Klieman, "The Israel-Jordan Tacit Security Regime," in Efraim Inbar, ed., *Regional Security Regimes: Israel and its Neighbors* (New York: State University of New York Press, 1995), pp. 127–49. Also see Klieman, *Statecraft in the Dark: Israel's Practice of Quiet Diplomacy* (Boulder, Colo: Westview Press, 1988) and *Israel and the World After 40 Years* (Washington, D.C.: Pergamon-Brassey's, 1990).
13. On this point, and for an overview of various bilateral CSBMs, see Yair Evron, "Confidence-and Security-Building Measures in the Arab-Israeli Context," in

Efraim Inbar and Shmuel Sandler, eds., *Middle Eastern Security: Prospects for An Arms Control Regime* (London: Frank Cass, 1995), pp. 152–72, esp. p. 161.

14. For a comprehensive study on measures to facilitate the establishment of a NWFZ in the Middle East predating ACRS, see *Establishment of a Nuclear-Weapon-Free-Zone in the Region of the Middle East*, Report of the Secretary-General, United Nations General Assembly, October 10, 1990, Forty-fifth session. For an assessment of the prospects for a WMDFZ in the Middle East in light of peace process developments, see Jan Prawitz and James F. Leonard, *A Zone Free of Weapons of Mass Destruction in the Middle East*, United Nations Institute for Disarmament Research (New York and Geneva: United Nations, 1996).

15. For a comprehensive study of NWFZ proposals from an Egyptian perspective, see Mahmoud Karem, *A Nuclear-Weapon-Free Zone in the Middle East* (New York: Greenwood Press, 1988). Also see Karem, "A Nuclear-Weapon-Free Zone in the Middle East: A Historical Overview of the Patterns of Involvement of the United Nations," in Tariq Rauf, ed., *Regional Approaches to Curbing Nuclear Proliferation in the Middle East and South Asia* (Ottawa: The Canadian Centre for Global Security, 1992), pp. 55–68. Karem's writing is particularly significant because he has played an influential role in the formation of Egyptian arms control policy in general and ACRS in particular as Director of the Disarmament Division at the Ministry of Foreign Affairs in Cairo. Also see Mohamed Nabil Fahmy (a senior Egyptian official in the Foreign Ministry), "Egypt's Disarmament Initiative," *Bulletin of the Atomic Scientists*, 46, no. 9: 9.

16. For an analysis of Israel's policy of ambiguity and its implications for regional arms control, see Avner Cohen, "Patterns of Nuclear Opacity in the Middle East: Understanding the Past, Implications for the Future," in Rauf, *Regional Approaches*, pp. 13–54. On the general issue of Israel's nuclear capability, see Avner Cohen, *Israel and the Bomb* (New York: Columbia University Press, 1999).

17. Israel proposed a NWFZ on October 30, 1980, to the General Assembly as a draft resolution. For the full text, see *Briefing Book*, pp. 9.8–9.9. In 1988, Israeli Prime Minister Yitzhak Shamir proposed a chemical-weapon-free-zone in the Middle East. See Address by Yitzhak Shamir to the UN General Assembly, June 7, 1988, reprinted in *Briefing Book*, pp. 9.9–9.14.

18. Avner Cohen, "The Nuclear Issue in the Middle East in a New World Order," in Inbar and Sandler, *Middle Eastern Security: Prospects for An Arms Control Regime*, p. 55.

19. For an analysis of alternative economic arrangements among Israel, Jordan, and the Palestinian territories under conditions of peace, see Patrick Clawson and Howard Rosen, *The Economic Consequences of Peace for Israel, the*

*Palestinians and Jordan*, Policy Paper No. 25 (Washington, D.C.: Washington Institute for Near East Policy, 1991).

20. For details of the ALPHA operation, see *Foreign Relations of the United States (FRUS), 1955–1957*, vol. 14, The Arab-Israeli Dispute (Washington, D.C.: U.S. Government Printing Office, 1989), pp. 1–401. Also see Evelyn Shuckburgh, *Descent to Suez, Diaries 1951–56* (New York: Norton, 1987), esp. pp. 242–67.

21. See Isaac Alteras, *Eisenhower and Israel: U.S.-Israeli Relations, 1953–1960* (Gainesville: University Press of Florida, 1993), p. 131.

22. See *FRUS, 1958–1960*, vol. 13 (1992), The Arab-Israeli Dispute, pp. 2–5.

23. Specifically, many believed any proposals that encouraged Arab unity, such as a development fund, would undermine the influence of oil companies in the region. This concern was made clear by Secretary of State John Foster Dulles in a conversation with John J. McCloy (Chairman of Chase Manhattan Bank), when Dulles briefed McCloy on the U.N. proposed plan for a regional development fund: "Arab unity may make it more difficult for the oil companies to maintain a decent position there [the Middle East]. The Sec would not want to dissuade M[cCloy] from doing it [providing credits for regional projects] but throws out this warning. M said it has a lot of imponderables and he does not like to be associated with something so vague." Quoted in *FRUS, 1958–1960*, vol. 12 (1993), Near East Region, p. 1.

24. See Jonathan E. Sanford, *U.S. Foreign Policy and Multilateral Development Banks* (Boulder, Colo.: Westview Press, 1982), p. 57.

25. For an account of the origins and evolution of the Arab boycott, see Aaron J. Sarna, *Boycott and Blacklist: A History of Arab Economic Warfare Against Israel* (New Jersey: Rowman & Littlefield, 1986).

26. Ibid., p. 74.

27. For a more detailed discussion of the implications of peace on foreign investment and foreign direct investment (FDI) in Israel, see Steve A. Yetiv, "Peace, Interdependence, and the Middle East," *Political Science Quarterly*, 112, no. 1 (Spring 1997): 29–49.

28. See Gary Clyde Hufbauer and Jeffrey J. Schott (assisted by Kimberly Ann Elliott), *Economic Sanctions Reconsidered: History and Current Policy* (Washington, D.C.: Institute for International Economics, 1985), p. 184.

29. For an analysis of evolving economic relations among the triad since the Oslo Accords (and more specifically the Paris protocols of April 1994) and the Israel-Jordan peace treaty, see Hisham Awartani and Ephraim Kleiman, "Economic Interactions Among Participants in the Middle East Peace Process," *Middle East Journal*, 51, no. 2 (Spring 1997): 215–29.

30. Heba Handoussa and Nemat Shafik, "The Economics of Peace: The Egyptian Case," in Stanley Fischer, Dani Rodrik and Elias Tuma, eds., *The Economics*

*of Middle East Peace: Views From the Region* (Cambridge, Mass.: MIT Press, 1993), p. 36.
31. Ibid.
32. For more on the Egyptian-Israeli trade relationship in the wake of their peace treaty, including potential areas where economic relations can expand, see Meir Merhav, ed., *Economic Cooperation and Middle East Peace* (London: Weidenfeld and Nicolson, 1989), pp. 16–21.
33. For examples of these views, see Ephraim Kleiman, "Some Basic Problems of the Economic Relationships between Israel, and the West Bank, and Gaza," pp. 305–33, and Osama A. Hamed and Radwan A. Shaban, "One-sided Customs and Monetary Union: The Case of the West Bank and Gaza Strip under Israeli Occupation," pp. 19–54, both in Fischer, Rodrik, and Tuma, *Economics of Middle East Peace*.
34. Kleiman, "Some Basic Problems," p. 309.
35. Hamed and Shaban, "One-sided Customs," p. 121.
36. Ibid.
37. The total public sector investment in the territories from 1982 to 1987 averaged just $60 million. See Fischer, Rodrik, and Tuma, *Economics of Middle East Peace*, p. 316.
38. See Awartani and Kleiman, "Economic Interactions," p. 223. Also see Marlise Simons, "Gaza-Jericho Economic Accord Signed by Israel and Palestinians," *New York Times*, April 30, 1994, p. A1.
39. For example, see Joyce R. Starr (with Addeane S. Caelleigh), *A Shared Destiny: Near East Regional Development and Cooperation* (New York: Praeger, 1983) and Merhav, *Economic Cooperation*.
40. On the Johnston Plan, see: "Jordan Waters," chap. 5 in Michael Brecher, *Decisions in Israel's Foreign Policy* (New Haven, Conn.: Yale University Press, 1975), pp. 173–224; "The Johnston Mission to the Middle East," chap. 4 in Miriam R. Lowi, *Water and Power: The Politics of a Scarce Resource in the Jordan River Basin* (Cambridge: Cambridge University Press, 1993), pp. 79–114; and Alteras, *Eisenhower and Israel*, esp. pp. 118–25.
41. See, for example, Daniel Hillel, *Rivers of Eden: The Struggle for Water and the Quest for Peace in the Middle East* (Oxford: Oxford University Press, 1994).
42. Lowi, *Water and Power*, p. 105.
43. For a detailed discussion of the Israeli-Jordanian water sharing scheme, see Jeffrey K. Sosland, *Cooperating Rivals: The Politics of Water Scarcity, Protracted Conflict, and Complex Cooperation in the Jordan River Basin* (Ph.D. diss., Georgetown University, 1998).
44. See Hillel, *Rivers of Eden* and Miriam Lowi, "Rivers of Conflict, Rivers of Peace," *Journal of International Affairs*, 49, no. 1 (Summer 1995): 123–45.

Notes to Chapter 3

45. For more details on these negotiations, see Lowi, "Rivers of Conflict," esp. pp. 130–34.
46. See Robert B. Abel, *The Influence of Technical Cooperation on Reducing Tensions in the Middle East* (Lanham, Md.: University Press of America, 1997), p. 29.
47. For an analysis of the Mediterranean Action Plan drawing on the epistemic communities approach, see Peter M. Haas, *Saving the Mediterranean: The Politics of International Environmental Cooperation* (New York: Columbia University Press, 1990); and P. Haas, "Do Regimes Matter? Epistemic Communities and Mediterranean Pollution Control," *International Organization*, 43, no. 3 (Summer 1989): 377–403.

*Chapter 3*

1. Prepared statement by Secretary Baker for the organizational meeting for multilateral negotiations on the Middle East, Moscow, January 28, 1992, reproduced in *Israel Information Service* <gopher://israel-info.gov.il:70/00/mad/multi/multi.2>. For Baker's delivered remarks to the conference (both opening and closing), see "Organizational Meeting for Multilateral Negotiations on the Middle East," *US Department of State Dispatch*, 3, no. 5 (February 3, 1992): 79–80.
2. See Nelson W. Polsby, "The Foreign Policy Establishment: Toward Professionalism and Centrism," in Eugene R. Wittkopf, ed., *The Domestic Sources of American Foreign Policy: Insights and Evidence*, 2nd ed. (New York: St. Martin's Press, 1994), pp. 208–215.
3. See Heclo, "Issue Networks and the Executive Establishment," in Anthony King, ed., *The New American Political System* (Washington, D.C.: American Enterprise Institute for Public Policy Research, 1978), pp. 87–124. According to Heclo, an issue network exists where a group of experts with shared knowledge, in or out of government, focus on a particular policy area as policymaking becomes a much more complex and fluid process. The experts in the issue network do not require professional training; they need only be issue-skilled, or be "well informed about the ins and outs of a particular policy debate." (p. 103).
4. Author interview with senior U.S. official, May 6, 1996, Washington, D.C.
5. Author interview with senior U.S. official, May 8, 1996, Washington, D.C.
6. Shlomo Avineri, "From World Struggle to Regional Conflict," *Ha'aretz*, January 16, 1996, reproduced in *Israel Information Service*, February 20, 1996 <gopher://israel-info.gov.il:70/00/archive/dps96/96021ba.dps>.
7. Muhammad Faour, *The Arab World After Desert Storm* (Washington, D.C.: The United States Institute of Peace Press, 1993), p. 118.

8. See, for example, Fouad Ajami, *The Arab Predicament: Arab Political Thought and Practice Since 1967* (Cambridge: Cambridge University Press, 1981) and Malcolm H. Kerr, *The Arab Cold War* (Oxford: Oxford University Press, 1970).
9. See Michael N. Barnett, *Dialogues in Arab Politics* (New York: Columbia University Press, 1998).
10. James A. Baker III, *The Politics of Diplomacy* (New York: Putnam, 1995), p. 412.
11. Federal News Service, March 6, 1991. Printed in *The Arab-Israeli Peace Process Briefing Book* (Washington, D.C.: Washington Institute for Near East Policy, 1991), p. 2.1.
12. Author interview with Israeli official, August 21, 1995, Washington, D.C.
13. For early discussion of the two track idea, see "The Middle East Peace Process," *US Department of State Dispatch*, 3, supplement no. 2 (February 1992), esp. Baker's comments at a news conference en route from Riyadh to Cairo, March 10, 1991 (pp. 16–17).
14. The State Department, for example, issued a document as early as 1979 suggesting Arab-Israeli regional cooperation projects. See Abdul-Monem Al-Mashat, *The Economics of Regional Security in the Middle East* (Cairo University, November 1994). Also see Joyce R. Starr (with Addeane S. Caelleigh), *A Shared Destiny: Near East Regional Development and Cooperation* (New York: Praeger, 1983).
15. As the invitation states, "Those parties who wish to attend multilateral negotiations will convene two weeks after the opening conference to organize those negotiations. The co-sponsors believe that those negotiations should focus on region-wide issues such as arms control and regional security, water, refugee issues, environment, economic development, and other subjects of mutual interest." Reprinted in "Recent Developments in the Middle East Peace Process," *US Department of State Dispatch*, 4, supplement no. 4 (September 1993): 25–26. The fact that the Moscow organizational session did not occur until late January of 1992 (rather than two weeks after Madrid as the invitation stipulated) reflects in part the lack of thought and planning put into the process until after Madrid (although the breakup of the Soviet Union between Madrid and Moscow also slowed the process).
16. For details of peace process initiatives and diplomacy before the Madrid conference, see William B. Quandt, *Peace Process: American Diplomacy and The Arab-Israeli Conflict Since 1967* (Washington, D.C.: The Brookings Institution, 1993).
17. On the U.S.-PLO dialogue and Reagan policy toward the Arab-Israeli peace process, see ibid., pp. 367–80.
18. Baker, *Politics of Diplomacy*, p. 115.

19. For the full text of the Shamir Plan, see *Briefing Book*, p. 4.27. Also reprinted in *Jerusalem Post*, April 14, 1989, p. 8.
20. Author interviews with senior U.S. officials, January 3, 1996 and May 6, 1996, Washington, D.C.
21. However, Shamir denies that he viewed the multilaterals as an incentive to attend the Madrid conference. For him, the question of Palestinian representation was at the heart of the issue, and ultimately dictated his position on Israeli participation at the conference. Author interview with Yitzhak Shamir, August 28, 1996, Tel Aviv, Israel.
22. Author interview with senior U.S. official, May 6, 1996, Washington, D.C.
23. For example, the EU, Japan, and Canada were given working groups to chair — REDWG, the Environment, and Refugees respectively.
24. According to one senior State Department official and former Baker aide — confirmed by Baker himself in an interview with the author — Baker was prepared to give up the multilaterals in exchange for Syrian acceptance to attend Madrid. Baker's aides avoided this by creating the compromise that attendance at the multilaterals would be optional, thus keeping the process afloat even without Syrian (and Lebanese) participation. Author interview with senior U.S. official, May 8, 1996, Washington, D.C. Also see Baker, *Politics of Diplomacy*, p. 505.
25. Author interview with senior State Department official, January 3, 1996, Washington, D.C.
26. By the eve of the Moscow conference, the Palestinians changed their position on this and subsequently supported the inclusion of the Refugee group in the process. The Israelis continued to express concern about including this issue but had little choice given Baker's insistence on its inclusion.
27. Israel was also concerned that arms control would dominate the process. Author interview with senior State Department official, January 3, 1996, Washington, D.C.
28. The steering group included: the United States, Russia, Israel, Egypt, Jordan, the Palestinians, Saudi Arabia (representing the GCC states), Tunisia, (representing the Arab Maghreb Union states), and the European Union, Japan, and Canada (all serving as lead organizers for various working groups).
29. For more details regarding the structure of the multilaterals and the operations of its various working groups, see Joel Peters, *Building Bridges: The Arab-Israeli Multilateral Talks* (London: The Royal Institute of International Affairs, 1994), esp. pp. 6–11, and Peters, *Pathways to Peace: The Multilateral Arab-Israeli Talks* (London: The Royal Institute of International Affairs, 1996).
30. Speech by Assistant Secretary for Near Eastern Affairs Edward P. Djerejian, *US Department of State Dispatch*, 4, no. 41 (October 11, 1993): 696.

31. Israel was concerned about the arms control aspect of ACRS, particularly Arab pressure on the nuclear issue. The Arab parties, especially Egypt, were adamant that the arms control (and nuclear) aspects of the group predominate. The Refugee group was a concession to the Palestinians (although they were initially opposed to it) and received cooly by the Israelis, who boycotted the first meeting in May 1992 because of controversy over the participation of diaspora Palestinians. Still, to satisfy the Israelis, the mandate for this group was limited to improving the conditions of the refugees in their present locations; the issue of the right of return and resettlement was left for the final status talks in bilateral Israeli-Palestinian negotiations.
32. For the Palestinian representation controversy at the Moscow conference, see David Makovsky, "US, Israel Deadlocked on Status of 'Outside' Palestinians in Regional Talks," *Jerusalem Post*, January 29, 1992, and Makovsky, "US, Russia Back Israeli Stand on Palestinian Delegation; Multilateral Talks Opening in Moscow Today," *Jerusalem Post*, January 28, 1992.
33. For expectations on the financing of the multilaterals, see Cairo MENA, November 17, 1991, " 'Sources' on Plan for Multilateral Talks in Rome," cited in *Foreign Broadcast Information Service-Near East and South Asia*-91-222 (hereafter *FBIS-NES*), November 18, 1991, p. 1 and Cairo *Al-Wafd*, November 18, 1991, p. 1, "Multilateral Talks to Examine Regional Concord," cited in *FBIS-NES*-91-226, November 22, 1991, p. 1. As David Makovsky explained, "The idea of the talks is that the richest industrialized countries will in time set aside a multi-billion dollar regional development fund, which will be offered to Arabs and Israelis as a potential benefit should they resolve their political conflicts." In Makovsky, "Levy Going to Moscow Today After Dedicating Embassy in Beijing," *Jerusalem Post*, January 26, 1992.
34. In negotiations between the Madrid and Moscow conferences to convene the multilateral talks, the linkage between bilateral progress and regional cooperation was a dominant theme. See, for example, David Makovsky, "International Funding for Regional Projects Linked to Peace Progress; 17 Non-Mideast States Likely to Join Multilateral Talks," *Jerusalem Post*, November 18, 1991.
35. Concluding remarks by Secretary Baker, Moscow, January 28, 1992. Reprinted in *US Department of State Dispatch*, 3 (February 1992): 27.
36. Author interview with senior U.S. official, May 8, 1996, Washington, D.C.
37. Author interview with Israeli official, August 21, 1995, Washington, D.C.
38. From the outset, the Syrians (and consequently the Lebanese) refused to attend a regional forum with Israel before all bilateral disputes had been settled, which is why the United States made participation in the multilaterals voluntary in the Madrid letter of invitation. Since the Moscow conference, Syria has maintained this position and has attempted to convince other Arab states to follow

suit. For an early statement of the Syrian position on the multilaterals, see London MBC Television, December 5, 1991, "Syrian Sees 'No Benefit' in Multilateral Talks," cited in *FBIS-NES*-91–235, December 6, 1991, pp. 2–3. Also see Baker, *Politics of Diplomacy*, p. 502.

39. See Jerusalem *Qol Yisra'el*, December 11, 1991, "U.S., Israel 'At Odds' Over Multilateral Talks," cited in *FBIS-NES*-91–238, December 11, 1991, p. 45 and Tel Aviv *Davar*, January 2, 1992, "Levi Sends Baker Position Paper on Multilaterals," cited in *FBIS-NES*-92–001, January 2, 1992, pp. 17–18. These points were also made in an author interview with a senior State Department official, January 3, 1996, Washington, D.C.

40. Indeed, according to a senior U.S. official, Egypt was initially supportive of the multilaterals, expressing enthusiasm for a process which it believed vindicated its decision to make peace with Israel. Author interview with senior U.S. official, May 6, 1996, Washington, D.C.

41. Hearing before Commission on Security and Cooperation in Europe, "CSCME: Prospects for Collective Security in the Middle East," One Hundred Third Congress, First Session, October 14, 1993. Crown Prince Hassan's plan is printed in the appendix, pp. 68–82.

42. See Paris Radio Monte Carlo, November 9, 1991, "Al-Masri on Bilateral, Multilateral Talks," cited in *FBIS-NES*-91–218, November 12, 1991, p. 37.

43. This dispute is what led to the Palestinian boycott of the Moscow conference and to the Israeli boycott of the first Refugee working group meeting in May 1992, when the cosponsors loosened restrictions on Palestinian participation and allowed diaspora Palestinians to participate. However, after Israeli elections the new Labor government agreed to include diaspora Palestinians in the Refugee group by the second plenary in November 1992 as long as they were not members of the PLO or the PNC. This issue became moot after Oslo.

44. Jon Immanuel, "Both Sides Claim Moscow Victory, and Now Await Next Round of Talks," *Jerusalem Post*, January 31, 1992.

45. As one Israeli official acknowledged, the Israeli participants knew the Palestinians were PLO members but did not publicly admit this. Author interview on September 27, 1995, Jerusalem.

46. The World Bank subsequently drafted a more detailed plan for Palestinian aid the following spring. See Thomas L. Friedman, "Agency Offering a Detailed Plan of Palestinian Aid," *New York Times*, May 3, 1994, p. A1.

47. This proposal was initiated with the Damascus Declaration of March 6, 1991, issued by the foreign ministers of Syria, Egypt, and the six Gulf Cooperation Council (GCC) states. For analysis of the failure of the Damascus Declaration, see Kim Murphy and Robin Wright, "Setbacks Widen U.S. Role in Gulf Security," *Los Angeles Times*, May 12, 1991, p. A1; Peter F. Sisler, "All-Arab

Defense of Gulf Unravels," *Washington Times*, May 9, 1991, p. A1; and "Damascus Declaration Put on Ice till April," in *Mideast Mirror*, November 12, 1991, p. 9.
48. Author interview with senior State Department official, January 3, 1996, Washington, D.C.
49. For instance, Oman was the first Gulf country to sponsor a multilateral working group (Water), in April 1994. Qatar and Bahrain have also hosted plenary sessions. In contrast, the Saudis have yet to sponsor a multilateral session.
50. *Mideast Mirror*, February 9, 1993. However, in private conversations with the author, other Arab officials noted that despite the Syrians' public stance on the multilaterals, they were extremely interested in the process, and were regularly briefed by other Arab participants on the proceedings of all working groups. The Americans encouraged these informal briefings because they hoped they would better prepare the Syrians for joining the process at a later stage without having to rework existing agreements.
51. For instance, in the Gulf, the Damascus Declaration (an attempt to establish a regional security force) failed because GCC states ultimately preferred the political risks of bilateral security ties to the West to the creation of a regional, pan-Arab security regime. On the demise of the Damascus Declaration, see Bruce Maddy-Weitzman and Joseph Kostiner, "The Damascus Declaration: An Arab Attempt At Regional Security," in Efraim Inbar, ed., *Regional Security Regimes: Israel and Its Neighbors* (Albany: State University of New York Press, 1995), pp. 107–125. Israel also continued to depend on and strengthen its bilateral security relationship with the United States in the years following the Gulf War, and developed new bilateral security links and cooperation with Jordan and Turkey as well. One Palestinian critic observed the Israeli preference for bilateral security arrangements, arguing that bilateral deals are "maximizing its [Israel's] bargaining power in each bilateral track and making itself the primary locus of all regional arrangements. . . . Only the existence of collective institutions might limit its relative advantage at the regional level," in Yezid Sayigh, "Redefining the Basics: Sovereignty and Security of the Palestinian State," *Journal of Palestine Studies*, 24, no. 4 (Summer 1995): 15–16. While these bilateral alternatives do not preclude multilateral security cooperation, they underscore that such regional cooperation was not the preferred choice among regional players, and not highly valued among top security elites.
52. For a guns versus butter argument, see Yahya M. Sadowski, *Scuds or Butter? The Political Economy of Arms Control in the Middle East* (Washington, D.C.: The Brookings Institution, 1993).
53. See, for example, Kenneth R. Timmerman, "The New World Arms Market," *Wall Street Journal*, April 3, 1997, p. A18.
54. For example, Israel has been actively developing a missile defense system (the

Arrow). For more on Israel's altering defense strategy and the development of the Arrow, see Peter Hirschberg, "Hitting Back," *Jerusalem Report*, March 21, 1996, pp. 20–22.
55. Hisham Awartani and Ephraim Kleiman, "Economic Interactions Among Participants in the Middle East Peace Process," *Middle East Journal*, 51, no. 2 (Spring 1997): 217
56. This is Stanley Fischer's estimate for 1983, the last year complete data were available for all countries in the region. See Fischer, "Prospects for Regional Integration in the Middle East," in Jaime De Melo and Arvind Panagariya, eds., *New Dimensions in Regional Integration* (Cambridge: Cambridge University Press, 1993), p. 434. Alan Richards and John Waterbury have cited similar figures in Richards and Waterbury, eds., A *Political Economy of the Middle East*, 2d ed. (Boulder, Colo.: Westview Press, 1996), p. 366.
57. Fischer, "Prospects for Regional Integration," p. 435.
58. Ibid., p. 436.
59. Awartani and Kleiman, "Economic Interactions," p. 221.
60. International Monetary Fund (IMF) Working Paper, *Is MENA a Region? The Scope for Regional Integration*, prepared by Mohamed A. El-Erian and Stanley Fischer, April 1996, p. ii.
61. These claims, while prevalent in the Arab press, tend to be exaggerated. Author interview with Egyptian official, Washington, D.C., March 27, 1996. For an Israeli response to these charges, see Yossi Beilin, "The Economic Fruits of Peace," excerpts from Remarks to the Jerusalem Economic Forum, January 31, 1995. Reproduced as a Policy Paper in *Israel Information Service* <gopher://israel-info.gov.il:70/00/speech/sta/950131b.sta>, February 9, 1995.
62. For a more detailed account of the implications of a regional peace for Israeli economic activity in the region, see Nadav Halevi, "Economic Implications of Peace: The Israeli Perspective," in Stanley Fischer, Dani Rodrik, and Elias Tuma, eds., *The Economics of Middle East Peace* (Cambridge, Mass.: MIT Press, 1993), pp. 87–115.
63. One relatively successful example of such a joint venture is a garment plant established in Jordan producing, among other things, Victoria's Secret lingerie with a "Made in Israel" label. Israelis enjoy lower production costs (about 50 percent less than in Israel) while the Jordanians can take advantage of Israel's preferential trading status with key importers like the United States. See Douglas Jehl, "Whose Lingerie Is It? A New Mideast Secret," *New York Times*, December 25, 1996, p. A6.
64. Interview with Deputy Under Secretary Oded Eran by *Zaman*, October 21, 1996, cited in *FBIS-NES-96-210*, October 21, 1996, p. 4 (emphasis added), located in World News Connection <http://wnc.fedworld.gov>.
65. Remarks by Deputy Foreign Minister Yossi Beilin to the Jerusalem Economic

Forum, January 31, 1995. Reproduced in *Israel Information Service* <gopher:/
/israel-info.gov.il:70/00/speech/sta/950131b.sta>.
66. David Rosenberg, "Someone Say Boycott?," *Jerusalem Report*, May 1, 1997, p. 41.
67. Ibid.
68. Among the most prevalent subregional cooperation alternatives considered by economists is a free trade zone among Israel, Jordan, and a future Palestinian entity, with some proposals including Egypt as well. See Patrick Clawson and Howard Rosen, *The Economic Consequences of Peace for Israel, the Palestinians and Jordan*, Policy Paper No. 25 (Washington, D.C.: Washington Institute for Near East Policy, 1991). Former Israeli Finance Minister Dan Meridor raised this idea as well. See Israel Line, *Israel Information Service* <gopher://israel-info.gov.il:70/11/archive>, March 24, 1997.
69. El-Erian and Fischer, *Is MENA a Region?*, pp. ii, 14. For a similar argument that economic growth and prosperity depend on domestic policies and not peace process related activity, see Eliyahu Kanovsky, "The Middle East Economies: The Impact of Domestic and International Politics," *Middle East Report of International Affairs (MERIA)*, journal 2, article 1 (June 1, 1997) <www.biu.ac.il/soc/besa/meria.html>.
70. The study group held a conference from November 14–16, 1991 which produced papers that eventually became the edited volume by Fischer, Rodrik, and Tuma, *Economics of Middle East Peace*. The regional participants included Egyptians, Israelis, Jordanians, Palestinians, Syrians, Lebanese, and from 1992 (after the Moscow organizational session for the multilaterals), several Gulf states.
71. Fischer, Rodrik, and Tuma, "Introduction," *Economics of Middle East Peace*, pp. 1–16.
72. For another example of this argument, see John Page, "Securing the Peace Dividend in the Middle East: External Finance and Domestic Effort," *Middle East Executive Reports*, 17, no. 10 (October 1994): 9. Also see Fischer, "Prospects for Regional Integration," pp. 423–449.
73. For a similar story concerning the establishment of a new Arab-Israeli regional institution—the Middle East Development Bank—see Dalia Dassa Kaye, *Banking on Peace: Lessons from the Middle East Development Bank*, Policy Paper No. 43 (San Diego, Calif.: Institute on Global Conflict and Cooperation, October 1998).
74. For opinion polls in the Arab Levant on normalization with Israel, documenting the negative attitude toward normalization among Arab publics despite growing acceptance of Israel at official levels, see Hilal Khashan, "The Levant: Yes to Treaties, No to Normalization," *Middle East Quarterly*, 2, no. 2 (June 1995): 3–13.

75. See, for example, William A. Orme, Jr., "Israeli Business Flies Like a Dove," *New York Times*, October 18, 1998, section 4, p. 3.
76. For a detailed account of this tacit cooperation, see Jeffrey K. Sosland, *Cooperating Rivals: The Politics of Water Scarcity, Protracted Conflict, and Complex Cooperation in the Jordan River Basin* (Ph.D. diss., Georgetown University, 1998). On the Johnston Plan, see: "Jordan Waters," chap. 5 in Michael Brecher, *Decisions in Israel's Foreign Policy* (New Haven, Conn.: Yale University Press, 1975), pp. 173–224; "The Johnston Mission to the Middle East," chap. 4 in Miriam R. Lowi, *Water and Power: The Politics of a Scarce Resource in the Jordan River Basin* (Cambridge: Cambridge University Press, 1993), pp. 79–114; and Issac Alteras, *Eisenhower and Israel* (Gainesville: University Press of Florida, 1993), esp. pp. 118–25.
77. For an analysis of the Mediterranean Action Plan drawing on the epistemic communities approach, see Peter M. Haas, *Saving the Mediterranean: The Politics of International Environmental Cooperation* (New York: Columbia University Press, 1990); and P. Haas, "Do Regimes Matter? Epistemic Communities and Mediterranean Pollution Control," *International Organization*, 43, no. 3 (Summer 1989): 377–403.
78. Author interview with senior State Department official, January 3, 1996.
79. For an elaboration of this concept and empirical applications, see John Ruggie, "International Regimes, Transactions, and Change: Embedded Liberalism in the Postwar Economic Order," in Stephen D. Krasner, ed., *International Regimes* (Ithaca, N.Y.: Cornell University Press, 1983), pp. 195–231; Ruggie, "Multilateralism: The Anatomy of an Institution," in Ruggie, ed., *Multilateralism Matters* (New York: Columbia University Press, 1993), pp. 3–47; and Steven Weber, "Shaping the Postwar Balance of Power: Multilateralism in NATO," *International Organization*, 46, no. 3 (Summer 1992): 633–80.
80. For the agent problem in ideational analysis, see Thomas Risse Kappen, "Ideas Do Not Float Freely: Transnational Relations, Domestic Structures and the End of the Cold War," *International Organization*, 48, no. 2 (Spring 1994): 185–214.
81. Polsby, "Foreign Policy Establishment," p. 210.
82. For an account of the old establishment, see Walter Isaacson and Evan Thomas, *The Wise Men: Six Friends and the World They Made* (New York: Simon and Schuster, 1986). The six men referred to are: Robert Lovett; John McCloy; Averell Harriman; Charles Bohlen; George Kennan; and Dean Acheson. Also see Godfrey Hodgson, *The Colonel* (New York: Knopf, 1990). For an account of the establishment's position on the Middle East, see Clark Clifford (with Richard Holbrooke), *Counsel to the President: A Memoir* (New York: Random House, 1991). In Clifford's words (pp. 4–5), the attitude of Secretary of Defense James V. Forrestal (who opposed the policy of recognizing the new

state of Israel), "was typical of the foreign policy establishment, especially the pro-Arab professionals at the State Department, who, deeply influenced by the huge oil reserves in the Mideast, supported the side they thought would be the likely winner in the struggle between Arabs and Jews. . . . I sometimes felt, almost bitterly, that they preferred to follow the views of the British Foreign Office than those of the President."

83. The term "Arabist" is usually associated with career Foreign Service Officers (FSOs) in the Near East Affairs Bureau of the State Department who speak Arabic and have served in the Arab world. They are traditionally viewed as not only Arab experts but as pro-Arab. See Robert D. Kaplan, "Tales From the Bazaar," *The Atlantic Monthly* (August 1992), pp. 38–39, and William B. Quandt, *Decade of Decisions: American Policy Toward the Arab-Israeli Conflict, 1967–1976* (Berkeley: University of California Press, 1977), pp. 25–26.

84. Quoted in Laura Blumenfeld, "Three Peace Suits," *Washington Post*, February 24, 1997, p. D1.

85. For a more extensive argument about the nature and evolution of this policy community, see Dalia Dassa Kaye, "Learning in the Arab-Israeli Peace Process: The Emergence of an American Middle East Epistemic Community" (master's thesis, University of California, Berkeley, April 1993).

86. See Christopher Madison, "Baker's Inner Circle," *National Journal* (July 13, 1991), pp. 1733–1738, and Morton Kondracke, "Baker's Half Dozen," *New Republic* (February 24, 1992), p. 11.

87. David Hoffman, "Little Known Aide Plays Major Role in Foreign Policy," *Washington Post*, October 28, 1991, p. A1.

88. See, for example, Dennis Ross, *Acting With Caution: Middle East Policy Planning for the Second Reagan Administration*, Policy Paper No. 1 (Washington, D.C.: Washington Institute for Near East Policy, 1984), p. 40, and Dennis Ross, "The Peace Process—A Status Report," in *U.S. Policy and the Middle East Peace Process, Fourth Annual Conference* (Washington, D.C.: Washington Institute for Near East Policy, 1989), pp. 10–18.

89. Norman Kempster, "Insider; Baker Aide, Ex-Envoy to Syria, Pushes Doors Open in Mideast," *Los Angeles Times*, World Report, November 19, 1991, p. H2.

90. See *Building for Peace: An American Strategy for the Middle East* (Washington, D.C.: Washington Institute for Near East Policy, 1988).

91. See, for example, the Washington Institute's Study Group Report, *Pursuing Peace: An American Strategy for the Arab-Israeli Peace Process* (Washington, D.C.: Washington Institute for Near East Policy, 1992). See *After the Storm: Challenges for America's Middle East Policy* (Washington, D.C.: Washington Institute for Near East Policy, 1991).

92. Author interview with senior U.S. official, May 6, 1996, Washington, D.C.

93. Author interview with senior U.S. official, May 6, 1996. This point was repeated to the author in several interviews, when senior American officials emphasized the central role of Israeli integration and normalization above all else. Author interview with senior American official, Tel Aviv, October 19, 1995.
94. Author interview with senior U.S. official, May 8, 1996, Washington, D.C.

*Chapter 4*

1. For example, even after the Gulf War, the Middle East continued to lead the world in arms imports, accounting for over 30 percent of the world's arms market. See *Limiting Conventional Arms Exports to the Middle East* (Washington, D.C.: Congressional Budget Office, September 1992), pp. 7–10. For additional data on arms sales to the region, see *The Military Balance 1998/99* (Oxford: Oxford University Press for the International Institute for Strategic Studies, 1998).
2. For example, five states in the region have armed forces that approach or exceed half a million personnel (Iraq, Iran, Syria, Israel, and Egypt), tank inventories are estimated at 25,000 (ten times those of Africa or Latin America), and combat aircraft number over 4,000 (roughly four times those of Africa or Latin America). See Alfred B. Prados, *Middle East Arms Supply: Recent Control Initiatives*, Congressional Research Service (CRS) Issue Brief (Washington, D.C.: Congressional Research Service, April 16, 1992), p. 1. For more data on the region's military balance after the Gulf War, see Anthony H. Cordesman, *After the Storm: the Changing Military Balance in the Middle East* (Boulder, Colo.: Westview Press, 1993), and *The Military Balance 1998/99*.
3. See Michael N. Barnett, "Regional Security After the Gulf War," *Political Science Quarterly*, 111, no. 4 (Winter 1996–97): 597–618.
4. For other detailed accounts of empirical developments in ACRS, see Bruce W. Jentleson and Dalia Dassa Kaye, "Security Status: Explaining Regional Security Cooperation and Its Limits in the Middle East," *Security Studies* 8, no. 1 (autumn 1998): 204–38, and Bruce W. Jentleson, *The Middle East Arms Control and Regional Security (ACRS) Talks: Progress, Problems and Prospects*, IGCC Policy Paper No. 26 (San Diego: University of California Institute on Global Conflict and Cooperation, 1996). For a shorter account, see Shai Feldman, *Nuclear Weapons and Arms Control in the Middle East* (Cambridge, Mass.: MIT Press, 1997), pp. 7–15. For a strict chronological overview of ACRS's plenaries and intersessionals, see, "A Brief History of the Arms Control and Regional Security Working Group," in *The Arms Control Reporter* (Cambridge, Mass.: Institute for Defense and Disarmament Studies, 1996), pp. 453.A.6–453.A.13.

5. The Europeans were represented by the European Community. Israel agreed to European participation in ACRS in May 1992 (due to Israeli reservations, the EC was only an observer at the Moscow organizational conference), in return for a "non-interference pledge on sensitive security issues and EC efforts to improve cooperation with Israel." Initially, the Israeli Ministry of Defense opposed EC participation in ACRS. See David Makovsky, "Israel, EC in Agreement on Role in Arms Talks," *Jerusalem Post*, May 1, 1992. According to this report, Israeli Foreign Minister Levy viewed European participation as most critical in these early conceptual stages of ACRS, but did not envision an active European role "when talks get down to hard bargaining between Israelis and Arabs."
6. For a summary of the May 1992 and September 1992 plenaries, see "Middle East Peace, Arms Control Talks on Hold," *Arms Control Today*, 23, no. 1 (Jan./Feb., 1993): 25.
7. For a detailed discussion of applying the East-West arms control experience to the Middle East context (including the ACRS process), see Keith R. Krause, "The Evolution of Arms Control in the Middle East," in Gabriel Ben-Dor and David B. Dewitt, eds., *Confidence Building in the Middle East* (Boulder, Colo.: Westview Press, 1994), pp. 267–290.
8. See Alon Pinkas, "Ivri, Mitzna to head arms control panel at Moscow Talks," *Jerusalem Post*, January 23, 1992.
9. See, for example, Steven L. Spiegel and David J. Pervin, eds., *Practical Peacemaking in the Middle East*, vol. 1, Arms Control and Regional Security (New York: Garland, 1995).
10. See Alan Platt, ed., *Arms Control and Confidence Building in the Middle East* (Washington, D.C.: United States Institute of Peace Press, 1992).
11. For more details on the European CBMs and their application to the Middle East, see Richard E. Darilek and Geoffrey Kemp, "Prospects for Confidence- and Security-Building Measures in the Middle East," in Platt, *Arms Control and Confidence Building in the Middle East*, pp. 9–42. Also see Ambassador Lynn Hansen, "CSBMs: The Ugly Duckling Remains a Duck—but a Pretty Good One," in Fred Tanner, ed., *Arms Control, Confidence-Building and Security Cooperation in the Mediterranean, North Africa and the Middle East* (Malta: Mediterranean Academy of Diplomatic Studies, 1994), pp. 51–66.
12. Etel Solingen, "Arms Control Negotiations in the Middle East: The Issue of Sequencing," *Peace and Change*, 20, no. 3 (July 1995): 367.
13. It is important to note that this consensual view in the arms control community based on the European experience was not accepted by all regional ACRS parties, particularly Egypt. For example, Ahmed Fakhr, a member of the Egyptian delegation to ACRS, has written on the Egyptian perspective and has emphasized the Egyptian preference for arms reduction and disarmament

agreements, not CBMs, because "the Middle East is not Europe.... First deal with arms control in the region because that is what is needed most urgently to enhance peace and security." See Ahmed Fakhr, "An Egyptian Perspective on Arms Control," in Richard Eisendorf, ed., *Arms Control and Security in the Middle East* (Washington, D.C.: Initiative for Peace and Cooperation in the Middle East, June 1995), p. 37.

14. For a discussion of the regional definition problem, see Abdullah Toukan, "The Middle East Peace Process and Arms Control and Regional Security." Paper presented to the ACRS plenary in Washington, D.C., May 1993, p. 3.

15. For an analysis of this problem in the context of the second ACRS plenary session in Moscow (September 1992), see Gerald Steinberg, "Trouble for Peace Process as Multilaterals Resume," *Jerusalem Post*, September 18, 1992.

16. For a discussion of the broader definition of arms control as a political, and not just a military, mechanism, see Abdullah Toukan, "The Middle East Peace Process and Arms Control and Regional Security." Dr. Toukan served on the Jordanian delegation to ACRS, participated in numerous track two security initiatives, and served as an advisor to King Hussein. He also has written extensively about arms control in the Middle East as an academic. See, for example, Toukan, "The Middle East Peace Process, Arms Control, and Regional Security," in Spiegel and Pervin, *Practical Peacemaking*, pp. 21–42, and Toukan, "A Jordanian Perspective on Arms Control," in Eisendorf, *Arms Control and Security in the Middle East*, pp. 89–99.

17. See Gerald Steinberg, "Major Boost for Arms Control Talks," *Jerusalem Post*, April 7, 1993.

18. Ibid.

19. For example, because the Defense rather than Foreign Ministry ran ACRS, the group's work tended to be less public than the other working groups' activities. One expression of this is the fact that in the Israeli position paper on the eve of the Moscow organizing conference on multilateral regional cooperation, in late January 1992, a discussion of all issues except arms control was included. See Israeli Foreign Ministry Background Paper, "Multilateral Regional Cooperation," January 27, 1992, Jerusalem, *Israel Information Service* <gopher://israel-info.gov.il:70/00/mad/multi/multi.6>.

20. See Ambassador Eytan Bentsur, "Israel's Vision of the Goals and Principles of the Regional Security and Arms Control Process," in Tanner, *Arms Control*, pp. 69–75.

21. For the text of Peres's address, see Efraim Inbar and Shmuel Sandler, eds., *Middle Eastern Security: Prospects for an Arms Control Regime* (London: Frank Cass, 1995), pp. 186–88.

22. Ibid., p. 187.

23. Feldman, *Nuclear Weapons and Arms Control*, p. 8.

24. Bentsur, "Israel's Vision," p. 70.
25. Ibid., p. 71.
26. Ibid., p. 74.
27. Author interview with senior Egyptian official, Egyptian Foreign Ministry, October 12, 1995, Cairo.
28. Author interview with Israeli Ministry of Defense official, October 1, 1995, Tel Aviv.
29. Treaty of Peace Between the Hashemite Kingdom of Jordan and The State of Israel, October 26, 1994, Article Four, Section 1 (b). For the full text of the treaty, see *The Jordan-Israel Peace Treaty, October 26, 1994: What Is It?* (Jordan Media Group, August 1995).
30. Author interview with Israeli Ministry of Defense official, October 1, 1995, Tel Aviv. However, according to the official, Israel believed that this objection was based on an Arab misperception of Helsinki, since the territorial status quo could be changed according to CSCE language through "peaceful means."
31. This assessment of various regional vision papers is based on an author interview with an Israeli official, September 27, 1995, Israeli Foreign Ministry, Jerusalem.
32. This point came up in a number of author interviews with regional security officials. Many officials noted how military-to-military contacts were much more productive, because military representatives tended to be less ideological than political officials, and were more willing to engage in substantive work.
33. Author interview with senior Jordanian official, February 16, 1996, Washington, D.C.
34. Author interview with U.S. official, February 16, 1996, Washington, D.C. According to the official, the Gulf states were much more comfortable with the CBM concept when they understood that CBMs were not just arms reduction measures. However, the Saudis were the most conservative among the Gulf participants, withholding addressing the Israelis directly until the last ACRS plenary in Tunis in December 1994.
35. The Palestinians—in contrast to other Arab parties—were the least interested in ACRS as a forum to further regional security interests (in their case, bilateral cooperation with Israel was most critical), particularly considering they had no standing army (only a Palestinian police force after Oslo), navy, or other military infrastructure embodied in statehood. Rather, the Palestinians were interested in ACRS as another means to legitimate their status as an independent actor vis-à-vis the Israelis, and to influence the group's activities so that ACRS's progress would always be sensitive and contingent on progress in the Palestinian negotiations. Based on author interview with senior Palestinian official, October 24, 1995, Jerusalem.
36. Choosing regional venues was particularly important to the Israelis because it underscored the political purpose of ACRS and other multilateral working

groups in legitimizing Israel's presence in the regional order. Arab parties were often more than willing to host plenaries or intersessionals in their capitals, which was perceived as enhancing a state's status.

37. Editorial in *Al-Ahram* "Paper Praises Choice for Multilateral Seminar," July 13, 1993, cited in *Foreign Broadcast Information Service-Near East and South Asia* (hereafter *FBIS-NES*)-93–132 July 13, 1993, p. 16.
38. Author interview with senior Jordanian official, February 16, 1996, Washington, D.C.
39. Jentleson, *Middle East Arms Control and Regional Security Talks*, p. 8.
40. "Analysis on the Appropriate Scope/Extent of the Middle East Region for Purposes of the Arms Control and Regional Security Process," Co-sponsor paper, ACRS plenary session, November 3–4, Moscow.
41. For Palestinian and other Arab assessments of the January 30–February 3 meeting, see "Palestinians Reject US-Russian Arms Ideas," *Reuters*, February 2, 1994, p. 2. Also see *The Arms Control Reporter* (1994), p. 453.B.172 for a review of this Cairo intersessional.
42. See Spokesman of the Ministry of Defense, "Regional Crisis Resolution Center to be Established," *Israeli Information Service* <gopher://israel-info.gov.il:70/00/mad/multi/941017.mul>, October 17, 1994. For a detailed account of the October 9–14 Paris intersessional, including different proposed language by Israel, Jordan, Egypt, and the United States for a WMDFZ in an ACRS conceptual text, see *The Arms Control Reporter* (1994), pp. 453.B.182–453.B.183.
43. The full text of the DoP was published after the May 1994 ACRS plenary in Doha, Qatar. See *Mideast Mirror*, May 3, 1994, 8, no. 83, pp. 18–19.
44. See Jerusalem *Qol Yisra'el*, "Israel Official: Qatar Talks 'Encumbered' by Saudis," May 7, 1994, cited in *FBIS-NES*-94–089, May 9, 1994, p. 5. According to this report, the Israeli delegation held meetings and conversations outside the formal talks with the Tunisians, Omanis, and Qataris, including the Qatari foreign minister.
45. One Egyptian commented to an American official at Doha, for example, that he had not visited Qatar since Camp David, which underscored Egyptian isolation. This also might help explain Egypt's aggressive position in ACRS, given its long absence from its leadership position in the Arab world. Author interview with U.S. official, February 16, 1996, Washington, D.C.
46. "Riyadh Says It Won't Host Multilaterals After Spearheading Opposition to 'Normalization' with Israel at Doha Round," *Mideast Mirror*, 8, no. 86, May 6, 1994, pp. 13–14.
47. Ibid.
48. See *The Arms Control Reporter* (1994), p. 453.B.176 for a summary of Arab positions at the Doha plenary.
49. However, privately, the Saudis have taken more interest in a regional security

agenda. According to a senior Jordanian member of the delegation to ACRS, the Saudis expressed a desire at the Cairo intersessional (as did the UAE representative) to support Jordan's position in the talks. Author interview, February 16, 1996, Washington, D.C.
50. According to a U.S. official on the ACRS delegation, the Saudis were upset that the plenary was held in Qatar. However, he noted that the Israelis also interpreted the Saudis' objection as a positive development, in that it demonstrated they cared about the process itself. Author interview, August 25, 1995, Washington, D.C.
51. Excerpted from an address at Georgetown University, April 7, 1994, in Steve Rodan, "Talks Explore Indirect Path to Arms Pact," *Jerusalem Post*, May 2, 1994, p. 7.
52. See Jerusalem *Qol Yisra'el*, "Israel Official: Qatar Talks 'Encumbered' by Saudis," May 7, 1994, cited in *FBIS-NES-94-089*, May 9, 1994, p. 5.
53. Author interview with State Department Official, August 25, 1995, Washington D.C.
54. See "Riyadh Says It Won't Host Multilaterals," *Mideast Mirror*. Also see *Al Hayat*, London, "Saudi Arabia Refuses to Host Multilateral Committees," May 6, 1994, pp. 1, 4, cited in *FBIS-NES-94-089*, May 9, 1994, p. 5.
55. Author interview with State Department official, August 25, 1995, Washington, D.C.
56. Author interview with U.S. official, Feb. 16, 1996, Washington, D.C.
57. See Along Pinkas, "Ivri: Arms Control Talks Irrelevant Unless Syria Joins In," *Jerusalem Post*, December 14, 1994, p. 2.
58. See Hamida ben Saleh, "Nuclear Issue Blocks Talks on Mideast Arms Control," *Agence France Presse*, December 14, 1994.
59. See "Riyadh Says It Won't Host Multilaterals," *Mideast Mirror*.
60. Although I characterize the RSC as a conceptual basket project, once established it would cover both conceptual and operational activities.
61. See "Mideast Conflict Prevention Centre To Be Set Up in Amman," *Agence France Presse*, December 15, 1994.
62. According to a Jordanian document outlining its vision on a regional center, the RSC's mission is to "contribute to the efforts being made to enhance security and stability in the Middle East, within the framework of the Middle East peace process." The RSC's "Initial Functions" were stipulated as follows: "a) Facilitate and provide a venue for seminars on topics that support ACRS working group activities. b) Facilitate training and education in support of the ACRS's process. c) Facilitate and support work on Arms Control and Regional Security arrangements agreed or being pursued in the ACRS process. d) Function as an integral part of ACRS communications and databank system." Ultimately, the Jordanians envisioned the RSC as a regional institution facilitating

the proposal for a CSCME, where security issues would be linked to issues like economic development or humanitarian concerns in order to promote a "Common Security Culture."
63. According to a U.S. official present at the meeting, the Egyptians sent their representative to Amman with one prepared statement about the purpose of the center that deadlocked the entire process because it focused only on the nuclear issue. According to the official, much Arab division was apparent at the meeting, with Qatar joining Jordan in a desire to move ahead with the project against Egyptian opposition. Author interview with U.S. official, Feb. 28, 1996, Washington, D.C.
64. Author interview with U.S. official, Feb. 28, 1996, Washington, D.C.
65. Author interview with Jordanian official, February 16, 1996, Washington, D.C. The funds were minimal, however, totaling under $200,000 according to this official's estimate.
66. See "Riyadh Says It Won't Host Multilaterals," *Mideast Mirror*.
67. See Amman Radio Jordan, "Multilateral Armament, Security Talks Open," November 8, 1994, cited in *FBIS-NES*-94-216, November 8, 1994, p. 1. Also see "Preparatory Arms-Control Talks in Jordan," *Jerusalem Post*, November 8, 1994.
68. See "Regional Military Communication Network Begins Operation," Israel Line, *Israeli Information Service* <gopher://israel-info.gov.il:70/00/archive/is-line95/950413.isl>, April 13, 1995.
69. See *The Arms Control Reporter* (1994), p. 453.B.185.
70. See Geoffrey Kemp and Jeremy Pressman, "The Middle East: continuation of the peace process," in *SIPRI Yearbook 1995* (Oxford: Oxford University Press, 1995), p. 192.
71. Shai Feldman, *Nuclear Weapons and Arms Control*, p. 14. Also see Sharon Sade (cited in Feldman, p. 34), "Arab Representatives Will Accept Ivri's Invitation to Visit IDF Bases," *Ha'aretz*, December 16, 1994, and Sade, "Israel Prepared to Permit Arab Representatives to Visit Defense Installations," *Ha'aretz*, December 14, 1994.
72. For a review of the December 12–15 Tunis plenary, see *The Arms Control Reporter* (1994), pp. 453.B.186–453.B.187.
73. For the full text of this agreement as agreed to at the December Tunis plenary, see *The Arms Control Reporter* (1994), pp. 453.D.17–453.D.20.
74. *SIPRI Yearbook 1995*, p. 192. Also see "Israel, Arab Nations Reach Tension-Easing Pacts," *Washington Post*, December 21, 1994, p. A21.
75. Peter Jones, "Maritime Confidence-Building Measures in the Middle East," in Jill R. Junnola, ed., *Maritime Confidence Building in Regions of Tension* (Washington, D.C.: The Henry L. Stimson Center, 1996), p. 58. For a similarly detailed discussion and excellent analysis of maritime confidence-building, see

Peter Jones, "Maritime Confidence-Building in the Middle East," in Tanner, *Arms Control*, pp. 103–11.

76. In "Maritime Confidence-Building Measures," p. 59, Jones documents a series of incidents between 1972 and 1989, with three of them between regional navies (two between Israel and Egypt in the Suez before the 1973 war and one between Iran and Kuwait in 1985), eleven incidents between regional navy ships and those of an extraregional power (not including the U.S.-Libyan "tanker war" incidents), and ten recorded cases of regional navies (by and large Israel) firing on or capturing suspected terrorists. Moreover, according to background interviews Jones conducted with Israeli and Egyptian naval officers, many other unrecorded incidents have taken place between the Israeli, Egyptian, and Syrian navies, sometimes because of navigation mistakes but also often because of aggressive surveillance by one of the parties leading to friction and even conflict.

77. Jones, "Maritime Confidence-Building Measures," p. 61.

78. Ibid.

79. Ibid., p. 62.

80. Ibid.

81. Similar disagreements over specific operational arrangements occurred with respect to detailing range limitations, or exclusion zones, which would specify how close regional ships could be to one another. In the end, the ACRS parties agreed not to include specific range limitation provisions or prohibit particular devices aboard ships. See Jones, "Maritime Confidence-Building Measures," p. 67.

82. Ibid., p. 64.

83. Ibid., p. 66.

84. Ibid.

85. Ibid., p. 69.

86. The formal title of this agreement, which was finalized at the April meeting, became "Guidelines for Operating Procedures for Maritime Cooperation and Conduct in the Prevention of Incidents on and over the Sea in the Middle East."

87. The head of the Israeli delegation to ACRS, David Ivry, revealed the plans for the joint naval demonstration in an interview with an Israeli newspaper in February 1995. See "Arab States Deny Plans for Naval Exercises with Israel," *Jerusalem Post*, February 21, 1995, p. 2. The exercise was supposed to include Israel and a number of Arab parties. The Arab navies scheduled to participate were: Egypt, Saudi Arabia, Qatar, Oman, Bahrain, Algeria, Tunisia, and Morocco. The news of such an exercise was negatively viewed in the Arab press, which argued that such activity went beyond normalization to treating Israel as a military ally, and also noted the poor timing of the exercise in the midst

of the NPT controversy. See "Arab Commentators Aghast at Israeli Involvement in North African Security Plans," *Mideast Mirror*, February 20, 1995, 9, no. 35, pp. 21–22.

88. For an elaboration of this problem, as well as a good overview of other problems ACRS faced, see Michael D. Yaffe, "An Overview of the Middle East Peace Process Working Group on Arms Control and Regional Security," in Tanner, *Arms Control.* Yaffe served on the American delegation to ACRS.

89. On Israel's nuclear weapon capabilities and policy of ambiguity, see Avner Cohen, *Israel and the Bomb* (New York: Columbia University Press, 1999); "Patterns of Nuclear Opacity in the Middle East: Understanding the Past, Implications for the Future," in Rauf, ed., *Regional Approaches to Curbing Nuclear Proliferation in the Middle East and South Asia* (Ottawa: The Canadian Centre for Global Security, 1992), pp. 13–54. Also see Yair Evron, *Israel's Nuclear Dilemma* (Ithaca, N.Y.: Cornell University Press, 1994); Shlomo Aronson and Oded Brosh, *The Politics and Strategy of Nuclear Weapons in the Middle East* (Albany: State University of New York Press, 1992); Ariel E. Levite and Emily B. Landau, *Israel's Nuclear Image: Arab Perceptions of Israel's Nuclear Posture* (in Hebrew) (Tel Aviv: Papyrus, 1994); and Shai Feldman, *Israeli Nuclear Deterrence* (New York: Columbia University Press, 1982).

90. For an overview of the Egyptian-Israeli dispute on the nuclear issue and the NPT, see "Israel, the NPT, and the ACRS Talks," in *The Arms Control Reporter* (1994), pp. 453.B.184–453.B.185.

91. For details on this dispute, see Gerald M. Steinberg, "The 1995 NPT Extension and Review Conference and the Arab-Israeli Peace Process," *NonProliferation Review*, 1, no. 1 (Fall 1996): 17–29. Essentially, Egypt threatened to withhold its signature and bring the nonaligned movement along if Israel did not sign. In the end, U.S. pressure, including congressional threats to cut Egyptian aid and the personal intervention of Vice President Al Gore, forced the Egyptians to back down.

92. See, for example, "Israel Has Agreed to Raise Level of Multilateral Talks on Arms Control," Israel Line, *Israel Information Service* <gopher://israel-info.gov.il:70/00/archive/isline95/950428.isl>, April 28, 1995.

93. See Fawaz Gerges, "Egyptian-Israeli Relations Turn Sour," *Foreign Affairs*, 74, no. 3 (May/June 1995): 69–78.

94. Author interviews with Jordanian and American officials, February 16, 1996, Washington, D.C.

95. Author interview with senior Israeli official, September 27, 1995, Israeli Foreign Ministry, Jerusalem.

96. For example, Yezid Sayigh (initially the head of the Palestinian delegation to ACRS) does not mention the nuclear issue in his review of threats to Palestinian security, and instead emphasizes nonmilitary threats like political, economic,

and social forces. See Sayigh, "Redefining the Basics: Sovereignty and Security of the Palestinian State," *Journal of Palestine Studies* 24, no. 4 (Summer 1995): 5–19. The issue also arose in a discussion with a senior Palestinian official. As he put it, the Palestinians would be in the same boat as Israel under a nuclear attack, so they fear the use of unconventional weapons on Israel as much as the Israelis do. Author interview with senior Palestinian official, October 24, 1995, Jerusalem.

97. The role of personal contacts in reducing threat perceptions of the "other" is often emphasized by American officials, particularly those who have had experience in U.S.-Soviet arms control. See, for example, Ambassador Lynn Hansen, "CSBMs: Ugly Duckling," pp. 51–66. Hansen observes that despite his initial skepticism, confidence-building measures carried an important psychological component critical to improving his relations with and perceptions of his Soviet counterparts (see esp. pp. 65–66).

98. Author interview with senior Israeli official, October 23, 1995, Jerusalem.

99. Author interview, August 6, 1996, Jerusalem.

100. Author interview with U.S. official, February 28, 1996, Washington, D.C.

101. Ibid.

102. For an elaboration of the status argument, see Jentleson and Kaye, "Security Status."

103. For an interesting elaboration on the sources of Egypt's identity and its struggle to define itself, see "Egypt as State, as Arab Mirror," chap. 2 in Fouad Ajami, *The Arab Predicament* (Cambridge: Cambridge University Press, 1981), and Anwar Sadat, *In Search of Identity* (New York: Harper Colophon Books, 1977).

104. Ron McLaurin, Lewis W. Snider, and Don Peretz, *Middle East Foreign Policy* (New York: Praeger, 1982), p. 54.

105. Ajami, *Arab Predicament*, p. 80.

106. A. I. Dawisha, *Egypt in the Arab World: The Elements of Foreign Policy* (New York: Wiley, 1976), p. 136. For another discussion of the role of dignity and honor in Egyptian foreign policymaking and negotiation style, see Raymond Cohen, *Culture and Conflict in Egyptian-Israeli Relations: A Dialogue of the Deaf* (Bloomington: Indiana University Press, 1990), esp. pp. 118–22.

107. Dawisha, for example, argues that prestige played a role in Egypt's decision to nationalize the Suez Canal, which was "not merely a response to the withdrawal of American aid, but also a function of decision-makers' perception of the manner in which it was done, which was deemed 'insulting to the dignity of Egypt,'" in *Egypt in the Arab World*, p. 137. Fawaz A. Gerges argues that the main reason for Nasser's military intervention in Yemen in 1962 was "to improve his position in the Arab world, and his international standing, after suffering the humiliating secession of Syria from the United Arab Republic (UAR)," in "The Kennedy Administration and the Egyptian-Saudi Conflict in

Yemen: Co-Opting Arab Nationalism," *Middle East Journal*, 49, no. 2 (Spring 1995): 292.

108. For a comprehensive study of NWFZ proposals from an Egyptian perspective, see Mahmoud Karem, *A Nuclear-Weapon-Free Zone in the Middle East* (New York: Greenwood Press, 1988) and "A Nuclear-Weapon-Free Zone in the Middle East: A Historical Overview of the Patterns of Involvement of the United Nations," in Rauf, *Regional Approaches*, pp. 55–68. Also see Mohamed Nabil Fahmy (a senior Egyptian official in the Foreign Ministry), "Egypt's Disarmament Initiative," *Bulletin of the Atomic Scientists*, 46, no. 9: 9. For a comprehensive study on measures to facilitate the establishment of a NWFZ in the Middle East, see *Establishment of a Nuclear-Weapon-Free-Zone In the Region of the Middle East*, Report of the Secretary-General, United Nations General Assembly, October 10, 1990, Forty-fifth session. For an assessment of the prospects for a WMDFZ in the Middle East in light of peace process developments, see Jan Prawitz and James F. Leonard, *A Zone Free of Weapons of Mass Destruction in the Middle East*, United Nations Institute for Disarmament Research (New York and Geneva: United Nations, 1996), esp. chap. 4, "The Middle East as a NWFZ or WMDFZ." On Egypt's position toward the NPT, see Gerald M. Steinberg, "Middle East Arms Control and Regional Security," *Survival*, 36, no. 1 (Spring 1994): 126–41.

109. While the Egyptians ultimately backed down and Prime Minister Peres issued some ambiguous statements on Israel's nuclear capabilities to diffuse tension, the nuclear issue remains the primary obstacle to progress in ACRS. See Jerusalem *Qol Yisra'el*, "Peres: 'Will Give Up the Atom' if Peace Achieved," December 22, 1995, cited in *FBIS-NES-95-247*, December 26, 1995, p. 51.

110. For an example of a traditional security perspective of Egyptian national security policy (focusing largely on military power considerations), see Gabriel Ben-Dor, "Egypt," in E. Kolodziej and R. Harkavy, eds., *Security Policies of Developing Countries* (Lexington, Ky.: Lexington Books, 1982), pp. 179–202.

111. For an elaboration of these systemic changes and their impact on regional security cooperation, see Jentleson and Kaye, "Security Status."

112. These fears were reflected in the Arab press, particularly at the time of the first regional economic summit in Casablanca when discussions of Israeli hegemony, both economic and military, were widespread. See, for example, *Al-Sha'b*, "Labor Party Rejects Morocco Economic Conference," October 4, 1994, p. 3, cited in *FBIS-NES-94-197*, October 4, 1994 and *Al-Sha'b*, "Opposition Parties Denounce Casablanca Conference," October 28, 1994, p. 3, cited in *FBIS-NES-94-212*, October 28, 1994 (both located in World News Connection <http://wnc.fedworld.gov>).

113. Statement by Mohamed Hasanayn Heikal, quoted in Feldman, *Israeli Nuclear Deterrence*, p. 87.

114. Quoted from an interview with El-Baz in *Al Ahram Weekly*, June 15–21, 1995, p. 1.
115. *Al Ahram*, "Egypt's Musa Comments on Nuclear Arms, Peace Issues," January 24, 1996, p. 9, cited in *FBIS-NES*, January 30, 1996, p. 5.
116. Thomas L. Friedman, "Exodus Part II," *New York Times*, February 15, 1995, p. A21.
117. Fouad Ajami, "The Sorrows of Egypt," *Foreign Affairs*, 74, no. 5 (September/October 1995): 86–87.
118. Ibid., p. 88.
119. Ze'ev Schiff, "An Israeli Umbrella for the Gulf," *Ha'aretz*, January 31, 1996, p. B1, News Analysis, *Israel Information Service* <gopher://israel-info.gov.il:70/00/archive/dps96/960131s.dps>, Feb. 8, 1996.
120. "Egypt Mounts Defense of Its Regional Role," *Mideast Mirror*, 11, no. 42, February 28, 1997, p. 9.
121. Cited in ibid., p. 10.
122. William B. Quandt, "Egypt: A Strong Sense of National Identity," in Hans Binnendijk, ed., *National Negotiating Styles* (Washington, D.C.: Foreign Service Institute, U.S. Department of State, 1987), p. 121.

*Chapter 5*

1. However, some analysts have demonstrated the limited effect of peace process developments on enhancing economic development in the region, which is more contingent on the respective national economic and social policies of the states within the region. See, for example, Eliyahu Kanovsky, *Assessing the Mideast Peace Economic Dividend* (Ramat Gan, Israel: The BESA Center, Bar-Ilan University, 1994) and Kanovsky, "The Middle East Economies: The Impact of Domestic and International Politics," *Middle East Report of International Affairs (MERIA)*, Journal 2, Article 1, June 1, 1997 <www.biu.ac.il/soc/besa/meria.html>.
2. This term is associated with notions of an integrated Middle East following the European Union model and was presented by Shimon Peres in his book, *The New Middle East* (New York: Henry Holt, 1993).
3. The full REDWG membership, in addition to the European Union gavelholder, includes: the four core regional parties (Egypt, Israel, Jordan, and the Palestinian Authority); other regional parties (Algeria, Bahrain, Kuwait, Mauritania, Morocco, Oman, Qatar, Saudi Arabia, Tunisia, United Arab Emirates, Yemen); extraregional parties (Australia, Austria, Belgium, Canada, China, Cyprus, Czech Republic, Denmark, Finland, France, Germany, Greece, Hungary, Iceland, India, Ireland, Italy, Japan, Korea, Luxembourg, Netherlands, Norway, Portugal, Romania, Russia, Spain, Sweden, Switzerland, Turkey,

Ukraine, United Kingdom, the United States; and three nonstate actors (the European Commission, United Nations, and World Bank).
4. See David Makovsky and Allison Kaplan, "Israel to Boycott Multilateral Talks over Palestinians from Abroad," *Jerusalem Post*, May 8, 1992.
5. See Jerusalem Israel Television Network in Hebrew, "Crisis over Participation in Multilateral Talks: EC Finds Levi Meeting 'Inconvenient,' " April 27, 1992, cited in *Foreign Broadcast Information Service-Near East and South Asia* (hereafter *FBIS-NES*)-92-082, April 28, 1992, p. 27.
6. See Makovsky and Kaplan, "Israel to Boycott Multilateral Talks."
7. David Makovsky and Alisa Odenheimer, "US: Israel Likely to Boycott Multilaterals," *Jerusalem Post*, March 27, 1992.
8. See Moshe Zak, "The Peril of Pseudo-UN Forums," *Jerusalem Post*, May 22, 1992.
9. Peres's writings, particularly *The New Middle East*, are replete with references to economic development following the European model. Also see David Makovsky, "Mixed Feelings in Ministry About Peres Appointment," *Jerusalem Post*, July 13, 1992. As Makovsky notes, "Peres will seek to make the multilateral peace talks on regional issues an integral part of Mideast peace talks, and not a footnote. On the campaign trail, Peres always spoke about the need for an economic 'common market' in the Middle East, and therefore they [foreign ministry officials] expect he will tackle regional issues with gusto."
10. See David Makovsky, "Foreign Ministry Boss Preparing Extensive Organizational Changes," *Jerusalem Post*, May 5, 1993.
11. See David Makovsky, "Multilaterals Okayed as Moussa Brokers Deal," *Jerusalem Post*, October 9, 1992.
12. "Mr. Rabin, Meet Mr. Peres," Opinion Section, *Jerusalem Post*, August 7, 1992.
13. Asher Wallfish and Dan Izenberg, "Upbeat Baker Leaves Israel in Search of New Arab Ideas; Speaks of 'New Opportunity to Move Forward,' " *Jerusalem Post*, July 22, 1992.
14. See Evelyn Gordan, "Israeli Delegation Leaves for Paris for Multilateral Economic Talks," *Jerusalem Report*, October 29, 1992.
15. Jerusalem *Qol Yisra'el*, "Peres Briefs Cabinet on Multilateral Talks," November 8, 1992, cited in *FBIS-NES*-92-217, November 9, 1992, p. 33.
16. Author interview with U.S. official, August 26, 1996, Jerusalem.
17. However, the bank idea resurfaced and developed into a concrete initiative in the aftermath of Oslo, as discussed later in the chapter.
18. See David Makovsky, "Mideast Reconstruction Bank Proposed at Paris Multilaterals," *Jerusalem Post*, October 30, 1992.
19. *Jordan Times*, "Chief Delegate Interviewed on Multilateral Talks," November 5–6, 1992, p. 3, cited in *FBIS-NES*-92-216, November 6, 1992, pp. 43–44.
20. Ibid., p. 44.

21. For more on various projects proposed by the extraregionals, see "Chief Delegate Interviewed on Multilateral Talks," p. 44.
22. See the World Bank study, *Developing the Occupied Territories: An Investment in Peace* (Washington, D.C., November 1993).
23. Quoted in David Makovsky, "Beilin: Israel Likely to Attend Talks in Tunisia," *Jerusalem Post*, June 1, 1993.
24. See "The Copenhagen Action Plan for Regional Economic Development," in *Mideast Mirror*, November 11, 1993, 7, no. 219. For an update of the Copenhagen Action Plan, see Joel Peters, *Pathways to Peace* (London: The Royal Institute of International Affairs, 1996), appendix 5, pp. 97–101.
25. "Multilateral Peace Talks Working Group on Regional Economic Development, Copenhagen," November 9, 1993, in the *Israel Information Service* <gopher://israel-info.gov.il:70/00/mad/multi/multi.16>. Also see *Jerusalem Israel Television Network*, Interview by Hayim Yavin and Ehud Ya'ari, "Savir Views Progress in Economic Multilaterals," November 9, 1993, cited in *FBIS-NES-93-216*, November 10, 1993, pp. 2–3.
26. The projects included feasibility studies and workshops on the following types of areas: improving regional highway infrastructure, railways and ports; linking electricity grids of Israel, the Palestinian territories, Jordan, and Egypt; hydroelectric canal projects (with the Mediterranean-Dead Sea and the Red-Dead Sea Canals as possible alternatives); an Egypt-Gaza gas pipeline; tourism ventures; training banking personnel in the Palestinian Authority; regional conferences on financial markets; increased regional business contacts; and cooperative networks among universities and the media, including symposia on regional education. For details of the canal project proposals, see Government of Israel, *Development Options for Cooperation: The Middle East/East Mediterranean Region 1996* (Israel: Ministry of Foreign Affairs and Finance, August 1995, Version 4), chap. 16.
27. The EC provided $125 million in funding for one of the projects focused on protecting natural resources like desert plants. For an overview of these projects, see Cairo MENA (in Arabic), "Economic Development Committee Approves Projects," December 15, 1993, cited in *FBIS-NES-93-240*, December 16, 1993, p. 1.
28. Ibid., p. 4.
29. However, it was not until May 1996 that the MC Secretariat was formally inaugurated and institutionalized.
30. Amman Declaration, October 31, 1995. For the text of the declaration, see FBIS-NES, November 1, 1995, pp. 11–13. The full text is also reproduced in the *Israel Information Service* <gopher://israel-info.gov.il:70/00/mad/pce/amman.pce>.
31. Author interview with U.S. official, August 26, 1996, Jerusalem.

32. The Mediterranean participants are: Egypt, Israel, Jordan, the Palestinian Authority, Syria, Lebanon, Tunisia, Morocco, Algeria, Turkey, Cyprus, and Malta.
33. This process created a forum for economic, political, and social cooperation between the EU members and the Mediterranean parties, including Israel and Syria. The participants agreed to a final declaration at the end of the conference, which outlined a series of political, social, and economic principles to guide regional relations. See "Barcelona Declaration Emphasizes Regional Peace and Security," Israel Line, *Israel Information Service* <gopher://israel-info.gov.il:70/00/archive/isline95/951129.isl>, November 29, 1995, and "Barcelona Conference," cited in *FBIS-NES*, November 29, 1995, pp. 1–3. For extended excerpts from the Declaration, see *Mideast Mirror*, November 29, 1995, pp. 11–12. A second follow-up meeting in Malta on April 15–16, 1997, followed this conference. For more detailed accounts of the Barcelona conference and subsequent Euro-Med partnership, see: Cairo MENA, "Foreign Minister on Barcelona Summit, Issues," cited in *FBIS-NES-95-227*, November 25, 1995, pp. 18–20 and *FBIS-NES-95-228*, November 28, 1995, pp. 1–2, 47. For more general overviews of recent European initiatives in the Middle East/Mediterranean region, see François D'Alancon, "The EC Looks to a New Middle East," *Journal of Palestine Studies*, 23, no. 2 (Winter 1994): 41–51 and Rosemary Hollis, "Europe and the Middle East: Power by Stealth?" *International Affairs*, 73, no. 1 (January 1997): 15–29.
34. See David Makovsky, "Saudis to Establish Ties After Peace with Syria," *Jerusalem Post*, October 14, 1994, p. 3A.
35. See Peters, *Pathways to Peace*, p. 47.
36. Quoted in David Makovsky, "Hot Air Keeps Regions Talks Afloat but Moving in Circles," *Jerusalem Post*, July 15, 1994, p. 3B.
37. The idea for a regional economic forum focused on private sector investment apparently originated with a conversation between Israeli Foreign Minister Shimon Peres and King Hassan of Morocco. Author interview with a senior U.S. official, May 8, 1996, Washington, D.C.
38. After its next plenary in Bonn on January 18–19, 1995, the full REDWG plenary met less often, with yearly rather than semiannual meetings. The plenary after Bonn met the following year in May 1996 in Amman. The next REDWG plenary was scheduled for June 1997 in Cyprus, but was postponed.
39. For further details on REDWG's structure and the role of the MC secretariat, see the REDWG concept paper, "REDWG: Establishment of a Permanent, Regional Economic Institution for the Middle East." By October 1995, the secretariat began issuing the *REDWG Update*, a bimonthly newsletter, to keep parties involved in REDWG activities informed of meetings and progress across its four sectors (infrastructure, tourism, trade, and finance). Four individuals representing each core party played a particularly critical role in furthering the

secretariat's work. It was not uncommon for the secretariat's executive secretary (from the European Commission) to speak to each of these individuals several times a day in efforts to coordinate activities and agendas. The secretariat also issued its first *Annual Report* for the REDWG plenary meeting in Amman in May 1996, which provided an overview of all its subcommittees' work from December 1994 to May 1996. The secretariat's offices opened on the sidelines of the REDWG plenary on May 7, 1996 in an Amman suburb.

40. Finance dealt with the MENABANK; Trade covered the RBC; and Tourism directed MEMTTA. The MC's infrastructure subcommittee prepared reports on all other projects that were not embodied in a regional institution. This interpretation of REDWG's relationship to the MENA summits is based on an author interview with an American official, August 26, 1996, Jerusalem.

41. According to one account, Peres raised the idea as early as October 1993 — in the wake of the Oslo Accord — in secret discussions with the Jordanians, whom he wanted to host the conference. However, given that Jordan had not yet signed a peace treaty with Israel, Peres turned to King Hassan of Morocco, who agreed to be the host. Peres wanted to have an Arab country host the summit to emphasize Arab acceptance of Israel in the region. Author interview with senior Jordanian official, August 19, 1996, Amman.

42. See Craig R. Whitney, "Hobnobbing at Very High Levels; Political and Corporate Elite Pay Handsomely at Davos," *New York Times*, January 28, 1997, p. C1.

43. Secretary Christopher, "Building the Structures of Peace and Prosperity in the New Middle East," Remarks at the Royal Palace, Casablanca, Morocco, October 30, 1994, issued by U.S. Department of State, Bureau of Public Affairs, Office of Public Communication.

44. See Statement by the Cooperation Council of the Arab States of the Gulf on the Cancellation by the GCC of the Secondary/Tertiary Arab Boycott of Israel, October 1, 1994. Reproduced in the *Israel Information Service* <gopher://israel-info.gov.il:70/00/mad/pce/941001.pce>, October 2, 1994. In the statement, the GCC notes the bilateral progress made on the Palestinian and Jordanian tracks, arguing that "for all practical purposes, secondary and tertiary boycotts are no longer a threat to the interests of these partners [the GCC's trading partners]."

45. Some parties, notably the Israelis, issued project books for widespread distribution. See Government of Israel, *Development Options for Regional Cooperation*, Submitted to the Middle East and North Africa Economic Summit, October, 1994.

46. See, for example, Government of Israel, *Development Options for Regional Cooperation*, p. II-3. The breakdown of the Israeli proposed financing, totaling between $18 and $27 billion, was as follows (in billions of dollars): water, 4–6; agriculture, 1–1.5; combating desertification, 1; tourism, 2–2.5;

transportation, 3–4; energy, 3–6; communication, 1; environment, 0.5–1; industry, 0.5–1; and canal projects, 2–3.

47. "The Economic Summit Conference for the Middle East and North Africa, Casablanca, October 30–November 1, 1994: From Peace-Making to Peace-Strengthening," *Israel Information Service* <gopher://israel-info.gov.il:70/00/mad/pce/941017.pce>, October 18, 1994.

48. On this point, also see Oded Granot, "The Interconnection Between Statecraft and Economics," *Ma'ariv*, October 28, 1994, p. 5. Reproduced in *Israel Information Service* <gopher://israel-info.gov.il:70/00/archive/dps/941028g.dps>, November 1, 1994.

49. See "Eight Ministers Led by Peres and 130 Businessmen Head for Casablanca," *Mideast Mirror*, 8, no. 209, October 28, 1994, pp. 2–14.

50. As a senior IDF intelligence official explained, Israel "revealed its full economic potential and made a negative impression on Arabs" at Casablanca. Quoted in Ora Koren, "Lowering Their Profile Because of Jerusalem," *Globes*, May 15, 1995, pp. 49–50.

51. Address by Prime Minister Yitzhak Rabin to the Middle East/North Africa Economic Summit in Casablanca, October 30, 1994. Reproduced in *Israel Information Service* <gopher://israel-info.gov.il:70/00/speech/sta/94103or.sta>, November 1, 1994.

52. Quoted in Koren, "Lowering Their Profile," pp. 49–50.

53. Casablanca Declaration, Middle East/North Africa Economic Summit, October 30–November 1, 1994 (State Department Copy). A full text of the Declaration was also printed in *Middle East Executive Reports*, 17, no. 11 (November 1994), p. 23.

54. Casablanca Declaration, October 30–November 1, 1994.

55. For further details about the MENA Summit Executive Secretariat and documents related to the MENA process, see the Secretariat's home page on the World Wide Web: <http://www.mena.org/newweb/general.html>.

56. See John Lancaster, "Beating Swords into Shares in the Future: Mideast Economic Summit Opens on Hopeful Note Despite Lingering Arab Concerns," *Washington Post*, October 30, 1995, p. A12. For a complete list of all government and private sector participants attending the Amman summit, see the home page of the Middle East and North Africa Economic Summit Executive Secretariat, MENAnet: <http://www.mena.org/newweb/general.html>.

57. Israel limited its delegation to one hundred individuals, with forty officials and sixty private sector representatives. See David Makovsky, "Beilin: Nation to Take a 'Lower Profile' at Summit," *Jerusalem Post*, October 26, 1995, p. 12, in FBIS-NES-95-208, October 27, 1995, pp. 35–36.

58. See, for instance, London *Al-Quds Al-Arabi*, "Summit Seen as Attempt to Strengthen Israel," October 30, 1995, p. 11, cited in *FBIS-NES-261*, November

1, 1995, p. 14 and "Amman Summit Aimed to Achieve Israeli 'Hegemony,'" cited in *FBIS-NES*, November 2, 1995, p. 51. For an excellent analysis of the Arab perception of Israeli hegemony, see Ze'ev Schiff, "The Arabs, In Their Own Eyes," *Ha'aretz*, February 1, 1995, p. B1. However, some Arab officials concede that the hegemony rhetoric is based more on the perception among the Arab public of the slow pace of economic development and their frustration with it than on hard economic facts, given the general consensus that Israel has little interest in dominating the Arab world economically or politically. One Jordanian official explained that the hegemony rhetoric was part of the "old literature" and a "silly concept." Author interview, August 19, 1996, Amman. In an interview on the eve of the Amman Summit, an Egyptian businessman brushed aside assertions of the Israeli desire for hegemony, arguing that Egypt has nothing to fear from Israeli economic competition and that Israel itself would be hesitant to integrate itself with an Arab state for fear of losing its own national identity. See interview by Ghada Ragab with Egyptian businessman Sherif Delawer, "Modest Goals, not Grand Designs," *Al Ahram Weekly*, October 12–18, 1995.

59. See "Government, Professional Associations Locked in Bitter Struggle About Normalization, Politicization," *Jordan: Issues and Perspectives*, no. 21 (Washington, D.C.: Jordan Information Bureau, September/October 1995), p. 12.
60. For an American overview of the Amman Summit, including its themes and agenda, see "Amman Middle East/North Africa Economic Summit," Fact Sheet, U.S. Department of State, Bureau of Public Affairs, October 25, 1995.
61. "Amman Economic Summit Seen as Milestone on Road to Achieving Economic Promise of Peace," *Jordan: Issues and Perspectives*, no. 21, p. 1.
62. "Modest Goals, not Grand Designs," p. 4.
63. Government of Jordan, *Building a Prosperous Peace, Amman '95, October 29–31, 1995* (Amman, Jordan: International Press Office, The Royal Hashemite Court, 1995), section 6, "Logistics."
64. The second Israeli volume prepared for the Amman Summit includes regional project proposals (none of which target Israel alone) for several subregions (the Jordan Rift Valley, the Gulf of Aqaba, and the Southeast Mediterranean) as well as across a variety of economic sectors (water, agriculture, desertification, tourism, regional parks, transportation, energy, telecommunications, trade and industry, human resources, public health, environment, and canals). For detailed analysis of these numerous project proposals, see Government of Israel, *Development Options for Cooperation, 1996* (Version 4, August 1995).
65. See Government of Jordan, *Building a Prosperous Peace*, esp. section 4, "Jordan's MENA Conference Priority Projects," for a detailed review of the project proposals for the Amman summit. The proposals cover the following sectors:

energy, environment, minerals and industry, transport, telecommunications, tourism, water.

66. Moreover, like most other parties at the MENA summits, Jordan encouraged its private sector to actively participate in the conference and offer its own initiatives to augment the official conference proposals, arguing that "the most important contacts will be far more numerous and on a smaller scale — in closed meeting rooms away from the public eye, between Jordanian businessmen and interested investors." See Government of Jordan, *Building a Prosperous Peace*, section 3.

67. Address by Prime Minister Yitzhak Rabin to the Amman Economic Summit, Amman, Jordan, October 29, 1995. Reproduced in *Israel Information Service* <gopher://israel-info.gov.il:70/00/speech/sta/951029.sta>, October 29, 1995.

68. For a Palestinian perspective on economic developments, see the press conference at the Amman Summit with Nabil Sha'th, *Amman Jordan Television Network*, October 31, 1995, cited in *FBIS-NES-95-211*, November 1, 1995, pp. 1–4.

69. For a response to the publicity received by his remarks, see interview with Foreign Minister Moussa, *Cairo MENA*, October 31, 1995, cited in *FBIS-NES-95-210*, October 31, 1995, p. 39. For further clarification by Moussa on his statement, see *Cairo MENA*, "Musa Comments on Outcome of Amman Conference; Clarifies Reference to 'Rushing,' " November 1, 1995, cited in *FBIS-NES-95-211*, November 1, 1995, pp. 41–42.

70. See Lancaster, "Beating Swords Into Shares."

71. Ultimately, a compromise was reached whereby the parties agreed Egypt would host the 1996 conference, while Qatar would host the fourth summit in 1997. See *Amman Jordan Television Network*, "King Husayn Reconciles Qatari, Egyptian stands," October 31, 1995, cited in *FBIS-NES-95-211*, November 1, 1995, p. 8.

72. Quoted in John Lancaster, "Arabs, Israelis Talking Business at the 2nd Summit," *Washington Post*, November 1, 1995, p. A21.

73. Among the more visible deals emerging from Amman was the Israeli-Qatari natural gas agreement worth $4.5–5 billion (via an American corporation, Enron), which would be the first time Israel purchased gas from a Gulf country. The gas project called for the building of a gas terminal, possibly in Jordan's Aqaba port, which would receive liquefied natural gas exported on tankers from the Enron plant in Qatar, which could then be transported over land to Israel (and also meet natural gas demands in Jordan and the Palestinian territories). See *Amman Jordan Times*, "Further on Gas Memorandum," November 1, 1995, cited in *FBIS-NES-95-212*, November 2, 1995, pp. 11–12. Also see "Qatar to Enter Into Natural Gas Deal With Israel," Israel Line on *Israel*

*Information Service* <gopher://israel-info.gov.il:70/00/archive/isline95/951025.isl>, October 25, 1995. In addition to the natural gas deal, the Israeli potash company agreed to extract bromine from the Dead Sea in a joint project with Jordan. See Tova Cohen, "Israel Sees Regional Acceptance, Trade as Reality," *The Reuters European Business Report*, October 31, 1995. Other economic ventures resulting from the summit included: textile and garment cooperation projects between Israeli and Jordanian companies; energy-related cooperation between Jordan and the Palestinian Authority; a $2 million U.S.-financed study on laying a Jordan-Palestinian-Israeli fiber optics network to serve a Middle East "information highway"; a $250 million fund announced by Qatar for the Palestinian territories. For more details on the outcome of the Amman Summit, see *Amman Jordan Times*, "Roundup of Amman Summit Accomplishments," November 4, 1995, pp. 1, 7, cited in *FBIS-NES-95–215*, November 7, 1995, pp. 45–47.

74. See "Planning for the Region," *Al Ahram Weekly*, February 1–7, 1996 and Tel Aviv *Davar Rishon* (in Hebrew), "Arab-Israeli Regional Economic Planning Talks Held in Holland," January 31, 1996, p. 2, cited in *FBIS-NES-96–021*, January 31, 1996, p. 8. The four regional ministers leading high-level delegations were: Egyptian Economic Minister Nawal Tatawi; Jordanian Planning Minister Rima Khalaf; Palestinian Minister of International Cooperation Nabil Shaath; and the Israeli Minister in charge of peace process affairs, Yossi Beilin.

75. See, for example, *Al Riyadh Al-Jazirah*, "Daily Criticizes Amman Economic Summit," October 30, 1995, p. 33, cited in *FBIS-NES-95–215*, November 7, 1995, pp. 30–31; *Al Quds Al-'Arabi*, "Summit Seen as Attempt to Strengthen Israel," October 30, 1995, p. 11, cited in *FBIS-NES-95–211*, November 1, 1995, p. 14; *Al-Ba'th*, "Amman Summit Aimed to Achieve Israeli 'Hegemony,'" October 31, 1995, p. 3, cited in *FBIS-NES-95–212*, November 2, 1995, pp. 51.

76. Quoted from an editorial in the Saudi newspaper *al-Medina* by John Lancaster, "Arabs, Israelis Talking Business at the 2nd Summit," *Washington Post*, November 1, 1995, p. A21.

77. See "Cairo Threatens to Cancel the Party," *Middle East Economic Digest*, September 6, 1996, p. 6, and David Makovsky, "Mubarak Threatens Cancellation of Summit," *Jerusalem Post*, August 23, 1996, p. 1.

78. On Israeli reactions, see Summary of Editorials from the Hebrew Press, *Israel Information Service* <gopher://israel-info.gov.il:70/00/archive/eds96/961104.eds>, November 4, 1996 and Avraham Tal, "Who Needs the Cairo Conference?" *Ha' Aretz*, August 12, 1996, p. B1. For Arab views, see "Cairo Struggles to Defend 'Normalization' Conference," *Mideast Mirror*, November 6, 1996, pp. 12–17, "Whatever Happened to Arab Linkage Between Normalization and Peace?" *Mideast Mirror*, November 12, 1996, pp. 9–13, and a debate

between two Egyptian academics on the summit in *Mideast Mirror*, October 29, 1996, pp. 10–12.
79. "Cairo Threatens to Cancel the Party," p. 6.
80. Cairo ESC Television (in Arabic), "Egypt: Mubarak on Washington Summit, Economic Conference, Drill," October 6, 1996, cited in *FBIS-NES*-96–195, October 6, 1996, located in World News Connection <http://wnc.fedworld.gov>. Also see, "Mubarak: Economic Summit to Proceed on Schedule," Israel Line, *Israel Information Service* <gopher://israel-info.gov.il:70/00/archive/isline96/961002.isl>, October 2, 1996; "Egypt to Hold Regional Summit," *Washington Post*, September 13, 1996, p. A36; and Cairo Arab Republic of Egypt Radio Network (in Arabic), "Egypt: Mubarak on European Role in Peace Process, Arab Summit," cited in *FBIS-NES*-96–204, October 21, 1996, located in World News Connection <http://wnc.fedworld.gov>.
81. See "The Sinking Palestinian Economy," *New York Times*, November 12, 1996, p. A24. While Israeli closures of the territories in the wake of terrorist activity are most associated with the plight of the Palestinian economy, other factors (particularly internal inefficiencies) have also contributed to the drastic economic situation in the West Bank and Gaza. See U.S. Undersecretary of Commerce Stuart E. Eizenstat, "Special Policy Forum Report." For a Palestinian view, see *Al-Sharq Al-Awsat*, "Palestinian Affairs: Economy Minister Laments Falling Investments," September 24, 1996, p. 12, cited in *FBIS-NES*-96–188, September 24, 1996, located in World News Connection <http://wnc.fedworld.gov>.
82. See Suleiman al-Khalidi, "Jordan Business to Shy from Israel Ties in Summit," *Reuters*, October 30, 1996.
83. Jordanian officials and businessmen who had been involved with organizing the Amman summit were also widely displeased with Egypt's handling of the conference, complaining that the Egyptians were shutting the Jordanians out of the planning process, and were focusing on promoting the Egyptian economy more than promoting a regional agenda. Author interview with senior Jordanian official, August 19, 1996, Amman.
84. See Cairo Arab Republic of Egypt Radio Network (in Arabic), "Mubarak Addresses Parliamentary Session," cited in *FBIS-NES*-96–220, November 10, 1996, located in World News Connection <http://wnc.fedworld.gov>.
85. Two types of infrastructure projects were developed: 1) sectoral programs, including the Middle East Regional Transport Study and the Integration of Regional Electricity Grids; and 2) geographic-specific projects, including the Taba-Eilat-Aqaba region (TEAM), the South Eastern Mediterranean coastal region from El Arish in Egypt's Northern Sinai through Palestinian Gaza to Israeli Ashdod (SEMED), and the Jordan Rift Valley region (JRV), which

includes Lake Tiberias, the Dead Sea, Southern Ghors, Wadi Araba, and the Northern Red Sea shore. For details, see REDWG Monitoring Committee Secretariat's *Annual Report*, December 1994–May 1996, pp. 19–22. These subregions served as the principal focus areas of Israel's project book for the conference, which outlined the following types of proposals: the interconnection of electricity grids between Egypt, the PA, and Israel; a natural gas pipeline from Egypt to Israel, Jordan, and the PA; an East Mediterranean Riviera; a Red Sea Riviera; several joint tourism projects; a Red Sea-Dead Sea Canal; a JRV telecommunications superhighway; and joint water conservation and development projects. See Israeli Ministry of Foreign Affairs, *Programs for Regional Cooperation, 1997*, reproduced on the World Wide Web <http://www.israel-mfa.gov.il./peace/projects/intro.html>. For more on the Riviera idea, see Serge Schmemann, "The Middle East Riviera That Isn't—Not Yet," *New York Times*, November 5, 1995, p. D2.

86. For the complete text of Egypt's project proposals, see the web site: <http://www.cairo96.gov.eg>. For Jordanian project proposals, see "New Realism Is Hallmark of Wish List," *Middle East Economic Digest*, November 15, 1996, pp. 17–18.

87. "Star Scheme to Link Egypt and Israel," *Middle East Economic Digest*, November 15, 1996, pp. 12–13.

88. Interview with Raouf Sa'ad by Ghadah Rajab in *Al-Ahram Weekly*, October 17–23, 1996, p. 4, cited in FBIS-NES-96-210, October 23, 1996, located in World News Connection <http://wnc.fedworld.gov>.

89. Author interview with State Department official, May 15, 1997, Washington, D.C.

90. Thomas L. Friedman, "Pyramid Power," *New York Times*, November 13, 1996, p. A23.

91. For the full text of President Mubarak's address to the conference, see FBIS-NES-96-219, November 12, 1996, located in World News Connection <http://wnc.fedworld.gov>. Other speeches by high-level political representatives are also included in this *FBIS* volume, including addresses by Klaus Schwab, Israeli Foreign Minister David Levy, Palestinian Minister of Finance Muhammad Zuhdi al-Nashashibi, and Jordanian Minister of Industry and Trade 'Ali Abu-al-Raghib.

92. See "Levy Meets with Egyptian, Qatari, European and American Counterparts," *Israel Information Service* <gopher://israel-info.gov.il:70/00/archive/isline96/961113.isl>, November 13, 1996.

93. See "Mideast Conference Ends, Links Prosperity and Peace," *Reuters*, November 14, 1996.

94. See Ora Qoren, "Israelis Note 'Radical Change' in Business Ties to Egypt,

*Globes*, December 12, 1996, cited in *FBIS-NES-96-241*, December 12, 1996, located in World News Connection <http://wnc.fedworld.gov>.

95. David Lipkin and Ya'el Karmi-Daniyeli, "Egyptian-Turkish Gas Deal Seen as Result of Israel Stalling," *Ma'Ariv*, November 14, 1996, p. 7, cited in *FBIS-NES-96-221*, November 14, 1996, located in World News Connection <http://wnc.fedworld.gov>. For more on the Egyptian-Turkish gas deal, see "Gas Deal Sidelines Israel at Mideast Conference," *Reuters*, November 13, 1996.
96. "Mideast Conference Ends, Links Prosperity and Peace."
97. For the full text of the final Cairo communiqué, see *FBIS-NES-96-222*, November 14, 1996, located in World News Connection <http://wnc.fedworld.gov>.
98. The fourth MENA summit convened in Doha, Qatar, from November 16–18, 1997. Despite tremendous pressure from the Syrians and other Arab states to cancel or at least postpone the summit given the political crisis on the Israeli-Palestinian track, the Qataris were determined to proceed. Washington firmly backed Qatar's position, and hosted a number of planning meetings in Washington, D.C. However, the decision by key states like Saudi Arabia and particularly Egypt to boycott the Doha summit (announced on the eve of the conference) proved a major setback to the process. For the Arab debate over Qatar's decision to move ahead with the summit, see: "Qatar Gears Up to Host 4th Mideast Economic Summit," *Mideast Mirror*, May 30, 1997, pp. 7–8; "The Gulf States and Normalization with Israel—How Far and How Fast?" *Mideast Mirror*, June 17, 1997, pp. 7–10; "Qatar Shoots for Islamic Summit," *Mideast Mirror*, July 28, 1997, pp. 7–8; "Syria's Regional Diplomacy: Right Substance, Wrong Style," *Mideast Mirror*, July 25, 1997, pp. 7–10; "The Make-or-Break Doha Summit," *Mideast Mirror*, July 23, 1997, pp. 8–10; Douglas Jehl, "Arabs Cool to Meeting with Israel to Improve Ties," *New York Times*, July 11, 1997, p. A3; "Moving Toward Regional Entente?," *Mideast Mirror*, July 2, 1997, pp. 10–11. On Egypt's decision to boycott Doha, see John Lancaster, "Cairo Snubs U.S.-Backed Trade Talks," *Washington Post*, November 12, 1997, p. A1.
99. The Council on Foreign Relations sponsored one such meeting in June 1999, for example. See Council on Foreign Relations, *Calendar and Chronicle* (August 1999).
100. Several significant studies on regional trade potential were conducted under REDWG's initiative, including: a German study, *New Potentials for Cooperation and Trade in the Middle East* (IFO); *Trade for Peace in the New Middle East: Measures to Enhance Trade between Egypt, Israel, Jordan and the Palestinian Territories* (Cairo: Arab-German Chamber of Commerce, October 1995); and Washington's *Market Access Study: Approved by the Taba Trade*

*Leaders*, (Amman, Jordan, October 30, 1995). The first two studies were distributed at the Amman Economic summit in October 1995.
101. Casablanca Declaration, October 30–November 1, 1994.
102. See Jose Rosenfeld and Jon Immanuel, "Shaath: Closure Must End Before We Can Discuss Economic Cooperation," *Jerusalem Post*, February 8, 1995, p. 2.
103. See Israel Line, April 18, 1995 <gopher://israel-info.gov.il:70/00/archive/isline95/950418.isl> and Economic Survey, August 9, 1995 <gopher://israel-info.gov.il:70/00/econ/ecs/1995/950809.ecs>, both reproduced in *Israel Information Service*.
104. REDWG MC Secretariat, *Annual Report*, p. 33.
105. Author interview with State Department official, May 15, 1997, Washington, D.C.
106. STIMENA's report is titled *Trade Relations Among the Core Parties and With Key Third Parties*.
107. MEMTTA focused its activities on gaining the interest and confidence of private sector companies in three critical regions: the Americas, Europe, and the Asia/Pacific area. See U.S. State Department Fact Sheet, "Middle East-Mediterranean Travel and Tourism."
108. Casablanca Declaration, October 30–November 1, 1994.
109. U.S. State Department Fact Sheet, "Middle East-Mediterranean Travel and Tourism Association."
110. Carla Hunt, "Areas Team Up to Promote Peace," *Travel Weekly's Guide to the Middle East/Mediterranean*, March 7, 1997.
111. Author interview with State Department official, May 15, 1997, Washington, D.C.
112. For a more detailed analysis of the birth and development of the bank, see Dalia Dassa Kaye, *Banking on Peace: Lessons from the Middle East Development Bank*, Policy Paper No. 43 (San Diego, Calif.: Institute on Global Conflict and Cooperation, October 1998).
113. See, for example, Robert R. Nathan and Jerome I. Levinson, "A Development Fund for the Near East," in Joyce R. Starr with Addeane S. Caelleigh, *A Shared Destiny: Near East Regional Development and Cooperation* (New York: Praeger, 1983), pp. 103–13.
114. James A. Baker III (with Thomas M. DeFrank), *The Politics of Diplomacy* (New York: Putnam, 1995), p. 413.
115. See Hearing before the Commission on Security and Cooperation in Europe, "CSCME: Prospects for Collective Security in the Middle East," One Hundred Third Congress, First Session, October 14, 1993. Crown Prince Hassan's plan is printed in the appendix, pp. 68–82. See also an address delivered by Crown Prince El Hassan Bin Talal at the International Symposium, "Looking Beyond

the Gulf War: A Conference on Security and Cooperation in the Middle East," Prague, March 16, 1991.
116. Peres, *New Middle East*, p. 111.
117. See Said El-Nagger and Mohamed El-Erian, "The Economic Implications of a Comprehensive Peace in the Middle East," in Stanley Fischer, Dani Rodrik, and Elias Tuma, eds., *The Economics of Middle East Peace* (Cambridge, Mass.: MIT Press, 1993), pp. 219–220. For another argument outlining the economic and financial rationale for the MENABANK, see Wafik Grais and Lorenzo Savorelli, "Economic and Financial Rationale for a New International Financial Institution for the Middle East and North Africa," June 1, 1998, on the MENABANK web site: <http://www.menabank.org>.
118. Author interview with an Israeli official, October 23, 1995, Jerusalem.
119. David Makovsky, "US Not Backing Peres' Bank Plan," *Jerusalem Post*, October 11, 1994, p. 2.
120. See "Casablanca Parley Closes with Promise of 'New Partnership,'" *Mideast Mirror*, 8, no. 211, November 1, 1994, pp. 9–15.
121. Author interview with Israeli official, October 23, 1995, Jerusalem.
122. This work resulted in a joint "vision paper" offered by the core parties for consideration at Casablanca. The vision paper argued forcefully for the need to establish a regional bank, in order for the parties to "function effectively as a region," and to "create a viable and dynamic regional economic development programme in the region." See "Middle East Development Bank (MEDB): A Policy Position Paper," drafted by the regional parties in REDWG's Monitoring Committee (MC), Finance Subcommittee before the Casablanca Summit.
123. It is not clear how the idea of the bank reached President Clinton, although there is speculation that Peres personally raised the proposal with him. Author interviews with senior U.S. officials, May 8, 1996, Washington, D.C.
124. Casablanca Declaration, Section 9, Part (a).
125. "Shared Prosperity in the Middle East: Toward a Regional Development Bank," Remarks by Lawrence H. Summers, Treasury Undersecretary for International Affairs, at the Middle East/North Africa Economic Summit, Casablanca, Morocco, October 31, 1994. See "Casablanca Parley Closes with Promise of 'New Partnership,'" *Mideast Mirror*, 8, no. 211, November 1, 1994, p. 12.
126. Not all European Union member states opposed the bank, although the opposition of key states like France and Germany was significant. Moreover, the European Commission supported the proposal, and its representative who headed the MC Secretariat assisted the regional parties in advancing the institution.
127. See "Casablanca Parley Closes with Promise of 'New Partnership,'" p. 12.
128. For details of these projects, see Ambassador David J. Dunford, "MENABANK:

Would U.S. Membership Help the Peace Process?" *Peacewatch*, no. 159 (Washington, D.C.: Washington Institute for Near East Policy, March 20, 1998).
129. See, for example, "Can the Middle East Bank on Bibi?" *U.S. News and World Report*, July 15, 1996, p. 20.
130. Author interview with senior Israeli official, August 25, 1996, Israeli Foreign Ministry, Jerusalem.
131. The final Cairo conference communiqué included the following statement in reference to the bank: "They [the participants at Cairo] underscored the importance of the bank for economic cooperation and development in the Middle East and North Africa in Cairo and its potential contribution to the promotion of capital flow to the region, to building infrastructure projects, and to the development of the private sector in the region. The conclusion of the drafting of the agreement establishing the bank was welcomed. Countries were encouraged to sign the agreement and complete their funding and ratification procedures promptly in order to enable the bank to begin operations in 1997." For the full text of the communiqué, see *FBIS-NES-96–222*, November 14, 1996, located in World News Connection <http://wnc.fedworld.gov>.
132. The United States holds 21 percent of the shares, which constitutes a $52.5 million annual commitment for a five-year period. See Testimony of Treasury Secretary Robert E. Rubin before the House Appropriations Subcommittee on Foreign Operations, April 18, 1996.
133. For the debate over the conference and normalization, see "Cairo Struggles to Defend 'Normalization' Conference," *Mideast Mirror*, November 6, 1996, pp. 12–17, and *Mideast Mirror*, October 29, 1996, pp. 10–12 for pro-conference and anti-conference views from two Egyptian academics.
134. See, for example, Fahmi Howeidi's editorial in *Asharq al-Aswat* in *Mideast Mirror*, November 11, 1996, pp. 9–11.
135. Arab oil revenues, for example, declined from a peak of $213 billion in 1980 to a low of $53 billion in 1986. See Ishac Diwan and Nick Papandreou, "The Peace Process and Economic Reforms in the Middle East," in Fischer, Rodrik, and Tuma, *The Economics of Middle East Peace*, p. 223.
136. From 1985 to 1995, the Middle Eastern economy contracted more rapidly than any other region's, including sub-Saharan Africa. See John Page, "Economic Prospects and the Role of Regional Development Finance Institutions" in *Regional Economic Development in the Middle East: Opportunities and Risks* (Washington, D.C.: The Center for Policy Analysis on Palestine, 1995), p. 5. For an excellent overview of Middle Eastern economies and recent trends, see Alan Richards and John Waterbury, *A Political Economy of the Middle East*, 2d ed. (Boulder, Colo.: Westview Press, 1996). Also see the World Bank study,

*Claiming the Future: Choosing Prosperity in the Middle East and North Africa* (Washington, D.C.: International Bank for Reconstruction and Development, 1995). For a comparative study of the impact of economic institutions in both labor- and oil-exporting Middle East states, see Kiren Aziz Chaudhry, *The Price of Wealth: Economies and Institutions in the Middle East* (Ithaca, N.Y.: Cornell University Press, 1997).

137. For example, while 60 percent of global direct foreign investment goes to Asia, only 3 percent of the world flow reaches the Middle East. See Page, "Economic Prospects," p. 13.

138. A popular symbol of this phenomenon has been the spread of McDonald's across the globe. The McDonald's example as a symbol of growing globalization effects on the Middle East and elsewhere was popularized by *New York Times* columnist Thomas Friedman in his so-called Golden Arches Theory of Conflict Prevention. According to this tongue-in-cheek spin-off of democratic peace theory, "No two countries that both have a McDonald's have ever fought a war against each other." See Thomas L. Friedman, "Foreign Affairs Big Mac I," *New York Times*, December 8, 1996, p. 15. For another discussion of the impact of globalization on the Middle East, including its challenge to cultural identities, see Martin Kramer, "The Middle East, Old and New," *Daedalus* 126, no. 2 (Spring 1997): 89–112.

139. Page, "Economic Prospects," p. 8.

140. Whitney, "Hobnobbing at Very High Levels," pp. C1, C21.

141. David Butter, "Reform Ready Economy for Real Growth," *Middle East Economic Digest*, 40, no. 16, April 19, 1996, pp. 25–26.

142. Cairo ESC Television (in Arabic), "Mubarak Addresses Economic Conference," November 12, 1996, cited in *FBIS-NES*-96–219, November 12, 1996, located in World News Connection <http://wnc.fedworld.gov>.

143. For an overview of the changing nature of the Israeli economy with respect to privatization and greater integration into the global economy, see Benjamin Gaon (of Koor Industries), "Israel and the Future of Middle East Economic Development," in *Peace Through Entrepreneurship: Practical Ideas from Middle Eastern Business Leaders* (Washington, D.C.: Washington Institute for Near East Policy, January 1994), pp. 9–13.

144. Rami G. Khouri, "Voting with Our Stomachs: McDonald's, Markets, Culture and Sovereignty," *Jordan Times*, November 12, 1996, in *Mideast Mirror*, November 12, 1996, p. 15–16.

145. For a review of the secret but limited Arab-Israeli trade record since the 1980s, see Ephraim Kleiman, "Is There a Secret Arab-Israeli Trade?" *Middle East Quarterly* (June 1998): 11–18.

146. For a general analysis of the role of multilateral development banks that makes

such an argument, see Dani Rodrik, *Why Is There Multilateral Lending?*, International Macroeconomics and International Trade, Discussion Paper Series, No. 1207 (London: Centre for Economic Policy Research, July 1995).
147. See Serge Schmemann, "Shalom (and Salaam) as Tourist Lure," *New York Times*, January 24, 1997, p. A6.

*Chapter 6*

1. For an overview of the water scarcity problem in the wider Middle East and North Africa region, see "Special Report Water" in *Middle East Economic Digest* (MEED), January 24, 1997, pp. 7–12. For a discussion of the scarcity issue in the Israeli-Palestinian context, including the River Jordan basin, see Alwyn R. Rouyer, "The Water Issue in the Palestinian-Israeli Peace Process," *Survival*, 39, no. 2 (Summer 1997): 57–81.
2. On epistemic communities, see Peter M. Haas, "Introduction: Epistemic Communities and International Policy Coordination," *International Organization*, 46, no. 1 (Winter 1992): 1–35.
3. Examples include: Miriam R. Lowi, *Water and Power: The Politics of a Scarce Resource in the Jordan River Basin* (Cambridge: Cambridge University Press, 1993); Jeffrey K. Sosland, *Cooperating Rivals: The Politics of Water Scarcity, Protracted Conflict, and Complex Cooperation in the Jordan River Basin* (Ph.D. diss., Georgetown University, 1998); Thomas Naff and Ruth Matson, eds., *Water in the Middle East: Conflict or Cooperation?* (Boulder, Colo.: Westview Press, 1984); Joyce Starr and Daniel Stoll, eds., *The Politics of Scarcity: Water in the Middle East* (Boulder, Colo.: Westview Press, 1988); Joyce Starr, "Water Wars," *Foreign Policy*, 82 (Spring 1991): 17–36; Natasha Beschorner, *Water and Instability in the Middle East*, Adelphi Paper 273 (London: International Institute for Strategic Studies, Winter 1992/93); and Amikam Nachmani, "The Politics of Water in the Middle East," in Efraim Inbar, ed., *Regional Security Regimes* (Albany: State University of New York Press, 1995), pp. 231–51.
4. For example, an Israeli position paper on the Environment and the Peace Process argued, "Among the issues being discussed at the multilateral talks, the environment is the least controversial. It does not deal with territorial problems, does not pose questions of national sovereignty, nor does it involve competition over limited resources. It serves objectives which enjoy almost complete consensus of opinion, that will produce common benefits and prevent mutual harm." In Dror Amir, "The Environment and the Peace Process," *Israel Information Service* <gopher://israel-info.gov.il:70/00/govmin/envir/950100.evp>, January 1995.
5. Still, some issues—like making water data available—proved sensitive among

the Jordan River basin riparians, particularly the Israelis, who were cautious about how such data would prejudice bilateral negotiations with the Palestinians and the Jordanians.
6. After the water rights issue nearly scuttled the water talks at the Geneva plenary in April 1993, the Israelis and Palestinians reached an agreement at their bilateral negotiations in Washington to set up a special bilateral working group to deal solely with the issue of water sharing and rights in the Palestinian territories. See David Makovsky, "Katz-Oz 'Not Disappointed' by Water Talks," *Jerusalem Post*, May 4, 1993.
7. According to a U.S. official involved in these discussions, Oman came up with the idea to launch a desalination project on its own, an initiative that was enthusiastically embraced by Washington. Author interview with State Department official, August 22, 1995, Washington, D.C.
8. Author interview with State Department official, July 11, 1996, Washington, D.C.
9. The Hashemite Kingdom of Jordan, Jordan Delegation to Middle East Multilateral Peace Talks, The Environment Working Group, Tokyo, May 18–19, 1992, Position Paper.
10. This cautious attitude was expressed at the first plenary meeting in Tokyo in May 1992 when, according to one report, the Palestinian members of the delegation "anxiously rushed from the conference room after the meeting's conclusion." The report also noted that the delegation of Palestinian environmental experts left the meeting several times to consult with a senior PLO official waiting outside the conference room. See Laura Stern, "Environment Talks Hailed as Success," *Jerusalem Post*, May 20, 1992.
11. Ibid.
12. While Japan chaired the Environment group, Japanese and American officials worked closely together. Author interview with U.S. official, August 22, 1995, Washington, D.C.
13. See Liat Collins, "First Face-to-Face Arab-Israel Meeting in Environment Talks," *Jerusalem Post*, October 23, 1992.
14. For a description of this project and others related to the environment, see "The Environment in the Peace Process: The Multilateral Track," *Israel Information Service* <gopher://israel-info.gov.il:70/00/mad/multi/950301.mul>, February 1995.
15. Ibid.
16. Ibid.
17. Author interview with State Department official, August 21, 1995, Washington, D.C.
18. See Youssef Azmeh, "Oman Leads the Arab World in Contacts with Israel," *Jerusalem Post*, April 19, 1994, p. 4; Liat Collins, "Omani Sands Are Shifting

Toward Israel," *Jerusalem Post*, May 4, 1994, p. 8; and Press Conference with Israeli Deputy Foreign Minister Dr. Yossi Beilin (upon his return from Oman), Jerusalem, *Israel Information Service* <gopher://israel-info.gov.il:70/00/mad/multi/940421.mul>, April 21, 1994.

19. For a summary of the meeting's achievements, see the Statement of the Gavelholder (the United States), "Middle East Peace Process Multilateral Working Group on Water Resources, Muscat, Oman, April 17–19, 1994," Near East Affairs home page, U.S. State Department web site: <http://www.state.gov/www/regions/nea/ppmwg5.html>. Other gavelholder summaries of working group plenaries can be located from the Near East Affairs home page.

20. For example, in a development that mirrors the evolution of the REDWG MC, a smaller steering group emerged to better direct the agenda and projects of the working group, demonstrating greater regional initiative in shaping the development of the group. The steering group includes: Egypt, Israel, Jordan, the Palestinians, Saudi Arabia, Oman, and Tunisia from the region; and Germany, Norway, Russia, Japan, Canada, Italy, the European Union, and the United States from outside the region.

21. For example, at the June 1995 Water plenary in Amman, Jordan, the following pledges were made for regional projects: $2.5 million from the United Sates and EU for a data bank for the Palestinians; $3 million from Austria for brackish water irrigation; $7 million from the Netherlands to build a dam for the Gaza Strip's aquifer; $3 million each from the United States and Oman for a regional desalination center; and $5 million each from the United States, Japan, and Israel to treat waste water in small communities, reduce water loss in cities, and desalinate brackish water. See AP story reprinted in *Jerusalem Post*, June 23, 1995, p. 2; Mohammed Hasni, "US, EU Offer 2.5 Million Dollars for Data Bank on Mideast Water," *Agence France Presse*, June 22, 1995; and "Multilateral Working Group on Water Decides on Regional Projects," Communication by the Israeli Foreign Ministry Spokesman, *Israel Information Service* <gopher://israel-info.gov.il:70/00/mad/multi/950623.mul>, June 23, 1995.

22. For detailed project proposals presented at the MENA summits, see Government of Israel, *Development Options for Cooperation: The Middle East/East Mediterranean Region, 1996* (Version IV, August 1995) and *Building a Prosperous Peace*, Jordanian project book prepared for the Middle East and North Africa Summit, October 29–31, 1995 (Amman, Jordan: International Press Office, The Royal Hashemite Court, 1995). Also see "Amman Eager to Know Where Israel Stands on 'Red-Dead' Canal and 'Med-Dead' Plan," *Mideast Mirror*, 8, no. 123, June 29, 1994, pp. 9–11.

23. Details of the working group's progress in each of these areas is outlined in the Gavelholder's Summary (U.S.), Working Group on Water Resources, Hammamet, Tunisia, May 15–16, 1996.

24. Deutsche Gesellschaft für Technische Zusammenarbeit (GTZ), Middle East Regional Study on Water Supply and Demand Development (March 1995).
25. Author interview with Israeli Foreign Ministry official, August 27, 1996, Jerusalem.
26. See the Desalination Center's Newsletter, *Watermark*, Volume One, Issue One (July 1996).
27. See "Regional Center for Research in Desalination," *Israel Information Service* <gopher://israel-info.gov.il:70/00/mad/multi/961222.mul>, December 23, 1996.
28. Excerpted from Text of Ambassador Frances D. Cook's Statement on the Occasion of the Signing of the Establishment Agreement for the Middle East Desalination Research Center in Muscat, December 22, 1996.
29. See Jerusalem *Qol Yisra'el* (in Hebrew), "Arab-Israeli Talks: Israel, Jordan, PA Sign Regional Water Document," February 13, 1996, cited in *Foreign Broadcast Information Service-Near East and South Asia* (hereafter *FBIS-NES*)-96–031, February 14, 1996, p. 8.
30. See Liat Collins, "Delegation Leaves for Bahrain Environment Talks," *Jerusalem Post*, October 24, 1994, p. 2.
31. For a summary of the results of this meeting, see the Press Statement by the Gavelholder, "Middle East Peace Process, Multilateral Working Group on the Environment, Manama, Bahrain, October 25–26, 1994," reproduced by the U.S. State Department Office of Near East Affairs, <http://www.state.gov/www/regions/nea/ppmwg4.html>.
32. According to Israeli reports, Foreign Ministry officials were initially opposed to Sarid's attendance at the plenary session because they were reluctant to raise the multilateral talks to the ministerial level, believing that its low-key format facilitated progress. See Liat Collins, "Israeli Officials Leave for Bahrain," *Jerusalem Post*, September 28, 1994, p. 2.
33. According to a State Department official involved in the talks, the postponement of the plenary session was due to logistical, not substantive, reasons. Author interview, July 11, 1996, Washington, D.C. In any case, the general trend after Oslo was movement away from large plenary sessions toward smaller, more project-focused cooperative forums with smaller, subregional participation.
34. Concluding Remarks by the Gavelholder, The Intersessional Meeting, The Environment Working Group, Muscat, June 26–27, 1996.
35. Ibid.
36. For an overview of regional environmental hazards in the Aqaba area, including oil spills, sewage, fish farming and aquatic tourism damage, and potential solutions, see Philip Warburg, *Middle East Environmental Cooperation*, IGCC Policy Brief No. 4 (San Diego: Institute on Global Conflict and Cooperation, University of California, May 1995).

37. See Amir, "Environment and the Peace Process."
38. The Saudis did not participate in the project, although it was designed to include them at a later stage.
39. The Multilateral Middle East Peace Talks, Update Following the Fourth Round, October-November 1993, *Israel Information Service* <gopher://israel-info.gov.il:70/00/mad/multi/multi.13>, November 23, 1993.
40. Ibid.
41. The European Union financed Egypt's center and equipment while the Japanese financed Jordan's facility. Israel financed the procurement of its own equipment. By November 1996, the Japanese had supplied $5.5 million in equipment to set up the Jordanian station in Aqaba. See *FBIS-NES-96–231*, November 27, 1996, located in World News Connection <http://wnc.fedworld.gov>.
42. Author interview, July 11, 1996, Washington, D.C.
43. "Multilateral Steering Committee on Water Pollution Convenes Today," Communication by the Environment Ministry Spokesman, *Israel Information Service* <gopher://israel-info.gov.il>, March 14, 1995.
44. "Tripartite Panel Meets on Aqaba Gulf Projects," *Deutsche Presse-Agentur*, April 4, 1995.
45. See "Progress in Multilateral Talks in Amman." Communicated by Foreign Ministry Spokesman, *Israel Information Service* <gopher://israel-info.gov.il:70/00/mad/multi/950622.mul>, June 22, 1995.
46. Author interview with U.S. official, September 29, 1995, Tel Aviv, and author interview with Israeli official, Ministry of the Environment, October 5, 1995, Jerusalem. Both confirmed that the contingency plan was implemented as joint forces combated the spill using a communication hotline developed in the planning workshops for the project.
47. "Cyprus, Egypt, Israel Sign Accord to Combat Threats to Mediterranean," *The Bureau of National Affairs International Environment Daily*, June 12, 1995.
48. The Multilateral Middle East Peace Talks, Update Following the Fourth Round, October-November 1993, *Israel Information Service* <gopher://israel-info.gov.il:70/00/mad/multi/multi.13>, November 23, 1993.
49. See Amir, "Environment and the Peace Process."
50. Ibid.
51. Author interview with Israeli official who took part in the "wise men" discussions, October 5, 1995, Jerusalem.
52. Ibid.
53. "Environment Gets Peace Dividends," *Jerusalem Post*, October 27, 1994, p. 16.
54. For an interesting critique of the epistemic community approach that discusses the problem of assuming that consensual scientific knowledge drives policy

while neglecting the role of politics in policymaking, see Karen T. Litfin, *Ozone Discourses: Science and Politics in Global Environmental Cooperation* (New York: Columbia University Press, 1994), esp. chaps. 1 and 2.

55. The misconception that the working groups are vastly different was commented on in a number of interviews, but two in particular emphasized this point. Author interview with U.S. official, July 11, 1996, Washington, D.C.; author interview with Jordanian official, October 9, 1995, Amman.

56. For the widespread public sentiment against normalization, as reflected in the Arab press, see the following articles in *Mideast Mirror*: "Arab States Stand Up to Israel at Last . . . or Do They?" April 1, 1997; "The Arab-Israeli Peace Process, R.I.P.," March 24, 1997; "Time for the Arabs to Respond to Netanyahu with Actions Rather Than Words—but How?" March 21, 1997; "A Halt to Normalization with Israel Is Vital . . . but Doesn't Go Far Enough," March 27, 1997; "Time to Convene an Arab Summit and Halt Normalization with Israel," October 11, 1996; "Netanyahu Has Made Normalization Indefensible," October 10, 1996; "Dore Gold and the Likud's 'Daydreams,'" November 29, 1996. Also see "Arab States Threaten to Freeze Ties," *Jerusalem Post*, September 16, 1996; David Makovsky and Hillel Kutler, "Report: Syria Failed to Pass Anti-Israel Ultimatum," *Jerusalem Post*, September 17, 1996; "Oman Threatens to Sever Ties with Israel," Israel Line, *Israel Information Service* <gopher://israel-info.gov.il:70/00/archive/isline97/970325.isl>, March 25, 1997.

*Chapter 7*

1. See, for example, David Lake and Patrick Morgan, eds., *Regional Orders: Building Security in a New World* (University Park: Pennsylvania State University Press, 1997) and Louise Fawcett and Andrew Hurrell, eds., *Regionalism in World Politics* (Oxford: Oxford University Press, 1995). For a review of works focused on economic regionalism, see Edward D. Mansfield and Helen V. Milner, "The New Wave of Regionalism," *International Organization*, 53, no. 3 (Summer 1999): 589–627.

2. See John Lancaster, "Arabs Balk at Convening with Israelis: Economic Forum Tied to Peace Negotiations," *Washington Post*, November 7, 1997, p. A28.

3. Examples of track two dialogues include discussions and workshops sponsored by the Institute on Global Conflict and Cooperation (IGCC) since 1993 and less academic discussions and working groups formed by the Search for Common Ground's Initiative for Peace and Cooperation in the Middle East (IPCME). For IGCC's work, see Steven L. Spiegel and David J. Pervin, eds., *Practical Peacemaking in the Middle East* (New York: Garland, 1995). Also see the many papers from IGCC-sponsored conferences on the IGCC web site on

multilateral cooperation: <http://www.igcc.ucsd.edu/igcc/memulti/multi-lat.html>. While IPCME focuses more on fostering regional dialogues and less on producing papers, it has produced one significant report from its working group on security. See Ambassador Peter D. Constable, ed., *Common Ground on Re-deployment of Israeli Forces in the West Bank*, The Initiative Papers No. 3 (Washington, D.C.: Search for Common Ground, 1994). The Initiative also produces an informative newsletter outlining the developments among its own regional working groups in addition to official processes in the region. See *Bulletin of Regional Cooperation in the Middle East* (Washington, D.C.: Initiative for Peace and Cooperation in the Middle East) or their web site: <http://www.searchforcommonground.org>.

4. Jordan's version was promoted by Crown Prince Hassan Bin Talal beginning in March 1991. See Hearing before the Commission on Security and Cooperation in Europe, "CSCME: Prospects for Collective Security in the Middle East," One Hundred Third Congress, First Session (October 14, 1993). Crown Prince Hassan's plan is printed in the appendix, pp. 68–82. See also an Address delivered by Crown Prince Hassan at the International Symposium, "Looking Beyond the Gulf War: A Conference on Security and Cooperation in the Middle East" (Prague: March 16, 1991). Israeli Foreign Minister Shimon Peres outlined his own version of a CSCME which he presented to U.S. Secretary of State Warren Christopher in late May 1994, in addition to raising the idea in discussions with President Clinton. See Aluf Ben, Aquiva Eldar, and Nadav Shragay, "Peres Holds Meetings with UNSC Members, Clinton; Raises New Regional Security Initiative," *Ha'aretz* in Hebrew, Tel Aviv, May 26, 1994, pp. A1, A10, cited in *Foreign Broadcast Information Service-Near East and South Asia* (hereafter *FBIS-NES*)-94-102, May 26, 1994, p. 36. Even before his proposal, Peres had discussed ideas for new regional security structures. See, for example, "Peres Views Regional Structure for Middle East," Paris *Le Monde* in French, November 11, 1993, p. 1, cited in *FBIS-NES*-93-221, November 18, 1993, p. 39. A Palestinian academic and the first head of the Palestinian delegation to ACRS, Yezid Sayigh, also offered a similar proposal for regional cooperation, the MASCME. See Yezid Sayigh, "The Multilateral Middle East Peace Talks: Reorganizing for Regional Security," in Spiegel and Pervin, *Practical Peacemaking in the Middle East*, pp. 207–229. And finally, in the fall of 1996, Prime Minister Netanyahu and his top foreign policy adviser, Dore Gold, began promoting—in response to a British proposal by Foreign Secretary Malcolm Rifkind—a new regional security structure for the region drawing on the OSCE as a model. See the address by Prime Minister Benjamin Netanyahu at the Conference of the Organization on Security and Cooperation in Europe, Lisbon (December 3, 1996), cited in *FBIS-NES*-96-234, December 3, 1996, located in World News Connection <http://wnc.fedworld.gov>. Also see Udi

Segal, "PM to Urge Middle East Security, Cooperation Organization," IDF Radio in Hebrew, Tel Aviv, December 1, 1996, cited in *FBIS-NES*-96–232, December 1, 1996, located in World News Connection <http://wnc.fedworld.gov>.

*Appendix C*

1. This version is based on the draft that was presented to the ACRS plenary session in Doha, Qatar, in May 1994 by the United States and Russia, the group's cosponsors. The text excludes Section I (Fundamental Principles Governing Security Relations Among Regional Participants in the Arms Control and Regional Security Working Group), most of which was not agreed to by the group. A similar text was reprinted in *Mideast Mirror*, 8, no. 83 (May 3, 1994).

# Selected Bibliography

Abel, Robert B. 1997. *The Influence of Technical Cooperation on Reducing Tensions in the Middle East*. Lanham, Md.: University Press of America.
Adler, Emanuel. 1992. "The Emergence of Cooperation: National Epistemic Communities and the International Evolution of the Idea of Nuclear Arms Control." *International Organization*, 46, no. 1 (Winter): 101–45.
———. 1997. "Seizing the Middle Ground: Constructivism in World Politics." *European Journal of International Relations*, 3, no. 3: 319–63.
———. 1998. "Seeds of Peaceful Change: the OSCE's Security Community-Building Model." In Adler and Barnett, *Security Communities*, pp. 119–60.
Adler, Emanuel and Michael N. Barnett, eds. 1998. *Security Communities*. Cambridge: Cambridge University Press.
Ajami, Fouad. 1981. *The Arab Predicament: Arab Political Thought and Practice Since 1967*. Cambridge: Cambridge University Press.
———. 1995. "The Sorrows of Egypt." *Foreign Affairs*, 74, no. 5 (September/October): 72–88.
Al-Mashat, Abdul-Monem. 1994. *The Economics of Regional Security in the Middle East*. Cairo University.
Alteras, Isaac. 1993. *Eisenhower and Israel: U.S.-Israeli Relations, 1953–1960*. Gainesville: University Press of Florida.
Arab-German Chamber of Commerce. 1995. *Trade for Peace in the New Middle East: Measures to Enhance Trade between Egypt, Israel, Jordan and the Palestinian Territories*. Cairo (October).
Aronson, Shlomo and Oded Brosh. 1992. *The Politics and Strategy of Nuclear Weapons in the Middle East*. Albany: State University of New York Press.
Awartani, Hisham and Ephraim Kleiman. 1997. "Economic Interactions Among Participants in the Middle East Peace Process." *Middle East Journal*, 51, no. 2 (Spring): 215–29.

Baker III, James A. 1991. Testimony to the House Foreign Affairs Committee on February 6, 1991. In *US Department of State Dispatch*, 2, no. 6 (February 11, 1991): 81–85.

———. 1995. *The Politics of Diplomacy*. New York: Putnam.

Barnett, Michael N. 1992. *Confronting the Costs of War: Military Power, State and Society in Egypt and Israel*. Princeton, N.J.: Princeton University Press.

———. 1996–97. "Regional Security After the Gulf War." *Political Science Quarterly*, 111, no. 4 (Winter): 597–618.

———. 1998. *Dialogues in Arab Politics: Negotiations in Regional Order*. New York: Columbia University Press.

Barnett, Michael N. and Jack S. Levy. 1991. "Domestic Sources of Alliances and Alignments: the Case of Egypt, 1962–1973." *International Organization*, 45, no. 3 (Summer): 369–95.

Bartholomew, Reginald. 1992. "Progress in Middle East Arms Control." *U.S. Department of State Dispatch*, 3, no. 13 (March 30): 242.

Ben-Dor, Gabriel. 1982. "Egypt." In *Security Policies of Developing Countries*. pp. 179–202. Edited by Edward A. Kolodziej and Robert E. Harkavy. Lexington, Ky.: Lexington Books.

Bentsur, Eytan. 1994. "Israel's Vision of the Goals and Principles of the Regional Security and Arms Control Process." In *Arms Control*. pp. 69–75. Edited by Fred Tanner.

Beschorner, Natasha. 1992–93. *Water and Instability in the Middle East*. Adelphi Paper 273. London: International Institute for Strategic Studies (Winter).

Bookmiller, Robert J. and Kristen Nakjavani Bookmiller. 1996. "Behind the Headlines: The Multilateral Middle East Talks." *Current History*, 597 (January): 33–37.

Brecher, Michael. 1975. *Decisions in Israel's Foreign Policy*. New Haven, Conn.: Yale University Press.

Brynen, Rex. 1997. "Much Ado About Nothing? The Refugee Working Group and the Perils of Multilateral Quasi-negotiation." *International Negotiation*, 2, no. 2 (November): 279–302.

Bush, George. 1991. "The World After the Persian Gulf War." *US Department of State Dispatch*, 2, no. 10 (March 11): 161.

Carr, Christopher D. 1996. "False Promises and Prospects: The Middle East Arms Control Initiative." In *Arms Control Toward the 21st Century*, pp. 255–63. Edited by Jeffrey A. Larsen and Gregory J. Rattray. Boulder, Colo.: Lynne Rienner.

Chaudhry, Kiren Aziz. 1997. *The Price of Wealth: Economies and Institutions in the Middle East*. Ithaca, N.Y.: Cornell University Press.

Checkel, Jeffrey T. 1998. "The Constructivist Turn in International Relations Theory." *World Politics*, 50, no. 2 (January): 324–48.

Christopher, Warren. 1994. "Building the Structures of Peace and Prosperity in the New Middle East." Remarks at the Royal Palace, Casablanca, Morocco,

October 30. Washington, D.C.: US Department of State, Bureau of Public Affairs, Office of Public Communication.

Clawson, Patrick and Howard Rosen. 1991. *The Economic Consequences of Peace for Israel, the Palestinians and Jordan*, Policy Paper No. 25. Washington, D.C.: Washington Institute for Near East Policy.

Clifford, Clark with Richard Holbrooke. 1991. *Counsel to the President: A Memoir*. New York: Random House.

Cohen, Avner. 1992. "Patterns of Nuclear Opacity in the Middle East: Understanding the Past, Implications for the Future." In *Regional Approaches to Curbing Nuclear Proliferation in the Middle East and South Asia*, pp. 13–54. Edited by Tariq Rauf. Ottawa: Canadian Centre for Global Security.

———. 1995. "The Nuclear Issue in the Middle East in a New World Order." In *Middle Eastern Security*, pp. 49–69. Edited by Efraim Inbar and Shmuel Sandler.

———. 1999. *Israel and the Bomb*. New York: Columbia University Press.

Cohen, Raymond. 1990. *Culture and Conflict in Egyptian-Israeli Relations: A Dialogue of the Deaf*. Bloomington: Indiana University Press.

Congressional Budget Office. 1992. *Limiting Conventional Arms Exports to the Middle East*. Washington, D.C.: Congressional Budget Office.

Constable, Peter D., ed. 1994. *Common Ground on Re-deployment of Israeli Forces in the West Bank*, The Initiative Papers No. 3. Washington, D.C.: Search for Common Ground.

Cordesman, Anthony H. 1993. *After the Storm: the Changing Military Balance in the Middle East*. Boulder, Colo.: Westview Press.

D'Alancon, François. 1994. "The EC Looks to a New Middle East." *Journal of Palestine Studies*, 23, no. 2 (Winter): 41–51.

Darilek, Richard E. and Geoffrey Kemp. 1992. "Prospects for Confidence- and Security-Building Measures in the Middle East." In *Arms Control and Confidence Building*, pp. 9–42. Edited by Alan Platt.

David, Steven R. 1991. "Explaining Third World Alignment." *World Politics*, 43, no. 2 (January): 233–56.

Dawisha, A. I. 1976. *Egypt in the Arab World: The Elements of Foreign Policy*. New York: Wiley.

Deutsch, Karl et al. 1957. *Political Community and the North Atlantic Area*. Princeton, N.J.: Princeton University Press.

Deutsch, Karl. 1953. *Nationalism and Social Communication*. Cambridge, Mass.: MIT Press.

Deutsche Gesellschaft für Technische Zusammenarbeit (GTZ). 1995. Middle East Regional Study on Water Supply and Demand Development (March).

Diwan, Ishac and Nick Papandreou. 1993. "The Peace Process and Economic Reforms in the Middle East." In *Economics of Middle East Peace*, pp. 227–55. Edited by Stanley Fischer, Dani Rodrik, and Elias Tuma.

Djerejian, Edward P. "The Multilateral Talks in the Arab-Israeli Peace Process." In *US Department of State Dispatch*, 4, no. 41 (October 11, 1993): 696.

Dunford, David J. 1998. "MENABANK: Would U.S. Membership Help the Peace Process?" *Peacewatch*, no. 159, March 20. Washington, D.C.: Washington Institute for Near East Policy.

Eizenstat, Stuart E. 1996. "Special Policy Forum Report, Run-Up to the Cairo Economic Summit: A U.S. View." *Peacewatch*, no. 110, November 8. Washington, D.C. : Washington Institute for Near East Policy.

El-Erian, Mohamed A. and Stanley Fischer. 1996. *Is MENA a Region? The Scope for Regional Integration*. Washington, D.C.: International Monetary Fund (IMF) Working Paper (April).

El-Nagger, Said and Mohamed El-Erian. 1993. "The Economic Implications of a Comprehensive Peace in the Middle East." In *Economics of Middle East Peace*, pp. 205–25. Edited by Stanley Fischer, Dani Rodrik, and Elias Tuma.

Evron, Yair. 1977. *The Role of Arms Control in the Middle East*. London: International Institute for Strategic Studies.

———. 1994. *Israel's Nuclear Dilemma*. Ithaca, N.Y.: Cornell University Press.

———. 1995. "Confidence- and Security-Building Measures in the Arab-Israeli Context." In *Middle Eastern Security*, pp. 152–72. Edited by Efraim Inbar and Shmuel Sandler.

Fahmy, Mohamed Nabil. 1990. "Egypt's Disarmament Initiative." *Bulletin of the Atomic Scientists*, 46, no. 9 (November): 9–10.

Fakhr, Ahmed. 1995. "An Egyptian Perspective on Arms Control." In *Arms Control and Security in the Middle East: The Search for Common Ground*, pp. 29–39. Edited by Richard Eisendorf. Washington, D.C.: Initiative for Peace and Cooperation in the Middle East.

Faour, Muhammad. 1993. *The Arab World After Desert Storm*. Washington, D.C.: United States Institute of Peace Press.

Fawcett, Louise. 1995. "Regionalism in Historical Perspective." In *Regionalism in World Politics*, pp. 9–36. Edited by Louise Fawcett and Andrew Hurrell.

Fawcett, Louise and Andrew Hurrell, eds. 1995. *Regionalism in World Politics*. Oxford: Oxford University Press.

Feldman, Shai and Ariel Levite, eds. 1994. *Arms Control and the New Middle East Security Environment*. Tel Aviv: Jaffee Center for Strategic Studies.

Feldman, Shai. 1982. *Israeli Nuclear Deterrence*. New York: Columbia University Press.

———. 1997. *Nuclear Weapons and Arms Control in the Middle East*. Cambridge, Mass.: MIT Press.

Finnemore, Martha. 1996. *National Interests in International Society*. Ithaca, N.Y.: Cornell University Press.

———. 1996. "Constructing Norms of Humanitarian Intervention." In *Culture of National Security*, pp. 153–85. Edited by Peter J. Katzenstein.

Finnemore, Martha and Kathryn Sikkink. 1998. "International Norm Dynamics and Political Change." *International Organization*, 52, no. 4 (Autumn): 887–917.

Fischer, Stanley. 1993. "Prospects for Regional Integration in the Middle East." In *New Dimensions in Regional Integration*, pp. 423–49. Edited by Jaime De Melo and Arvind Panagariya. Cambridge: Cambridge University Press.

Fischer, Stanley, Dani Rodrik, and Elias Tuma. 1993. *The Economics of Middle East Peace*. Cambridge, Mass.: MIT Press.

*Foreign Relations of the United States (FRUS) 1955–1957*, vols. 14–15. 1989. Washington, D.C.: U.S. Government Printing Office.

*Foreign Relations of the United States (FRUS), 1958–1960*, vol. 13. 1992. Washington, D.C.: U.S. Government Printing Office.

*Foreign Relations of the United States (FRUS), 1958–1960*, vol. 12. 1993. Washington, D.C.: U.S. Government Printing Office.

Gaon, Benjamin (of Koor Industries). 1994. "Israel and the Future of Middle East Economic Development." In *Peace Through Entrepreneurship: Practical Ideas from Middle Eastern Business Leaders*, pp. 9–13. Washington, D.C.: Washington Institute for Near East Policy.

George, Alexander L., Philip J. Farley, and Alexander Dallin, eds. 1988. *U.S.-Soviet Security Cooperation*. Oxford: Oxford University Press.

Gerges, Fawaz A. 1995. "The Kennedy Administration and the Egyptian-Saudi Conflict in Yemen: Co-Opting Arab Nationalism." *Middle East Journal*, 49, no. 2 (Spring): 292–311.

———. 1995. "Egyptian-Israeli Relations Turn Sour." *Foreign Affairs*, 74, no. 3 (May/June): 69–78.

Gilpin, Robert. 1987. *The Political Economy of International Relations*. Princeton, N.J.: Princeton University Press.

Glaser, Charles L. 1994–95. "Realists As Optimists: Cooperation As Self-Help." *International Security*, 19, no. 3 (Winter): 50–90.

Goldstein, Judith. 1989. "The Impact of Ideas on Trade Policy." *International Organization*, 43, no. 1 (Winter): 31–71.

Goldstein, Judith and Robert O. Keohane, eds. 1993. *Ideas and Foreign Policy*. Ithaca, N.Y.: Cornell University Press.

———. 1993. "Ideas and Foreign Policy: An Analytical Framework." In *Ideas and Foreign Policy*, pp. 3–30. Edited by Judith Goldstein and Robert O. Keohane.

Government of Israel. 1994. *Development Options for Regional Cooperation*. Submitted to the Middle East and North Africa Economic Summit, Casablanca (October).

———. 1994. *The Refugee Issue: A Background Paper*. Jerusalem: Government Press Office.

———. 1995. *Development Options for Cooperation: The Middle East/East Mediterranean Region 1996*. Israel: Ministry of Foreign Affairs and Finance, Version 4 (August).

Government of Japan. 1994. Statement by the Gavelholder, Middle East Peace Process, Multilateral Working Group on the Environment (October 25–26). Manama, Bahrain.
———. 1996. Concluding Remarks by the Gavelholder, The Intersessional Meeting, The Environment Working Group (June 26–27). Muscat, Oman.
Government of Jordan. 1992. Jordan Delegation to Middle East Multilateral Peace Talks, Position Paper, The Environment Working Group (May 18–19). Tokyo, Japan.
———. 1995. *Building a Prosperous Peace, Amman '95, October 29–31, 1995*. Amman, Jordan: International Press Office, The Royal Hashemite Court.
Government of the United States. 1994. Statement of the Gavelholder, Middle East Peace Process Multilateral Working Group on Water Resources (April 17–19). Muscat, Oman.
———. 1996. Gavelholder's Summary: Working Group on Water Resources (May 15–16). Hammamet, Tunisia.
Grimmet, Richard. 1992. *Conventional Arms Transfers to the Third World, 1984–1991*. Washington, D.C.: Congressional Research Service.
Haas, Ernst B. 1958. *The Uniting of Europe: Political, Social and Economic Forces, 1950–1957*. Stanford, Calif.: Stanford University Press.
———. 1964. *Beyond the Nation-State: Functionalism and International Organization*. Stanford, Calif.: Stanford University Press.
———. 1970. "The Study of Regional Integration: Reflections on the Joy and Anguish of Pretheorizing." *International Organization*, 24, no. 4 (Autumn): 607–46.
———. 1975. *The Obsolescence of Regional Integration Theory*. Berkeley, California: Institute of International Studies.
———. 1975. "Is There a Hole in the Whole? Knowledge, Technology, Interdependence, and the Construction of International Regimes." *International Organization*, 29, no. 3 (Summer): 827–76.
———. 1980. "Why Collaborate: Issue-Linkage and International Regimes." *World Politics*, 32, no. 3 (April): 357–405.
———. 1990. *When Knowledge Is Power: Three Models of Change in International Organizations*. Berkeley: University of California Press.
Haas, Peter M. 1989. "Do Regimes Matter? Epistemic Communities and Mediterranean Pollution Control." *International Organization*, 43, no. 3 (Summer): 377–403.
———. 1990. *Saving the Mediterranean: The Politics of International Environmental Cooperation*. New York: Columbia University Press.
———. 1992. "Introduction: Epistemic Communities and International Policy Coordination." *International Organization*, 46, no. 1 (Winter): 1–35.
Haggard, Stephan and Beth A. Simmons. 1987. "Theories of International Regimes." *International Organization*, 41, no. 3 (Summer): 491–517.

Halevi, Nadav. 1993. "Economic Implications of Peace: The Israeli Perspective." In *The Economics of Middle East Peace*, pp. 87–115. Edited by Stanley Fischer, Dani Rodrik, and Elias Tuma.

Hall, Peter, ed. 1989. *The Political Power of Economic Ideas: Keynesianism Across Nations*. Princeton, N.J.: Princeton University Press.

Hamed, Osama A. and Radwan A. Shaban. 1993. "One-Sided Customs and Monetary Union: The Case of the West Bank and Gaza Strip Under Israeli Occupation." In *The Economics of Middle East Peace*, pp. 19–54. Edited by Stanley Fischer, Dani Rodrik, and Elias Tuma.

Hampson, Fen Osler with Michael Hart. 1995. *Multilateral Negotiations: Lessons from Arms Control, Trade, and the Environment*. Baltimore: Johns Hopkins University Press.

Handoussa, Heba and Nemat Shafik. 1993. "The Economics of Peace: The Egyptian Case." In *The Economics of Middle East Peace*, pp. 19–54. Edited by Stanley Fischer, Dani Rodrik, and Elias Tuma.

Hansen, Ambassador Lynn. 1994. "CSBMs: The Ugly Duckling Remains a Duck—but a Pretty Good One." In *Arms Control*, pp. 51–66. Edited by Fred Tanner.

Hearing before the Commission on Security and Cooperation in Europe. 1993. "CSCME: Prospects for Collective Security in the Middle East." One Hundred Third Congress, First Session, October 14.

Heclo, Hugh. 1978. "Issue Networks and the Executive Establishment." In *The New American Political System*, pp. 87–124. Edited by Anthony King. Washington, D.C.: American Enterprise Institute for Public Policy Research.

Hillel, Daniel. 1994. *Rivers of Eden: The Struggle for Water and the Quest for Peace in the Middle East*. Oxford: Oxford University Press.

Hodgson, Godfrey. 1990. *The Colonel*. New York: Knopf.

Hollis, Rosemary. 1997. "Europe and the Middle East: Power by Stealth?" *International Affairs*, 73, no. 1 (January): 15–29.

Hufbauer, Gary Clyde and Jeffrey J. Schott (assisted by Kimberly Ann Elliott). 1985. *Economic Sanctions Reconsidered: History and Current Policy*. Washington, D.C.: Institute for International Economics.

Hunt, Carla. 1997. "Areas Team Up to Promote Peace." *Travel Weekly's Guide to the Middle East/Mediterranean* (March 7).

Inbar, Efraim, ed. 1995. *Regional Security Regimes: Israel and its Neighbors*. Albany: State University of New York Press.

Inbar, Efraim and Shmuel Sandler, eds. 1995. *Middle Eastern Security: Prospects for an Arms Control Regime*. London: Frank Cass.

International Institute for Strategic Studies. 1998. *The Military Balance 1998/99*. Oxford: Oxford University Press.

Isaacson, Walter and Evan Thomas. 1986. *The Wise Men: Six Friends and the World They Made*. New York: Simon and Schuster.

Jacobsen, John Kurt. 1995. "Much Ado About Ideas: The Cognitive Factor in Economic Policy." *World Politics*, 47, no. 2 (January): 283–310.

Jentleson, Bruce W. 1996. *The Middle East Arms Control and Regional Security (ACRS) Talks: Progress, Problems and Prospects*, IGCC Policy Paper No. 26. San Diego: University of California Institute on Global Conflict and Cooperation.

Jentleson, Bruce W. and Dalia Dassa Kaye. 1998. "Security Status: Explaining Regional Security Cooperation and Its Limits in the Middle East." *Security Studies*, 8, no. 1 (Autumn): 204–38.

Jervis, Robert. 1982. "Security Regimes." *International Organization*, 36, no. 2 (Spring): 357–78.

———. 1983. "Security Regimes." In *International Regimes*, pp. 173–94. Edited by Stephen D. Krasner.

———. 1999. "Realism, Neoliberalism, and Cooperation: Understanding the Debate." *International Security*, 24, no. 1 (Summer): 42–63.

Jones, Peter. 1994. "Maritime Confidence-Building in the Middle East." In *Arms Control*, pp. 103–11. Edited by Fred Tanner.

———. 1996. "Maritime Confidence-Building Measures in the Middle East." In *Maritime Confidence Building in Regions of Tension*, pp. 57–73. Edited by Jill R. Junnola. Washington, D.C.: Henry L. Stimson Center.

Jönsson, Christer. 1995. "Cognitive Factors in Explaining Regime Dynamics." In *Regime Theory*, pp. 202–22. Edited by Volker Rittberger.

Jordan Information Bureau. 1995. *Jordan: Issues and Perspectives*. Washington, D.C.: Jordan Information Bureau, no. 21 (September/October).

Jordan Media Group. 1995. *The Jordan-Israel Peace Treaty, October 26, 1994: What Is It?*. Amman: Jordan Media Group.

Kanovsky, Eliyahu. 1994. *Assessing the Mideast Peace Economic Dividend*. Ramat Gan, Israel: BESA Center, Bar-Ilan University.

———. 1997. "The Middle East Economies: The Impact of Domestic and International Politics." *Middle East Report of International Affairs (MERIA)*, Journal 2, Article 1, June 1 <www.biu.ac.il/soc/besa/meria.html>.

Kaplan, Robert D. 1992. "Tales from the Bazaar." *Atlantic Monthly*, 270, no. 2 (August): 37–61.

Karem, Mahmoud. 1988. *A Nuclear-Weapon-Free Zone in the Middle East*. New York: Greenwood Press.

———. 1992. "A Nuclear-Weapon-Free Zone in the Middle East: A Historical Overview of the Patterns of Involvement of the United Nations." In *Regional Approaches to Curbing Nuclear Proliferation in the Middle East and South Asia*, pp. 55–68. Edited by Tariq Rauf. Ottawa: Canadian Centre for Global Security.

Katzenstein, Peter J., ed. 1996. *The Culture of National Security: Norms and Identity in World Politics*. New York: Columbia University Press.

Kaye, Dalia Dassa. 1993. "Learning in the Arab-Israeli Peace Process: The Emergence of an American Middle East Epistemic Community." Master's thesis, University of California, Berkeley.

———. 1997. "Madrid's Forgotten Forum: The Middle East Multilaterals." *Washington Quarterly*, 20, no. 1 (Winter): 167–86.

———. 1998. *Banking on Peace: Lessons from the Middle East Development Bank*. Institute on Global Conflict and Cooperation (IGCC), Policy Paper No. 43 (October).

Keck, Margaret E. and Kathryn Sikkink. 1998. *Activists Beyond Borders: Advocacy Networks in International Politics*. Ithaca, N.Y.: Cornell University Press.

Kemp, Geoffrey and Jeremy Pressman. 1995. "The Middle East: Continuation of the Peace Process." In *SIPRI Yearbook 1995*, pp. 171–210. Oxford: Oxford University Press.

Keohane, Robert O. 1983. "The Demand for International Regimes." In *International Regimes*, pp. 141–71. Edited by Stephen D. Krasner.

———. 1984. *After Hegemony: Cooperation and Discord in the World Political Economy*. Princeton, N.J.: Princeton University Press.

———. 1988. "International Institutions: Two Approaches." *International Studies Quarterly*, 32, no. 4 (December): 379–96.

———. 1990. "Multilateralism: An Agenda for Research." *International Journal*, 45, no. 4 (Fall): 731–64.

Kerr, Malcolm H. 1970. *The Arab Cold War*. Oxford: Oxford University Press.

Khashan, Hilal. 1995. "The Levant: Yes to Treaties, No to Normalization." *Middle East Quarterly*, 2, no. 2 (June): 3–13.

Kier, Elizabeth. 1997. *Imagining War: French and British Military Doctrine Between the Wars*. Princeton, N.J.: Princeton University Press.

Kindleberger, Charles P. 1973. *The World in Depression, 1929–39*. Berkeley: University of California Press.

King, Gary, Robert O. Keohane, and Sidney Verba. 1994. *Designing Social Inquiry*. Princeton, N.J.: Princeton University Press.

Kissinger, Henry. 1982. *Years of Upheaval*. Boston: Little, Brown & Company.

Kleiman, Ephraim. 1993. "Some Basic Problems of the Economic Relationships Between Israel, and the West Bank, and Gaza." In *The Economics of Middle East Peace*, pp. 305–33. Edited by Stanley Fischer, Dani Rodrik, and Elias Tuma.

———. 1998. "Is There a Secret Arab-Israeli Trade?" *Middle East Quarterly* (June): 11–18.

Klieman, Aharon. 1988. *Statecraft in the Dark: Israel's Practice of Quiet Diplomacy*. Boulder, Colo.: Westview Press.

———. 1990. *Israel and the World After 40 Years*. Washington, D.C.: Pergamon-Brassey's.

———. 1995. "The Israel-Jordan Tacit Security Regime." In *Regional Security Regimes: Israel and its Neighbors*, pp. 127–49. Edited by Efraim Inbar.
Klotz, Audi. 1995. *Norms in International Relations: the Struggle Against Apartheid*. Ithaca, N.Y.: Cornell University Press.
Kondracke, Morton. 1992. "Baker's Half Dozen." *New Republic*, 206, issue 8 (February 24): 11–12.
Kossaifi, George F. 1996. *The Palestinian Refugees and the Right of Return*, Information Paper No. 7. Washington, D.C.: Center for Policy Analysis on Palestine.
Kramer, Martin. 1997. "The Middle East, Old and New." *Daedalus*, 126, no. 2 (Spring): 89–112.
Krasner, Stephen D. 1976. "State Power and the Structure of International Trade." *World Politics*, 28, no. 3 (April): 317–45.
———. 1983. *International Regimes*. New York: Columbia University Press.
Krause, Keith R. 1994. "The Evolution of Arms Control in the Middle East." In *Confidence Building in the Middle East*, pp. 267–90. Edited by Gabriel Ben-Dor and David B. Dewitt. Boulder, Colo.: Westview Press.
Lake, David and Patrick Morgan, eds. 1997. *Regional Orders: Building Security in a New World*. University Park: Pennsylvania State University Press.
Lebovic, James H. 1995. "How Organizations Learn: U.S. Government Estimates of Foreign Military Spending." *American Journal of Political Science*, 39, no. 4 (November): 835–63.
Lebow, Richard Ned and Thomas Risse-Kappen, eds. 1995. *International Relations Theory and the End of the Cold War*. New York: Columbia University Press.
Legro, Jeffrey W. 1997. "Which Norms Matter? Revisiting the 'Failure' of Internationalism." *International Organization*, 51, no. 1 (Winter): 31–63.
Levite, Ariel E. and Emily B. Landau. 1994. *Israel's Nuclear Image: Arab Perceptions of Israel's Nuclear Posture* (in Hebrew). Tel Aviv: Papyrus.
Lindberg, Leon N. 1963. *The Political Dynamics of European Economic Integration*. Stanford, Calif.: Stanford University Press.
Lindblom, Charles. 1965. *The Intelligence of Democracy*. New York: Free Press.
Lipson, Charles. 1993. "International Cooperation in Economic and Security Affairs." In *Neorealism and Neoliberalism*, pp. 60–84. Edited by David A. Baldwin. New York: Columbia University Press.
Litfin, Karen T. 1994. *Ozone Discourses: Science and Politics in Global Environmental Cooperation*. New York: Columbia University Press.
Lowi, Miriam R. 1993. *Water and Power: The Politics of a Scarce Resource in the Jordan River Basin*. Cambridge: Cambridge University Press.
———. 1995. "Rivers of Conflict, Rivers of Peace." *Journal of International Affairs*, 49, no. 1 (Summer): 123–45.
Lynch, Marc. 1999. *State Interests and Public Spheres: The International Politics of Jordanian Identity*. New York: Columbia University Press.

Maddy-Weitzman, Bruce and Joseph Kostiner. 1995. "The Damascus Declaration: An Arab Attempt at Regional Security." In *Regional Security Regimes*, pp. 107–25. Edited by Efraim Inbar.

Madison, Christopher. 1991. "Baker's Inner Circle." *National Journal*, 23, no. 28 (July 13): 1733–38.

Makovsky, David. 1996. *Making Peace with the PLO: The Rabin Government's Road to the Oslo Accord.* Boulder, Colo.: Westview Press.

Mansfield, Edward D. and Helen V. Milner. 1999. "The New Wave of Regionalism." *International Organization*, 53, no. 3 (Summer): 589–627.

McLaurin, Ron, Lewis W. Snider, and Don Peretz. 1982. *Middle East Foreign Policy.* New York: Praeger.

Mearsheimer, John J. 1995. "A Realist Reply." *International Security*, 20, no. 1 (Summer): 82–93.

Merhav, Meir, ed. 1989. *Economic Cooperation and Middle East Peace.* London: Weidenfeld and Nicolson.

Milner, Helen. 1992. "International Theories of Cooperation Among Nations: Strengths and Weaknesses." *World Politics*, 44, no. 3 (April): 466–96.

Moore, John Norton, ed. 1977. *The Arab-Israeli Conflict: Readings and Documents.* Princeton, N.J.: Princeton University Press.

Nachmani, Amikam. 1995. "The Politics of Water in the Middle East." In *Regional Security Regimes*, pp. 231–51. Edited by Efraim Inbar.

Naff, Thomas and Ruth Matson, eds. 1984. *Water in the Middle East: Conflict or Cooperation?* Boulder, Colo.: Westview Press.

Nathan, Robert R. and Jerome I. Levinson. 1983. "A Development Fund for the Near East." In *Shared Destiny*, pp. 103–13. Edited by Joyce R. Starr with Addeane S. Caelleigh.

Nau, Henry R. 1990. *The Myth of America's Decline: Leading the World Economy into the 1990s.* Oxford: Oxford University Press.

Nolan, Janne E. 1988. "The U.S.-Soviet Conventional Arms Transfer Negotiations." In *U.S.-Soviet Security Cooperation*, pp. 510–23. Edited by Alexander George et al.

———., ed. 1994. *Global Engagement: Cooperation and Security in the 21st Century.* Washington, D.C.: Brookings Institution.

Nye, Joseph S. Jr. 1987. "Nuclear Learning and U.S.-Soviet Security Regimes." *International Organization*, 41, no. 3 (Summer): 371–402.

Olsen, Mancur. 1965. *The Logic of Collective Action: Public Goods and the Theory of Groups.* Cambridge, Mass.: Harvard University Press.

Page, John. 1994. "Securing the Peace Dividend in the Middle East: External Finance and Domestic Effort." *Middle East Executive Reports*, 17, no. 10 (October): 9–21.

———. 1995. "Economic Prospects and the Role of Regional Development Finance Institutions." In *Regional Economic Development in the Middle East:*

*Opportunities and Risks*, pp. 5–17. Washington, D.C.: Center for Policy Analysis on Palestine.

Peres, Shimon. 1993. *The New Middle East*. New York: Henry Holt.

Peters, Joel. 1994. *Building Bridges: The Arab-Israeli Multilateral Talks*. London: Royal Institute of International Affairs.

———. 1996. *Pathways to Peace: The Multilateral Arab-Israeli Peace Talks*. London: Royal Institute of International Affairs.

Platt, Alan, ed. 1992. *Arms Control and Confidence Building in the Middle East*. Washington D.C.: United States Institute of Peace Press.

Polsby, Nelson W. 1994. "The Foreign Policy Establishment: Toward Professionalism and Centrism." In *The Domestic Sources of American Foreign Policy: Insights and Evidence*, 2d ed., pp. 208–15. Edited by Eugene R. Wittkopf. New York: St. Martin's Press.

Prados, Alfred B. 1992. *Middle East Arms Supply: Recent Control Initiatives*, Congressional Research Service (CRS) Issue Brief. Washington, D.C.: Congressional Research Service.

Prawitz, Jan and James F. Leonard. 1996. *A Zone Free of Weapons of Mass Destruction in the Middle East*. United Nations Institute for Disarmament Research. New York and Geneva: United Nations.

Price, Richard and Christian Reus-Smit. 1998. "Dangerous Liaisons? Critical International Theory and Constructivism." *European Journal of International Relations*, 4, no. 3: 259–94.

Price, Richard and Nina Tannenwald. 1996. "Norms and Deterrence: The Nuclear and Chemical Weapons Taboos." In *Culture of National Security*, pp. 114–52. Edited by Peter J. Katzenstein.

Putnam, Robert. 1988. "Diplomacy and Domestic Politics." *International Organization*, 42, no. 3 (Summer): 422–60.

Quandt, William B. 1977. *Decade of Decisions: American Policy Toward the Arab-Israeli Conflict, 1967–1976*. Berkeley: University of California Press.

———. 1987. "Egypt: A Strong Sense of National Identity." In *National Negotiating Styles*, pp. 105–23. Washington, D.C.: Foreign Service Institute, U.S. Department of State.

———. 1993. *Peace Process: American Diplomacy and the Arab-Israeli Conflict Since 1967*. Washington, D.C.: Brookings Institution.

Rabinovich, Itamar. 1999. *Waging Peace: Israel and the Arabs at the End of the Century*. New York: Farrar, Straus and Giroux.

REDWG Monitoring Committee Secretariat. 1996. *REDWG Annual Report*. Amman, Jordan.

Richards, Alan and John Waterbury, eds. 1996. *A Political Economy of the Middle East*, 2d ed. Boulder, Colo.: Westview Press.

Risse, Thomas, Stephen C. Ropp, and Kathryn Sikkink. 1999. *The Power of Human Rights: International Norms and Domestic Change*. Cambridge: Cambridge University Press.

Risse-Kappen, Thomas. 1994. "Ideas Do Not Float Freely: Transnational Relations, Domestic Structures and the End of the Cold War." *International Organization*, 48, no. 2 (Spring): 185–214.

———. 1996. "Collective Identity in a Democratic Community: The Case of NATO." In *Culture of National Security*, pp. 357–99. Edited by Peter J. Katzenstein.

Rittberger, Volker, ed. 1995. *Regime Theory and International Relations*. Oxford: Oxford University Press.

Rittberger, Volker and Michael Zürn. 1991. "Regime Theory: Findings from the Study of 'East-West' Regimes." *Cooperation and Conflict*, 26, no. 4: 165–83.

Rodrik, Dani. 1995. *Why Is There Multilateral Lending?* International Macroeconomics and International Trade, Discussion Paper Series No. 1207. London: Centre for Economic Policy Research.

Rosecrance, Richard. 1986. *The Rise of the Trading State*. New York: Basic Books.

Ross, Dennis. 1984. *Acting with Caution: Middle East Policy Planning for the Second Administration*, Policy Paper No. 1. Washington, D.C.: Washington Institute for Near East Policy.

———. 1989. "The Peace Process—A Status Report." In *U.S. Policy and the Middle East Peace Process, Fourth Annual Conference*, pp. 10–18. Washington, D.C.: Washington Institute for Near East Policy.

Rouyer, Alwyn R. 1997. "The Water Issue in the Palestinian-Israeli Peace Process." *Survival*, 39, no. 2 (Summer): 57–81.

Rubin, Jeffrey Z. and Walter C. Swap. 1994. "Small Group Theory: Forming Consensus through Group Processes." In *International Multilateral Negotiation*, pp. 132–47. Edited by I. William Zartman.

Rubin, Robert E., Treasury Secretary. 1996. Testimony Before the House Appropriations Subcommittee on Foreign Operations. Washington, D.C. (April 18).

Ruggie, John Gerard. 1983. "International Regimes, Transactions, and Change: Embedded Liberalism in the Postwar Economic Order." In *International Regimes*, pp. 195–231. Edited by Stephen D. Krasner.

———., ed. 1993. *Multilateralism Matters: The Theory and Praxis of an Institutional Form*. New York: Columbia University Press.

———. 1993. "Multilateralism: The Anatomy of an Institution." In *Multilateralism Matters*, pp. 3–47. Edited by John Gerard Ruggie.

———. 1998. "What Makes the World Hang Together? Neo-Utilitarianism and the Social Constructivist Challenge." *International Organization*, 52, no. 4 (Autumn): 855–85.

Sadat, Anwar. 1977. *In Search of Identity*. New York: Harper Colophon Books.

Sadowski, Yahya M. 1993. *Scuds or Butter? The Political Economy of Arms Control in the Middle East.* Washington, D.C.: The Brookings Institution.

Sandholtz, Wayne. 1992. *High-Tech Europe: The Politics of International Cooperation.* Berkeley: University of California Press.

Sanford, Jonathan E. 1982. *U.S. Foreign Policy and Multilateral Development Banks.* Boulder, Colo.: Westview Press.

Sarna, Aaron J. 1986. *Boycott and Blacklist: A History of Arab Economic Warfare Against Israel.* New Jersey: Rowman & Littlefield.

Sayigh, Yezid. 1995. "Redefining the Basics: Sovereignty and Security of the Palestinian State." *Journal of Palestine Studies*, 24, no. 4 (Summer): 5–19.

———. 1995. "The Multilateral Middle East Peace Talks: Reorganizing for Regional Security." In *Practical Peacemaking*, pp. 207–29. Edited by Steven L. Spiegel and David J. Pervin.

Shuckburgh, Evelyn. 1987. *Descent to Suez, Diaries 1951–56.* New York: Norton.

Sikkink, Kathryn. 1991. *Ideas and Institutions: Developmentalism in Brazil and Argentina.* Princeton, N.J.: Princeton University Press.

*SIPRI Yearbook 1995: Armaments, Disarmament and International Security.* 1995. Oxford: Oxford University Press.

Snidal, Duncan. 1985. "The Limits of Hegemonic Stability Theory." *International Organization*, 39, no. 4 (Autumn): 579–614.

Solingen, Etel. 1995. "Arms Control Negotiations in the Middle East: The Issue of Sequencing." *Peace and Change*, 20, no. 3 (July): 364–78.

———. 1997. "Economic Liberalization, Political Coalitions, and Emerging Regional Orders." In *Regional Orders*, pp. 68–100. Edited by David A. Lake and Patrick M. Morgan.

———. 1998. *Regional Orders at Century's Dawn: Global and Domestic Influences on Grand Strategy.* Princeton, N.J.: Princeton University Press.

Sosland, Jeffrey K. 1998. *Cooperating Rivals: The Politics of Water Scarcity, Protracted Conflict, and Complex Cooperation in the Jordan River Basin.* Ph.D. diss., Georgetown University.

Spero, Joan E., Under Secretary of State for Economic, Business, and Agricultural Affairs, Department of State. 1996. "U.S. Foreign Policy and the International Financial Institutions." Testimony Before the House Committee on Banking and Financial Services, Subcommittee on Domestic and International Monetary Policy, Washington, D.C. (April 25).

Spiegel, Steven L. 1985. *The Other Arab-Israeli Conflict: Making America's Middle East Policy, from Truman to Reagan.* Chicago: University of Chicago Press.

Spiegel, Steven L. and David J. Pervin, eds. 1995. *Practical Peacemaking in the Middle East*, vol. 1, Arms Control and Regional Security. New York: Garland.

Starr, Joyce R. 1991. "Water Wars." *Foreign Policy*, 82 (Spring): 17–36.

Starr, Joyce R. and Daniel Stoll, eds. 1988. *The Politics of Scarcity: Water in the Middle East.* Boulder, Colo.: Westview Press.

Starr, Joyce R. with Addeane S. Caelleigh. 1983. *A Shared Destiny: Near East Regional Development and Cooperation.* New York: Praeger.

Stein, Arthur A. 1983. "Coordination and Collaboration: Regimes in an Anarchic World." In *International Regimes*, pp. 115–40. Edited by Stephen D. Krasner.

Steinberg, Gerald M. 1994. "Middle East Arms Control and Regional Security." *Survival*, 36, no. 1 (Spring): 126–41.

———. 1996. "The 1995 NPT Extension and Review Conference and the Arab-Israeli Peace Process." *NonProliferation Review*, 1, no. 1 (Fall): 17–29.

Summers, Lawrence H., Treasury Undersecretary for International Affairs. 1994. "Shared Prosperity in the Middle East: Toward a Regional Development Bank." Remarks at the Middle East/North Africa Economic Summit, Casablanca, Morocco (October 31).

Taba Trade Leaders. 1995. *Market Access Study.* Amman, Jordan (October 30).

Tamari, Salim. 1996. *Palestinian Refugee Negotiations: From Madrid to Oslo II.* Washington, D.C.: Institute for Palestine Studies.

Tanner, Fred. 1994. *Arms Control, Confidence-Building and Security Cooperation in the Mediterranean, North Africa and the Middle East.* Malta: Mediterranean Academy of Diplomatic Studies.

Telhami, Shibley. 1990. *Power and Leadership in International Bargaining.* New York: Columbia University Press.

Toukan, Abdullah. 1993. "The Middle East Peace Process and Arms Control and Regional Security." Paper presented to the ACRS plenary in Washington, D.C. (May).

———. 1995. "A Jordanian Perspective on Arms Control." In *Arms Control and Security in the Middle East: The Search for Common Ground*, pp. 89–99. Edited by Richard Eisendorf. Washington, D.C.: Initiative for Peace and Cooperation in the Middle East.

———. 1995. "The Middle East Peace Process, Arms Control, and Regional Security." In *Practical Peacemaking*, pp. 21–42. Edited by Steven L. Spiegel and David J. Pervin.

Tripp, Charles. 1995. "Regional Organizations in the Arab Middle East." In *Regionalism in World Politics*, pp. 283–308. Edited by Louise Fawcett and Andrew Hurrell.

United Nations. 1990. *Establishment of a Nuclear-Weapon-Free-Zone in the Region of the Middle East.* Report of the Secretary-General, United Nations General Assembly, October 10, Forty-fifth session.

U.S. Department of State, Bureau of Public Affairs. 1995. "Amman Middle East/North Africa Economic Summit." Fact Sheet (October 25). Washington, D.C.

———. 1995. "Middle East-Mediterranean Travel and Tourism Association." Fact Sheet (October 25). Washington, D.C.

Walt, Stephen M. 1987. *The Origins of Alliances*. Ithaca, N.Y.: Cornell University Press.

Waltz, Kenneth N. 1979. *Theory of International Politics*. Reading, Mass.: Addison-Wesley.

Warburg, Philip. 1995. *Middle East Environmental Cooperation*, IGCC Policy Brief No. 4. San Diego: Institute on Global Conflict and Cooperation, University of California.

Washington Institute for Near East Policy. 1988. *Building for Peace: An American Strategy for the Middle East*. Washington, D.C.: Washington Institute for Near East Policy.

———. 1991. *After the Storm: Challenges for America's Middle East Policy*. Washington, D.C.: Washington Institute for Near East Policy.

———. 1991. *The Arab-Israeli Peace Process Briefing Book*. Washington, D.C.: Washington Institute for Near East Policy.

———. 1992. *Pursuing Peace: An American Strategy for the Arab-Israeli Peace Process*. Washington, D.C.: Washington Institute for Near East Policy.

Weber, Steven. 1992. "Shaping the Postwar Balance of Power: Multilateralism in NATO." *International Organization*, 46, no. 3 (Summer): 633–80.

Wendt, Alexander E. 1987. "The Agent-Structure Problem in International Relations Theory." *International Organization*, 41, no. 3 (Summer): 335–70.

———. 1992. "Anarchy Is What States Make of It." *International Organization*, 46, no. 2 (Spring): 391–425.

———. 1995. "Constructing International Politics." *International Security*, 20, no. 1 (Summer): 71–81.

———. 1999. *Social Theory of International Politics*. Cambridge: Cambridge University Press.

World Bank. 1993. *Developing the Occupied Territories: An Investment in Peace*. Washington, D.C.: International Bank for Reconstruction and Development.

———. 1995. *Claiming the Future: Choosing Prosperity in the Middle East and North Africa*. Washington, D.C.: International Bank for Reconstruction and Development.

Yaffe, Michael D. 1994. "An Overview of the Middle East Peace Process Working Group on Arms Control and Regional Security." In *Arms Control*, pp. 93–100. Edited by Fred Tanner.

Yee, Albert. 1996. "The Causal Effects of Ideas on Policies." *International Organization*, 50, no. 1 (Winter): 69–108.

Yetiv, Steve A. 1997. "Peace, Interdependence, and the Middle East." *Political Science Quarterly*, 112, no. 1 (Spring): 29–49.

Young, Oran R. 1991. "Political Leadership and Regime Formation: On the Development of Institutions in International Society." *International Organization*, 45, no. 3 (Summer): 281–308.

Young, Oran and Gail Osherenko. 1993. "The Formation of International Regimes: Hypotheses and Cases." In *Polar Politics: Creating International Environmental Regimes*, pp. 1–21. Edited by Oran Young and Gail Osherenko. Ithaca, N.Y.: Cornell University Press.

Zabusky, Stacia E. 1995. *Launching Europe: An Ethnography of European Cooperation in Space Science*. Princeton, N.J.: Princeton University Press.

Zartman, I. William, ed. 1994. *International Multilateral Negotiation: Approaches to the Management of Complexity*. San Francisco: Jossey-Bass.

# Index

Abdel-Shafi, Haidar, 56
Acheson, Dean, 70, 257n82
Ad-hoc liaison committee (AHLC), 120; see also Regional Economic Development Working Group (REDWG)
Adler, Emanuel, 8
Ajami, Fouad, 106–107
Algeria, 58, 94; see also North African states
Amman Economic Summit (1995), xix, 130–133, 152, 216–219, 275n56, 276n64, 277–278n73; see also Regional Economic Development Working Group (REDWG)
Arab states, xiv; views toward ACRS, 59–61, 79, 91, 99, 266–267n87; views toward regional economic cooperation, 61–62, 111, 114–115, 129, 131, 155, 194, 275–276n58; positions toward multilateral talks, 22, 27, 50, 53, 58, 67, 187; Israeli normalization and, 25, 43, 59, 64, 130, 133, 147, 256n74, 291n56; views toward water and environmental cooperation, 161–163, 169
Arafat, Yasir, vii, 47, 151
Arms Control and Regional Security Working Group (ACRS), xviii, xix–xx, 24, 52, 58, 76–78, 161, 189–190, 195–198, 205–206, 261n19; achievements of, 99–102; breakdown of, 97–99; 102–109; communications network, 93; Declaration of Principles and Statements of Intent on Arms Control and Regional Security (ACRS DoP), 88–91, 100; Israel's nuclear capabilities, 4, 24, 26, 269n109; origins of, 59–61; post-Oslo activity, 86–97; pre-Oslo activity, 78–86; Prenotification of Certain Military Activities agreement, 94, 100; Prevention of Incidents at Sea (INCSEA) agreement, 95–97, 100; public

ACRS (*continued*)
opinion and, 27; regional security center (RSC), 92, 100, 264–265n62; Search and Rescue (SAR) agreement, 95–97, 100

arms control: Bush Administration arms control initiative (1991), 32; Carter Administration's Conventional Arms Transfer Talks (CAT), 32; conventional arms transfer register, 244n5; history of, 30–34; Johnson Administration proposal for an arms shipment register, 32; Multinational Force and Observers (MFO), 33; Near East Arms Coordinating Committee (NEACC), 31; Tripartite Declaration (1950), 31; *see also* Arms Control and Regional Security Working Group (ACRS); Nuclear Weapons Free Zone and Weapons of Mass Destruction Free Zone (NWFZ/WMDFZ) proposals

Bahrain, 57, 94, 106, 176, 178, 180, 254n49; *see also* Gulf states

Baker III, James A., xxii, 11, 13, 49, 71–72; regional arms control and, 32; economic cooperation and, 113–114, 142; post-Gulf War diplomacy and, 47–48, 245n9, 250n13; Madrid Peace Conference and, xii, 51, 67, 187, 251n24; Moscow organizational meeting for the multilateral talks and, xiv, 199–202, 251n26

Bank for Economic Cooperation and Development in the Middle East and North Africa (MENABANK). *See* Middle East Development Bank

Barcelona conference (1995), 120, 273n33; participants, 273n32, 273n33

Barnett, Michael, 18

Beilin, Yossi, 62–63, 116, 168, 278n74

Bilateral peace process tracks, xii–xiv, xviii–xx, 27, 48, 51, 53, 56–57, 193, 199–201, 252n34

Bohlen, Charles, 257n82

Brzezinski, Zbigniew, 70

Bush, George, 47; regional arms control and, 32, 245n9, 245n10; Madrid Peace Conference and, xii, 69

Cairo Economic Conference (1996), 133–137, 220–222, 279–280n85; *see also* Regional Economic Development Working Group (REDWG)

Camp David Accords. *See* Israeli–Egyptian Peace Treaty

Canada: and ACRS, 84, 94–96; and REDWG, 115, 216, 220; and Refugee Working Group, 201, 251n23

Casablanca Economic Summit (1994), 128–130, 211–215, 269n112; *see also* Regional Economic Development Working Group (REDWG)

Checkel, Jeffrey T., 21

Christopher, Warren, 128, 136, 292n4

Clifford, Clark, 257–258n82

Clinton, Bill, 128, 143, 211, 283n123, 292n4

Conference on Security and Cooperation in Europe (CSCE). *See* Organization for Security and Cooperation in Europe (OSCE)

confidence and security-building measures (CSBMs). *See* confidence-building measures (CBMs)
confidence-building measures (CBMs), xix, 31, 33, 52, 72, 197, 245–246n13, 268n97; ACRS and, 78–97, 100, 189, 260n11, 262n34, 266n81
constructivism, 2–3, 10, 20–22
cooperation, 1; definition of, 6–9; failure and, 26–28; as policy adjustment, 2, 5–6; as process, viii, xv, 2, 6–10, 77, 185; success and, 23–26
Copenhagen Action Plan (CAP), 117, 121
Council on Foreign Relations (CFR), 127, 215, 222, 281n99
Cyprus, 140, 145, 175

Damascus Declaration (1991), 253–254n47, 254n51
David, Steven, 18
Djerejian, Edward P., 72
Doha Economic Summit (1997), 28, 194, 281n98; *see also* Regional Economic Development Working Group (REDWG)
domestic politics, 17–19
Dulles, John Foster, 35, 70, 247n23

economic cooperation: ALPHA, 35; the Arab boycott, 36–37, 210, 213, 218, 247n25; the Eisenhower administration proposal for a Middle East Economic Development Fund, 35–36; history of, 34–40; Israeli–Egyptian economic relations, 38; Israeli–Palestinian economic relations, 38–39; *see also* Regional Economic Development Working Group (REDWG)
Eden, Anthony, 35
Egypt, 236n6, 259n2; views toward regional arms control, 27, 33–34, 78–79, 82–85, 90–91, 94, 100, 189–190, 195, 244n5, 252n31, 260–261n13, 263n45, 265n63; regional institutions and, 28, 93, 138, 140–141, 145, 153; Israel and, 38, 98–99, 103, 248n32, 267n91; Jordan and, 55, 77, 92, 105–106, 132–133, 179, 279n83; regional leadership concerns, 4, 28, 55, 77, 86, 103–109, 132, 148, 196, 220; multilateral track and, 55, 58, 253n40; REDWG and, 115, 118, 134–137, 151, 219, 275–276n58, 277n71, 281n98; water and environmental cooperation and, 170, 172–176, 178, 180–181
Eitan, Rafael, 135
El-Baz, Osama, 106
Environment Working Group, xix, 16, 24, 52–53, 57, 158–161, 189–190; Bahrain Environmental Code of Conduct, 164, 173, 176–177, 180, 230–234; origins of, 65–66; post-Oslo activity, 172–177, 290n41; pre-Oslo activity, 163–165
Eran, Oded, 129
Europe, 8, 48, 54, 64, 68–69; ACRS and, 78–80, 260n5; REDWG and, 113–116, 118–121, 143–144, 147, 155, 201, 216, 218, 220, 251n23, 272n27, 283n126; water and environmental cooperation and, 171–172, 174
European Community. *See* Europe
European Invesment Fund, 144
European Union. *See* Europe

Fakhr, Ahmed, 260–261n13
Forrestal, James V., 257n82
France, 115; *see also* Europe
Frenkel, Jacob, 114
Friedman, Thomas, 285n138

Ganzouri, Kamal, 137, 151
Geneva peace conference (1973), 236n6
Germany, 115, 170–171; *see also* Europe
Gold, Dore, 292n4
Goldstein, Judith, 19
Gore, Al, 267n91
Gulf Cooperation Council (GCC). *See* Gulf states
Gulf states, 25, 51, 55, 74, 191, 236n6, 254n51; views toward regional arms control, 59–61, 84, 90–91, 107, 262n34; economic cooperation and, 61, 120, 128, 210, 213; multilateral track and, 57; water and environmental cooperation and, 162, 171, 173; *see also* Arab states; Bahrain; Kuwait; Oman; Qatar; Saudi Arabia; United Arab Emirates
Gulf War (1990–1991), 46–48, 50, 57, 68, 150, 184, 187

Habermas, Jürgen, 6
Habib, Philip, 42
Harriman, Averell, 257n82
Hassan II, King, 211, 273n37, 274n41
Hassan, Crown Prince, 55, 142, 282–283n115, 292n4
Helsinki process (1975), 86, 88, 203, 262n30
Hussein, King, 47, 132, 215–216, 219, 261n16
Hussein, Saddam, 48

India, 80
Indyk, Martin, 72–73
Institute on Global Conflict and Cooperation (IGCC), 291–292n3
International Monetary Fund (IMF), 62–63, 150
International Relations theory, 1, 5, 10, 18; *see also* constructivism; domestic politics; neofunctionalism; neoliberal institutionalism; rational cognitivists; realism
Iran and Iraq, 52, 57, 80, 94, 97, 103, 196, 259n2
Israel, 236n6, 237n13, 254–255n54, 259n2; Arab acceptance of, 16, 25, 28, 48, 50–51, 53, 69, 73–74, 90, 136, 153–154, 169, 194, 262–263n36, 263n44; views toward regional arms control, 34, 60–61, 79–80, 82–83, 93–94, 100, 196, 252n31; views toward regional economic cooperation, 38–39, 62–65, 111, 113–114, 116, 118, 129, 135, 138–141, 145, 151, 153, 155; Egypt and, 38, 98–99, 103, 248n32; Jordan and, 55, 203–205, 212, 254n51, 255n63; multilateral track and, 54, 58–59, 251n27, 260n5; nuclear capabilities and, 4, 24, 34, 55, 82, 91, 105–106, 246n16, 267n89; refugee issue and, 51, 251n26, 252n31, 253n43; the United States and, 71, 254n51; water and environmental cooperation and, 161, 168, 170–176, 178, 180–181, 286n4, 286–287n5, 287n6
Israeli–Egyptian Peace Treaty (1979), 50, 90, 212

Israeli–Palestinian bilateral track. *See* bilateral peace process tracks
Italy, 116, 145; *see also* Europe
Ivry, David, 91, 98, 102, 266n87

Japan, 69, 115, 120–121, 140, 171, 216, 220; and Environment Working Group, 159–161, 164–165, 174–176, 201, 251n23, 287n12
Jassem, Hamed Bin, 137
Johnston, Eric, 41
Jones, Peter, 94–96, 266n76
Jordan, 236n6; views toward regional arms control, 83, 94, 101, 265n63; views toward regional economic cooperation, 116, 118, 130–132, 134, 141, 151–153, 155, 274n41, 277n66; Egypt and, 55, 77, 92, 105–106, 132–133, 179, 279n83; regional institutions and, 28, 93, 138, 140, 145, 153; Israel and, 55, 203–205, 212, 254n51, 255n63; multilateral track and, 55; water and environmental cooperation and, 161, 163, 170–176, 180

Karem, Mahmoud, 246n15
Kennan, George, 257n82
Keohane, Robert O., 5–6, 19, 239n20
Keynes, John Maynard, 13
Khalaf, Rima, 278n74
Kissinger, Henry, 70, 236n6
Korea, 171
Kozyrev, Andrei, 200, 202
Kurtzer, Daniel, 72
Kuwait, 57, 94; *see also* Gulf states

Lansing, Robert, 70
leadership, 12–13, 22–23

Lebanon, 52, 54, 56, 97, 128, 161, 172, 200, 212, 236n6, 251n24, 252n38
Levy, David, 113, 137, 260n5
Libya, 52, 80, 97, 196
Lovett, Robert, 257n82
Lowi, Miriam, 41

Madrid Peace Conference (1991), xii–xiii, 13, 44, 48–51, 53, 56, 58–59, 67–74, 187, 206, 212, 251n21, 251n24
Maghreb states. *See* North African states
Mauritania, 58; *see also* North African states
McCloy, John, 247n23, 257n82
Mead, Margaret, 6
Meridor, Dan, 136
Middle East and Mediterranean Travel and Tourism Association (MEMTTA), 121, 133, 140–141, 155, 214, 217, 221, 274n40, 282n107; *see also* Regional Economic Development Working Group (REDWG)
Middle East Development Bank, 16, 25, 114, 121, 133, 141–148, 155, 214, 217, 221–222, 256n73, 274n40, 282n112, 283n117, 284n131; *see also* Regional Economic Development Working Group (REDWG)
Middle East policy elites, 4, 23, 44–45, 68–75, 187–188
Miller, Aaron, 72
Morocco, 58, 94, 106, 140, 212; *see also* North African states

Moscow organizational meeting for the multilateral talks (1992), xiii–xiv, 44–45, 52–58, 66–74, 199–202, 213, 250n15, 252n32, 261n19
Moussa, 'Amr, 106, 132, 137, 277n69
Mubarak, Hosni, 104, 107, 134, 136, 151–152, 220
multilateral negotiations, 9
multilateral process, xi–xx; bilateral tracks and, xiii–xiv, xviii–xx, 27, 48, 51, 53, 56–57, 193, 199–201, 252n34; intersessional activities, xv, 25–26, 84, 115–116, 162, 165; origins of, 44–75; participants, xvi, 236n8; steering group, 52, 120, 201, 237n17, 251n28; *see also* multilateral working groups
multilateral working groups. *See* Arms Control and Regional Security Working Group (ACRS); Environment Working Group; Refugee Working Group; Regional Economic Development Working Group (REDWG); Water Working Group
multilateralism, 9–10
Multinational Force and Observers (MFO), 85

Nasser, Gamal, 104
neofunctionalism, 14–15
neoliberal institutionalism, 1, 14–17
Netanyahu, Benjamin, 132–134, 146, 151, 169, 173, 292n4
Netherlands, and ACRS, 84, 93; and REDWG, 145; *see also* Europe
New Middle East, 111, 142, 154, 156, 188, 240n36; *see also* Peres, Shimon

North African states, 51, 58, 74, 90, 236n6; *see also* Algeria; Mauritania; Morocco; Tunisia; Arab states
North Atlantic Treaty Organization (NATO), 86
Norway, 120, 169–170, 175, 223
Nuclear Nonproliferation Treaty (NPT), xx, 27, 83, 91–92, 97–100, 105; *see also* Arms Control and Regional Security Working Group (ACRS), breakdown of; Egypt, Israel and; Israel, Egypt and
Nuclear Weapons Free Zone and Weapons of Mass Destruction Free Zone (NWFZ/WMDFZ) proposals: ACRS and, 82, 89, 209, 263n42, 269n108; pre-Madrid initiatives, 31–34, 246n14, 246n15, 246n17; *see also* confidence-building measures (CBMs)

Oman, xix, 57, 94, 106, 136, 162, 171, 178, 180, 254n49, 263n44, 287n7; *see also* Gulf states
Organization for Security and Cooperation in Europe (OSCE, formerly CSCE), 8, 52, 54, 55, 79, 83, 92–93, 100, 142, 189, 196–198, 203, 262n30, 292–293n4
Oslo Accords, Oslo I (1993), vii, xviii–xix, 59, 85, 114, 162, 165, 236–237n13; Oslo II (1995), xix–xx, 130, 237n13

Pakistan, 80
Palestine Liberation Organization (PLO), 49, 56, 72, 113, 236n13; *see also* Palestinians
Palestinian Authority (PA). *See* Palestinians

Index 317

Palestinians: ACRS and, 93–94, 101, 262n35, 267–268n96; intifada, 49; economic relations with Israel, 38–39; multilateral track and, 56–57, 59, 67; REDWG and, 118, 134, 138–141, 151–153, 155, 212, 277n68; refugee issue and, 51, 251n26, 252n31; representation issues, 52, 56, 67, 85, 113–114, 200, 252n32, 253n43, 253n45; water and environmental cooperation and, 161, 163, 168–169, 171–172, 175–176, 180–181, 287n6, 287n10
Pelletreau, Robert, 90
Peres, Shimon, 82, 98, 113–114, 127, 129, 133, 142, 240n36, 269n109, 271n9, 273n37, 274n41, 283n123, 292n4
Persian Gulf War. *See* Gulf War (1990–1991)

Qatar, 57, 90, 92, 93–94, 101, 133, 219, 254n49, 263n44, 265n63, 277n71, 281n98; *see also* Gulf states
Quandt, William, 108

Rabin, Yitzhak, vii, 82, 98, 113, 129, 132–133, 181
Rabinovich, Itamar, xxii
rational cognitivists, 19–20
realism; cooperation and, 1, 5; hegemonic stability theory, 11–12
REDWG. *See* Regional Economic Development Working Group
Refugee Working Group, 51, 52, 56–57, 59, 201, 237n14, 251n26, 252n31
Regional Business Council (RBC), 121, 133, 138–139, 155, 214, 217, 222, 274n40; *see also* Regional Economic Development Working Group (REDWG)
Regional Economic Development Working Group (REDWG), 52–53, 59, 68, 110–112, 189–190, 273–274n39, 281–282n100; globalization and, 28, 149–157, 190, 195; impediments to, 147–148; regional institutions and, 25, 138–146; Israeli hegemony and, 24; membership, 270–271n3; Middle East and North Africa (MENA) summits, 111–112, 121, 127–137, 147, 153–155, 169, 174, 274n40, 275n55; Monitoring Committee (MC), 118, 121, 127, 130, 135, 138, 142, 214, 217–218, 222, 272n29; origins of, 61–65; post-Oslo activity, 117–121; pre-Oslo activity, 112–117; Palestinian development and, xix, 56, 115–116, 119, 132, 221; progress in, 149–154; regional projects and, 40; *see also* Amman Economic Summit (1995); Cairo Economic Conference (1996); Casablanca Economic Summit (1994); Doha Economic Summit (1997); Middle East Development Bank; Middle East and Mediterranean Travel and Tourism Association (MEMTTA); Regional Business Council (RBC)
Rifkind, Malcolm, 292n4
Ross, Dennis, 47, 71–72
Ruggie, John, 9–10
Russia, 202, 216, 220; and ACRS, 78, 84, 120, 144–145, 207

Saad, Raouf, 135
Sadat, Anwar, 104

Sandholtz, Wayne, 238n8
Sarid, Yossi, 173, 289n32
Saudi Arabia, 54–55, 57–58, 60, 64, 68, 191, 254n49; ACRS and, 90–91, 94, 101, 262n34, 263–264n49, 264n50; REDWG and, 120, 136, 281n98; water and environmental cooperation and, 171, 173–174, 179, 290n38; see also Gulf states
Savir, Uri, 11, 114, 117
Sayigh, Yezid, 267–268n96, 292n4
Search for Common Ground, 291–292n3
Shaath, Nabil, 278n74
Shamir, Yitzhak, xxii, 47, 49–51, 53, 59–60, 64, 67, 69, 246n17, 251n21
Sharansky, Natan, 136
Sharon, Ariel, 135
Shultz, George, 49, 72
Solingen, Etel, 18
Soviet Union, 46–47, 184, 236n6, 250n15
Spain, 115–116; see also Europe
State Department, 53, 70
Summers, Lawrence, 143
Switzerland, 139
Syria, 236n6, 254n50, 259n2; ACRS and, 94, 102–103, 196; opposition to the Madrid and multilateral peace process, 11, 24, 51–52, 54, 56, 58–59, 64, 67, 97, 161, 187, 200, 236n6, 251n24, 252–253n38; REDWG and, 128, 212, 281n98; water and environmental cooperation and, 172

Tarawneh, Fayez, 115
Tatawi, Nawal, 278n74
Toukan, Abdullah, 261n16

track two talks, 79, 102, 195–196, 291–292n3
Tunisia, 58, 91, 93–94, 106, 136, 140, 175, 212, 263n44; see also North African states
Turkey, 80, 84, 140, 254n51

United Arab Emirates, 57, 94, 264n49; see also Gulf states
United Kingdom, 115; see also Europe
United Nations, 48, 54, 81, 200
United States, 8, 11, 202, 236n6; ACRS and, 78–79, 81, 84, 99, 102, 201, 207, 267n91; Egypt and, 55; leadership and, 13, 22, 68, 188; formation of the multilateral process, xxi, 4, 16, 23, 48, 50–51, 53–54, 57, 186–188; REDWG and, 113, 115–116, 119–121, 138–140, 143–147, 155, 216, 220, 284n132; water and environmental cooperation and, 41–42, 159, 161–163, 165, 170–171, 176, 181, 287n12

Washington Institute for Near East Policy, 72–73
water and environmental cooperation: Eisenhower Administration water for peace program, 41; history of, 40–43, 66; the Johnston Plan, 41, 66, 248n40; Mediterranean Action Plan (Med Plan), 42, 66, 175, 249n47, 257n77; Middle East Regional Cooperation Program (MERC), 42; see also Environment Working Group; Water Working Group
Water Working Group, 16, 24, 52, 57, 158–161, 189–190, 201, 237n17, 288n21; Declaration of Principles

for Cooperation on Water-Related Matters and New and Additional Water Resources, 163, 172, 176, 180, 223–229; Middle East Desalination Research Center, 171–172; origins of, 65–66; post-Oslo activity, 168–172; pre-Oslo activity, 161–163; steering group members, 288n20

World Bank, 116, 128, 144, 164, 175, 253n46
World Economic Forum (WEF), 127, 151, 215, 216, 222

Yeltsin, Boris, 128, 211
Yemen, 94, 105
Young, Oran, 12

Zabusky, Stacia E., 6–7

GPSR Authorized Representative: Easy Access System Europe, Mustamäe tee
50, 10621 Tallinn, Estonia, gpsr.requests@easproject.com

www.ingramcontent.com/pod-product-compliance
Lightning Source LLC
Chambersburg PA
CBHW070808300426
44111CB00014B/2450